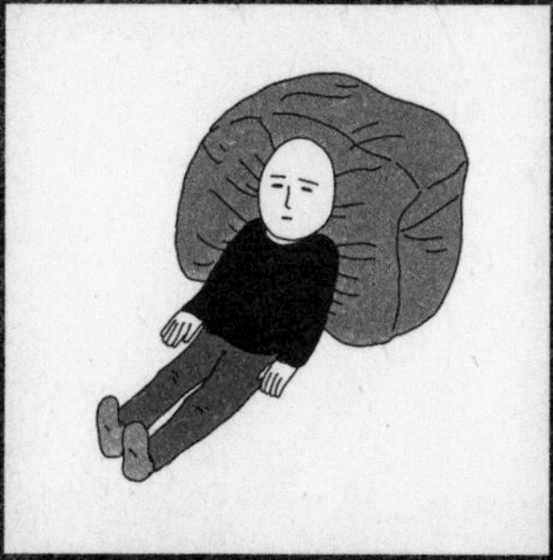

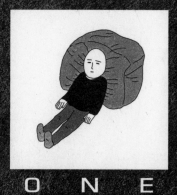

O N E

I have a cushion I don't use anymore, so I was thinking about throwing it away. But I leaned against it when I went to toss it out and remembered how comfortable it was, so now I can't throw it away.

—ONE

Manga creator ONE began *One-Punch Man* as a webcomic, which quickly went viral, garnering over 10 million hits. In addition to *One-Punch Man*, ONE writes and draws the series *Mob Psycho 100* and *Makai no Ossan*.

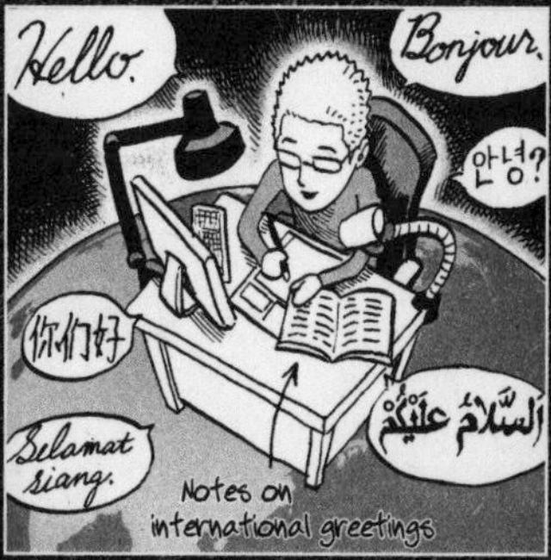
Hello.
Bonjour.
안녕?
你们好
السلام عليكم
Selamat siang.
Notes on international greetings

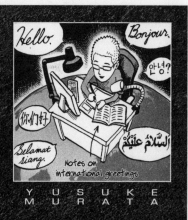

Y U S U K E M U R A T A

Sometimes I livestream myself drawing. Solitude used to be one of the perks of working late at night, but now I enjoy a raucous time with people from around the world while I work. It's amazing the way times change!

—Yusuke Murata

A highly decorated and skilled artist best known for his work on *Eyeshield 21*, Yusuke Murata won the 122nd Hop Step Award (1995) for *Partner* and placed second in the 51st Akatsuka Award (1998) for *Samui Hanashi*.

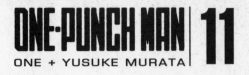

ONE-PUNCH MAN | 11

ONE + YUSUKE MURATA

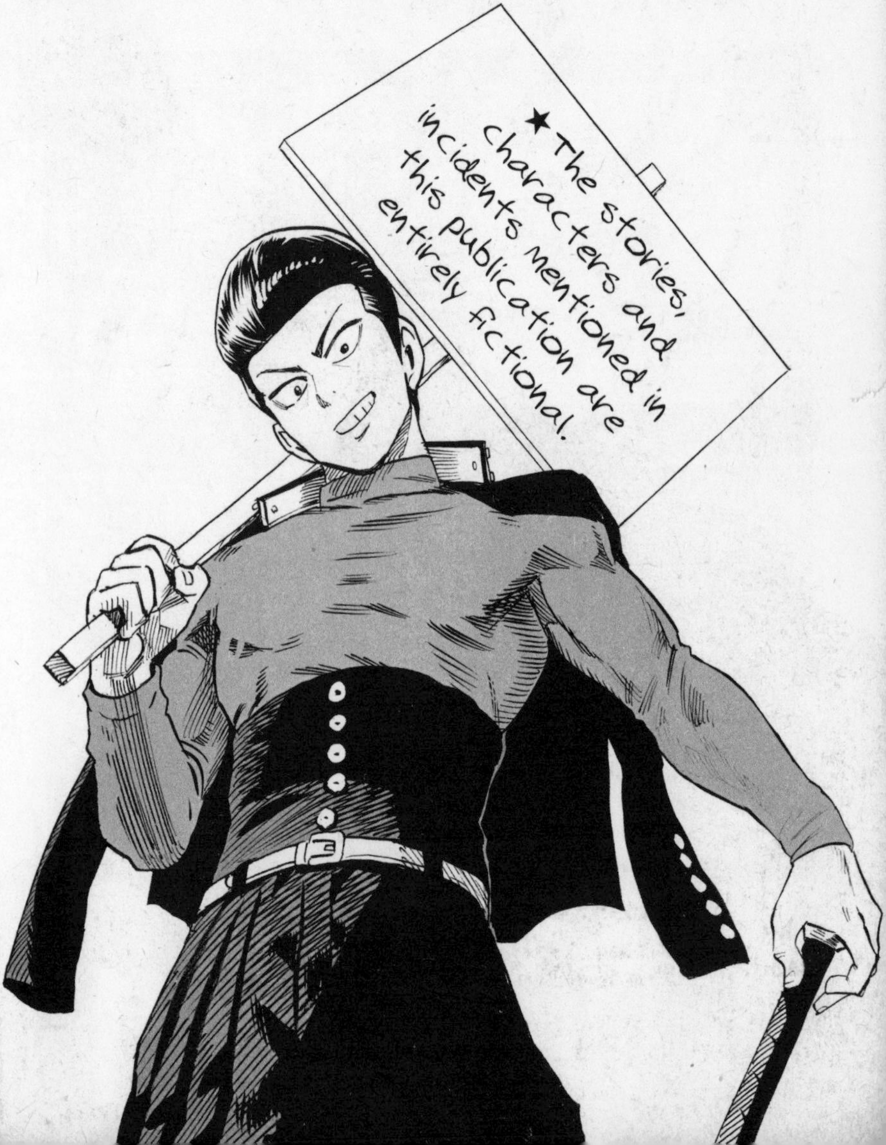
★ The stories, characters and incidents mentioned in this publication are entirely fictional.

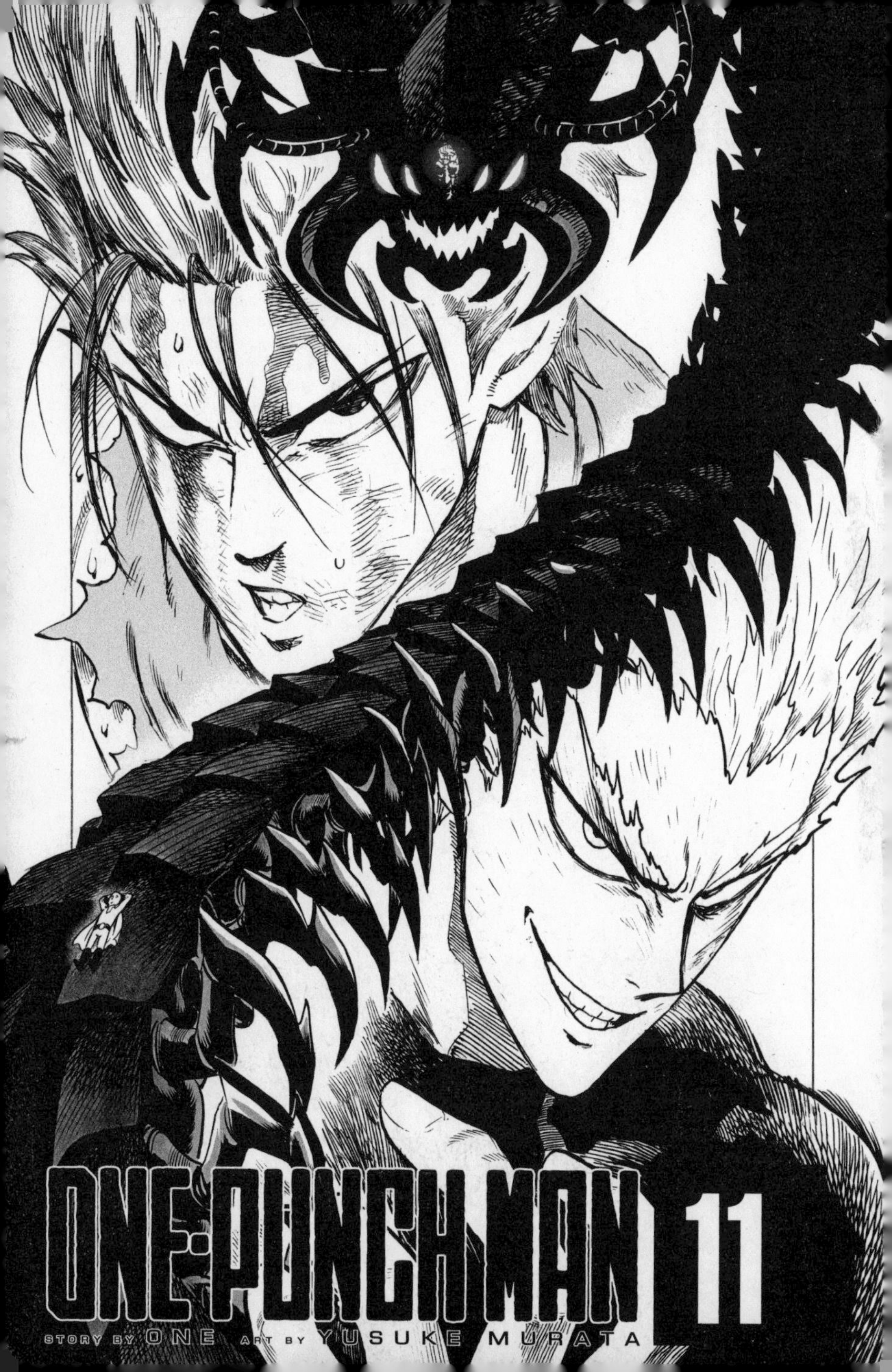

ONE-PUNCH MAN 11

STORY BY ONE ART BY YUSUKE MURATA

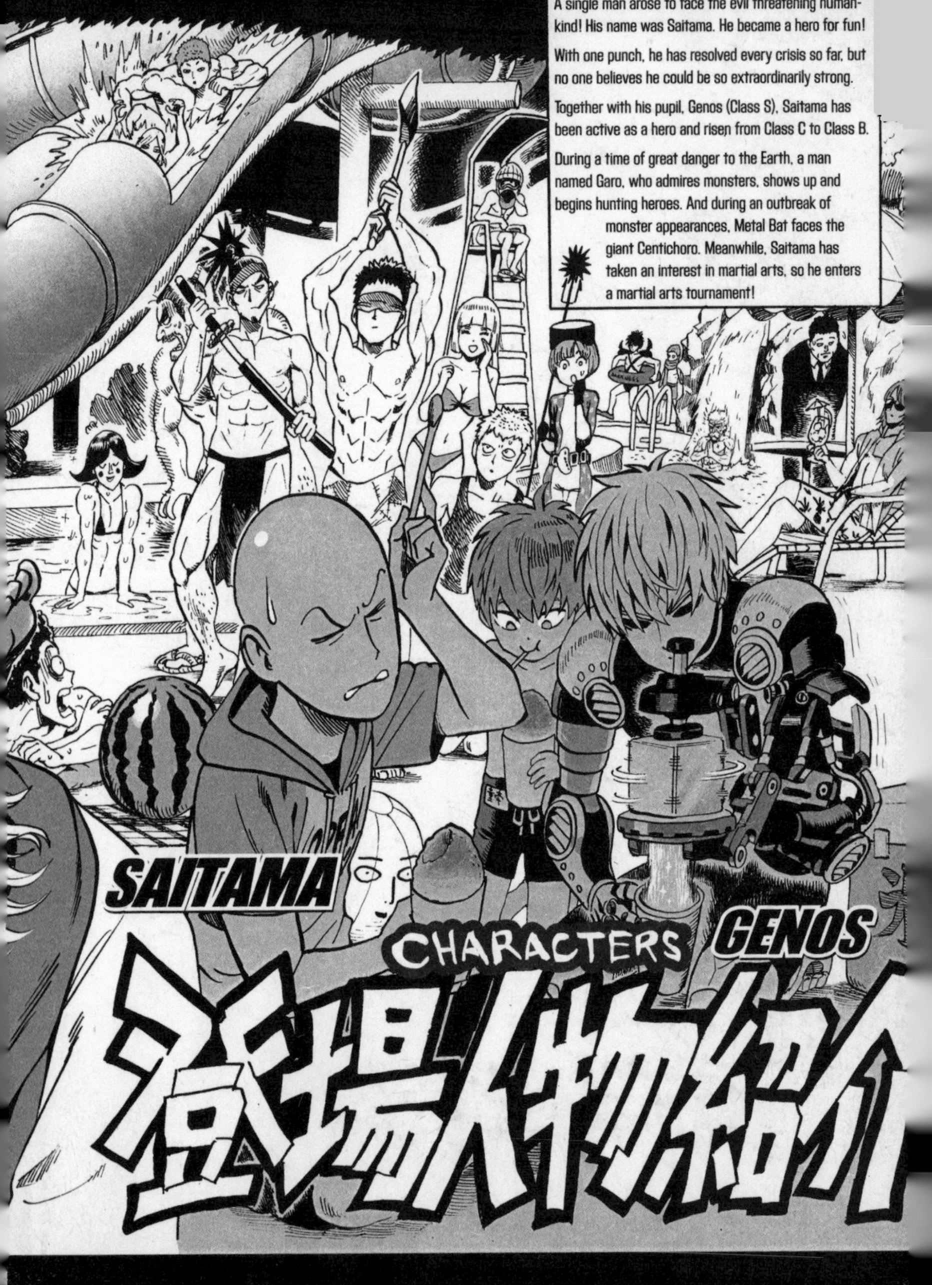
A single man arose to face the evil threatening humankind! His name was Saitama. He became a hero for fun!
With one punch, he has resolved every crisis so far, but no one believes he could be so extraordinarily strong.
Together with his pupil, Genos (Class S), Saitama has been active as a hero and risen from Class C to Class B.
During a time of great danger to the Earth, a man named Garo, who admires monsters, shows up and begins hunting heroes. And during an outbreak of monster appearances, Metal Bat faces the giant Centichoro. Meanwhile, Saitama has taken an interest in martial arts, so he enters a martial arts tournament!
SAITAMA
CHARACTERS
GENOS

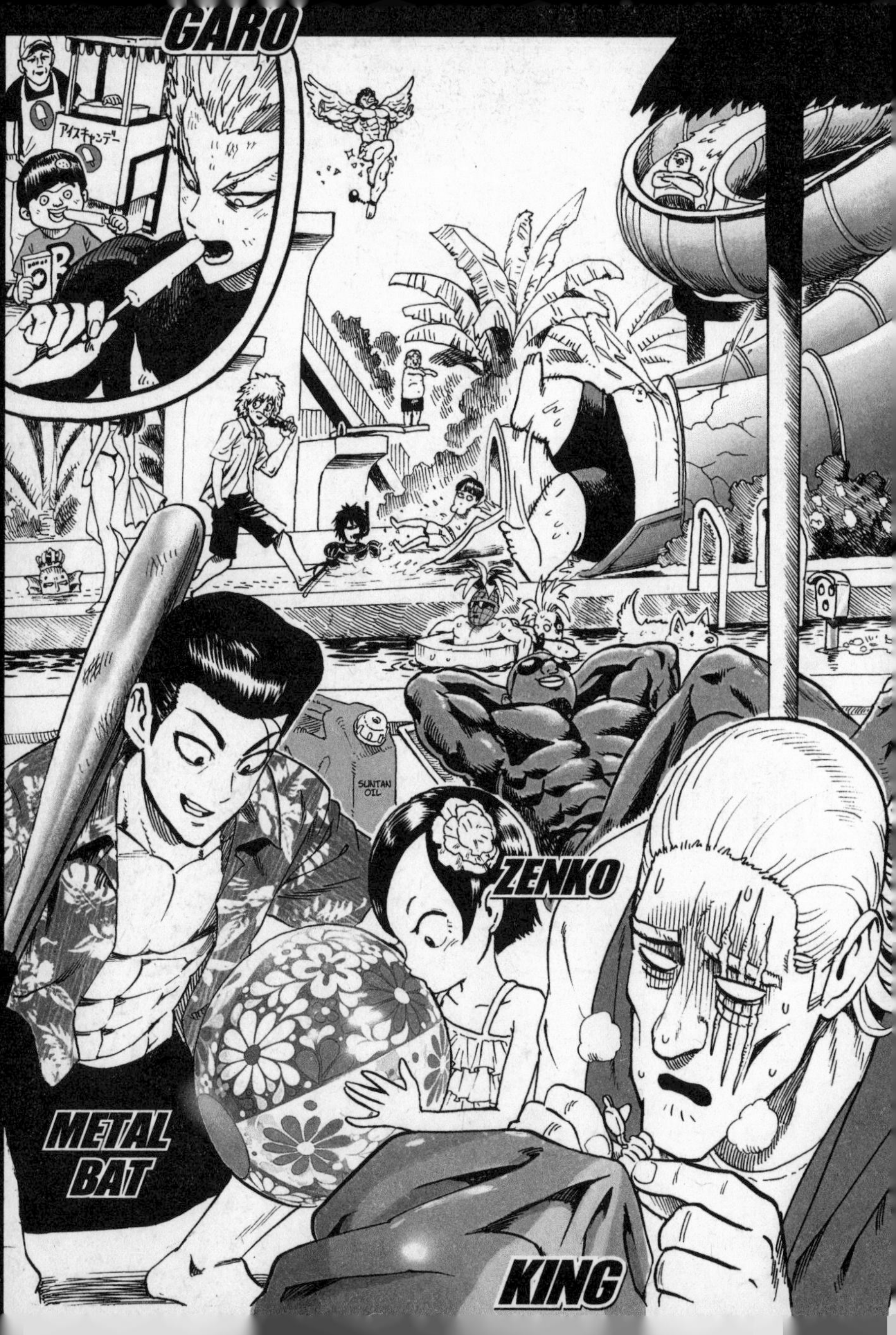
GARO
アイスキャンデー
SUNTAN OIL
ZENKO
METAL BAT
KING

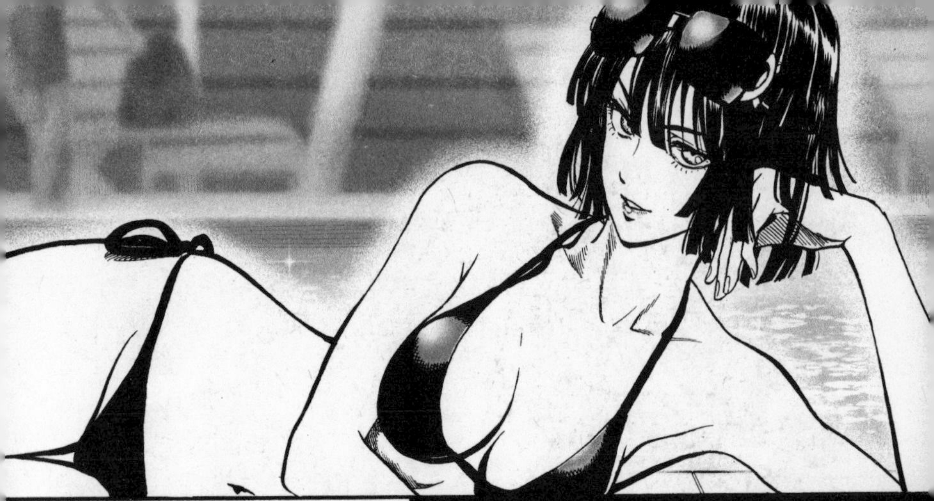

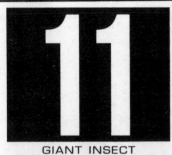

11

GIANT INSECT

ONE-PUNCH MAN

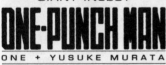

ONE + YUSUKE MURATA

My name is Saitama. I am a hero. My hobby is heroic exploits. I got too strong. And that makes me sad. I can defeat any enemy with one blow. I lost my hair. And I lost all feeling. I want to feel the rush of battle. I would like to meet an incredibly strong enemy. And I would like to defeat it with one blow. That's because I am One-Punch Man.

CONTENTS

ONE-PUNCH MAN VOLUME ELEVEN

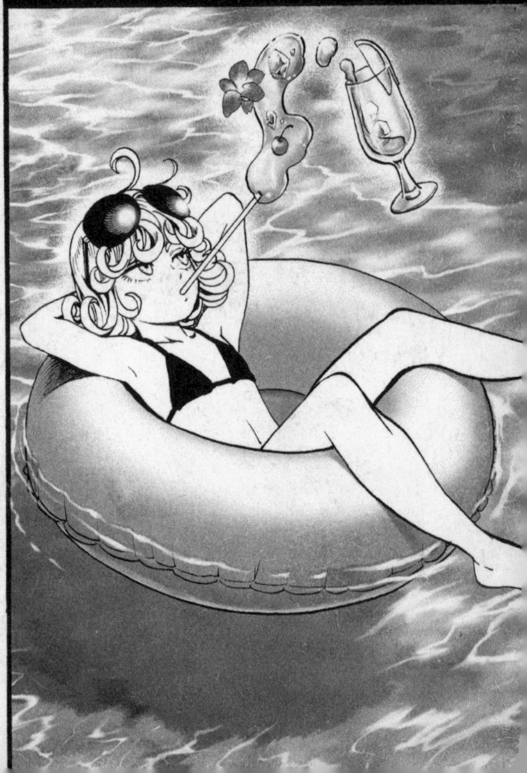

PUNCH 56: HEAD-ON

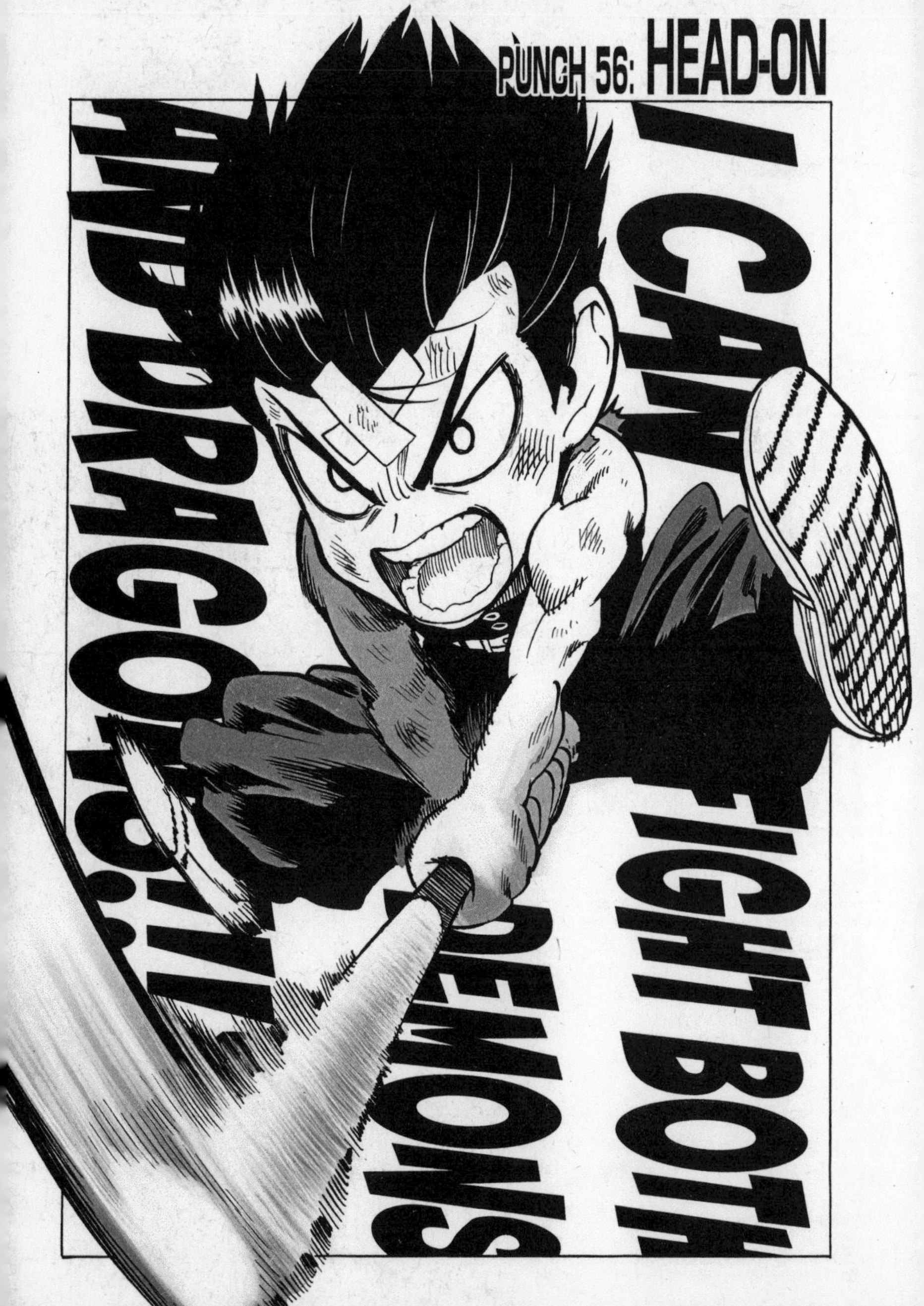
I CAN FIGHT BOTH
DEMONS
AND DRAGONS!!

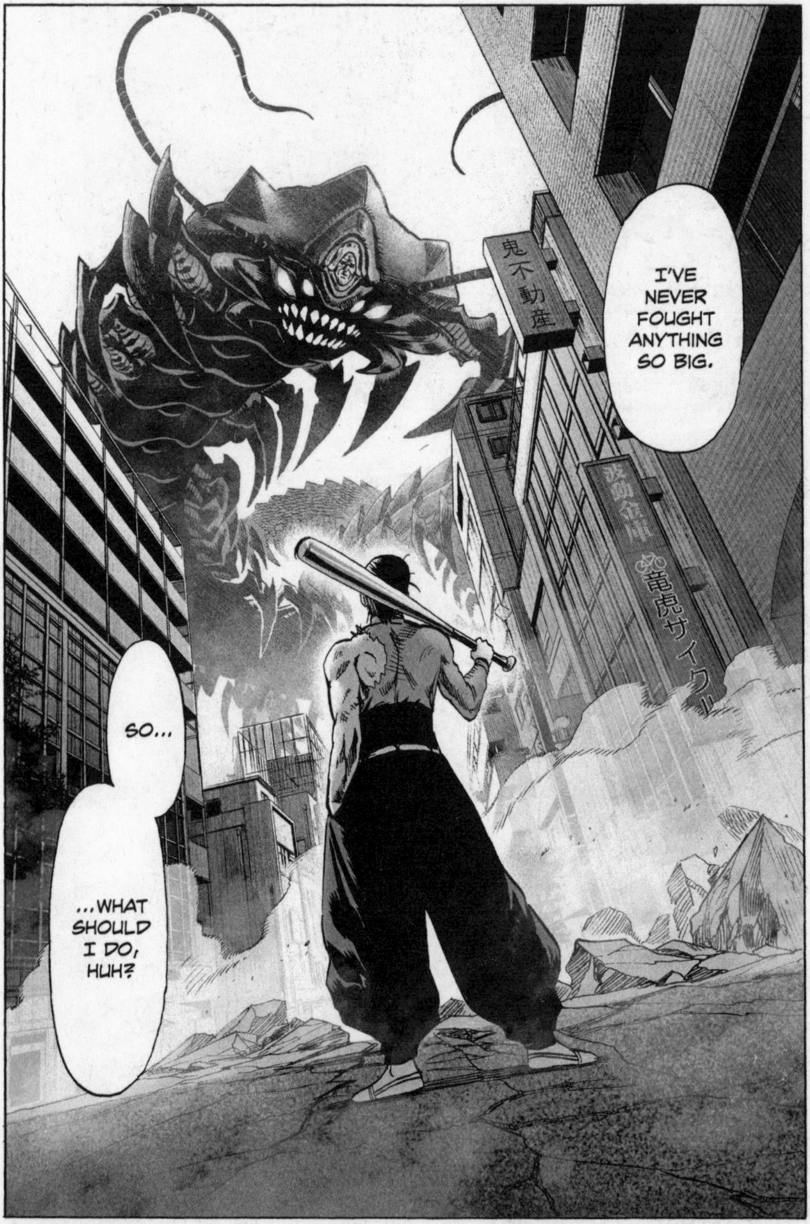
I'VE NEVER FOUGHT ANYTHING SO BIG.
鬼不動産
波動金庫
竜虎サイク
SO...
...WHAT SHOULD I DO, HUH?

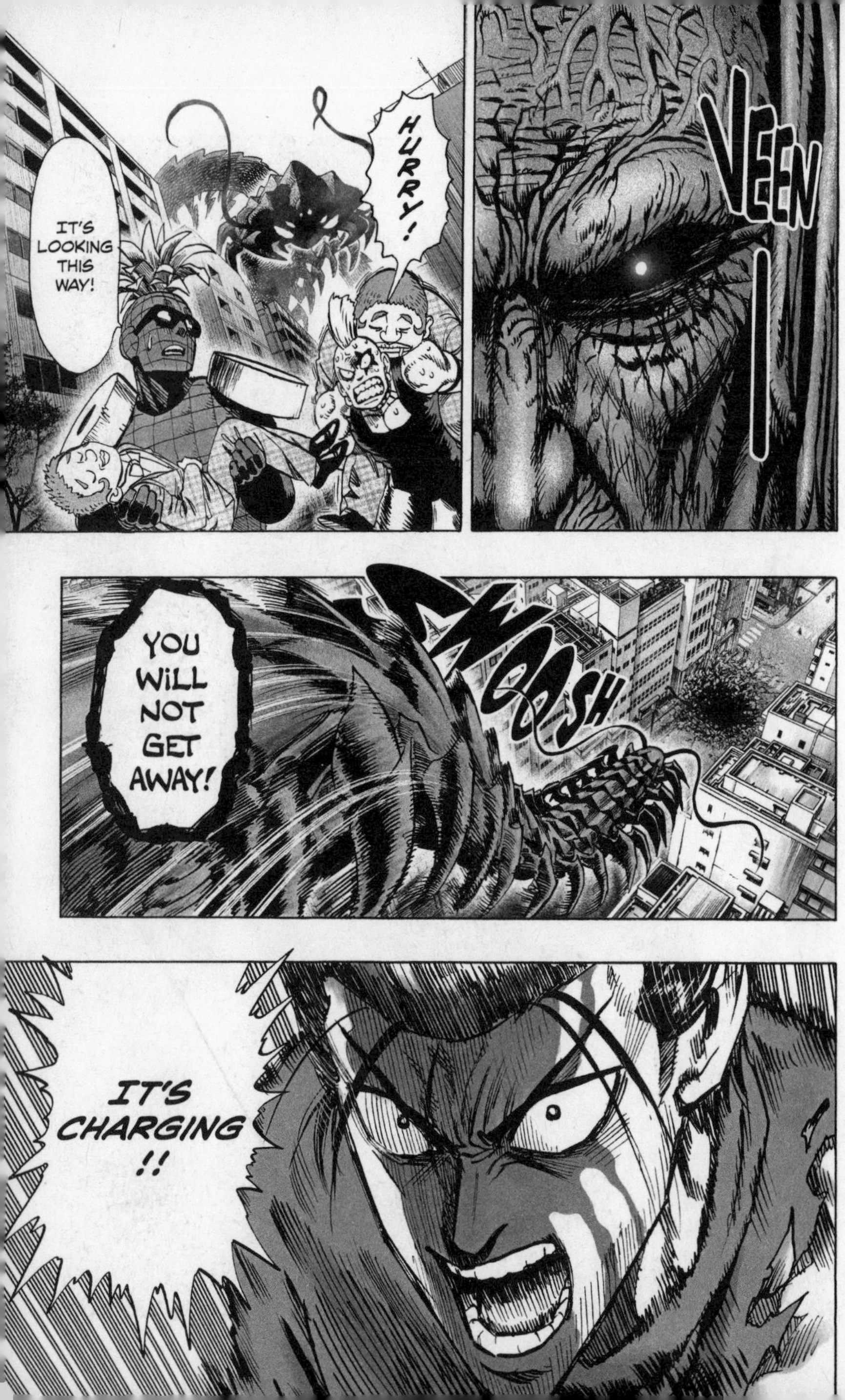
VEEN
HURRY!
IT'S LOOKING THIS WAY!
WHOOSH
YOU WILL NOT GET AWAY!
IT'S CHARGING!!

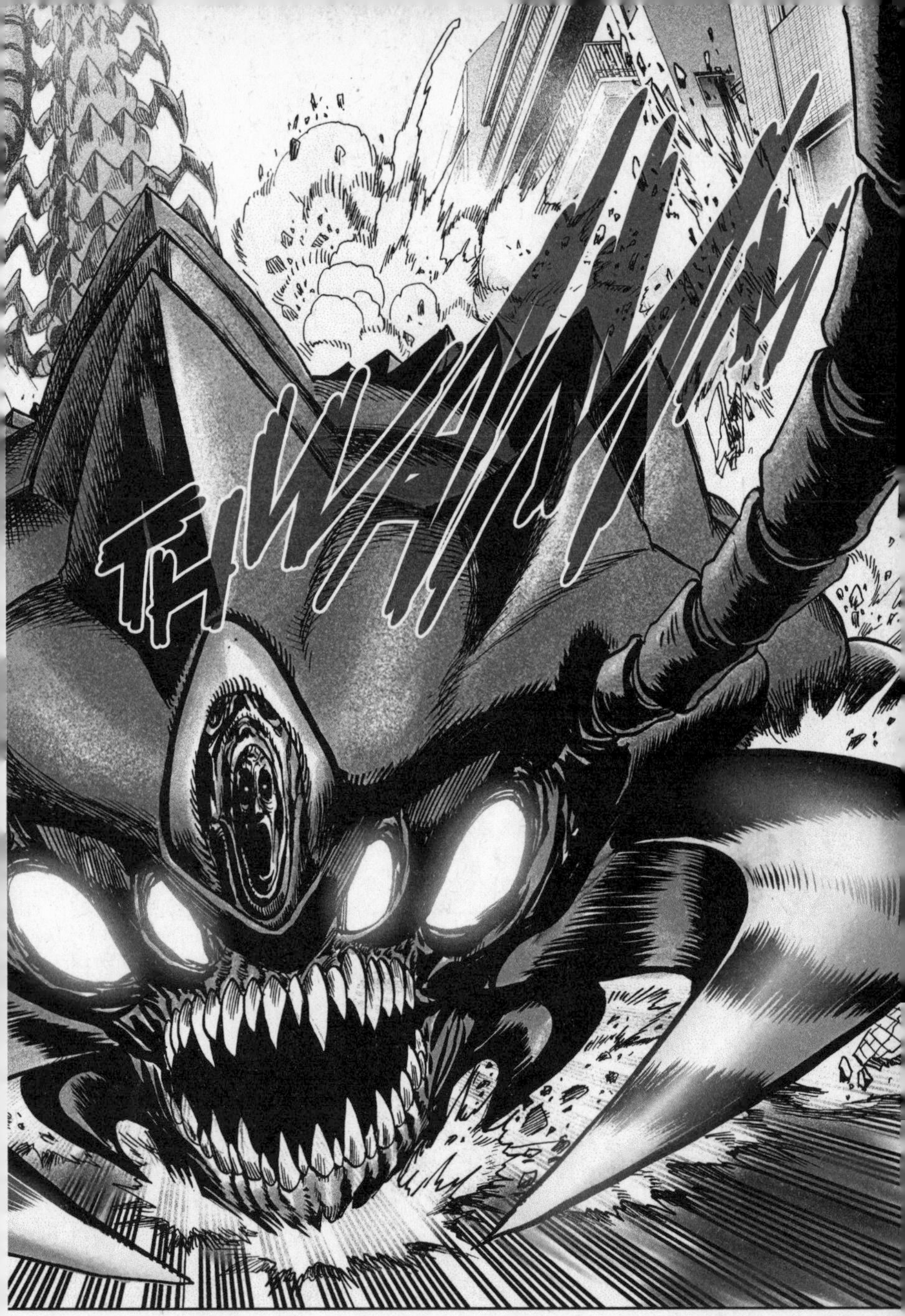
THWAM

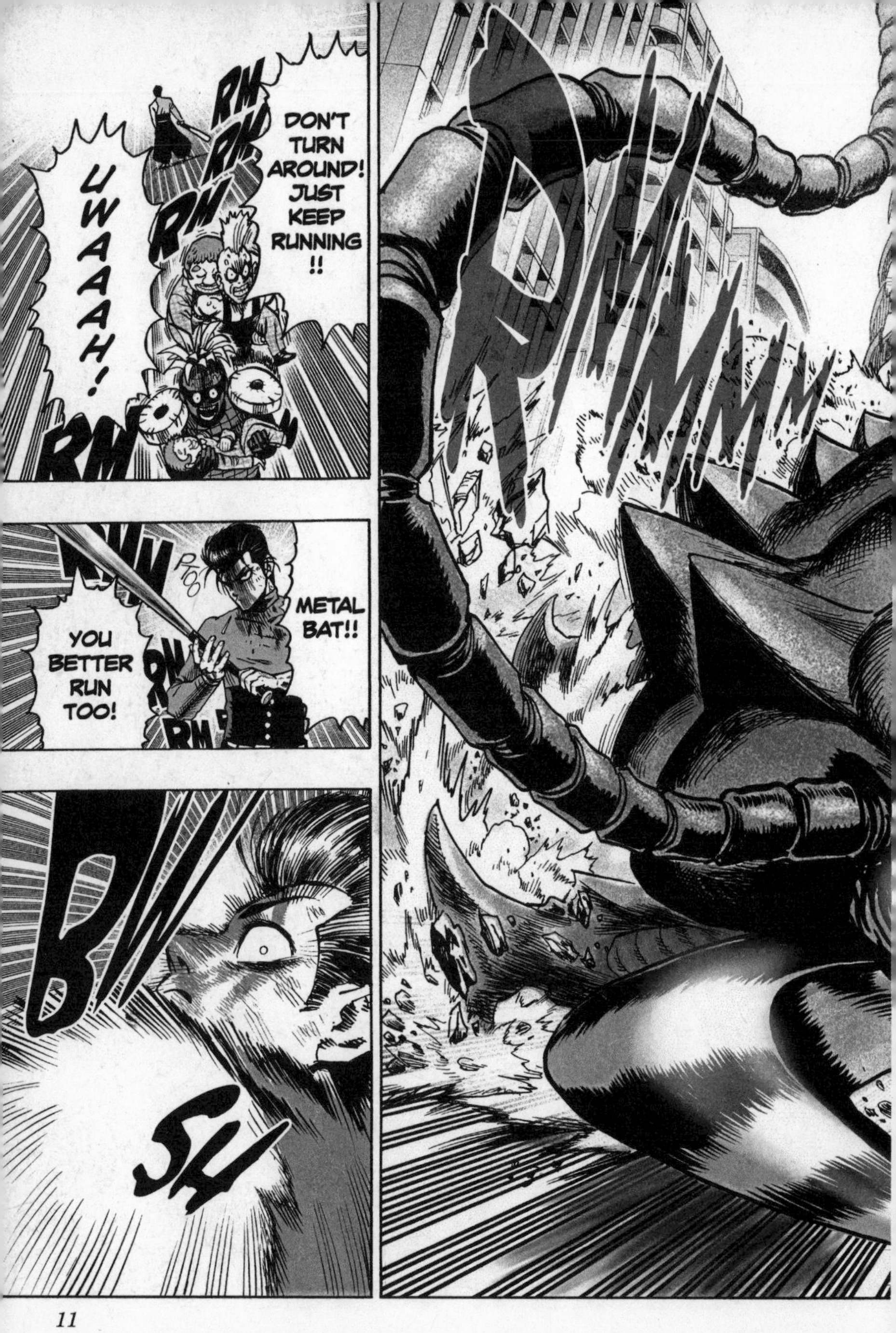

RMMMM
RM RM RM RM
DON'T TURN AROUND! JUST KEEP RUNNING!!
UWAAAAH!
RM
PTOO
METAL BAT!!
YOU BETTER RUN TOO!
RM

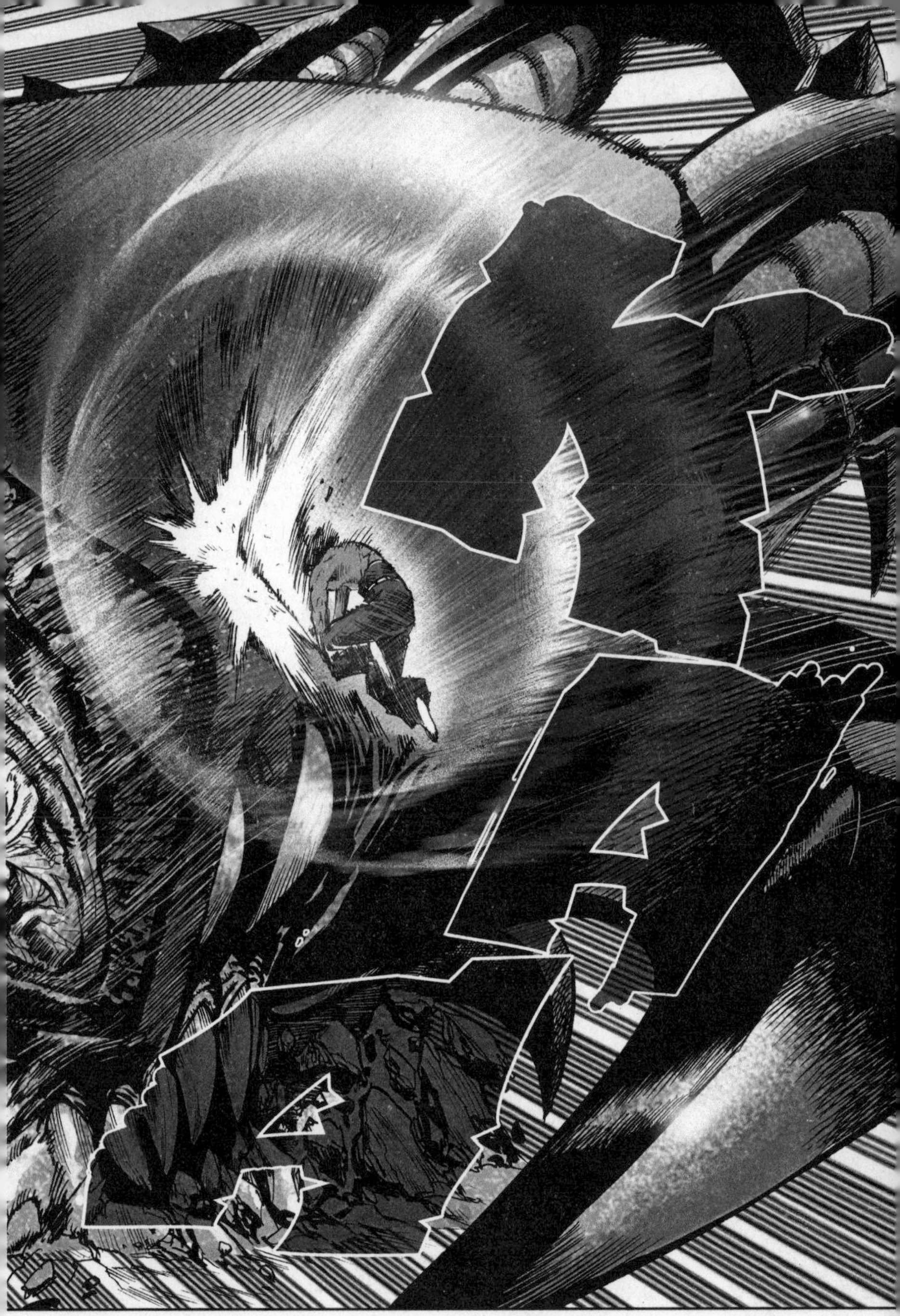

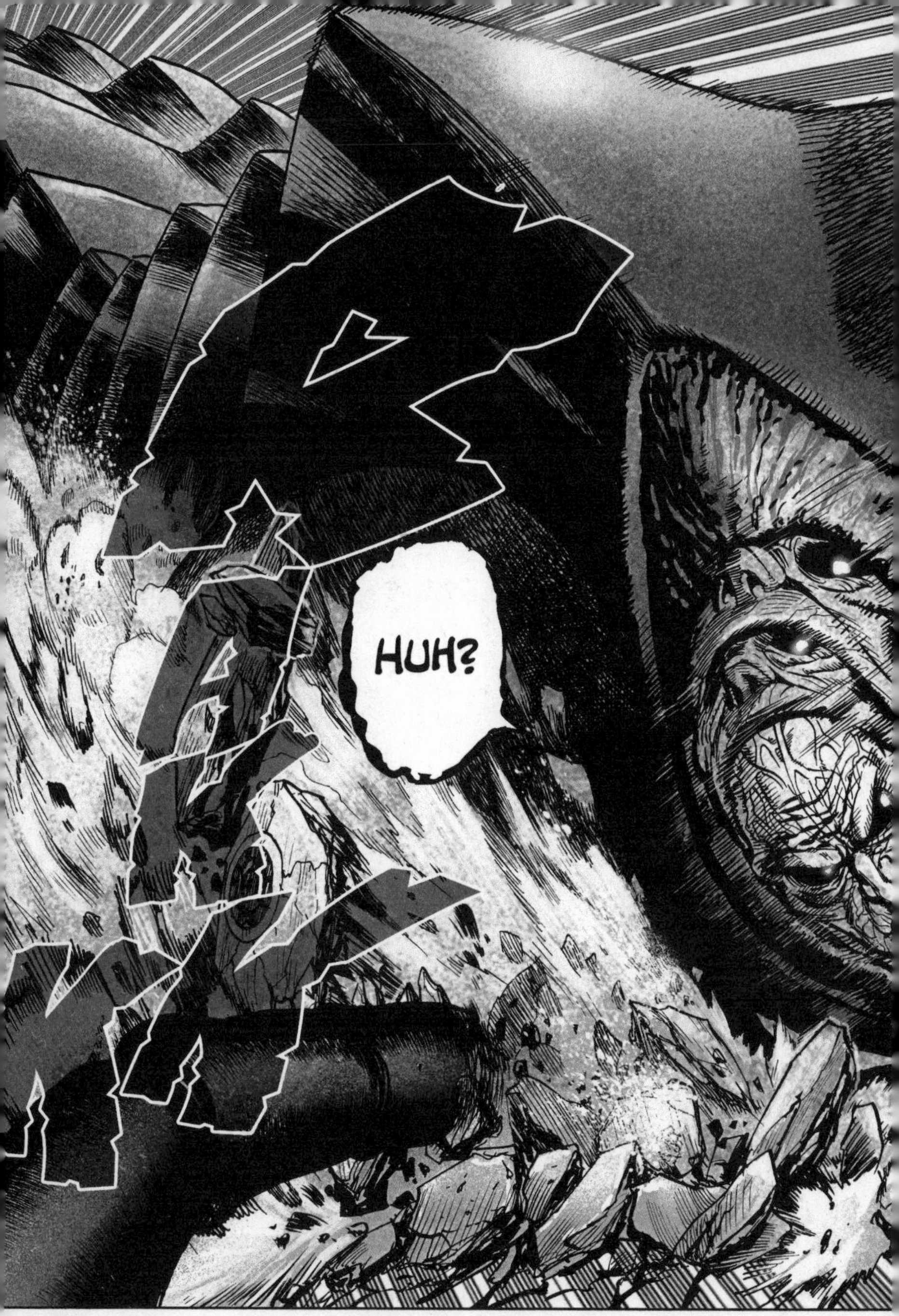
HUH?

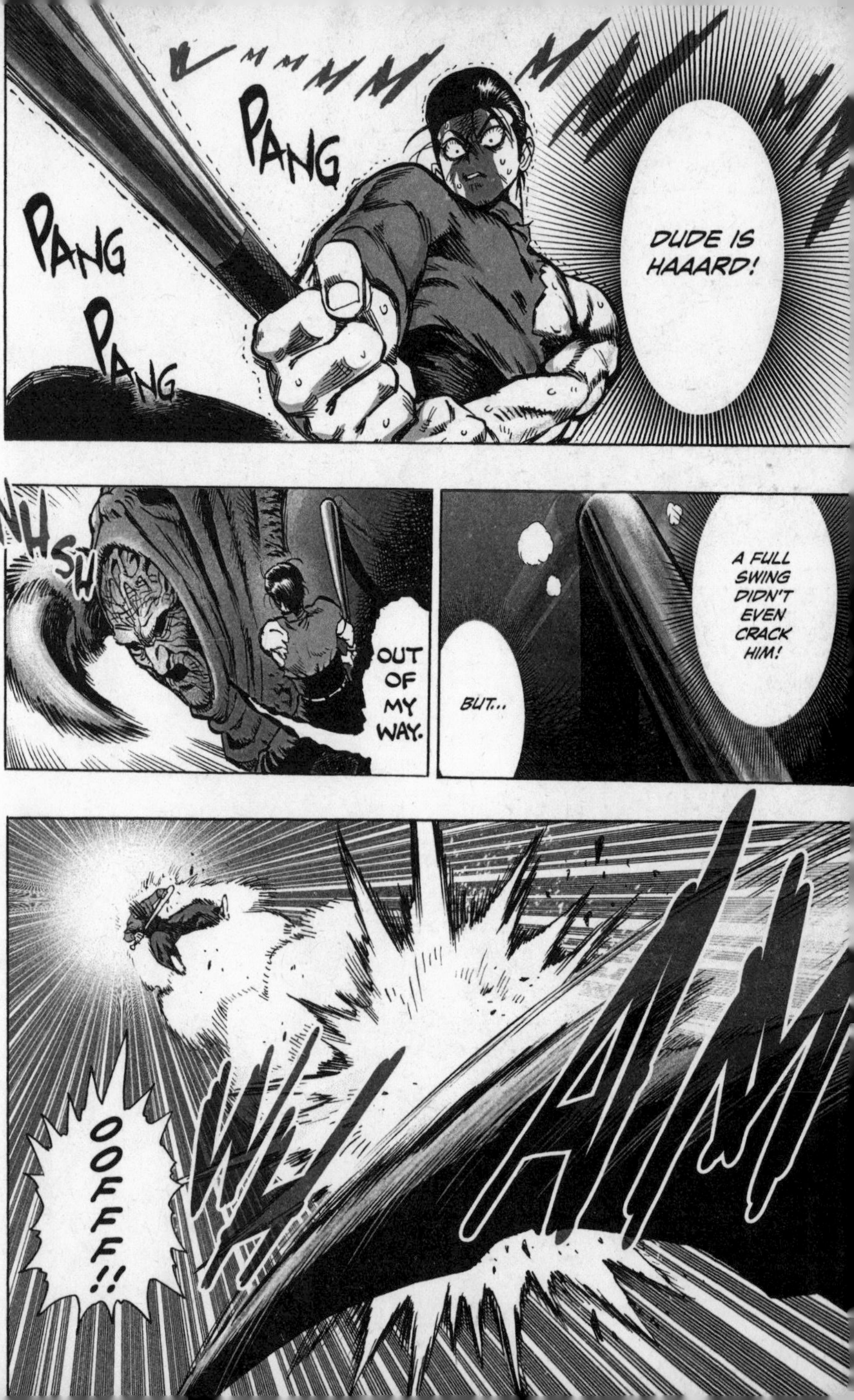
DUDE IS HAAARD!
PANG
PANG
PANG
PANG
A FULL SWING DIDN'T EVEN CRACK HIM!
BUT...
WHSH
OUT OF MY WAY.
OOFFF!!

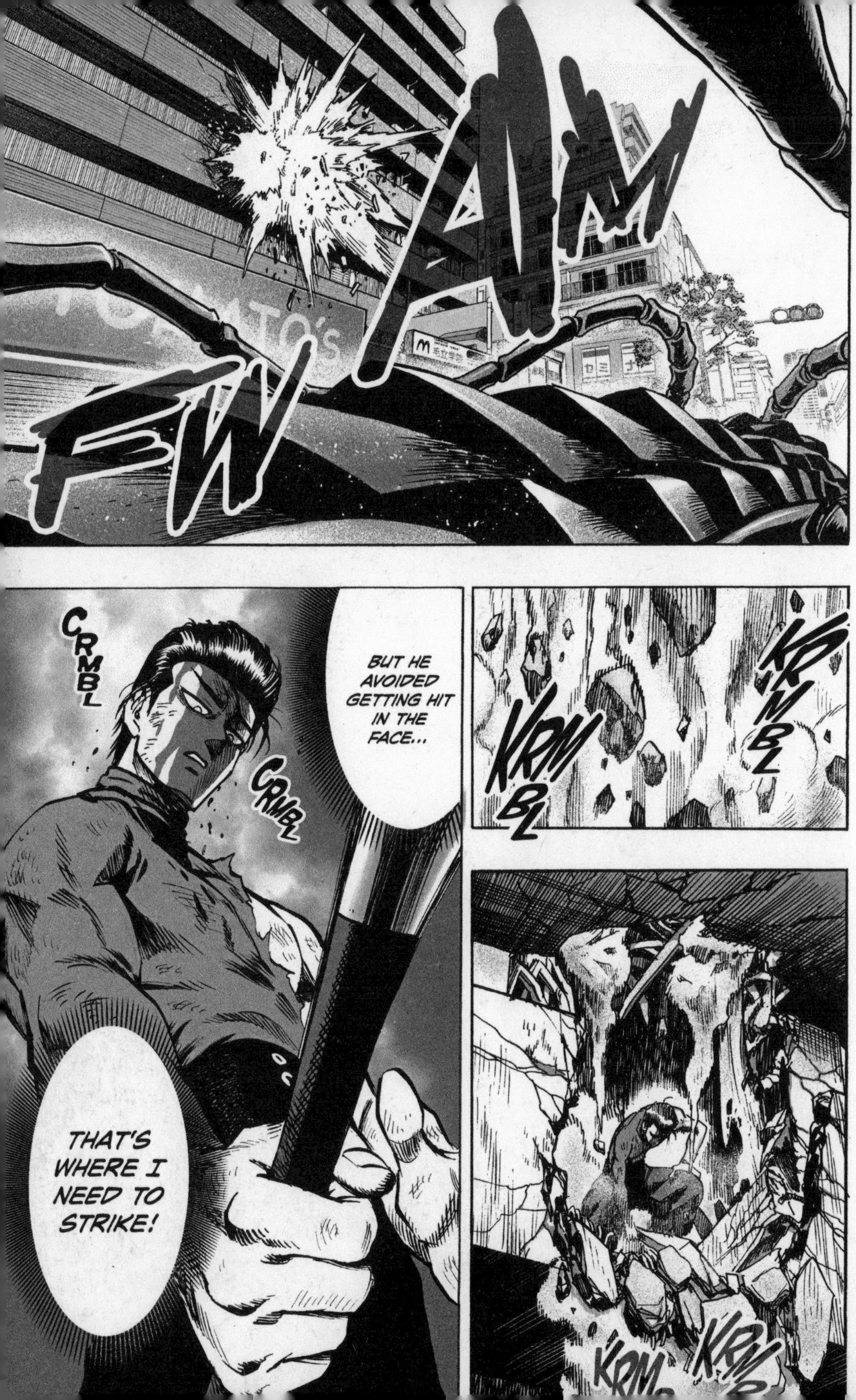

FWAM
KRMBL
KRMBL
KRM
KRM
CRMBL
BUT HE AVOIDED GETTING HIT IN THE FACE...
CRMBL
THAT'S WHERE I NEED TO STRIKE!

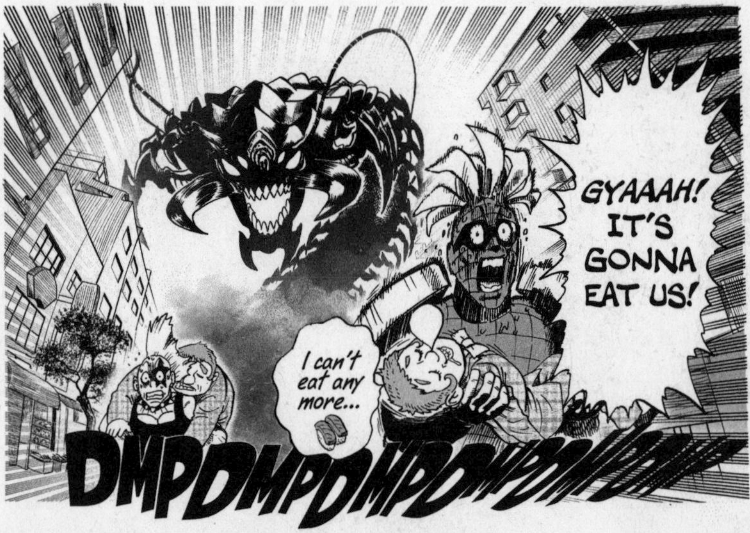
GYAAAH! IT'S GONNA EAT US!
I can't eat any more...
DMPDMPDMPDMPDMPDMPDMP

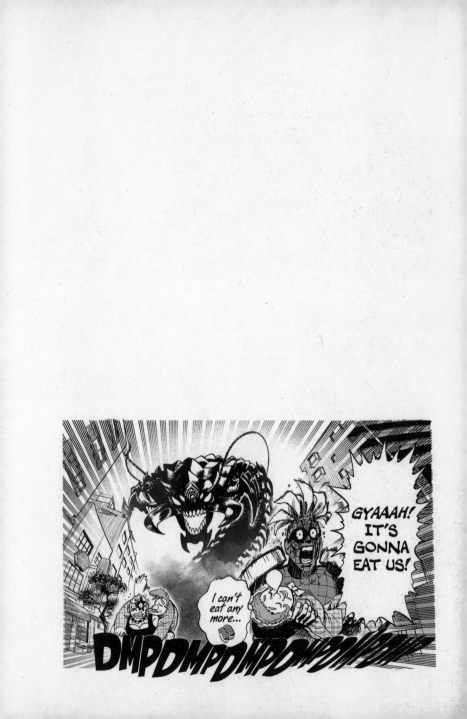

PUNCH 57: INTERRUPTION

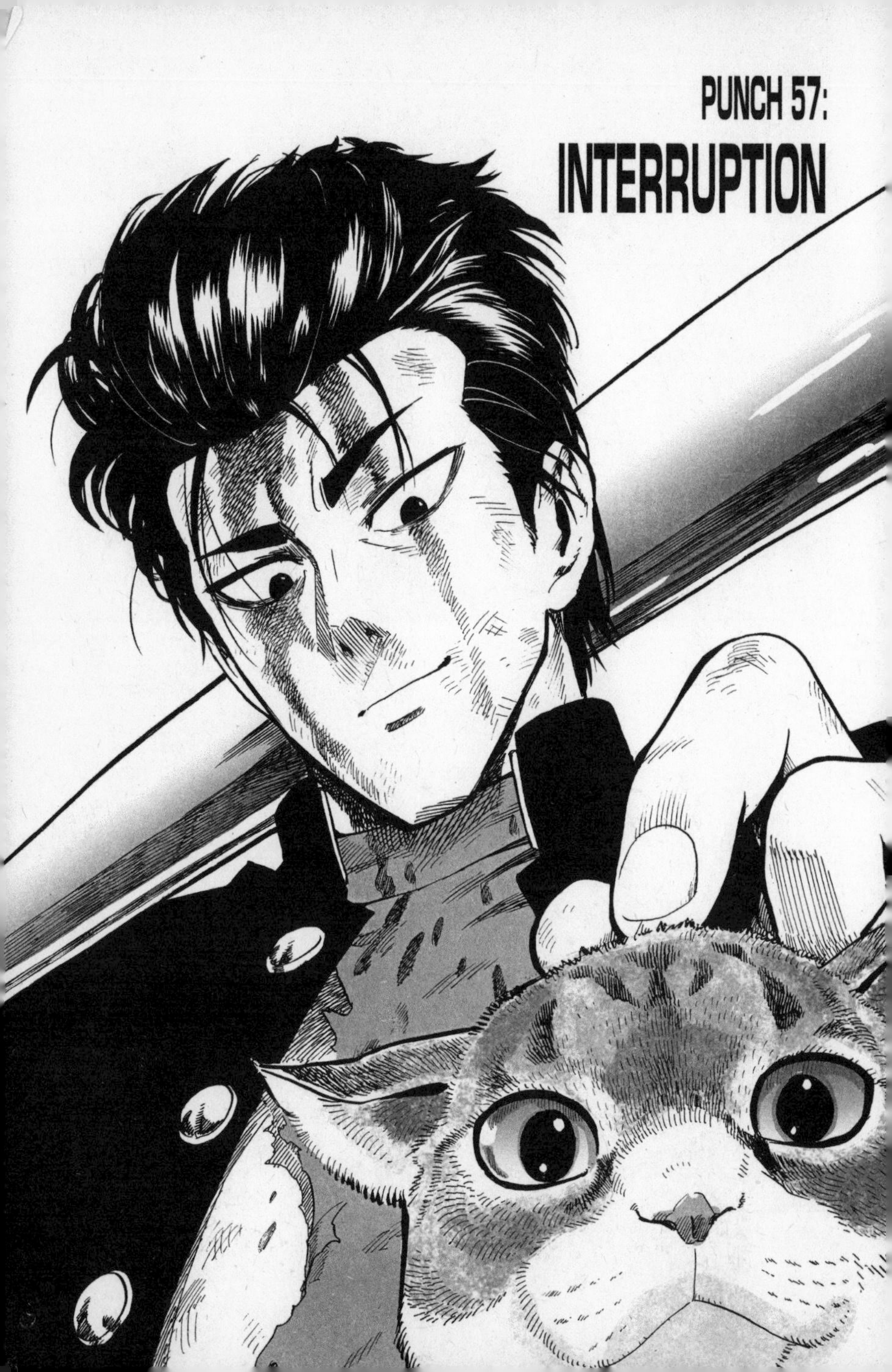

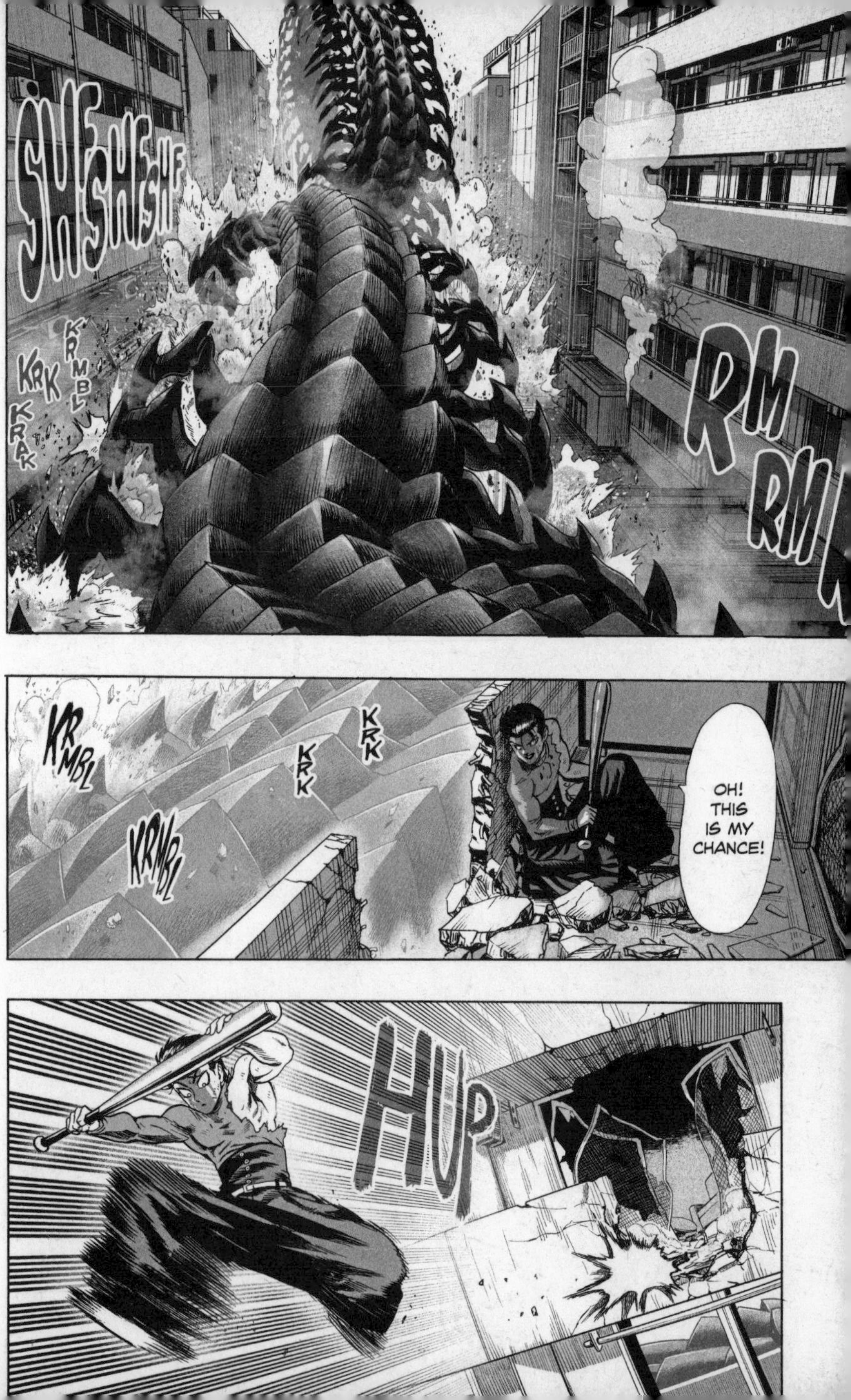
RM RM
SHISHISHF
KRMBL
KRK
KRAK
OH! THIS IS MY CHANCE!
KRK KRK
KRMBL
KRMBL
HUP

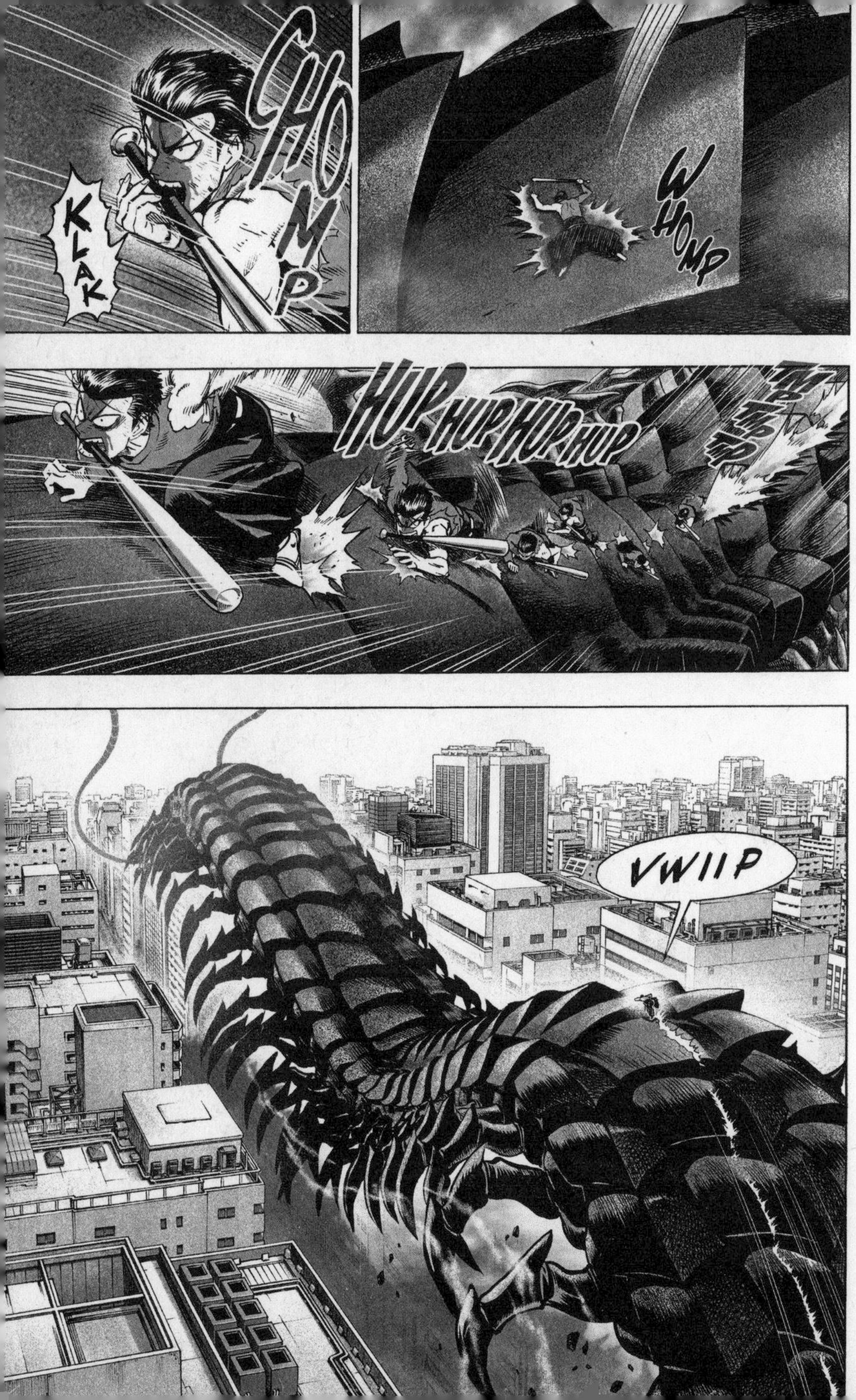
WHOMP
CHOMP
KLAK
TMP TMP TMP
HUP HUP HUP HUP
VWIIP

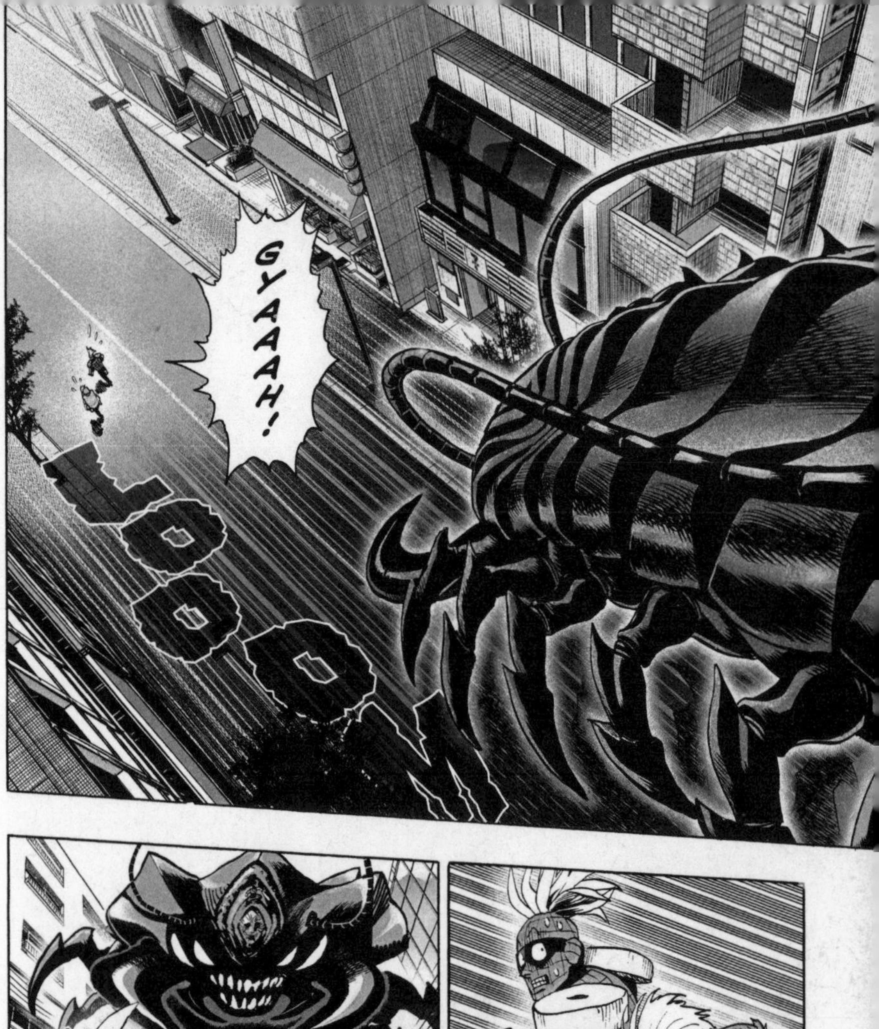
GYAAAH!

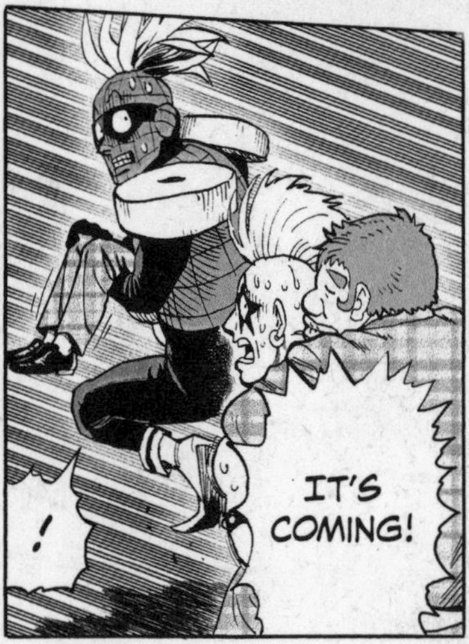
!
IT'S COMING!

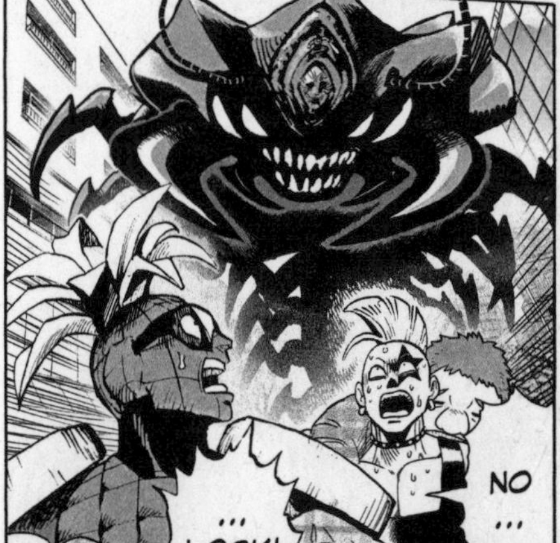
NO ...
... LOOK!

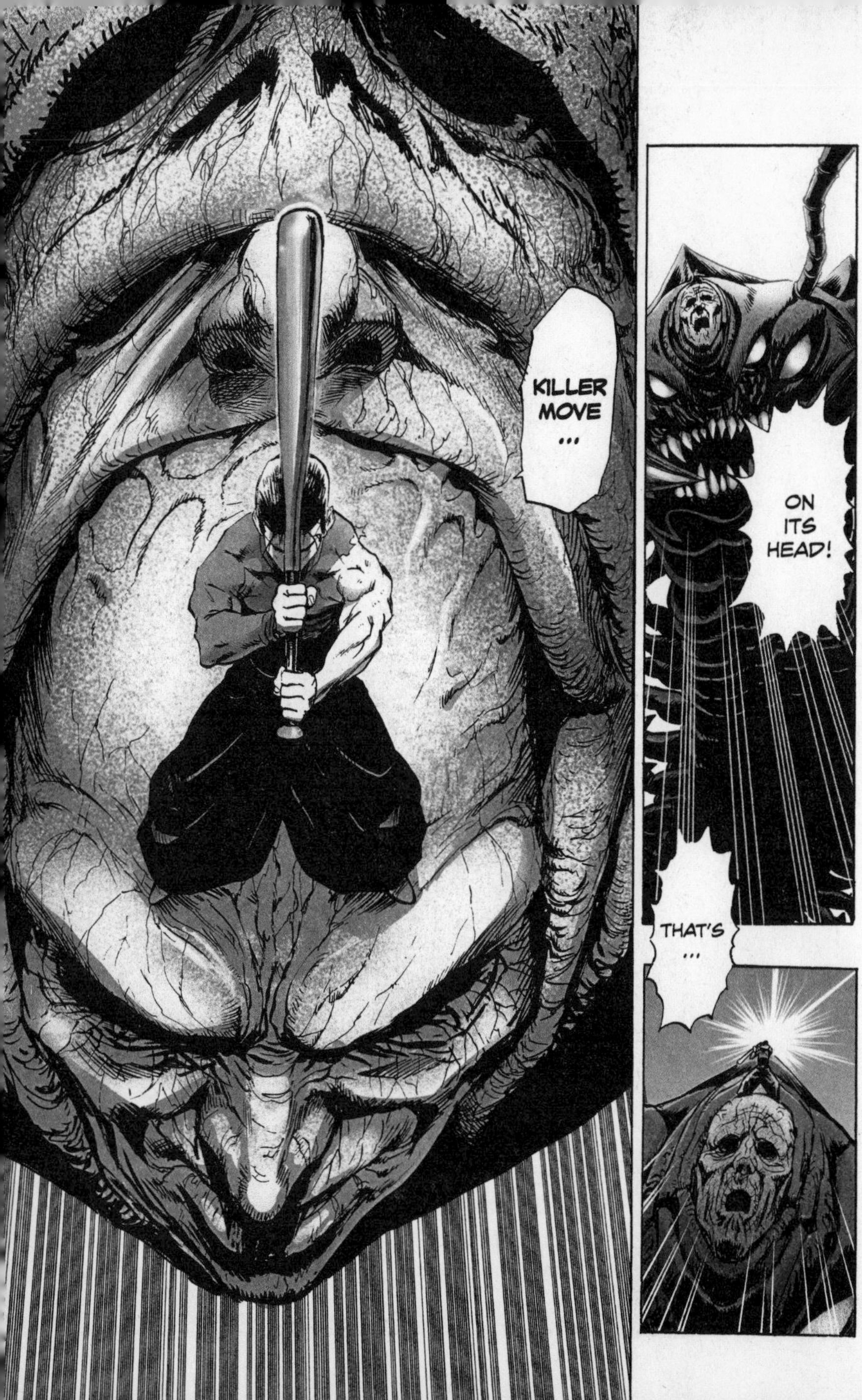
ON ITS HEAD!
THAT'S ...
KILLER MOVE ...

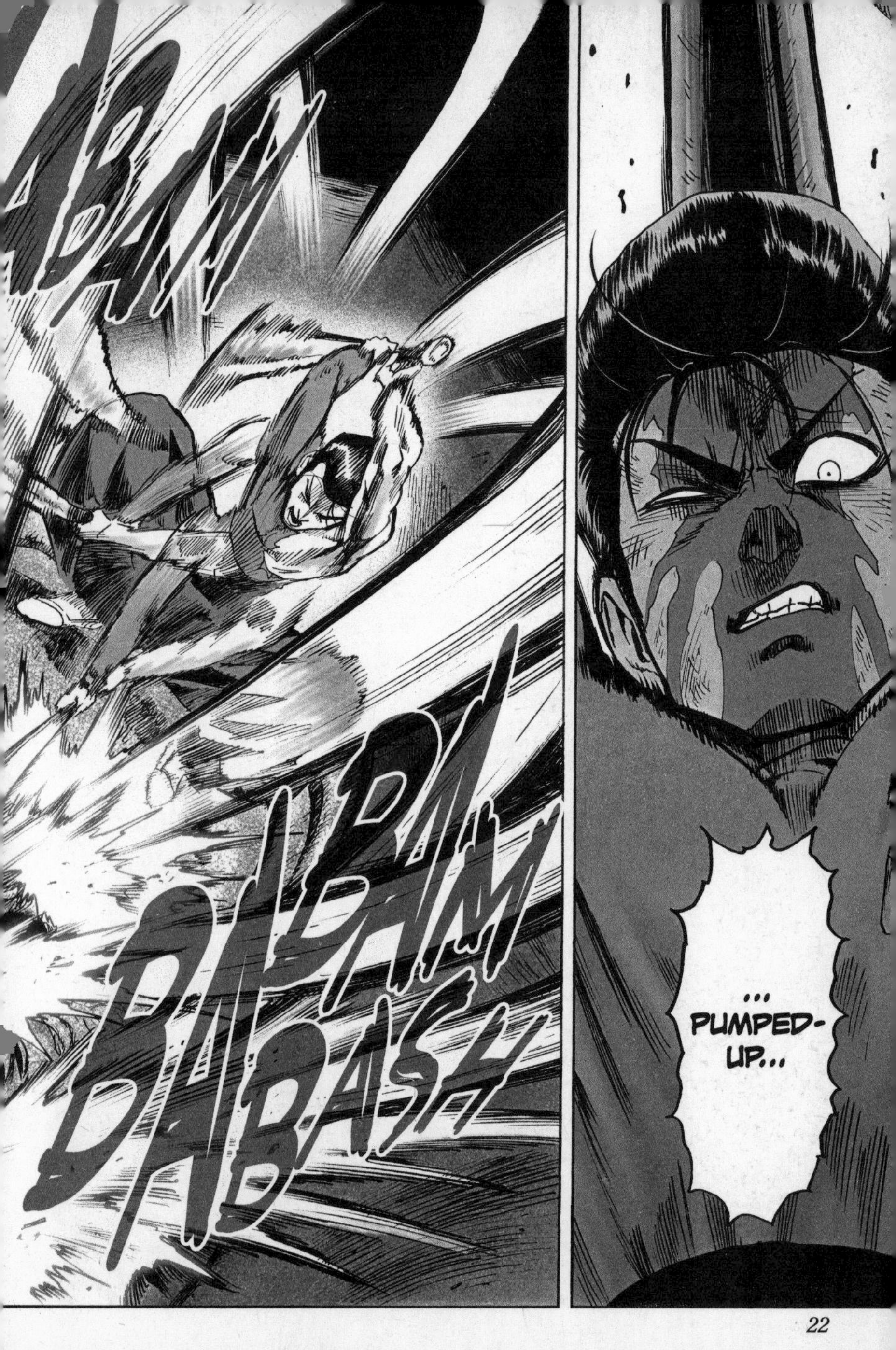
...PUMPED-UP...
DADAM
DADAM
DABASH

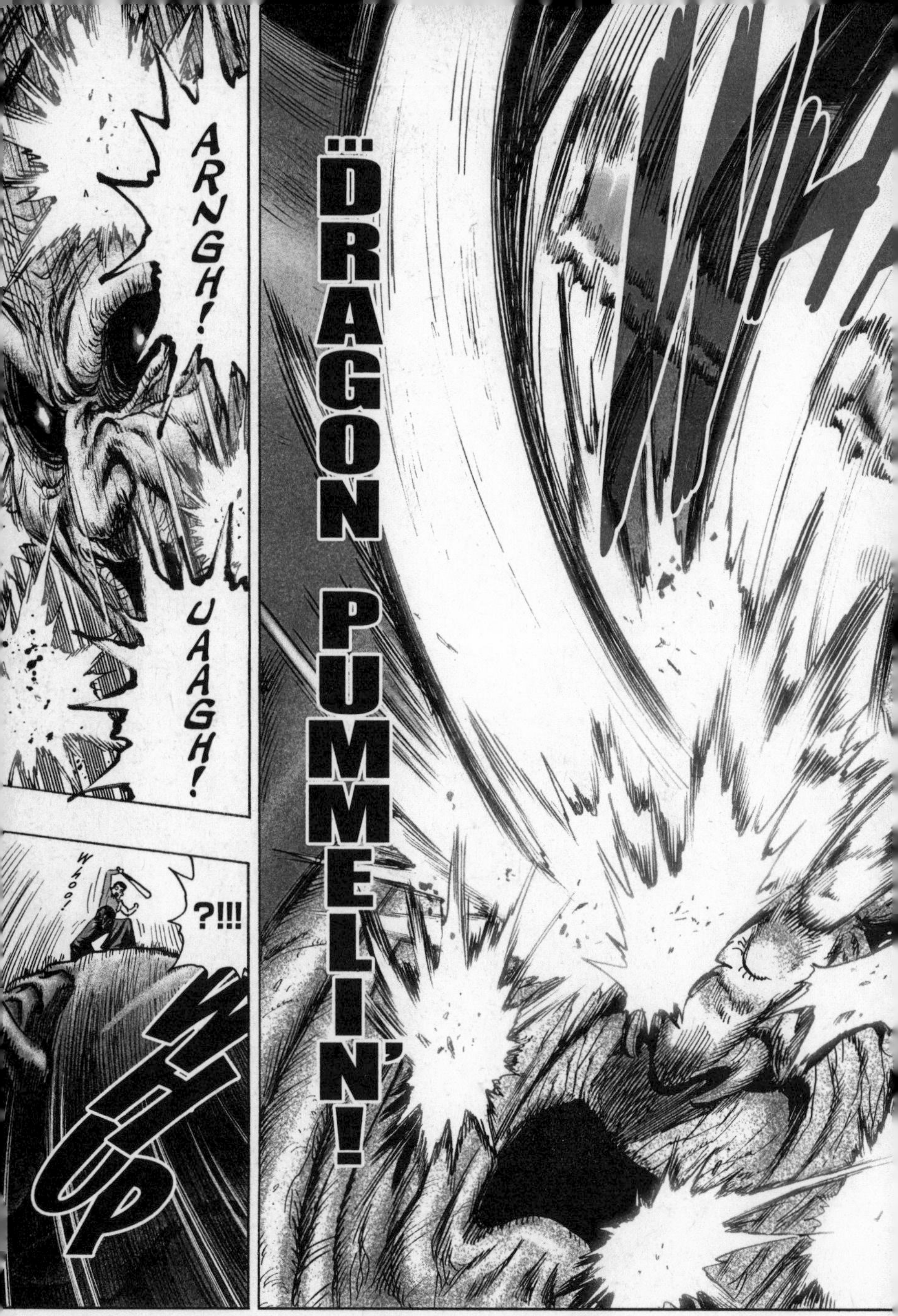
DRAGON PUMMELIN'!
ARNGH!
UAAGH!
Whoo!
?!!!
WHUP

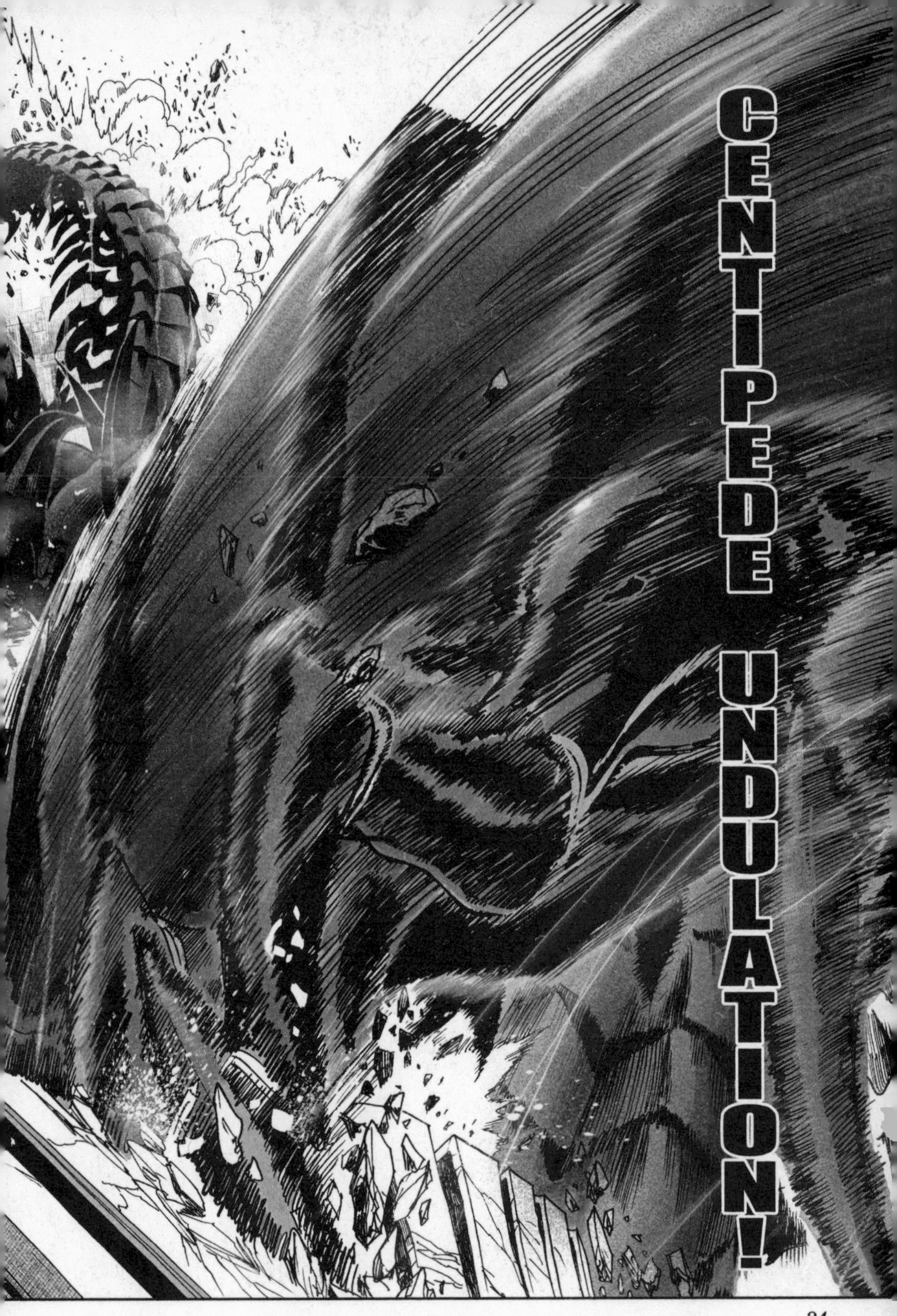
CENTIPEDE UNDULATION!

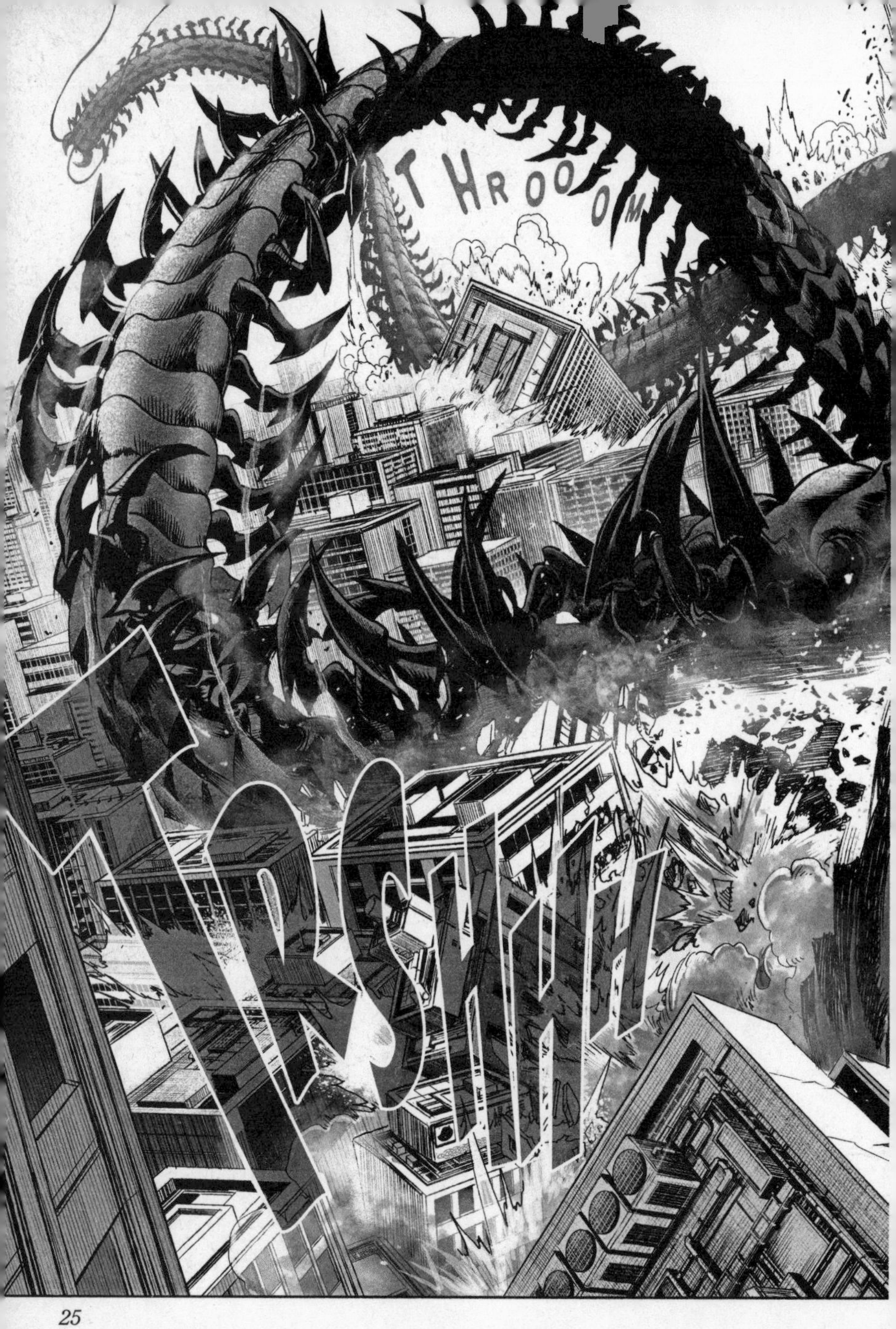
THROOOOM
WSHHH

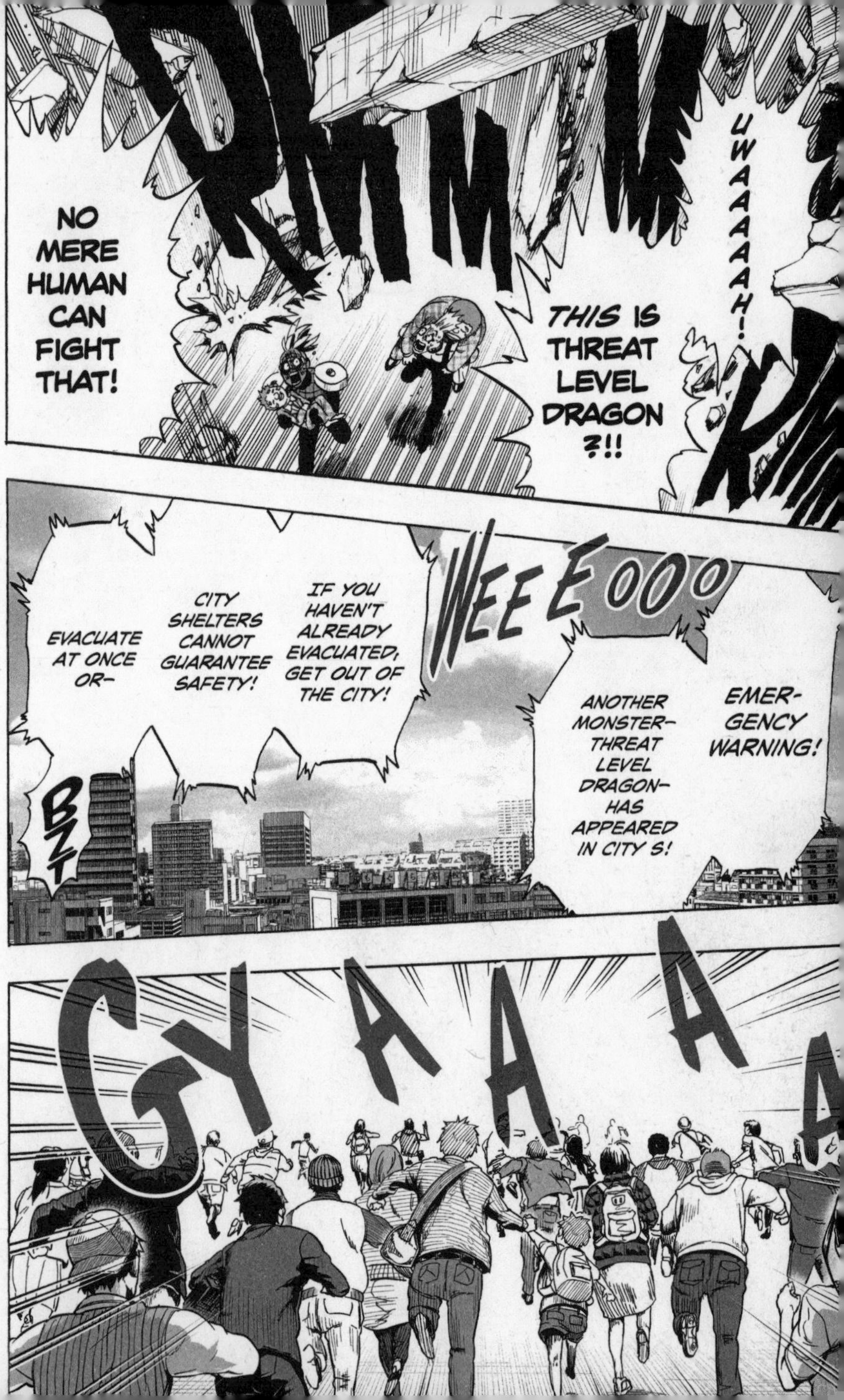
UWAAAAAAH!
THIS IS THREAT LEVEL DRAGON ?!!
NO MERE HUMAN CAN FIGHT THAT!
WEEE OOO
EMERGENCY WARNING!
ANOTHER MONSTER—THREAT LEVEL DRAGON—HAS APPEARED IN CITY S!
IF YOU HAVEN'T ALREADY EVACUATED, GET OUT OF THE CITY!
CITY SHELTERS CANNOT GUARANTEE SAFETY!
EVACUATE AT ONCE OR—
BZZT
GYAAA

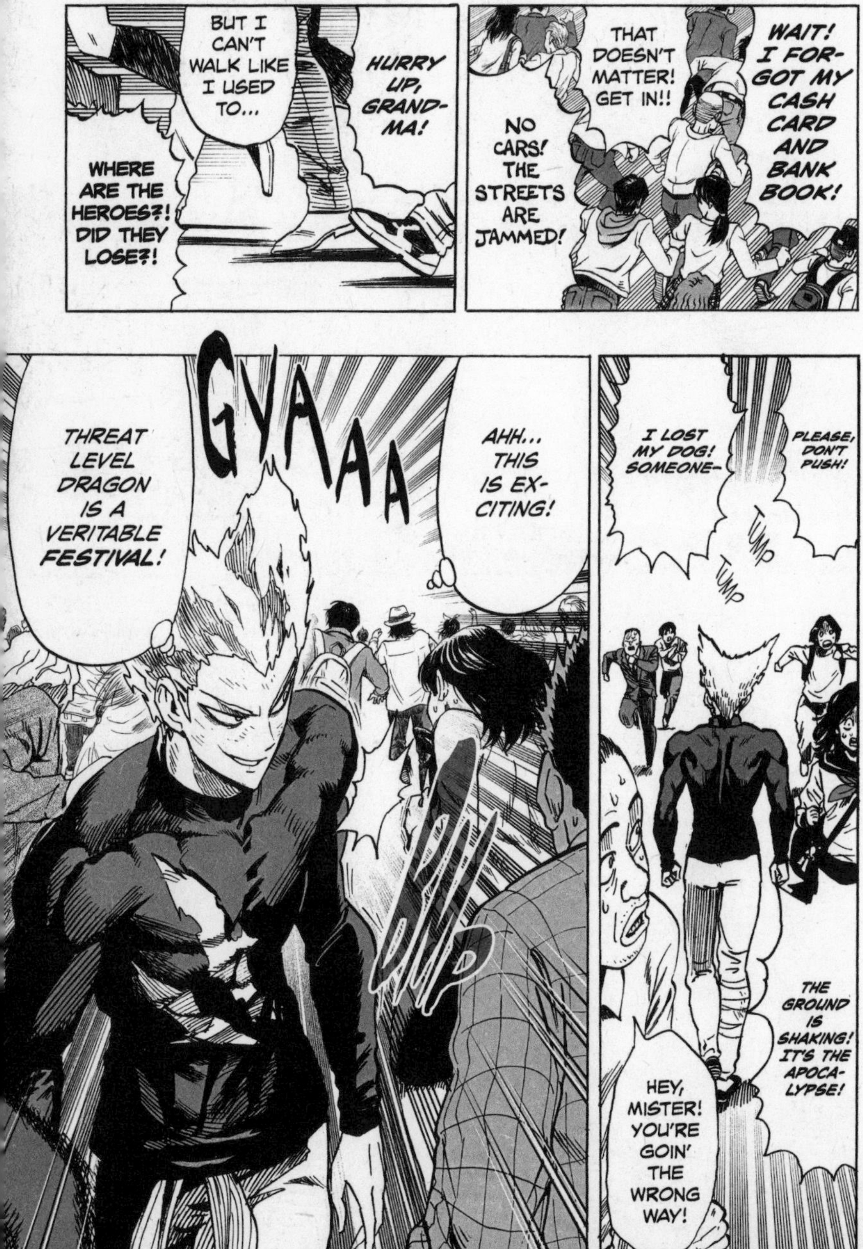
WAIT! I FORGOT MY CASH CARD AND BANK BOOK!
THAT DOESN'T MATTER! GET IN!!
NO CARS! THE STREETS ARE JAMMED!
HURRY UP, GRANDMA!
BUT I CAN'T WALK LIKE I USED TO...
WHERE ARE THE HEROES?! DID THEY LOSE?!
PLEASE, DON'T PUSH!
I LOST MY DOG! SOMEONE-
TUMP
TUMP
THE GROUND IS SHAKING! IT'S THE APOCALYPSE!
HEY, MISTER! YOU'RE GOIN' THE WRONG WAY!
AHH... THIS IS EXCITING!
GYAAAA
THREAT LEVEL DRAGON IS A VERITABLE FESTIVAL!

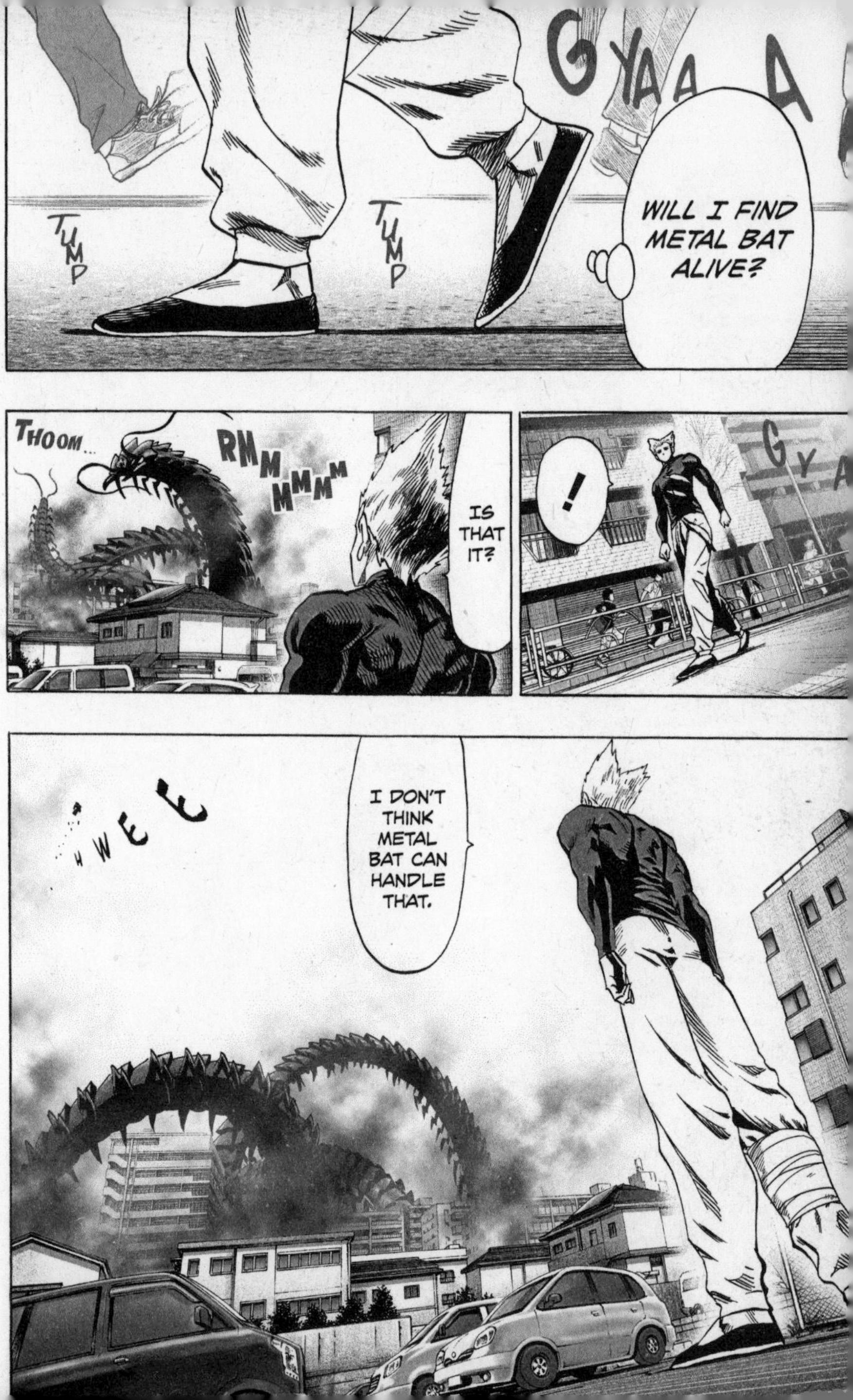
GYAAA
WILL I FIND METAL BAT ALIVE?
TUMP
TUMP
GYA
!
IS THAT IT?
RMMMMMMM
THOOM...
I DON'T THINK METAL BAT CAN HANDLE THAT.
HWEE

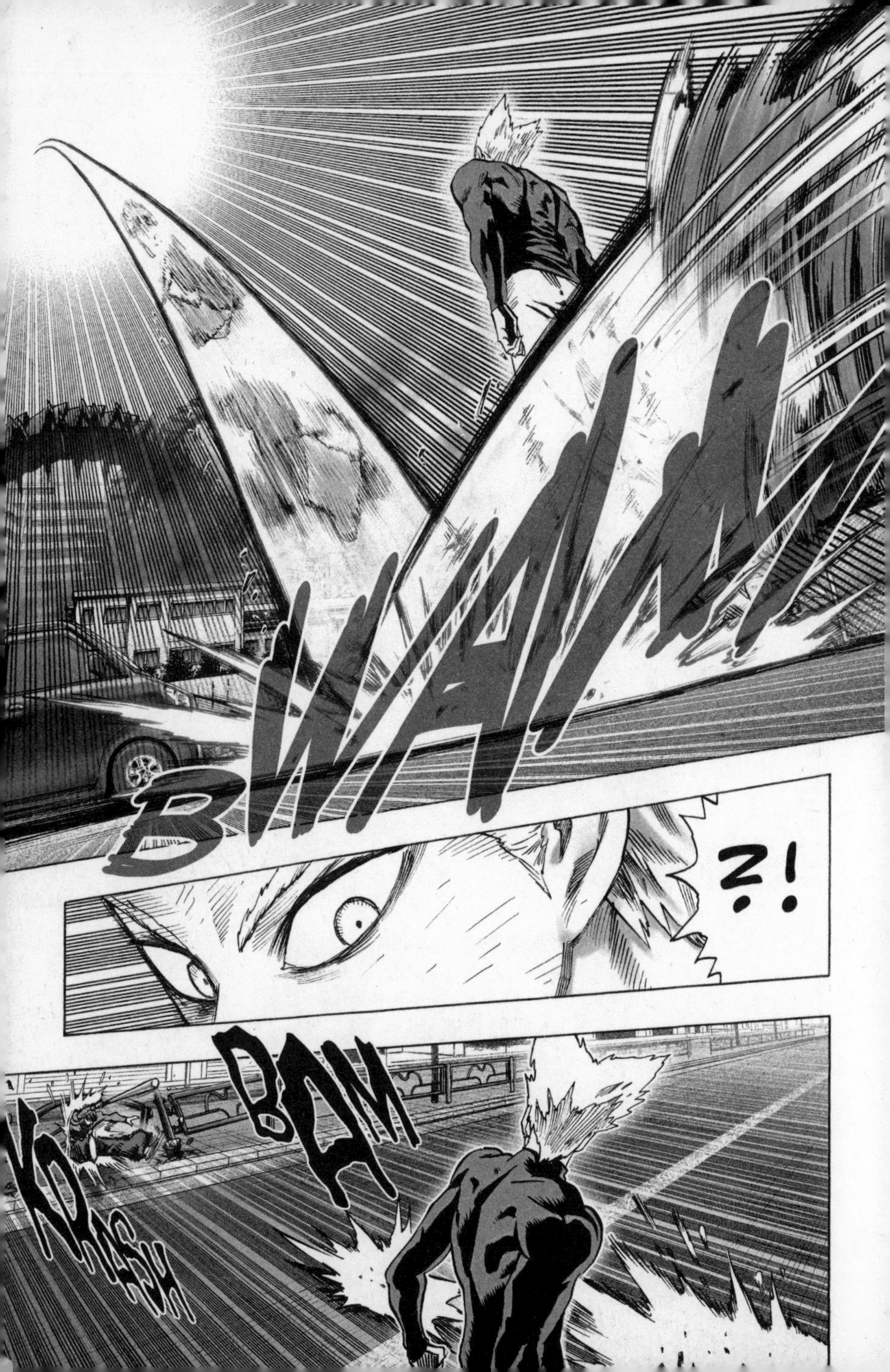
BWAM
?!
BOM
KRASH

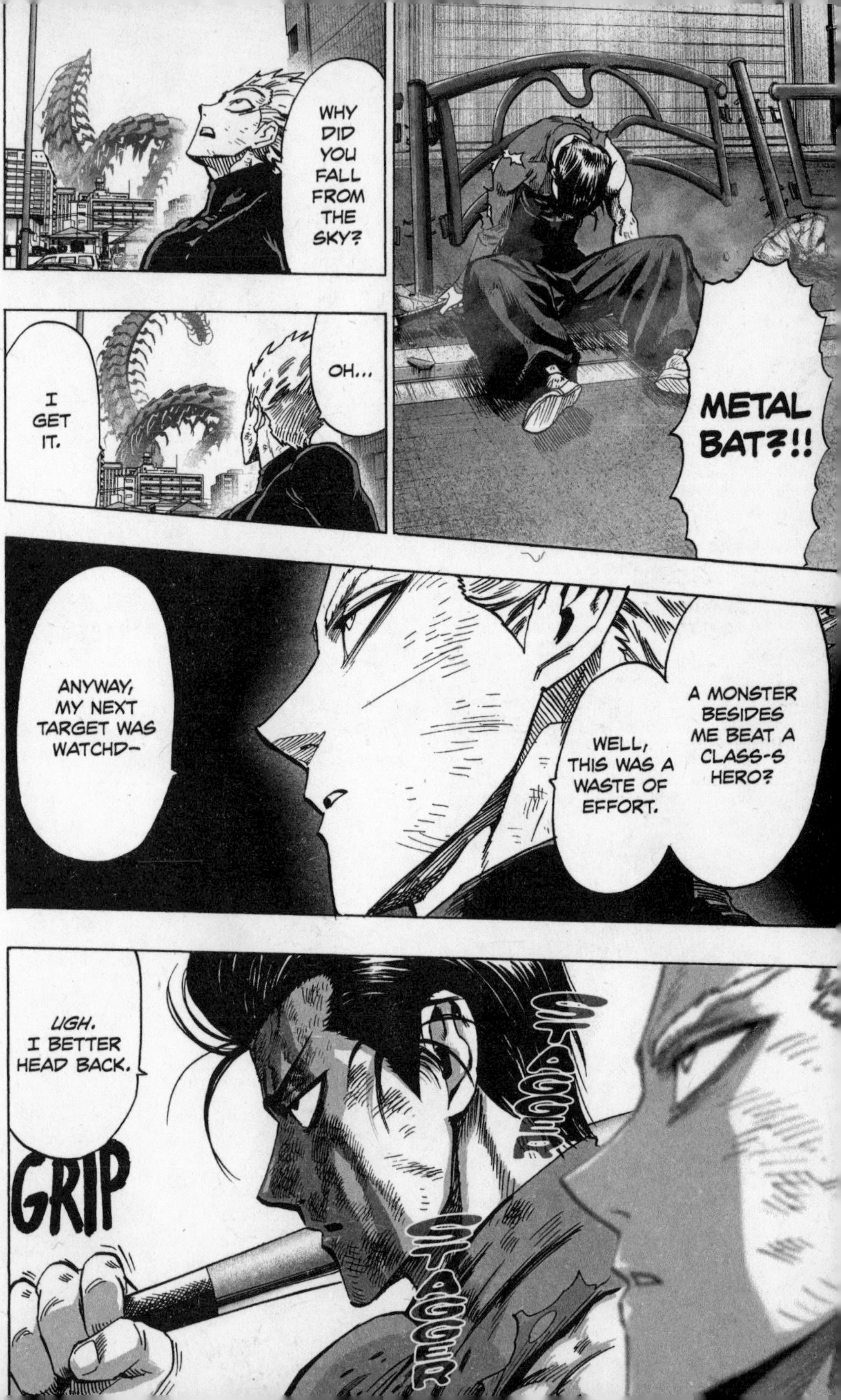
METAL BAT?!!
WHY DID YOU FALL FROM THE SKY?
OH...
I GET IT.
A MONSTER BESIDES ME BEAT A CLASS-S HERO?
WELL, THIS WAS A WASTE OF EFFORT.
ANYWAY, MY NEXT TARGET WAS WATCHD–
STAGGER
STAGGER
UGH. I BETTER HEAD BACK.
GRIP

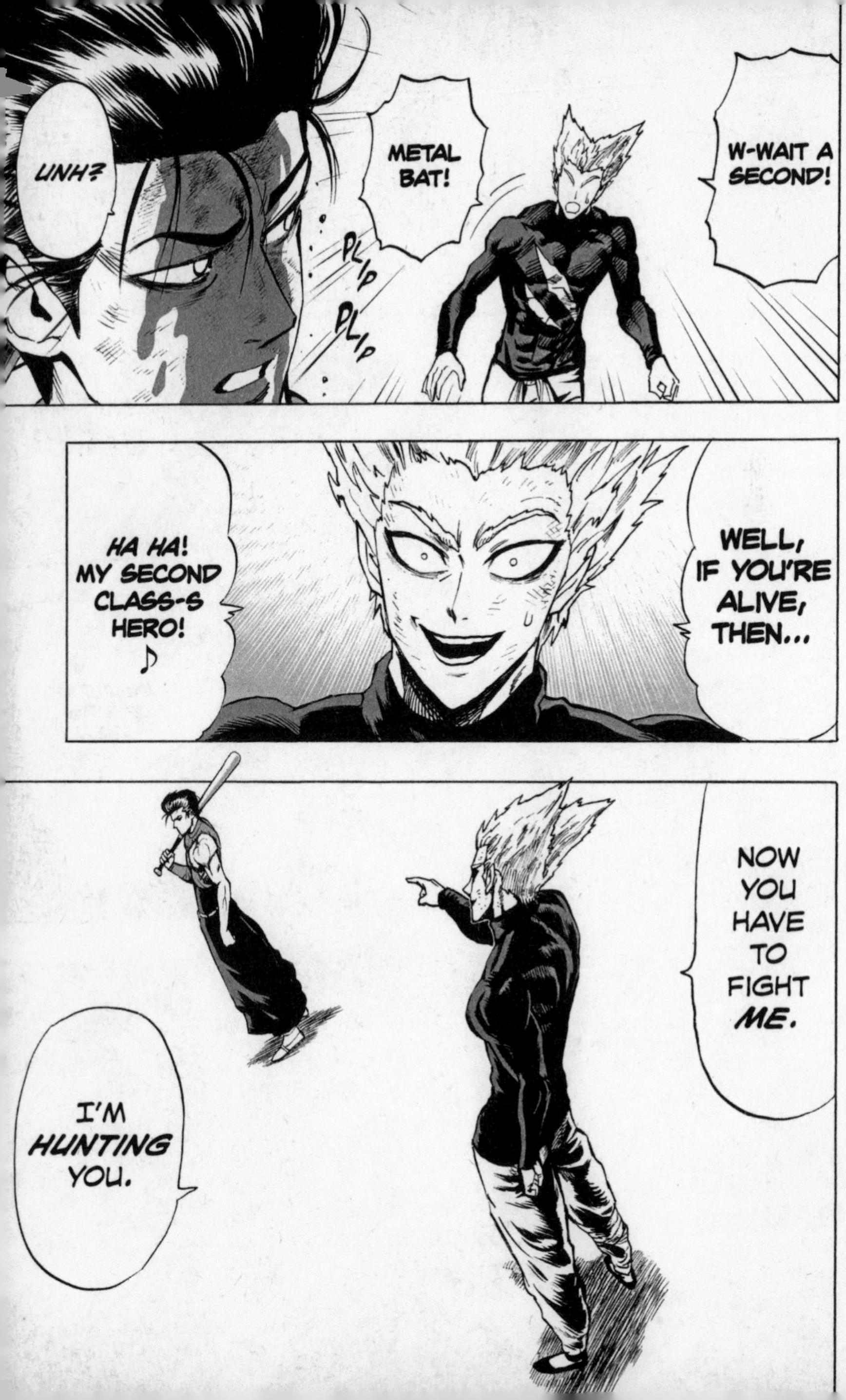
W-WAIT A SECOND!
METAL BAT!
PLIP
PLIP
UNH?
WELL, IF YOU'RE ALIVE, THEN...
HA HA! MY SECOND CLASS-S HERO! ♪
NOW YOU HAVE TO FIGHT ME.
I'M HUNTING YOU.

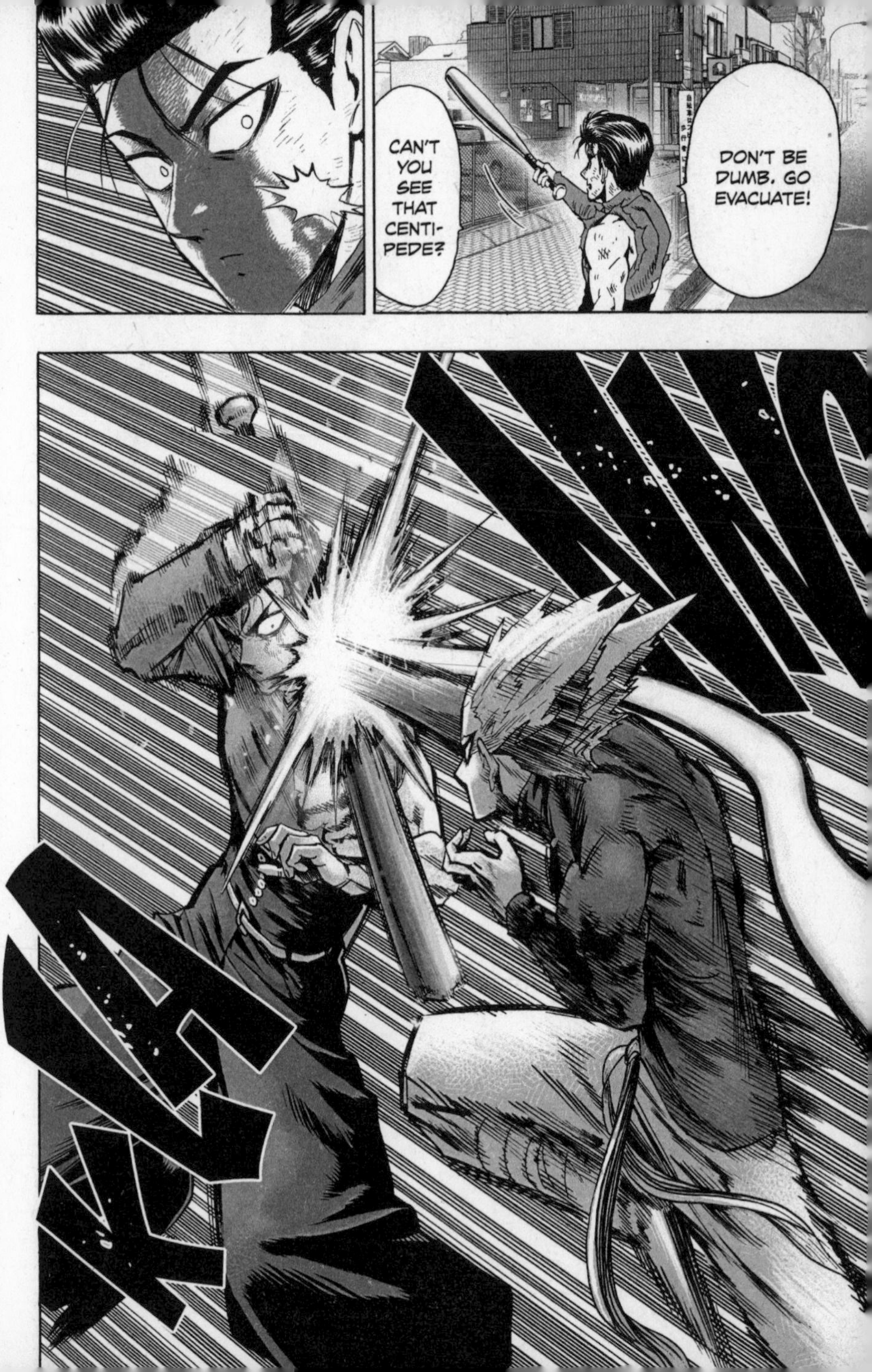
DON'T BE DUMB. GO EVACUATE!
CAN'T YOU SEE THAT CENTIPEDE?

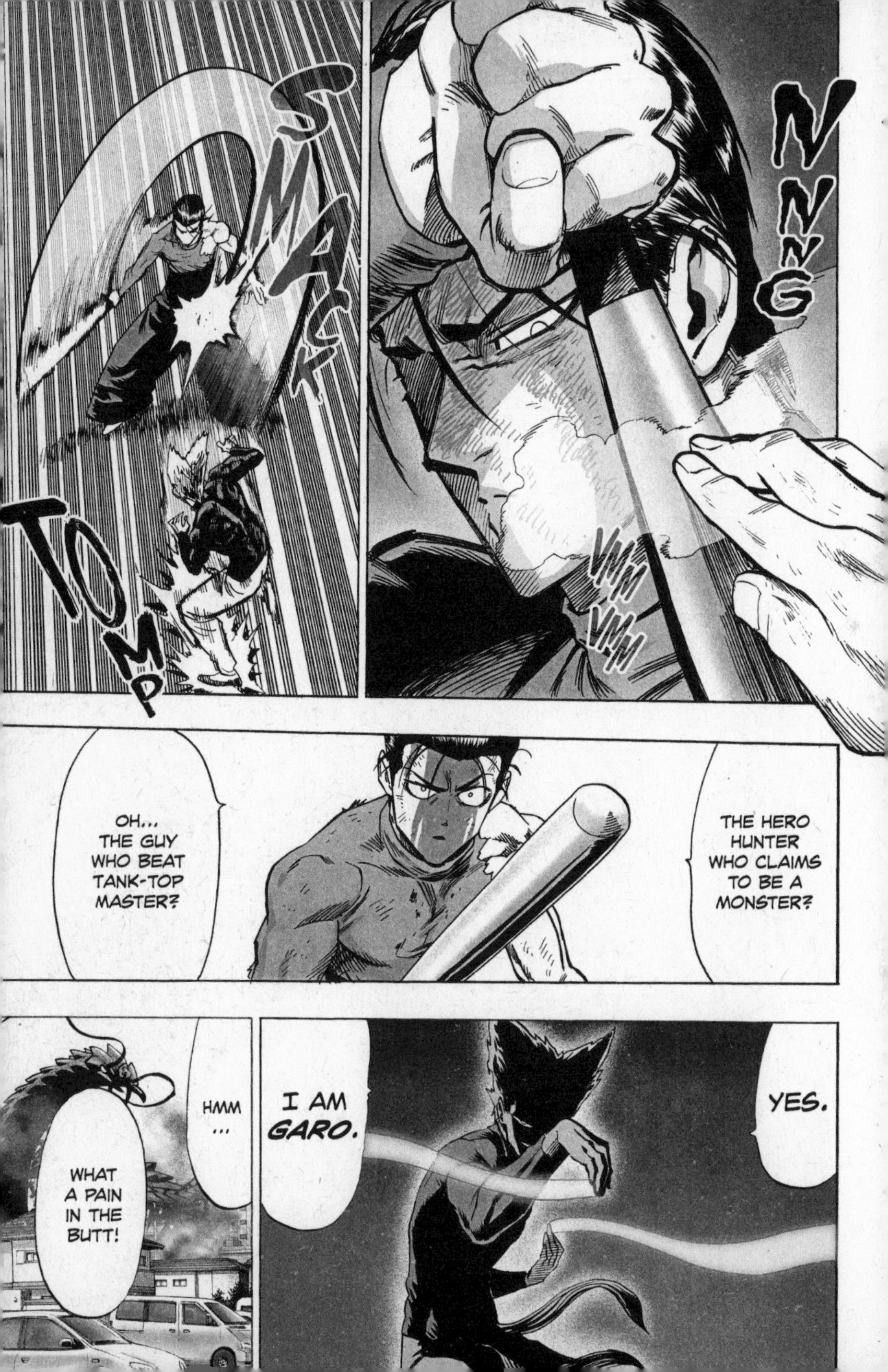
NNNNG
VMM VMM
SMACK
TOMP
THE HERO HUNTER WHO CLAIMS TO BE A MONSTER?
OH... THE GUY WHO BEAT TANK-TOP MASTER?
YES.
I AM GARO.
HMM...
WHAT A PAIN IN THE BUTT!

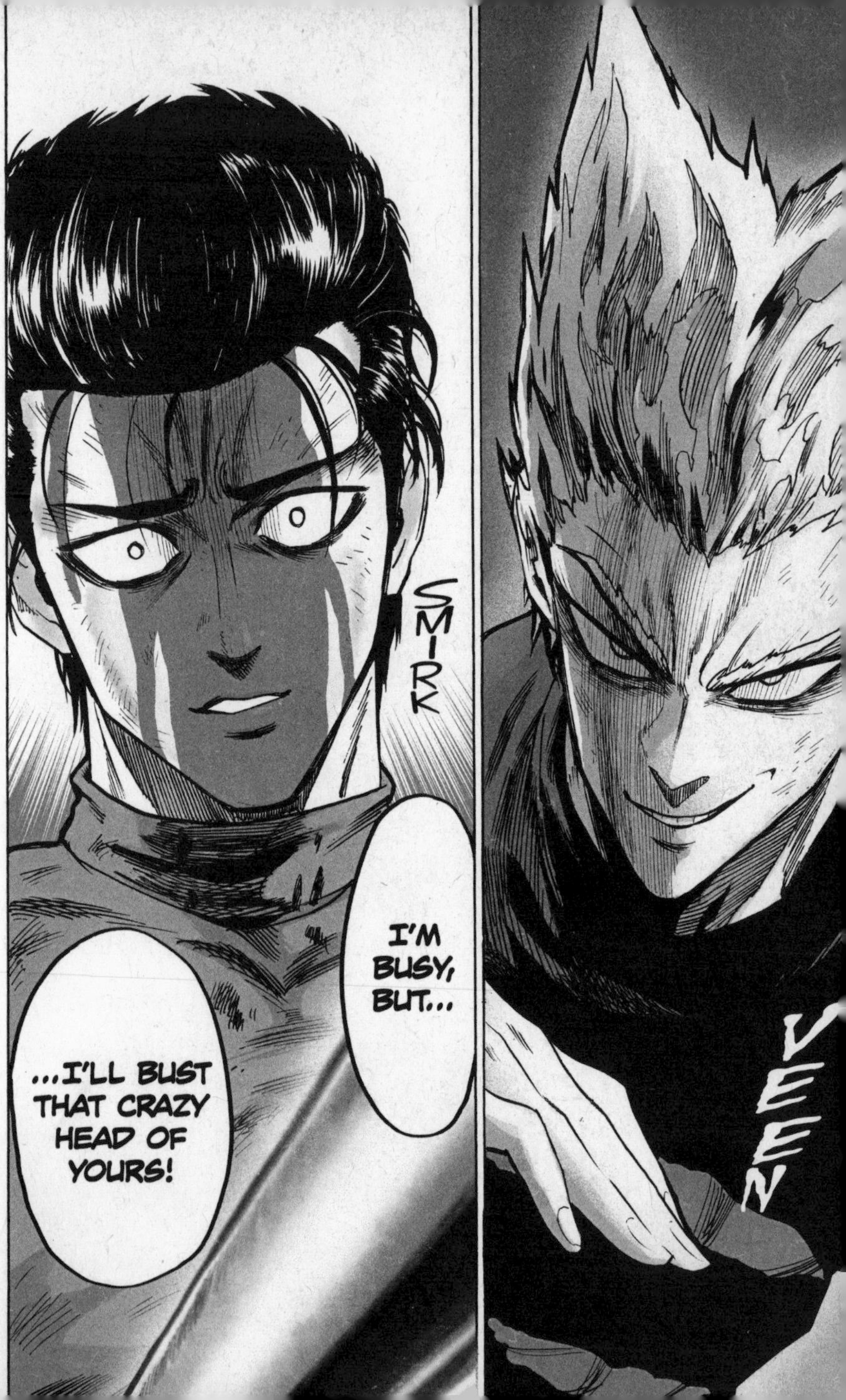
VEEN
SMIRK
I'M BUSY, BUT...
...I'LL BUST THAT CRAZY HEAD OF YOURS!

PUNCH 58: GIANT INSECT

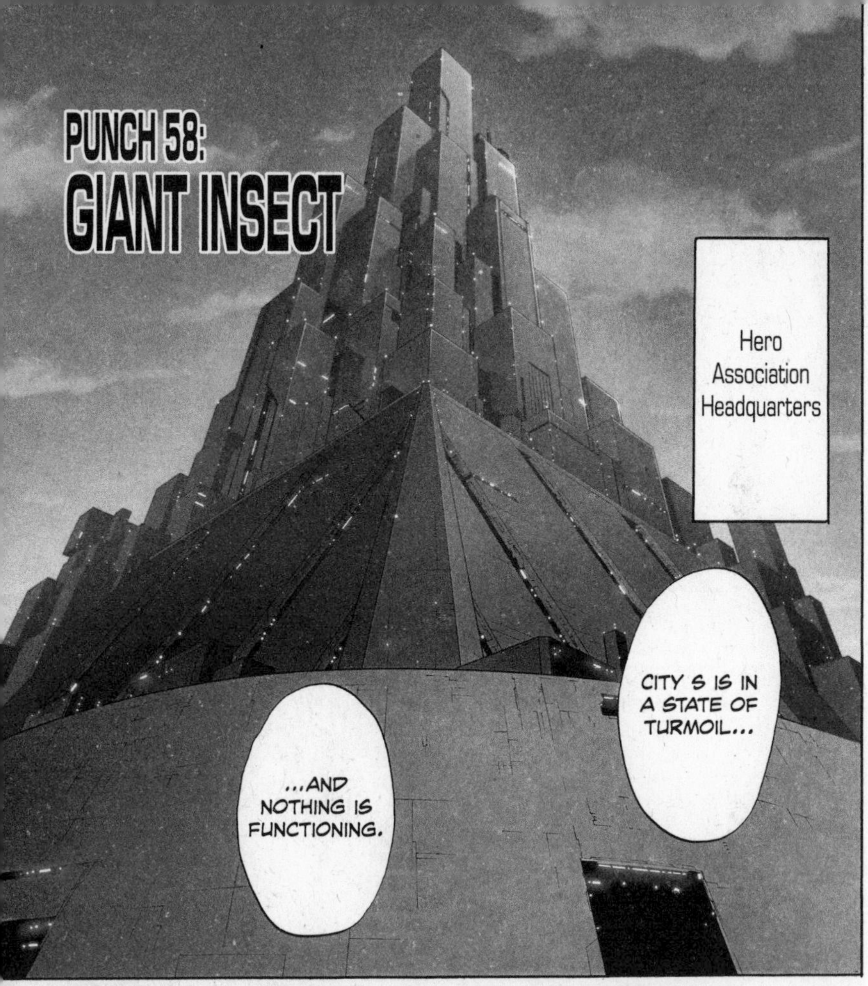

Hero Association Headquarters
CITY S IS IN A STATE OF TURMOIL...
...AND NOTHING IS FUNCTIONING.

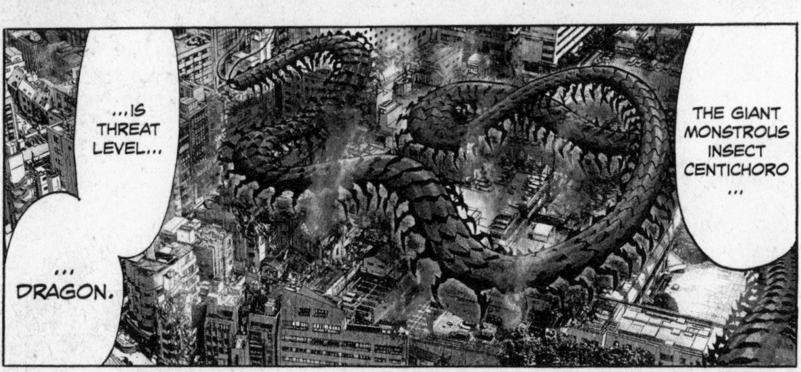

THE GIANT MONSTROUS INSECT CENTICHORO ...
...IS THREAT LEVEL...
... DRAGON.

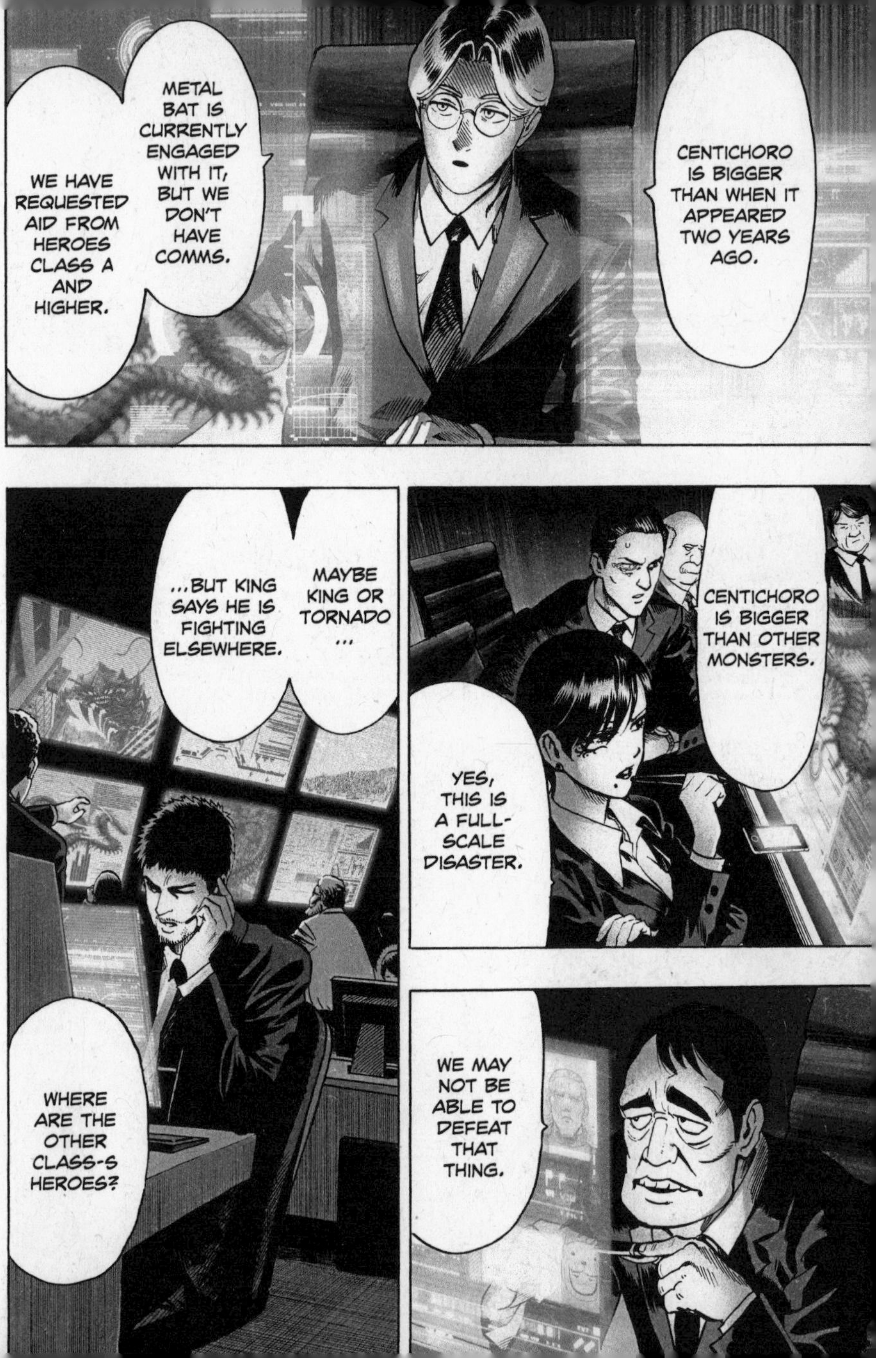
CENTICHORO IS BIGGER THAN WHEN IT APPEARED TWO YEARS AGO.
METAL BAT IS CURRENTLY ENGAGED WITH IT, BUT WE DON'T HAVE COMMS.
WE HAVE REQUESTED AID FROM HEROES CLASS A AND HIGHER.
CENTICHORO IS BIGGER THAN OTHER MONSTERS.
YES, THIS IS A FULL-SCALE DISASTER.
WE MAY NOT BE ABLE TO DEFEAT THAT THING.
MAYBE KING OR TORNADO ...
...BUT KING SAYS HE IS FIGHTING ELSEWHERE.
WHERE ARE THE OTHER CLASS-S HEROES?

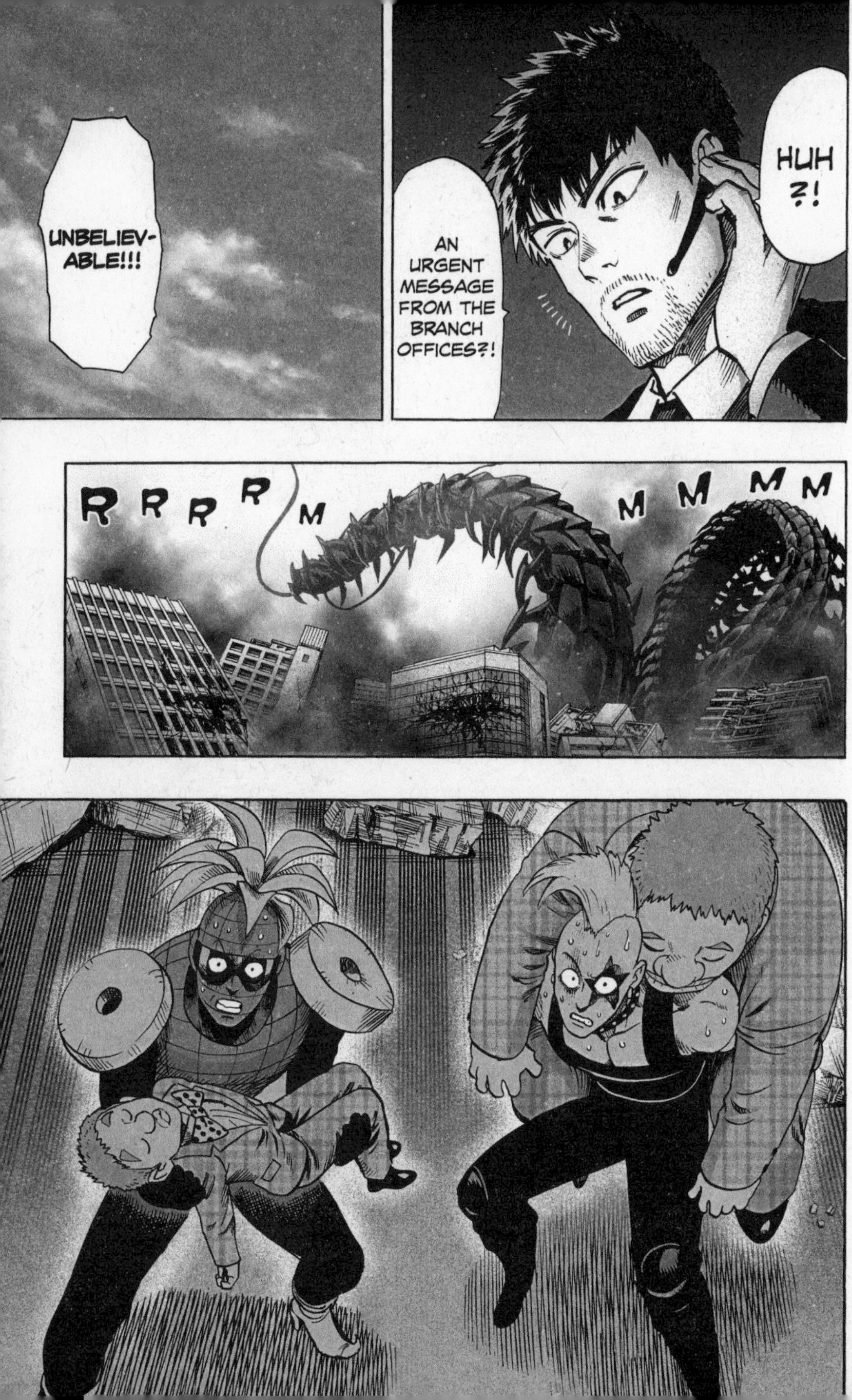
HUH ?!
AN URGENT MESSAGE FROM THE BRANCH OFFICES?!
UNBELIEV-ABLE!!!
RRRRM MMMMM

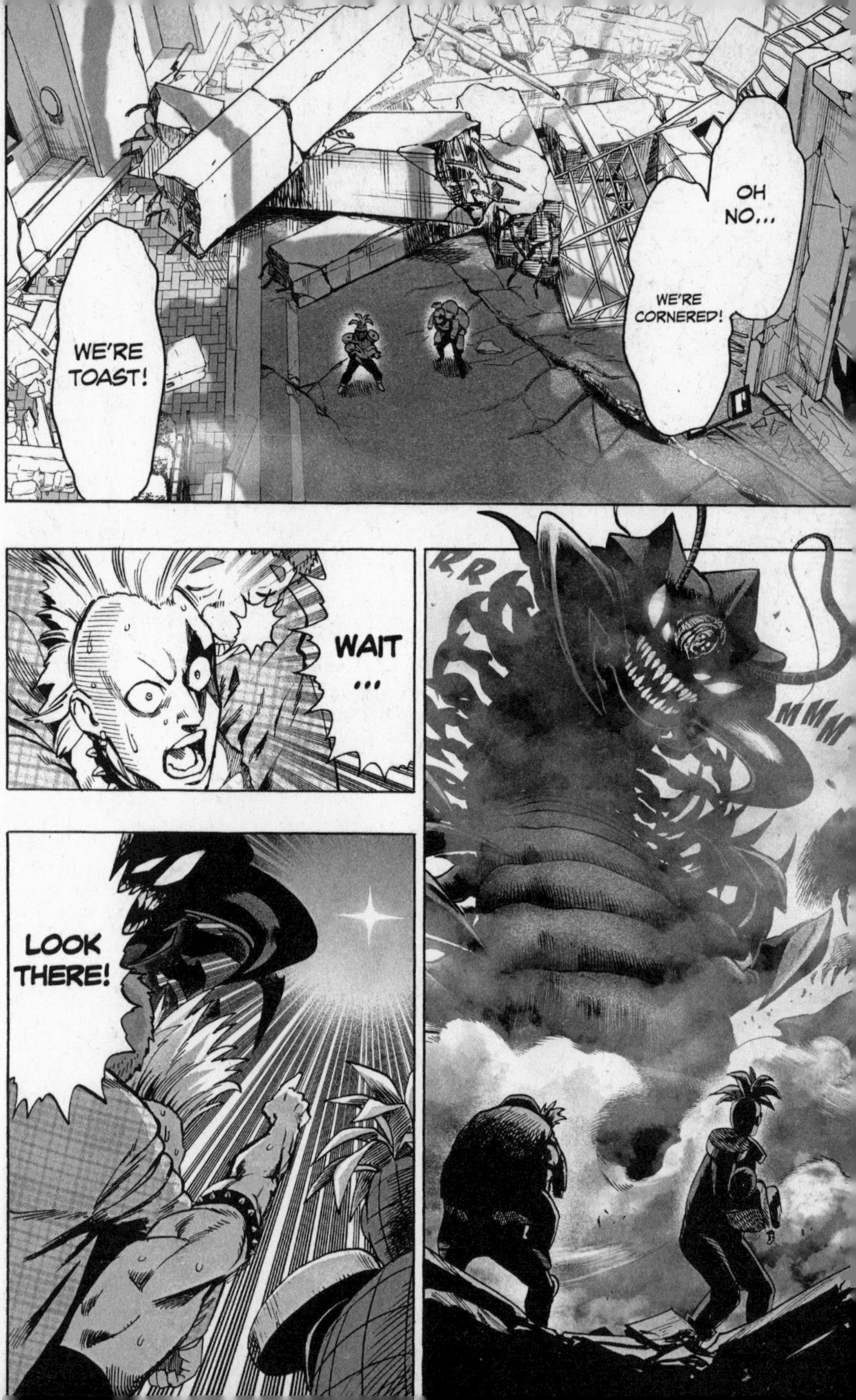
OH NO...
WE'RE CORNERED!
WE'RE TOAST!
RR
MMM
WAIT ...
LOOK THERE!

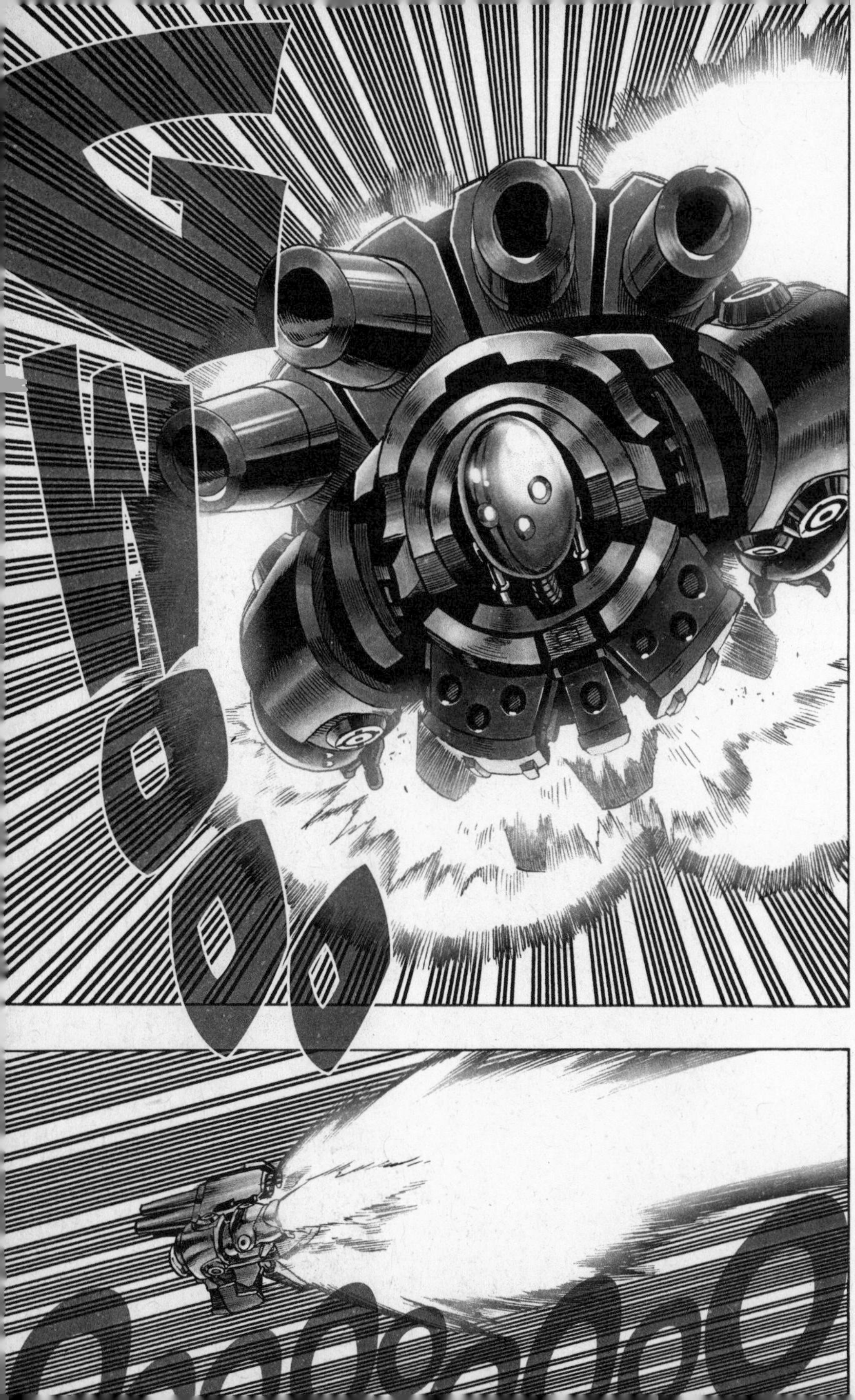
ZWOOO

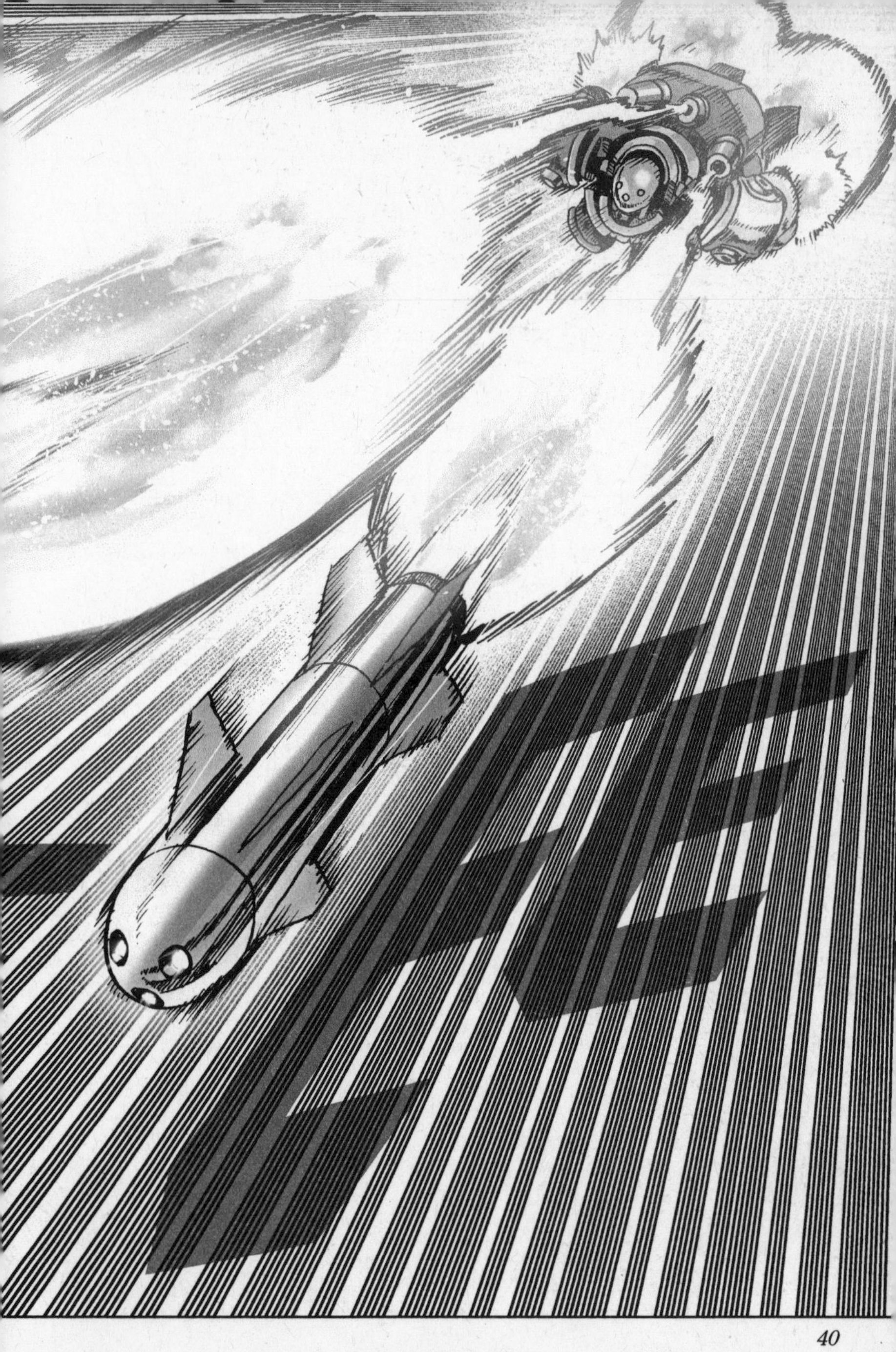

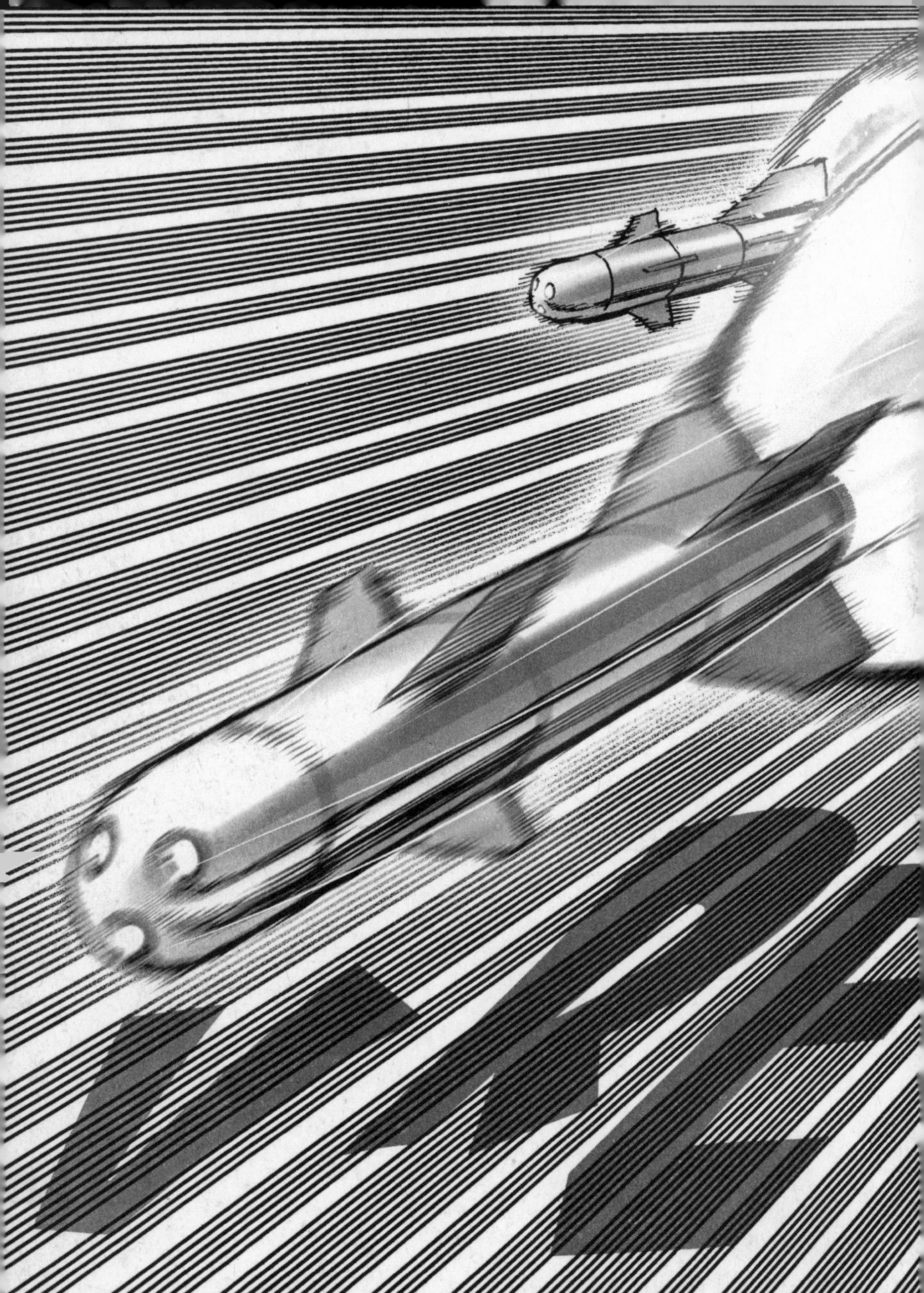

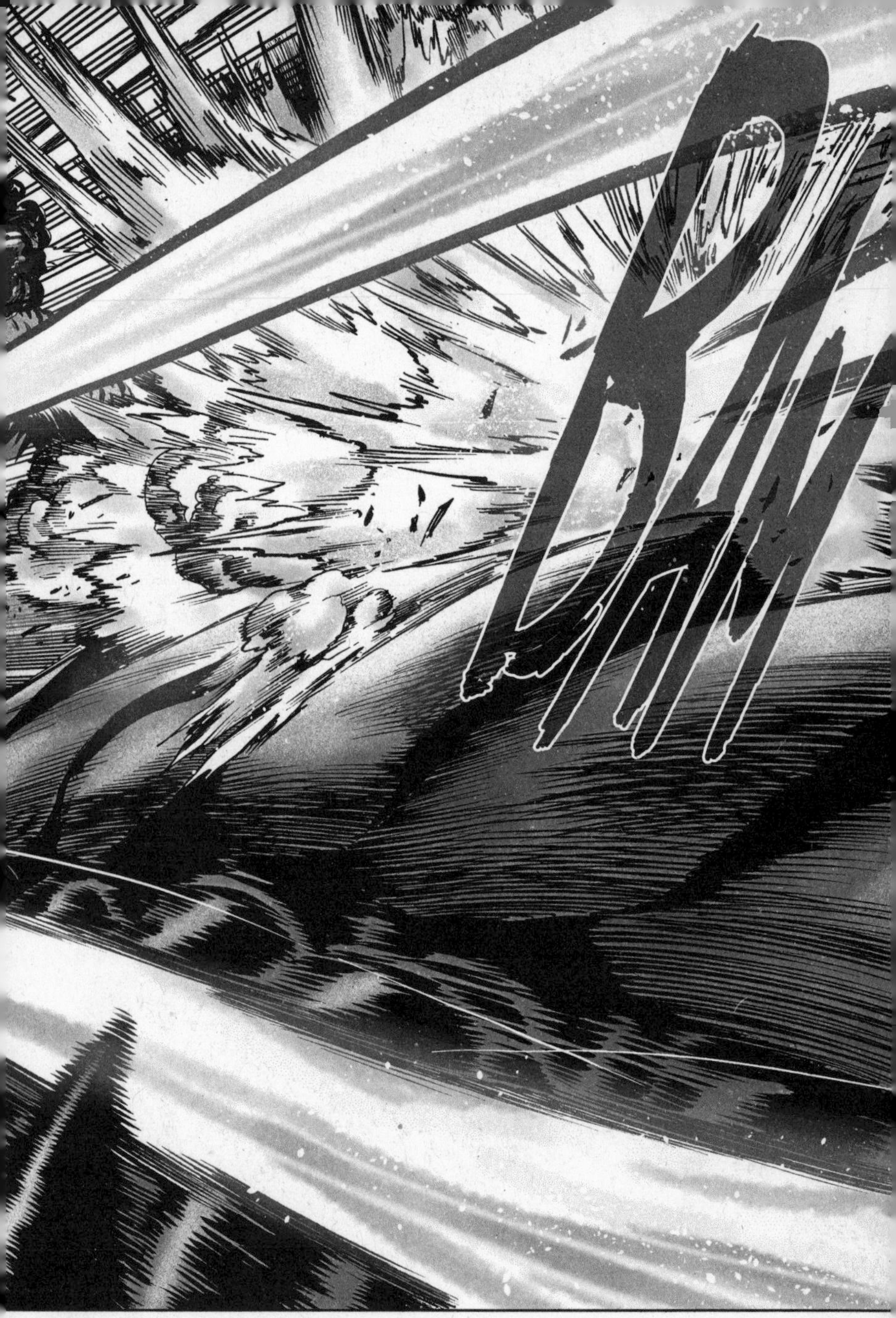

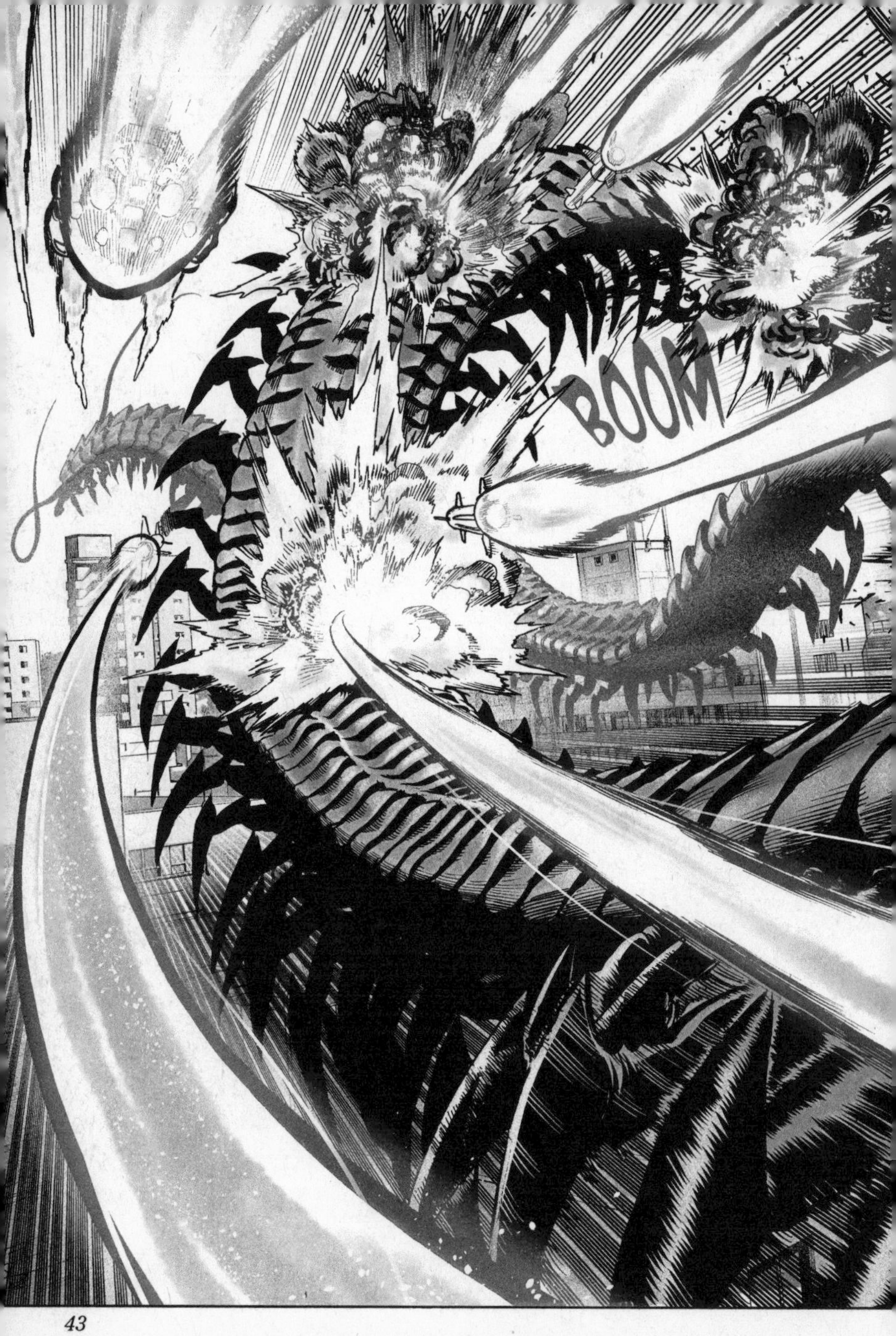
BOOM

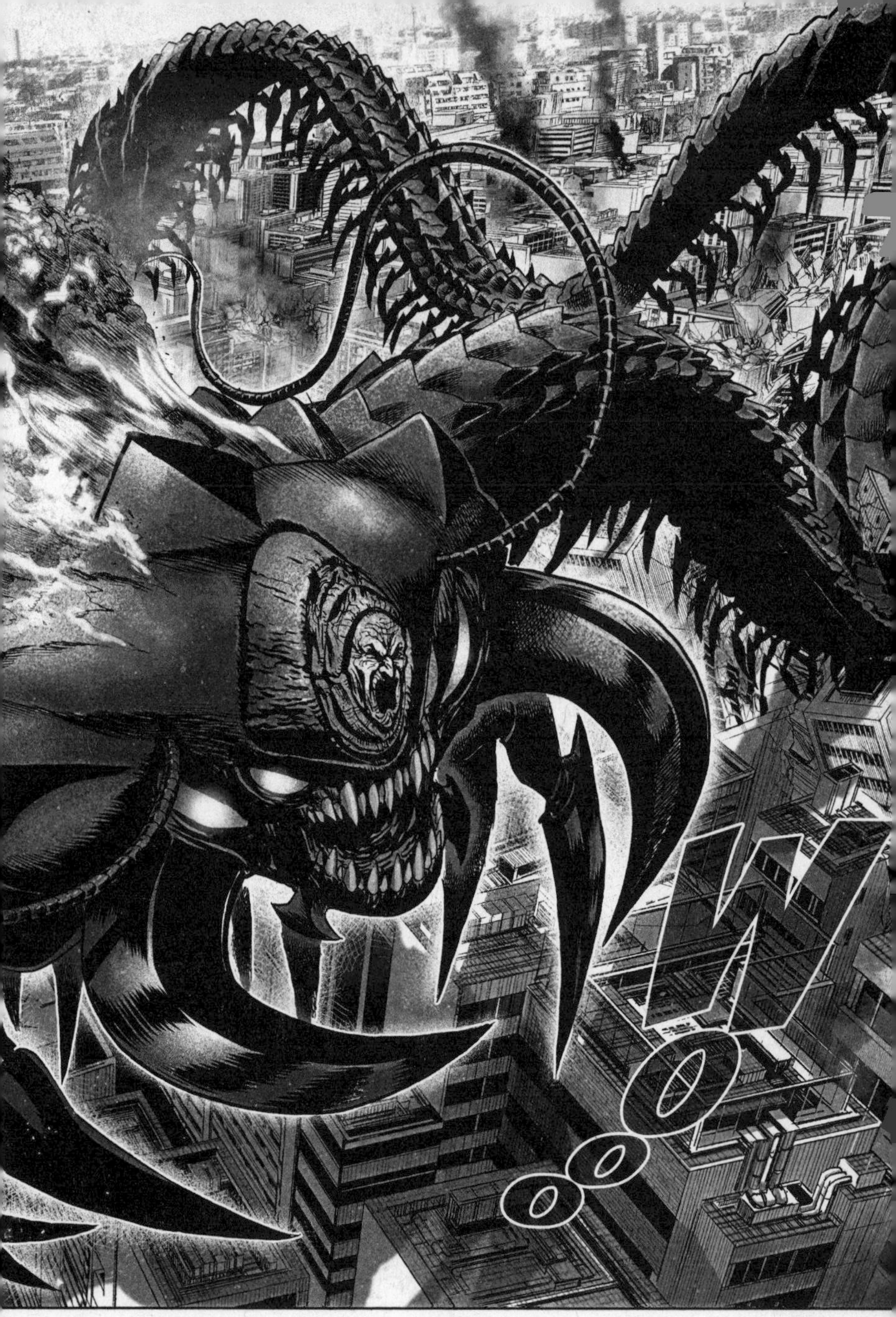
WOOO

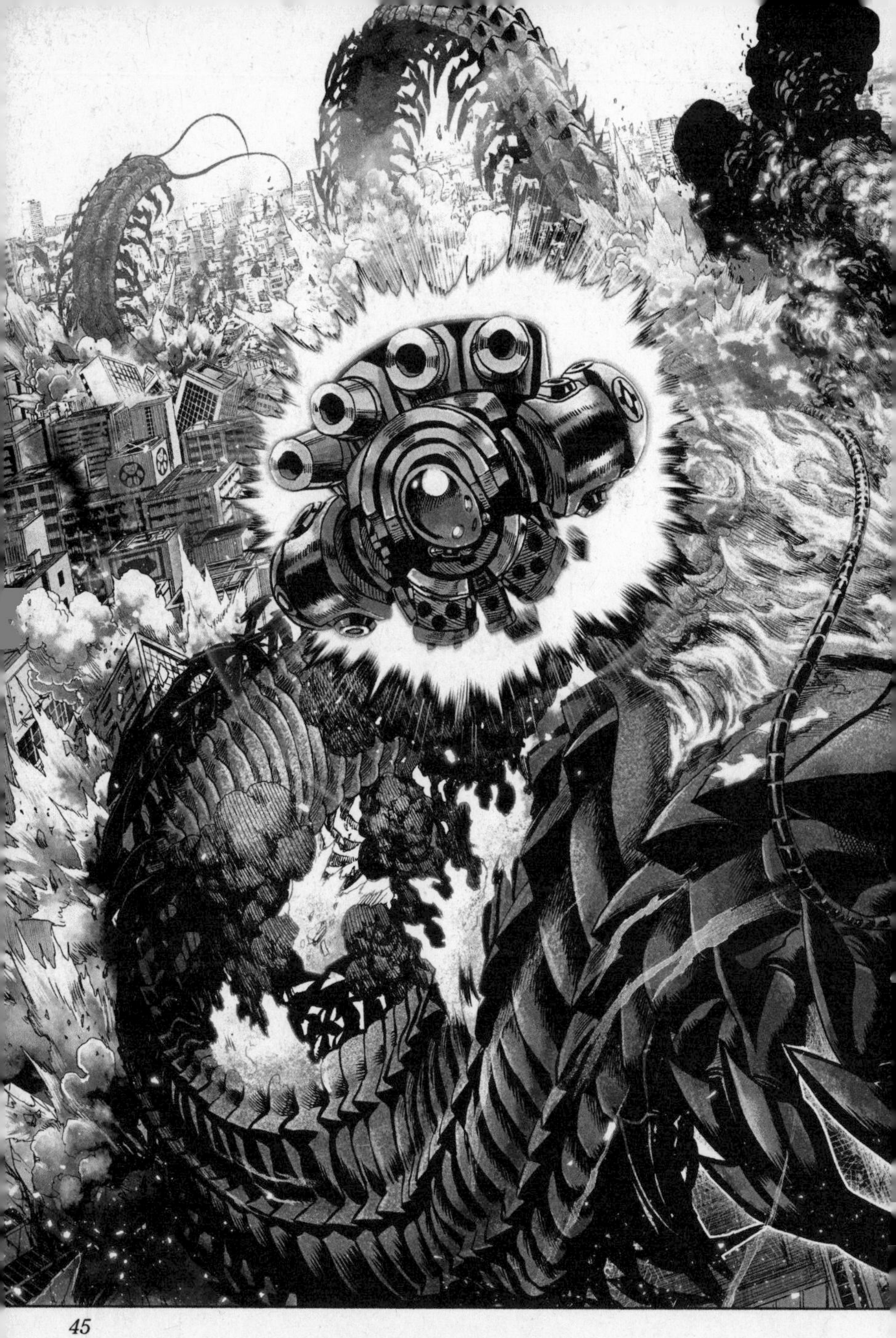

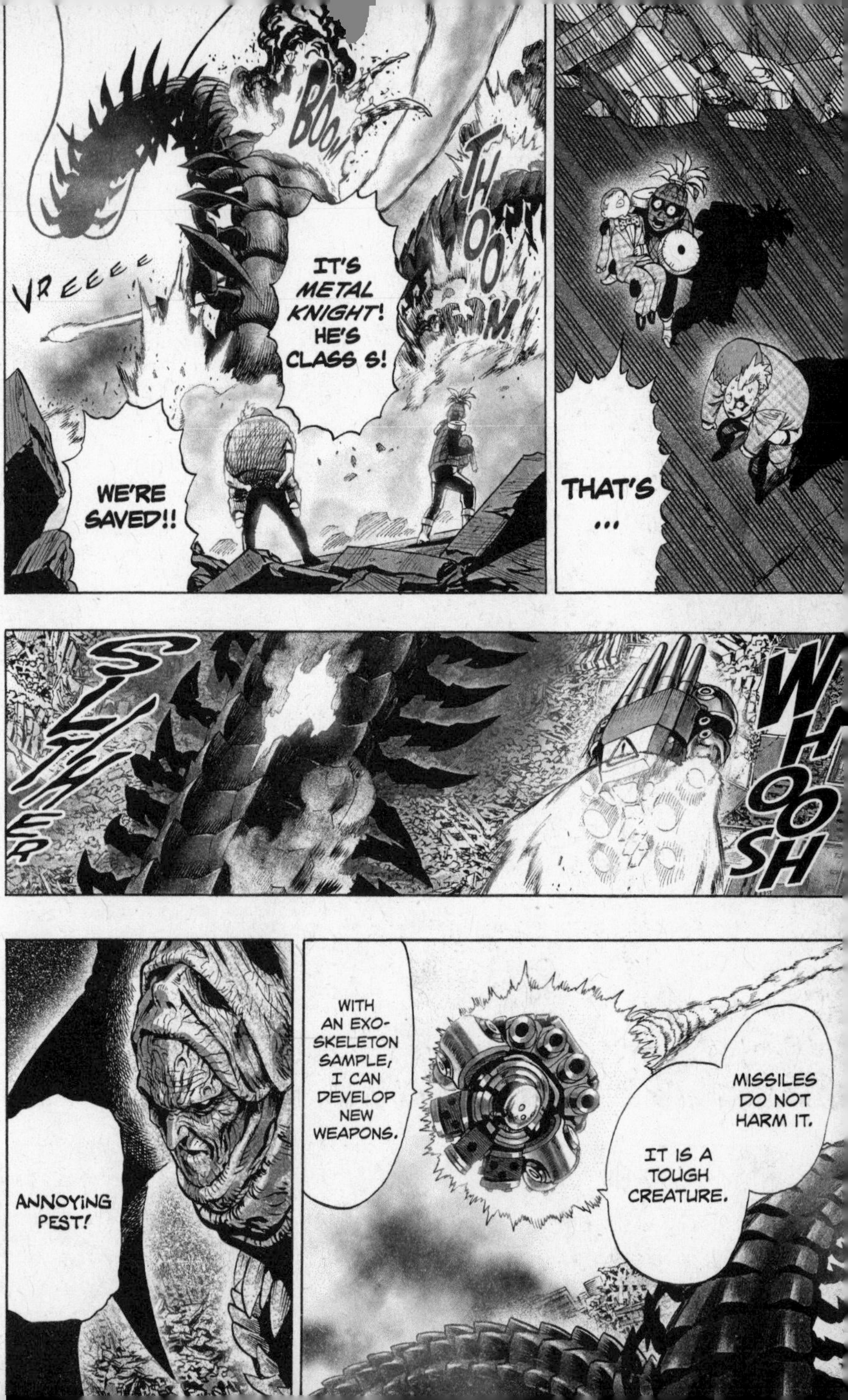
THAT'S ...
BOOM
THOOOM
IT'S METAL KNIGHT! HE'S CLASS S!
VREEEE
WE'RE SAVED!!
WHOOOSH
SLITHER
MISSILES DO NOT HARM IT.
IT IS A TOUGH CREATURE.
WITH AN EXO-SKELETON SAMPLE, I CAN DEVELOP NEW WEAPONS.
ANNOYING PEST!

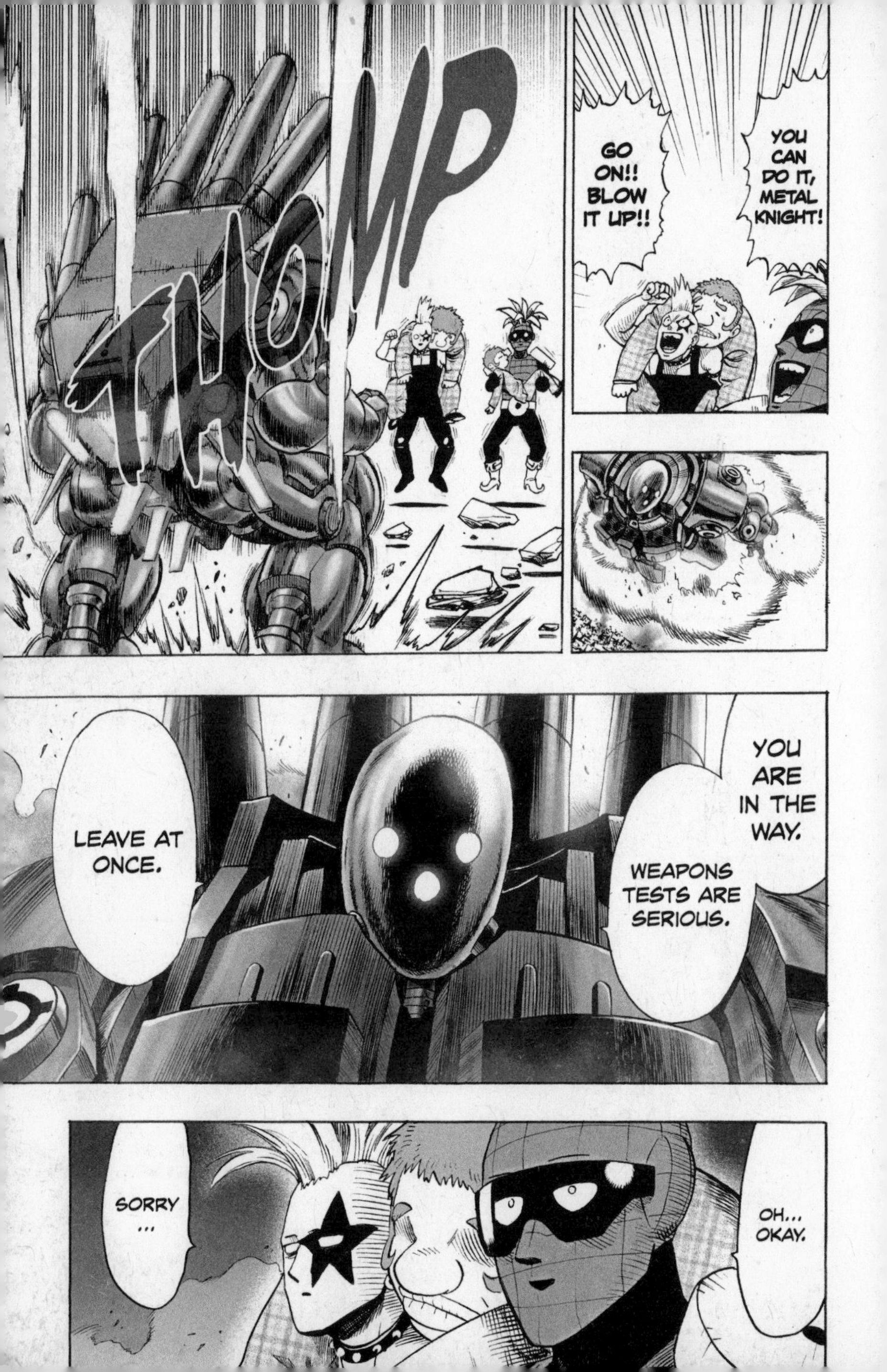
YOU CAN DO IT, METAL KNIGHT!
GO ON!! BLOW IT UP!!
THOMP
YOU ARE IN THE WAY.
WEAPONS TESTS ARE SERIOUS.
LEAVE AT ONCE.
OH... OKAY.
SORRY ...

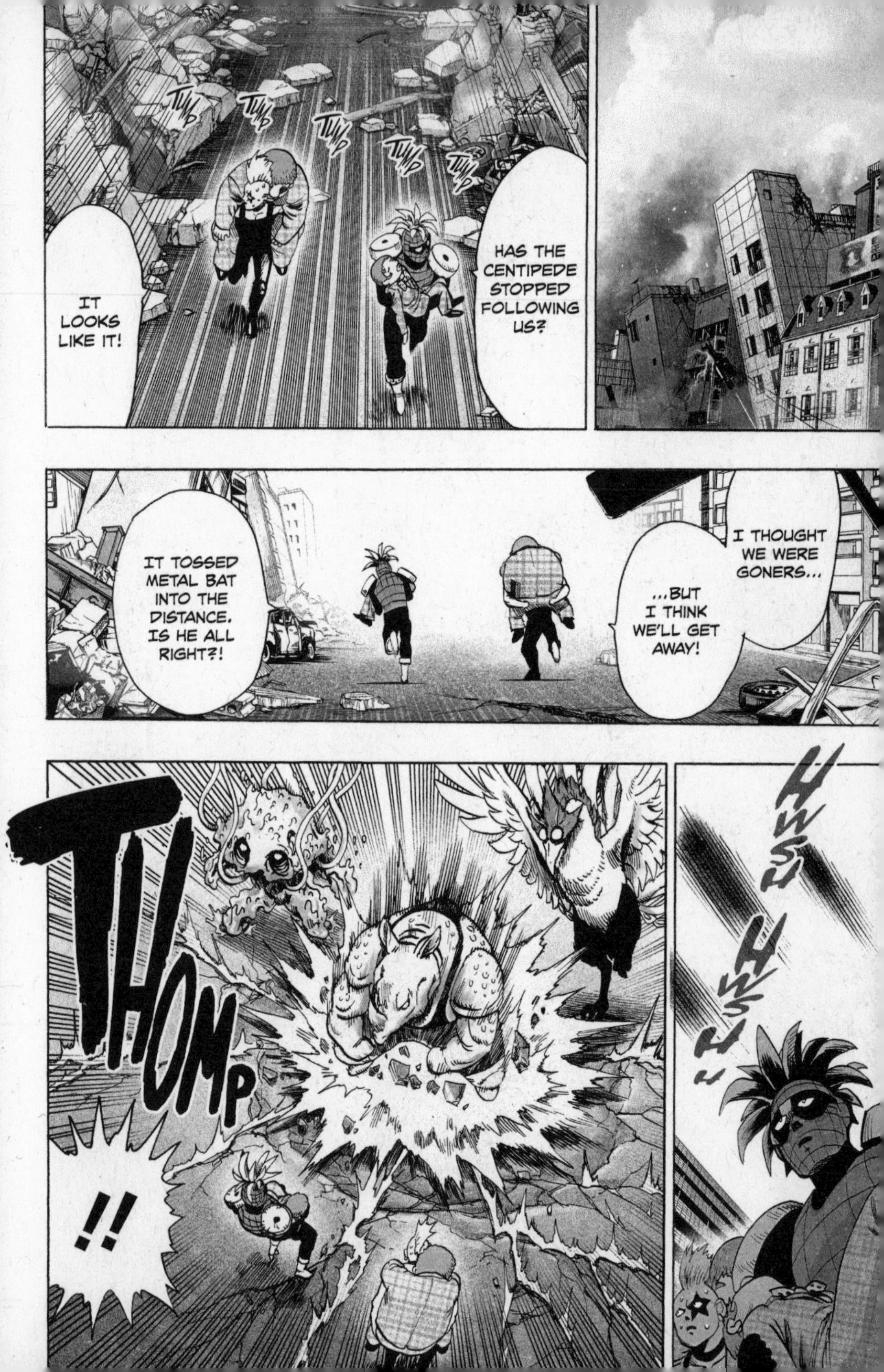
TUMP
TUMP
TUMP
TUMP
TUMP
HAS THE CENTIPEDE STOPPED FOLLOWING US?
IT LOOKS LIKE IT!
I THOUGHT WE WERE GONERS...
...BUT I THINK WE'LL GET AWAY!
IT TOSSED METAL BAT INTO THE DISTANCE. IS HE ALL RIGHT?!
HWSH
HWSH
THOMP
!!

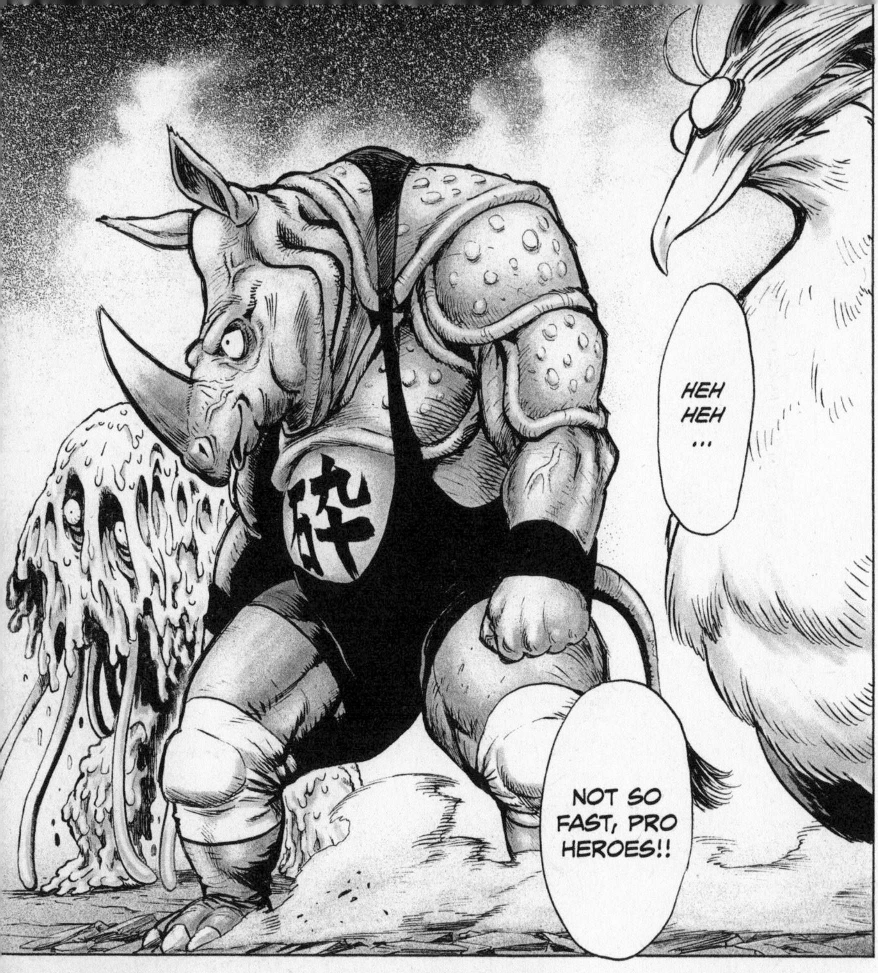
HEH HEH ...
砕
NOT SO FAST, PRO HEROES!!
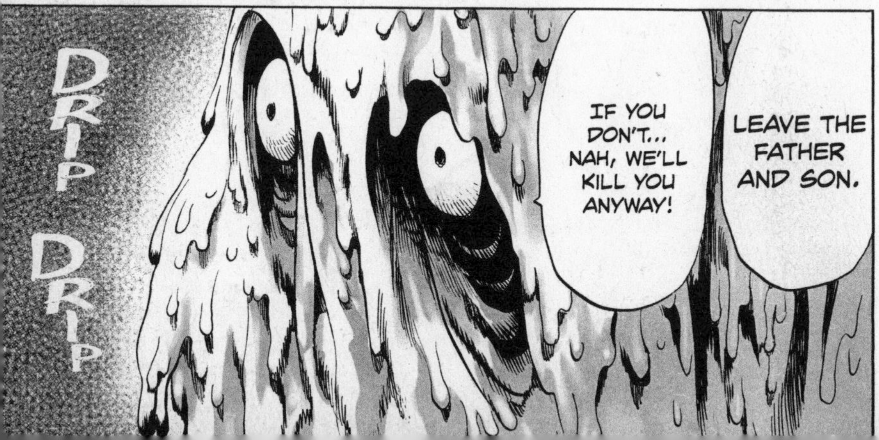
LEAVE THE FATHER AND SON.
IF YOU DON'T... NAH, WE'LL KILL YOU ANYWAY!
DRIP DRIP

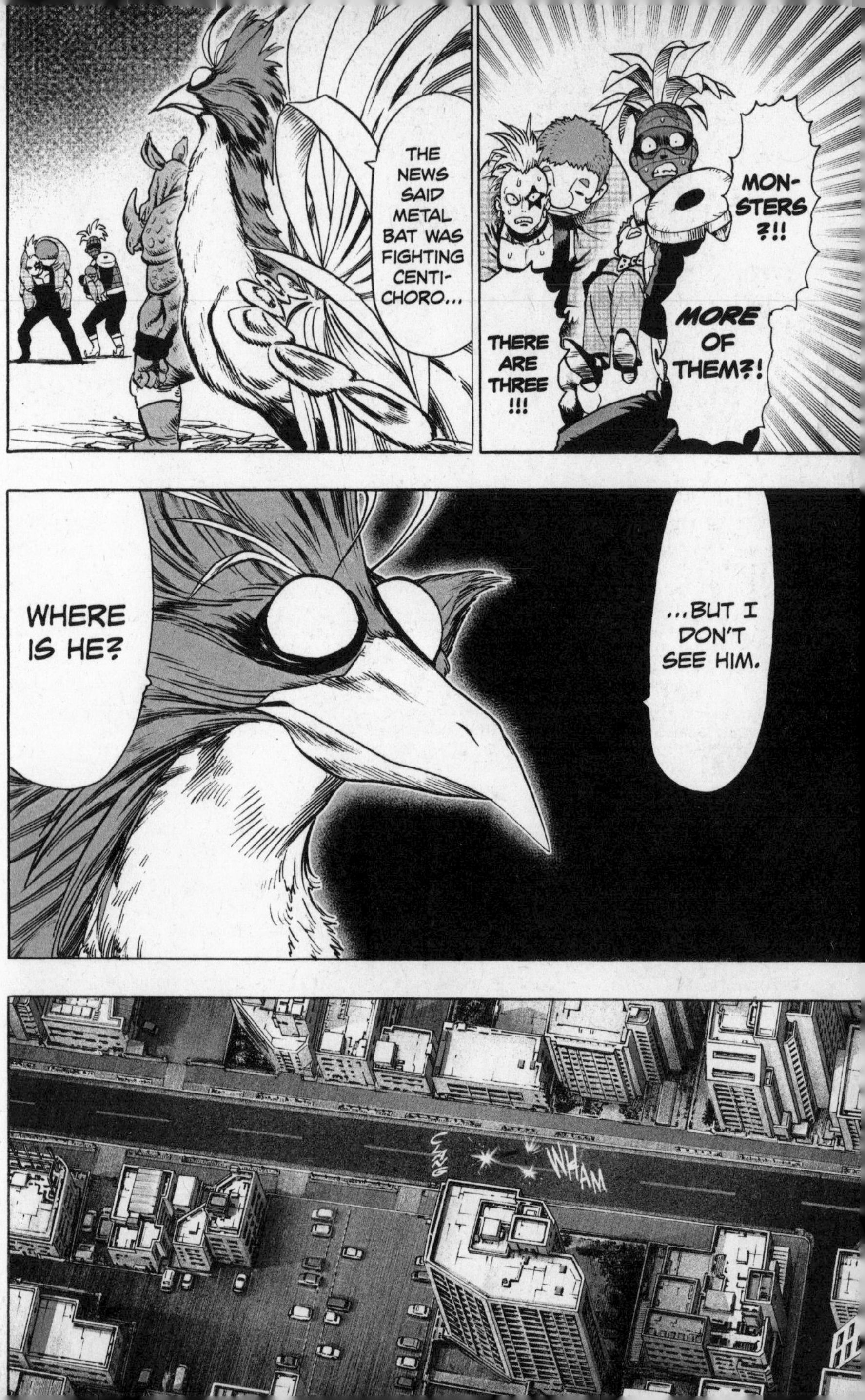
MON-
STERS
?!!
MORE
OF
THEM?!
THERE
ARE
THREE
!!!
THE NEWS SAID METAL BAT WAS FIGHTING CENTI-CHORO...
...BUT I DON'T SEE HIM.
WHERE IS HE?
WHAM
CLANG

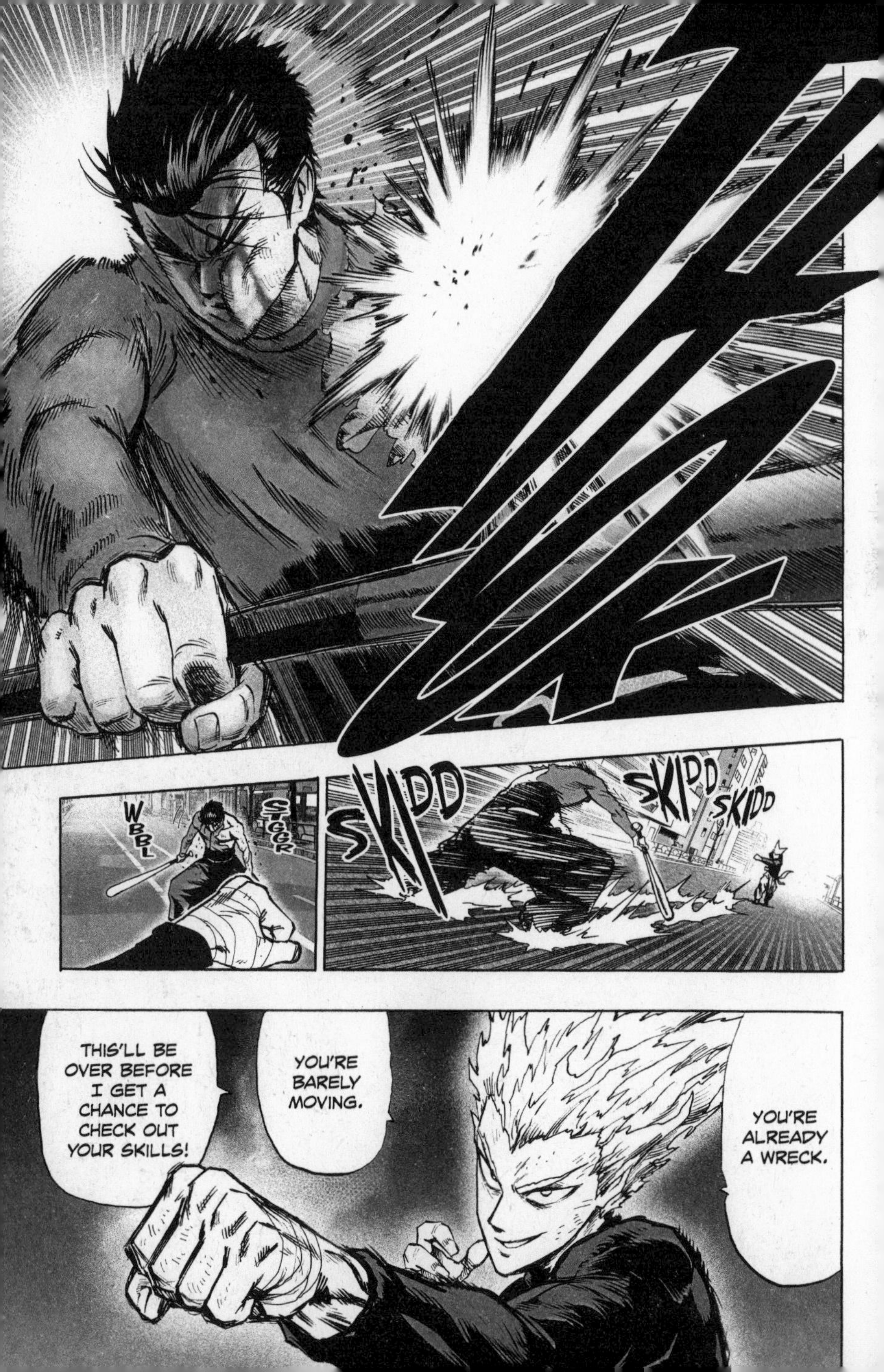
SKIDD
SKIDD
SKIDD
STGGR
WBBL
YOU'RE ALREADY A WRECK.
YOU'RE BARELY MOVING.
THIS'LL BE OVER BEFORE I GET A CHANCE TO CHECK OUT YOUR SKILLS!

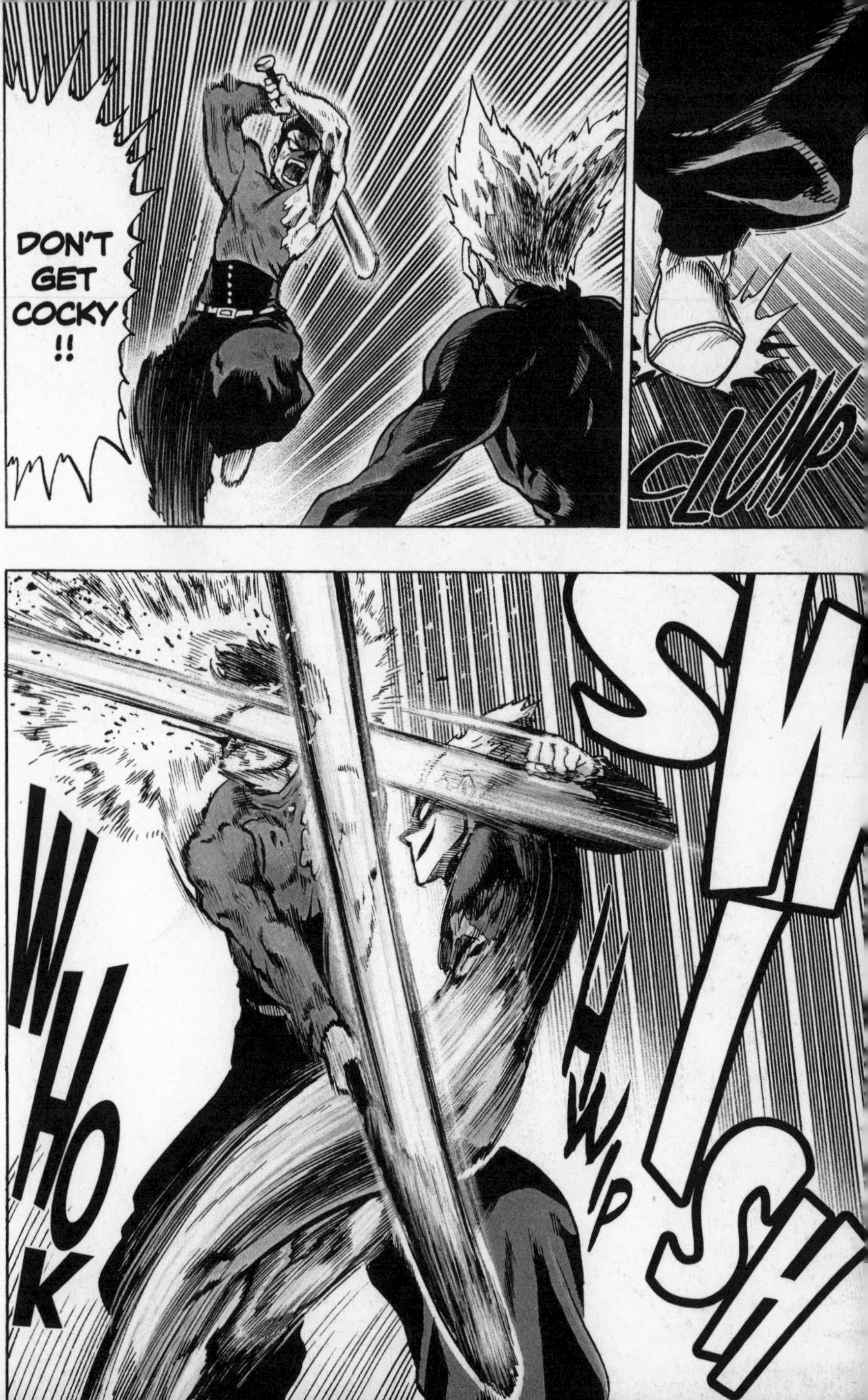
CLUMP
DON'T GET COCKY !!
SWISH
WHIP
WHOK

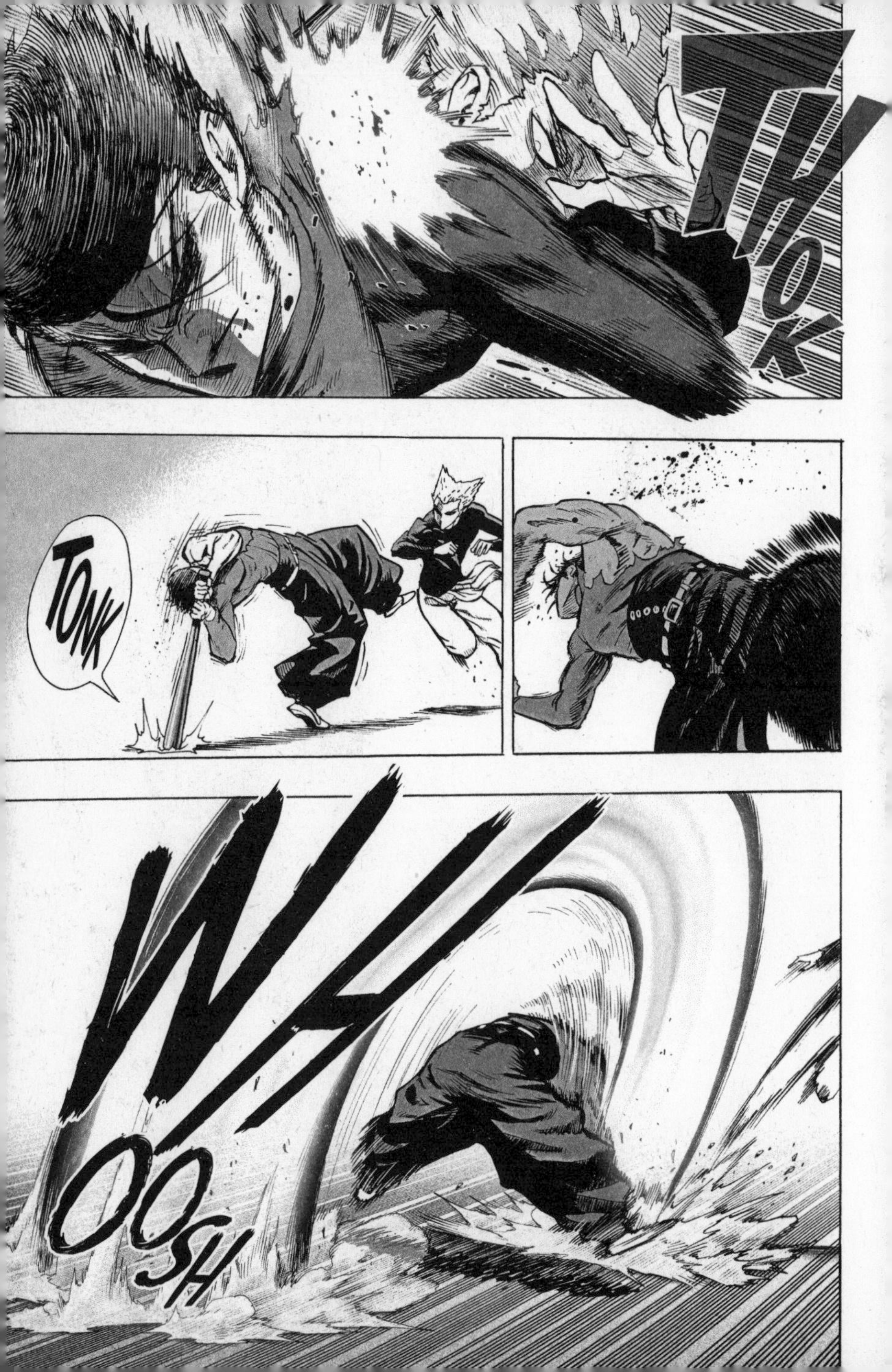
THWOK
TONK
WHOOSH

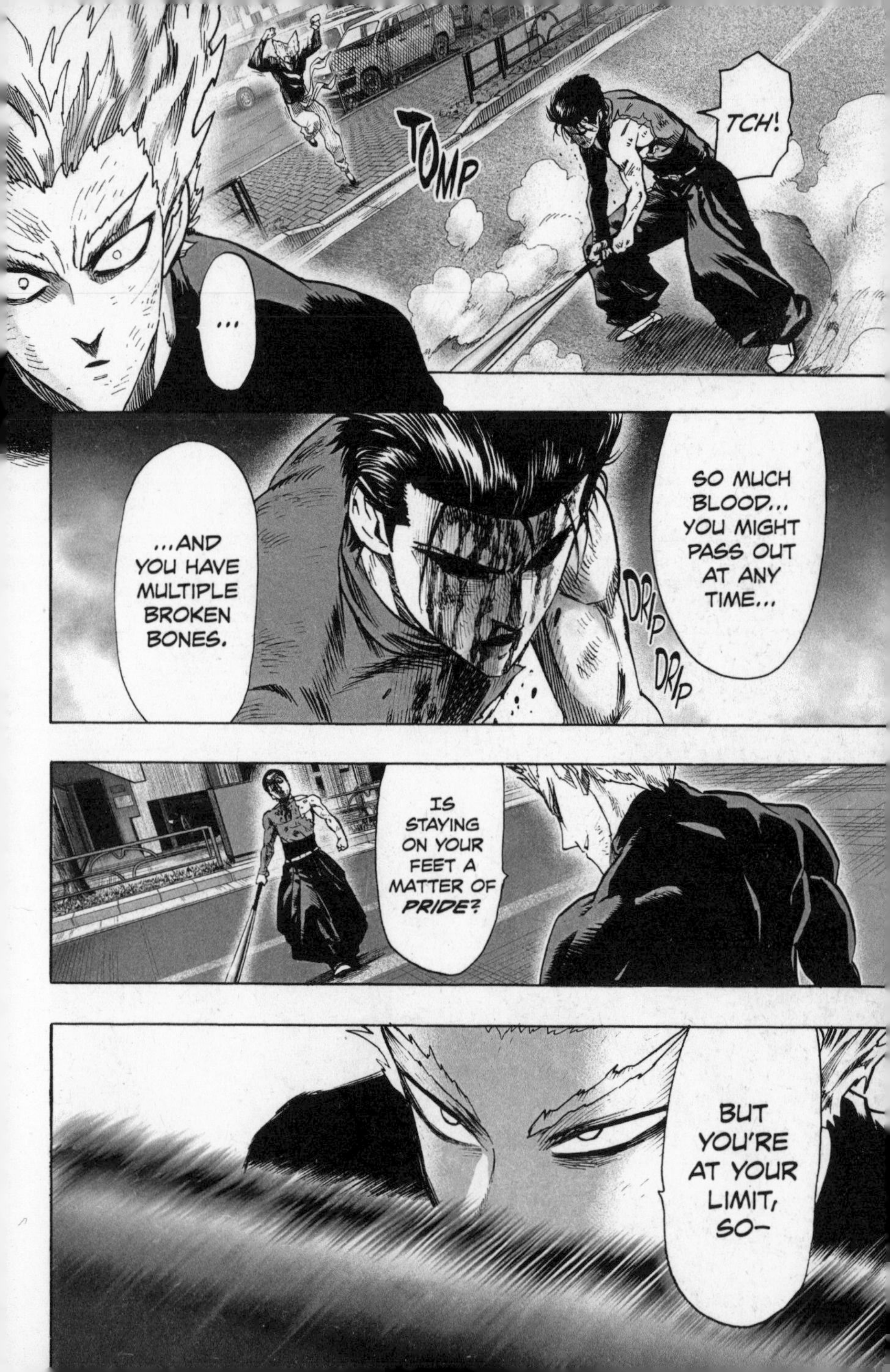
TCH!
TOMP
...
SO MUCH BLOOD... YOU MIGHT PASS OUT AT ANY TIME...
DRIP DRIP
...AND YOU HAVE MULTIPLE BROKEN BONES.
IS STAYING ON YOUR FEET A MATTER OF *PRIDE*?
BUT YOU'RE AT YOUR LIMIT, SO—

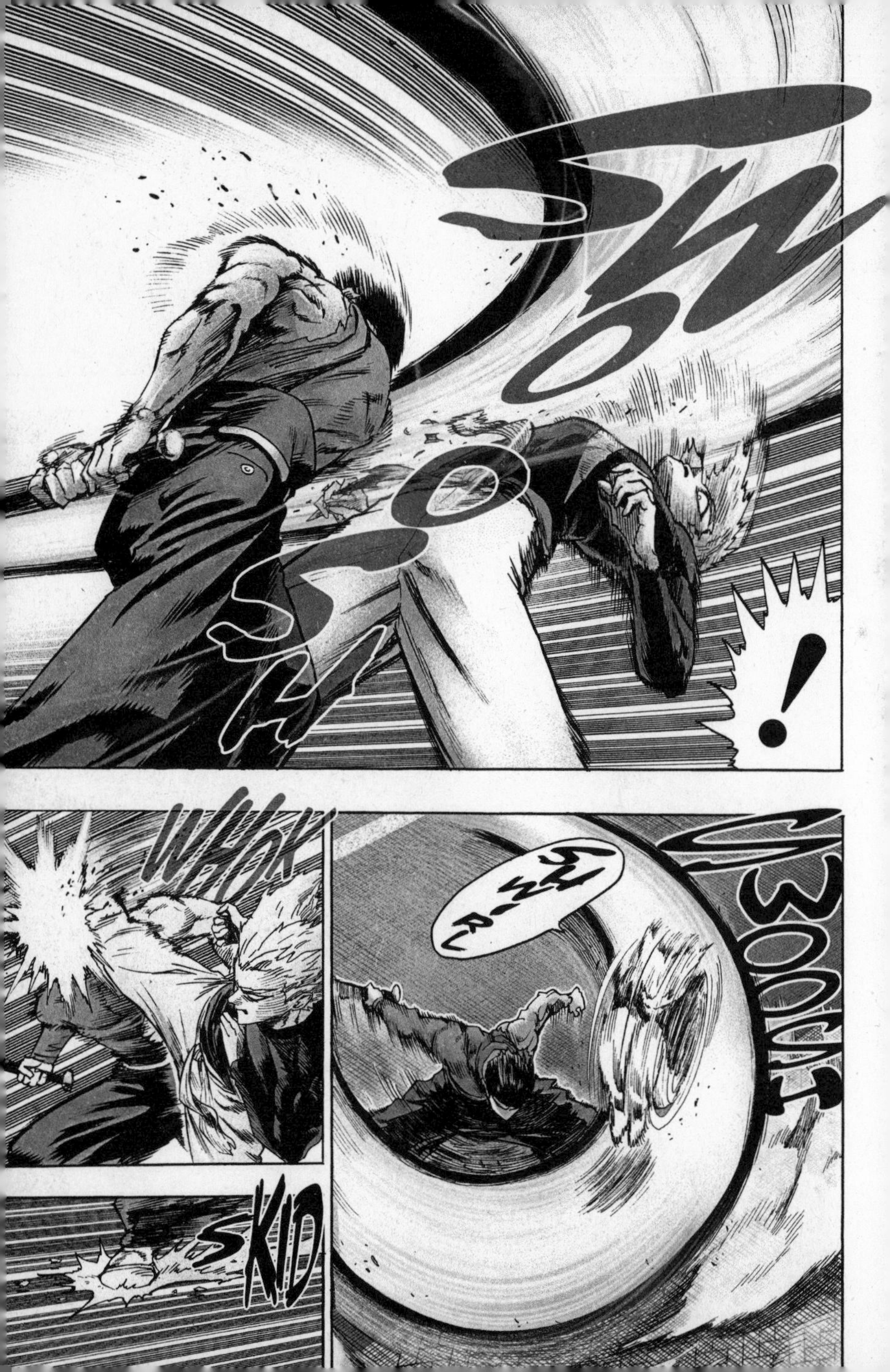
!
SHW-R-L
WHOK
SKID

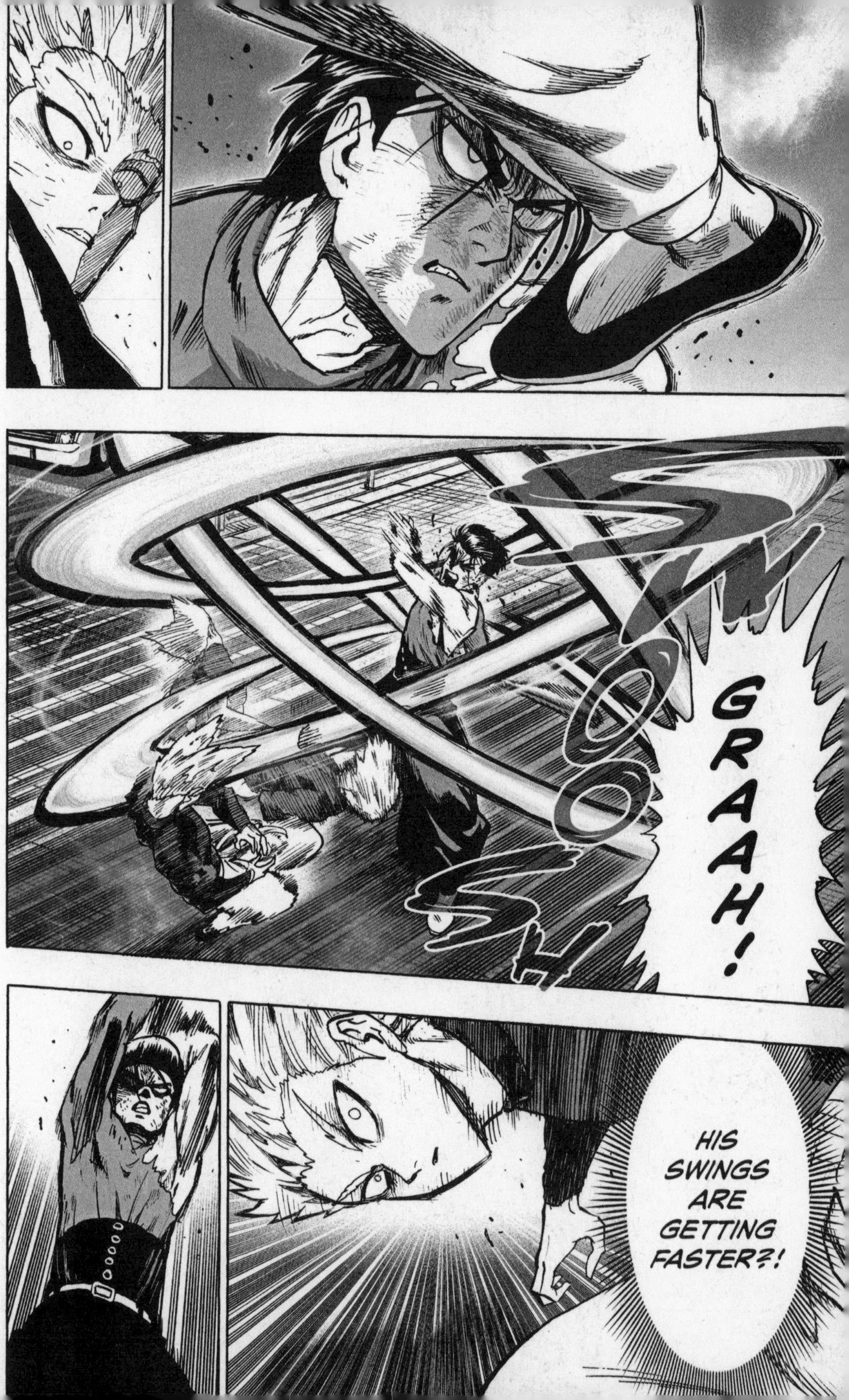

GRAAH!
SWOOSH
HIS SWINGS ARE GETTING FASTER?!

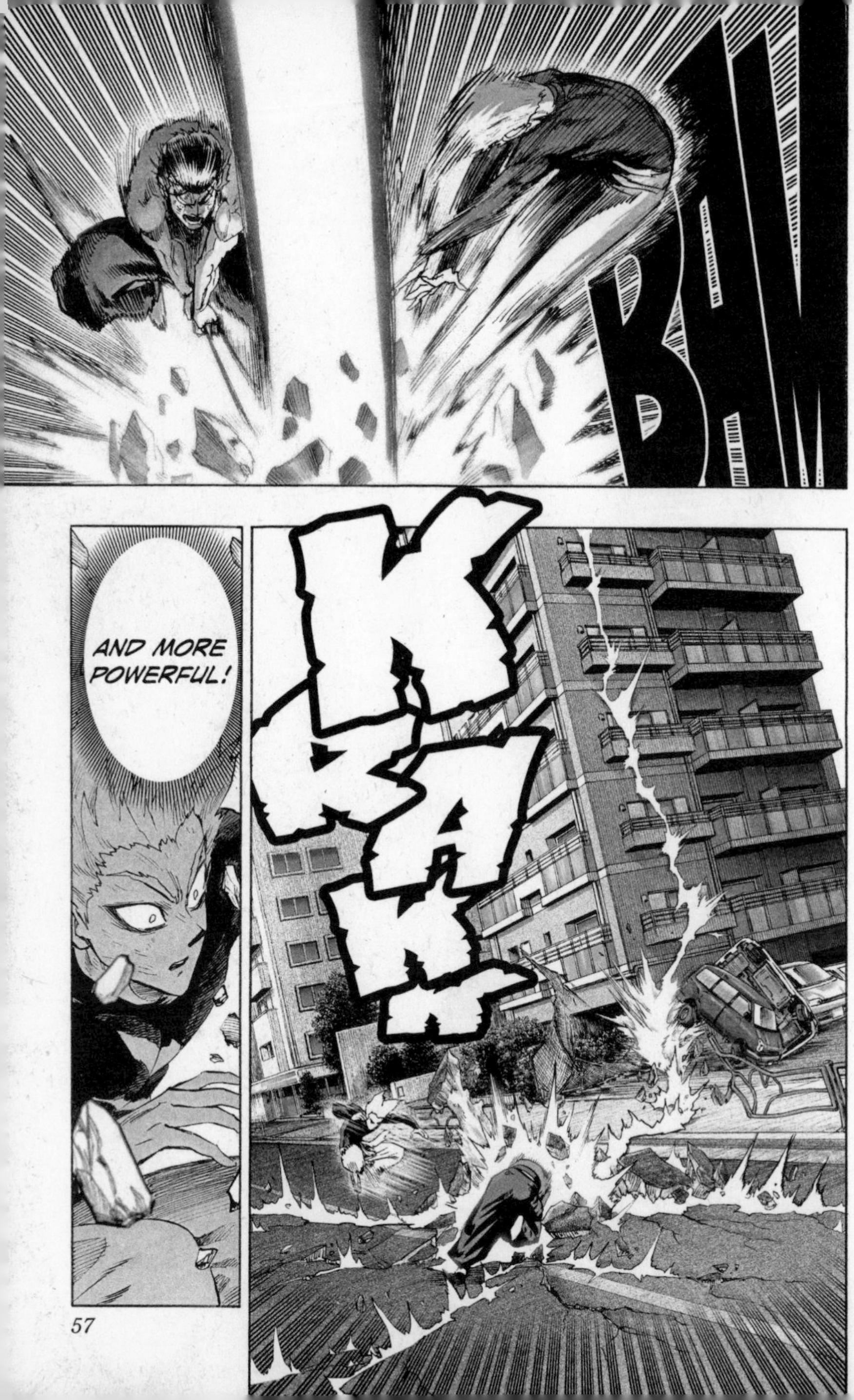
BAM
KRAK
AND MORE POWERFUL!

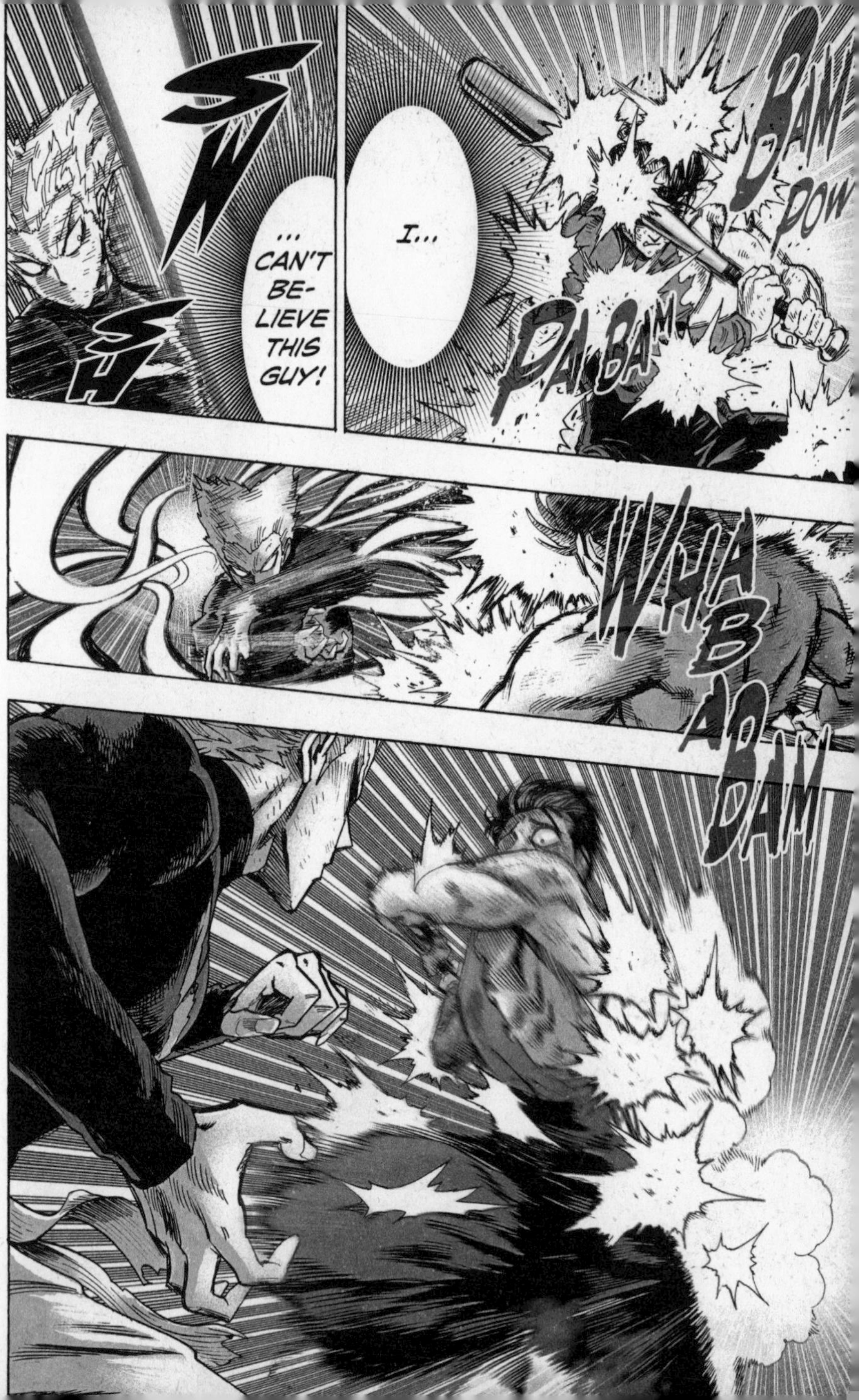
BAM
POW
DA BAM
I...
... CAN'T BE-LIEVE THIS GUY!
SW
SH
WHABABAM
BAM

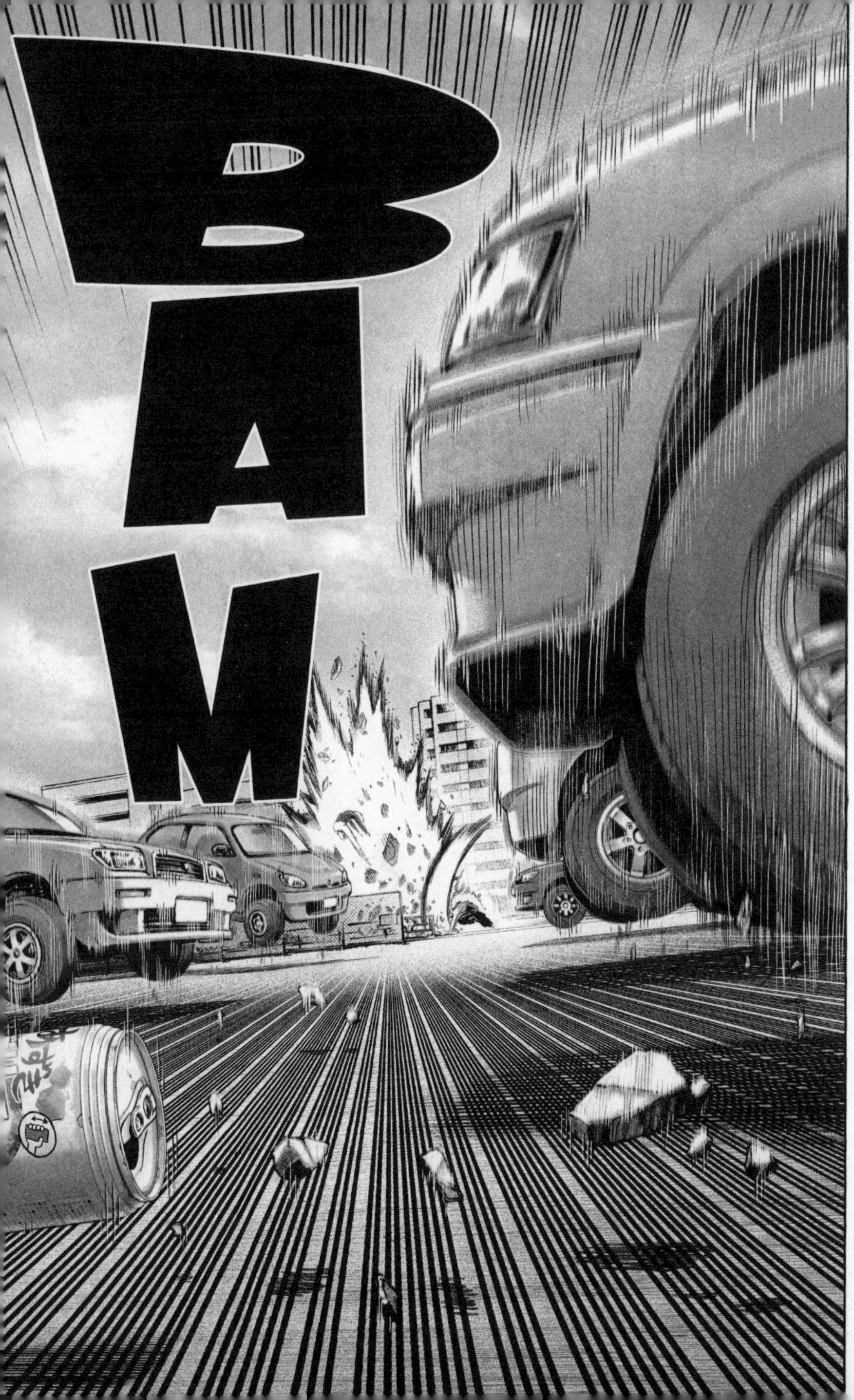
BAM

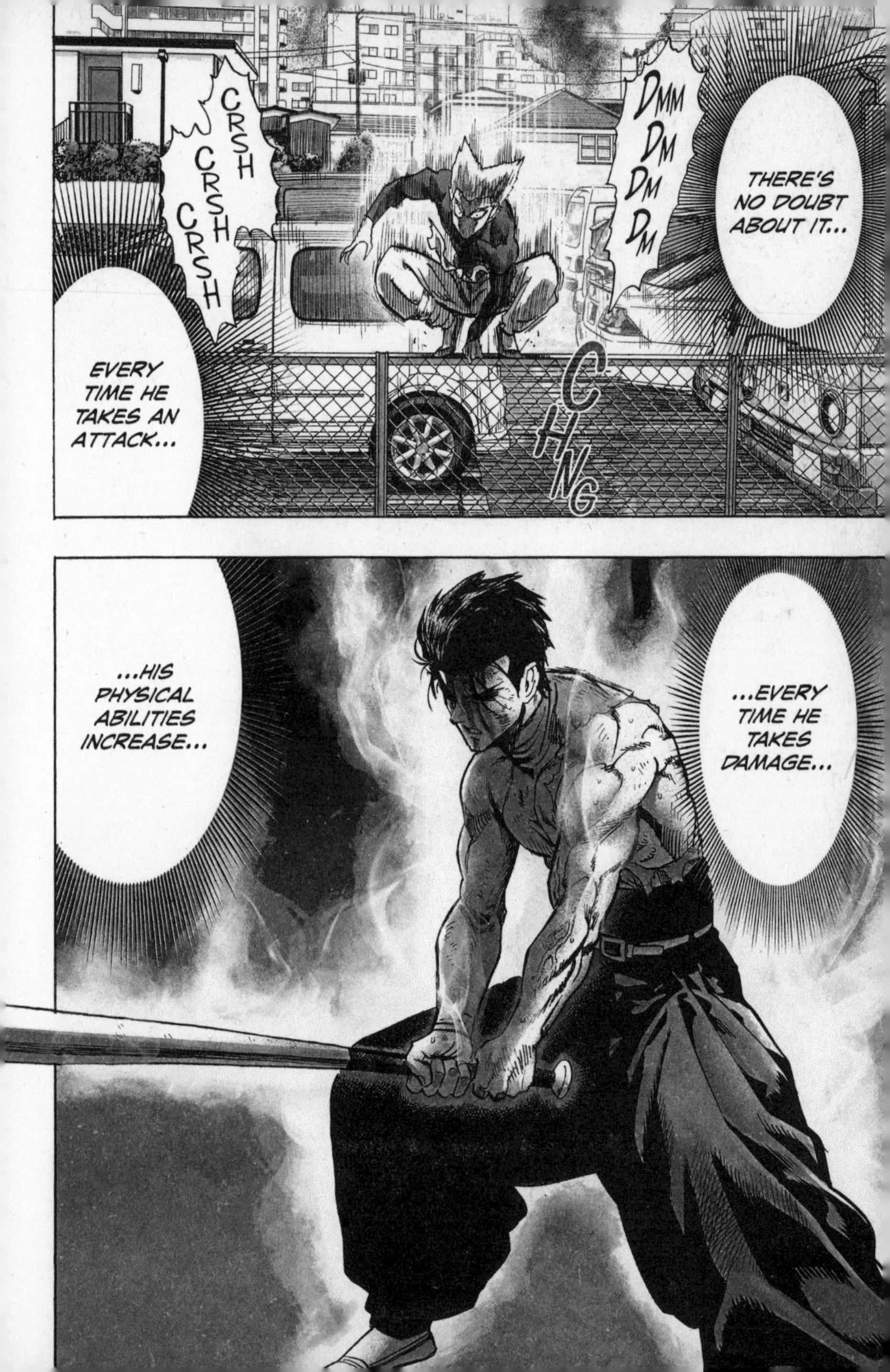
THERE'S NO DOUBT ABOUT IT...
DMM DM DM DM
CHING
CRSH CRSH CRSH
EVERY TIME HE TAKES AN ATTACK...
...EVERY TIME HE TAKES DAMAGE...
...HIS PHYSICAL ABILITIES INCREASE...

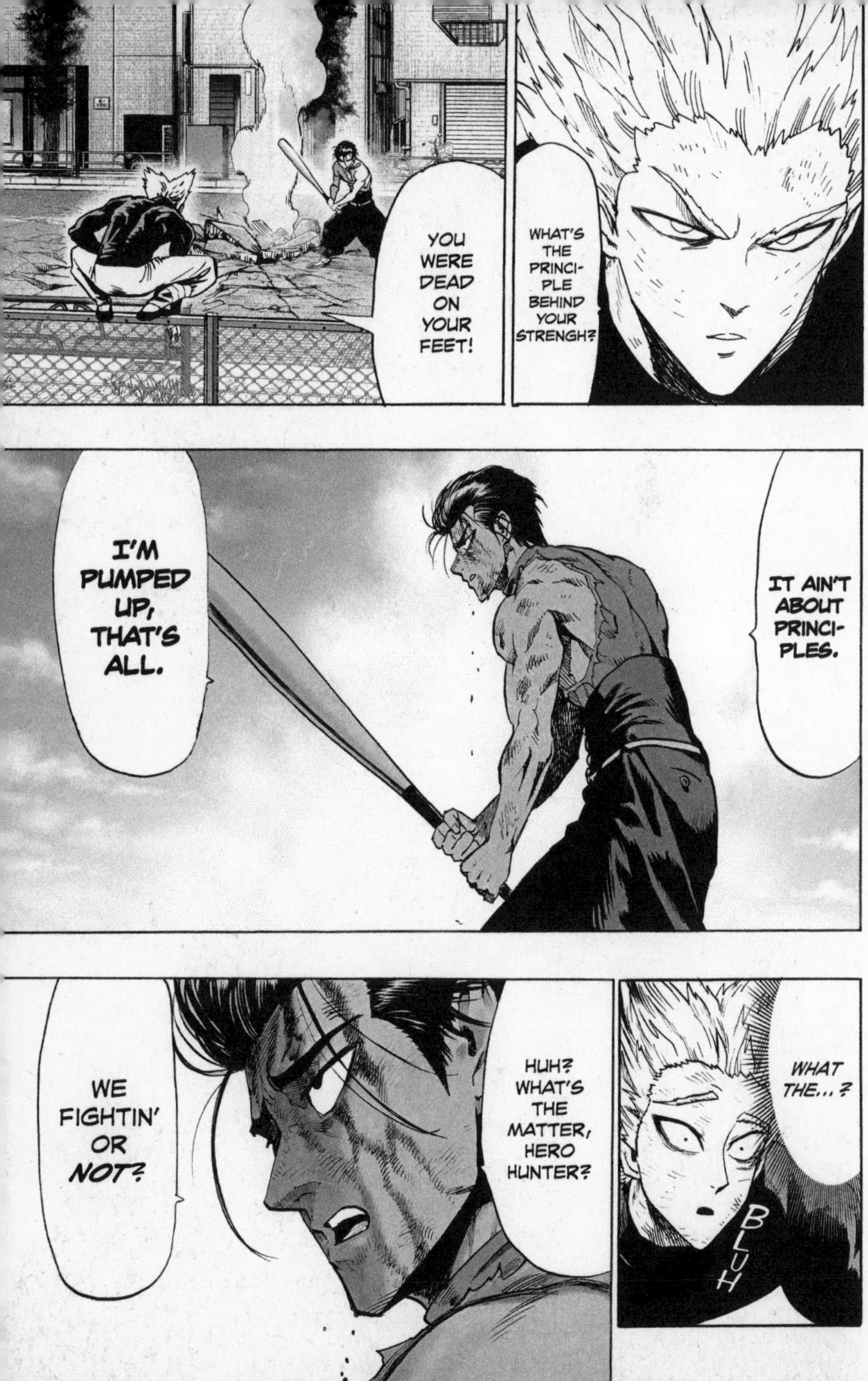
WHAT'S THE PRINCI-PLE BEHIND YOUR STRENGH?
YOU WERE DEAD ON YOUR FEET!
IT AIN'T ABOUT PRINCI-PLES.
I'M PUMPED UP, THAT'S ALL.
WHAT THE...?
BLUH
HUH? WHAT'S THE MATTER, HERO HUNTER?
WE FIGHTIN' OR *NOT*?

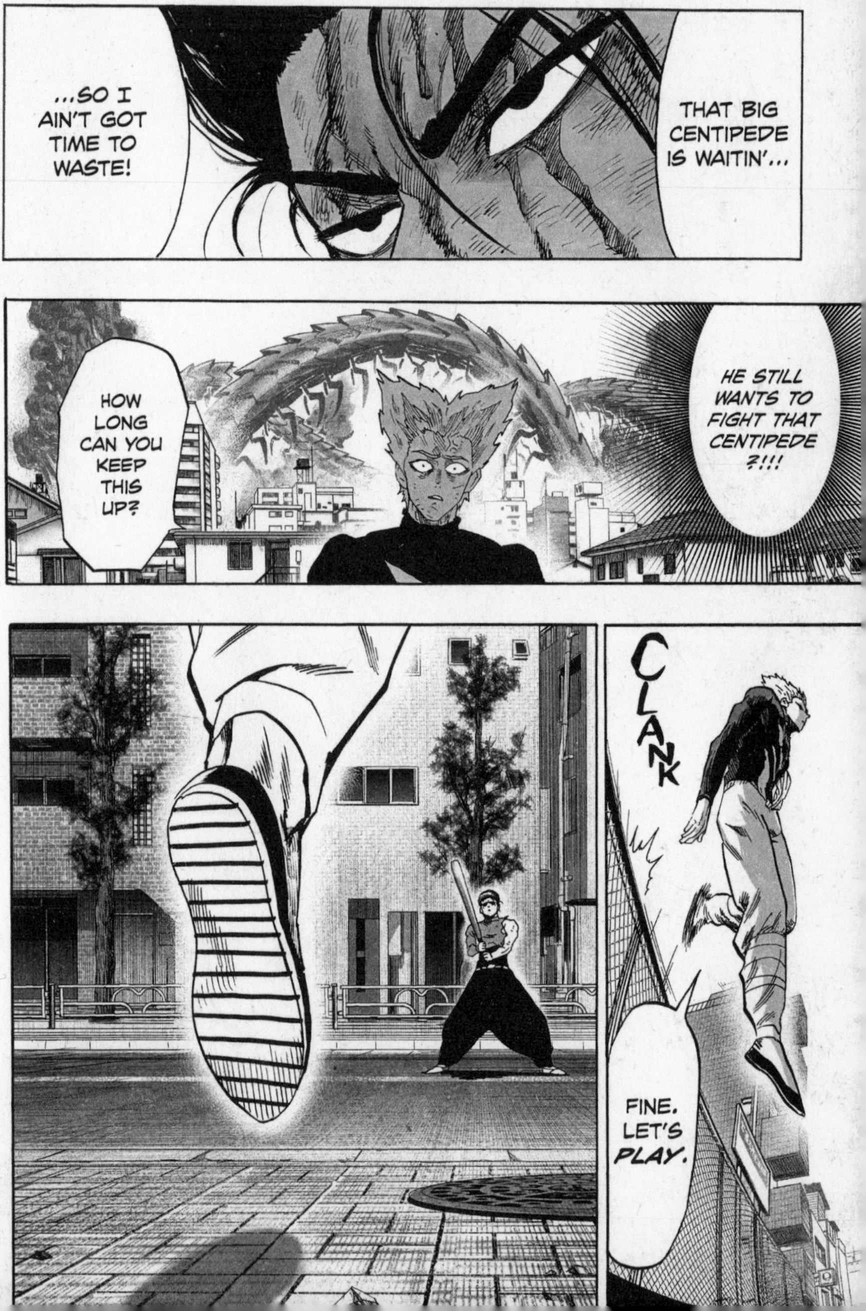
THAT BIG CENTIPEDE IS WAITIN'...
...SO I AIN'T GOT TIME TO WASTE!
HE STILL WANTS TO FIGHT THAT CENTIPEDE ?!!!
HOW LONG CAN YOU KEEP THIS UP?
CLANK
FINE. LET'S PLAY.

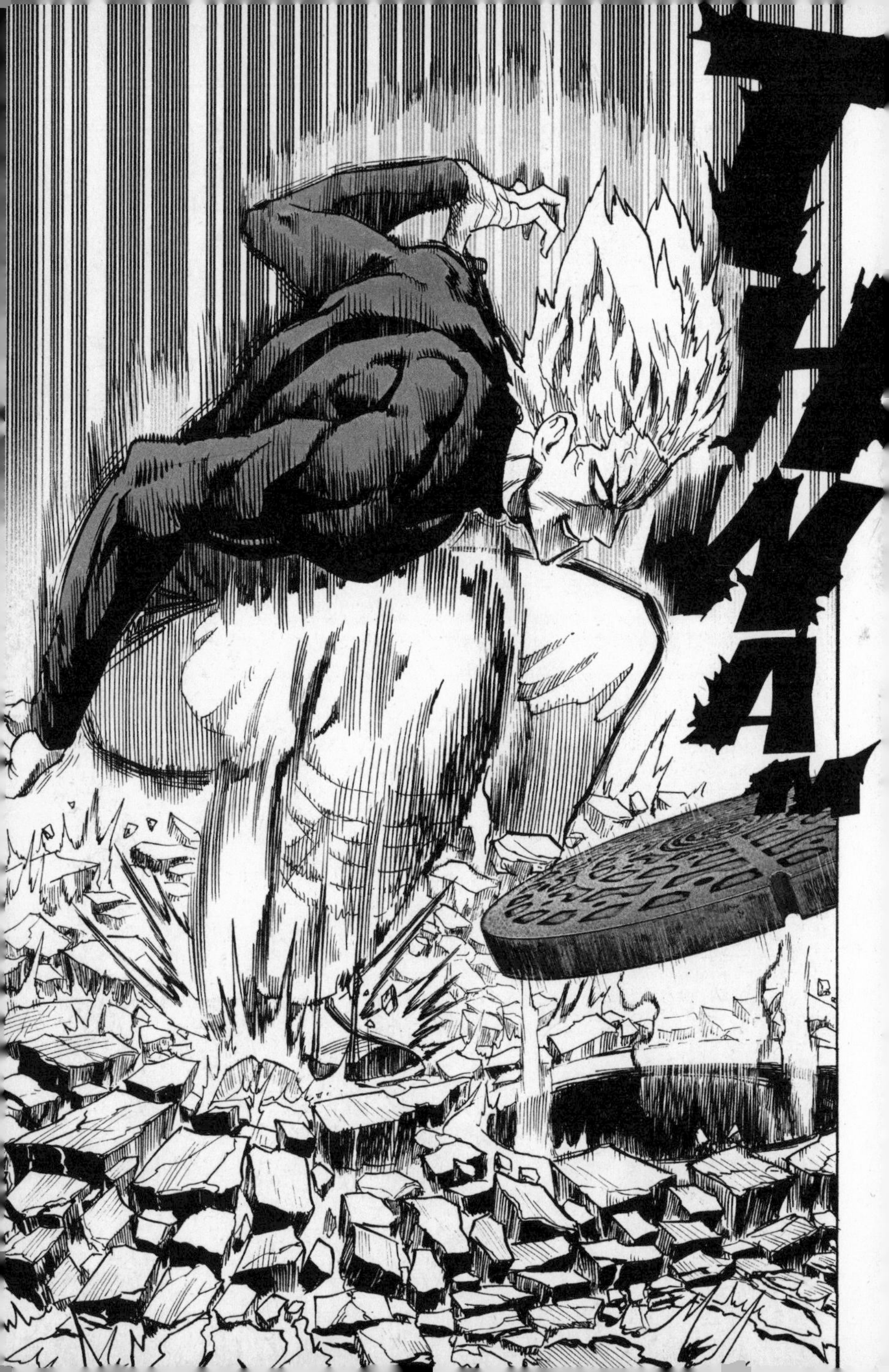
THWAM

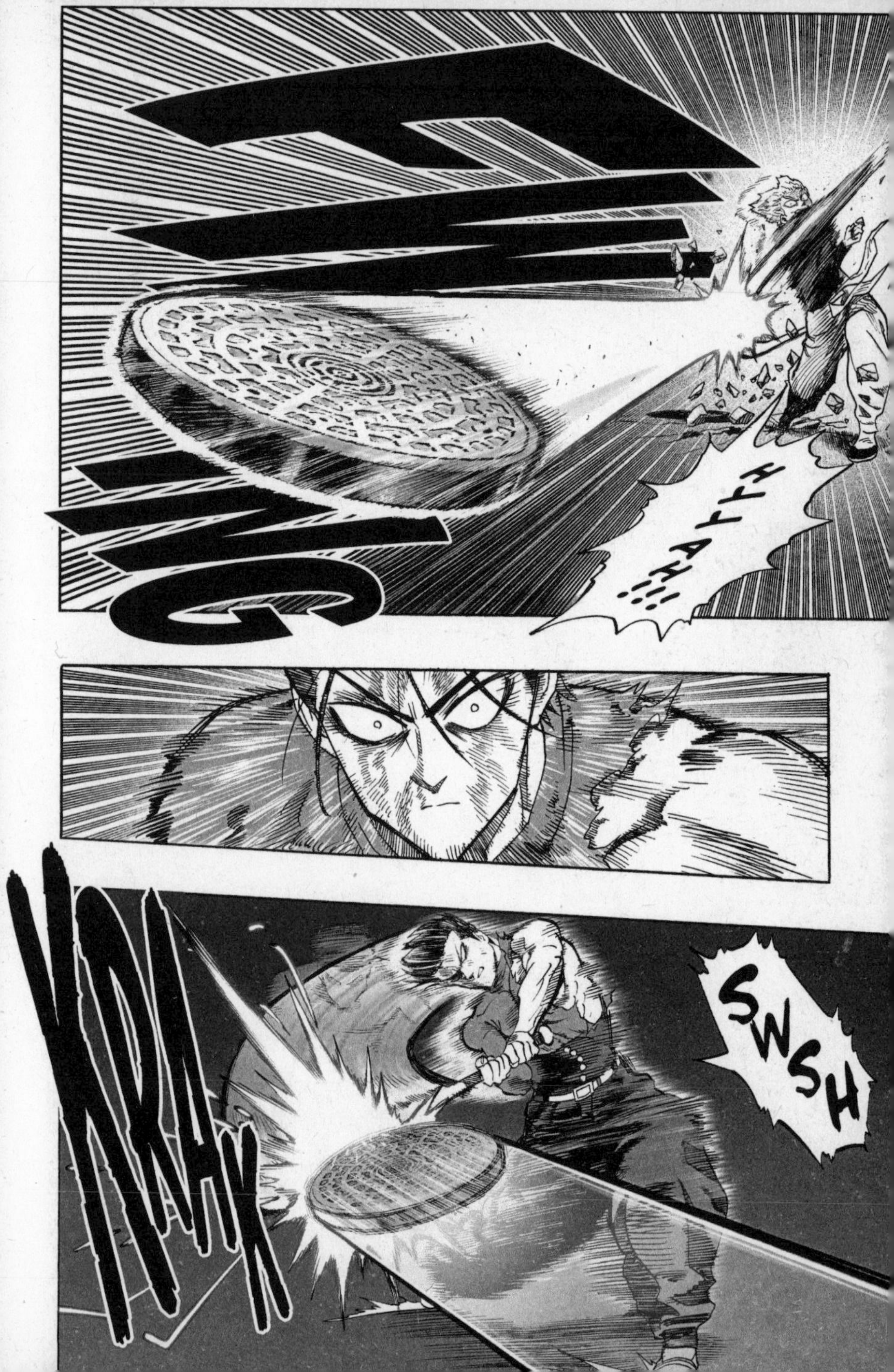
HIYAH!!!!
FWING
SWSH
KRAK

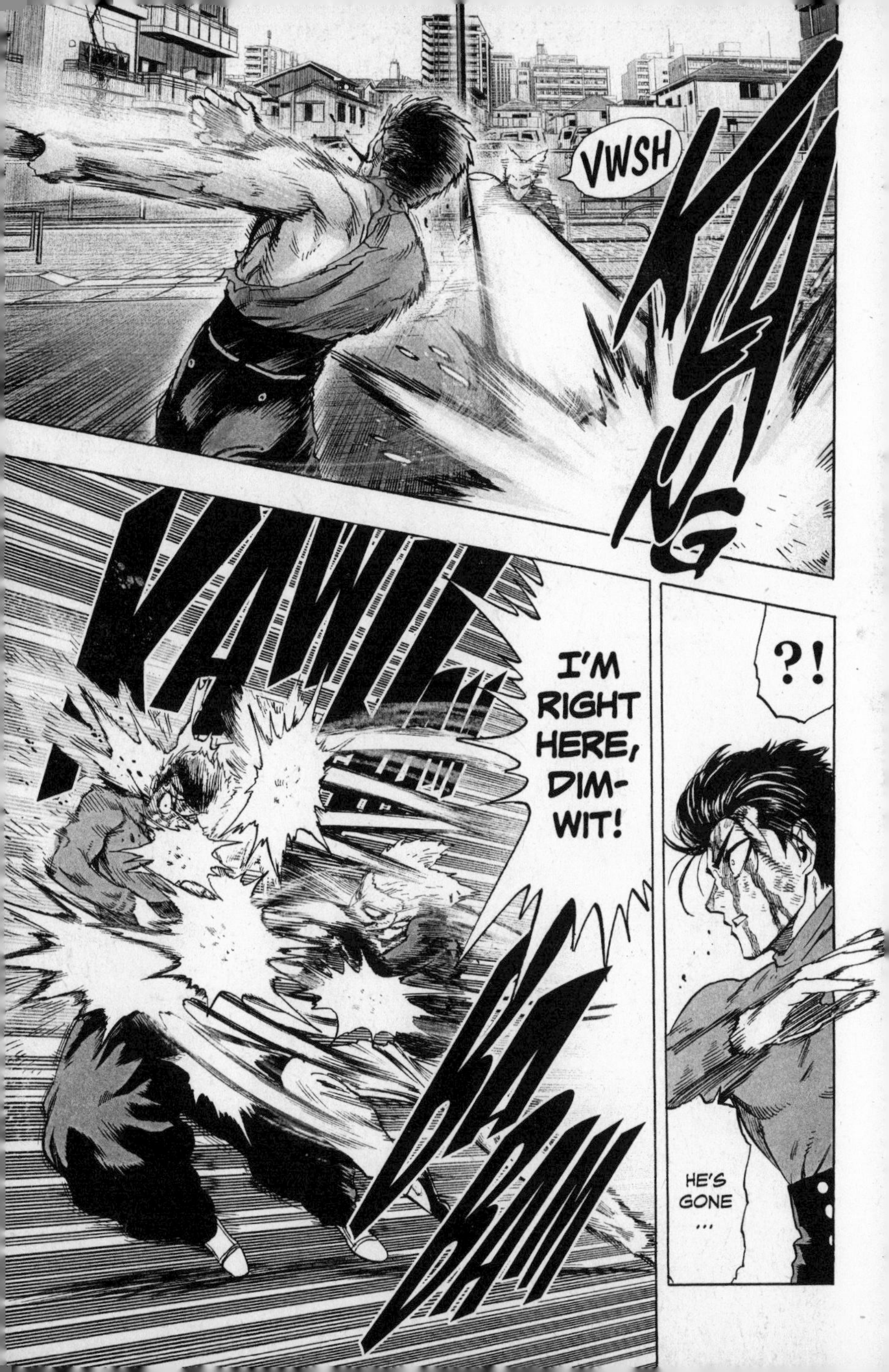
VWSH
?!
HE'S GONE ...
I'M RIGHT HERE, DIM-WIT!

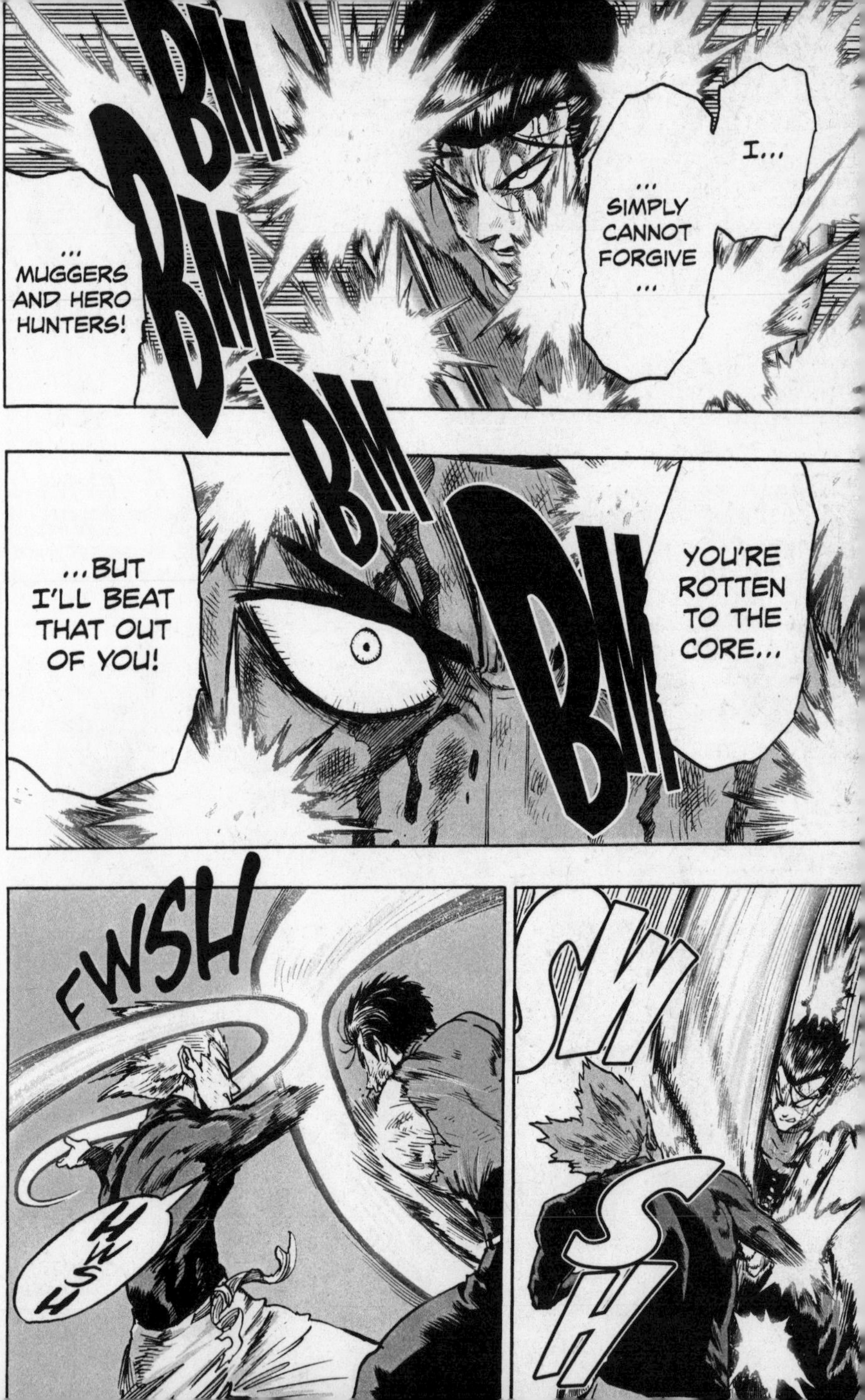
I...
... SIMPLY CANNOT FORGIVE ...
... MUGGERS AND HERO HUNTERS!
BM BM BM BM
YOU'RE ROTTEN TO THE CORE...
...BUT I'LL BEAT THAT OUT OF YOU!
BM BM
SWSH
FWSH
HWSH

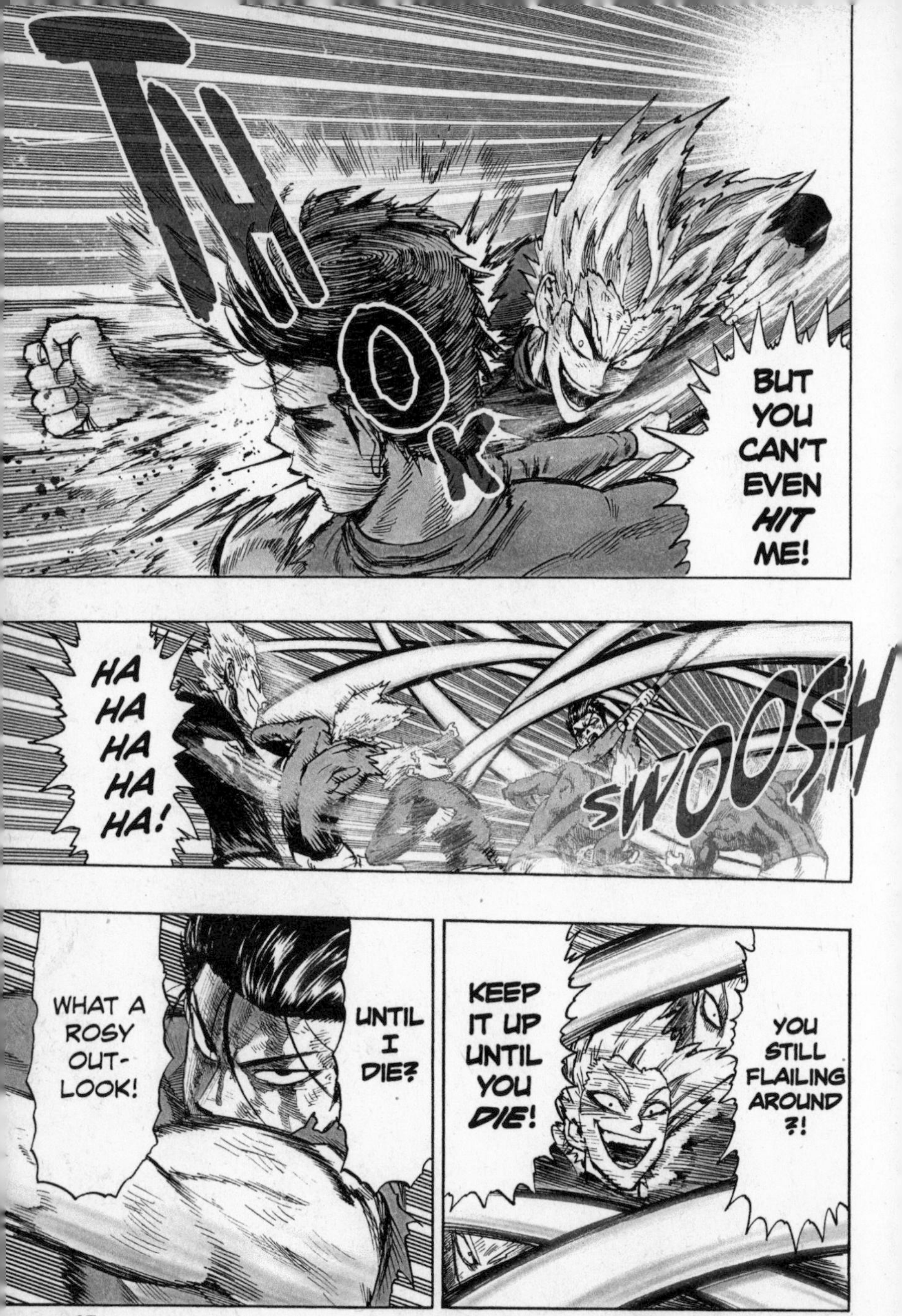
THOK
BUT YOU CAN'T EVEN *HIT* ME!
SWOOSH
HA HA HA HA HA!
YOU STILL FLAILING AROUND?!
KEEP IT UP UNTIL YOU *DIE*!
UNTIL I DIE?
WHAT A ROSY OUT-LOOK!

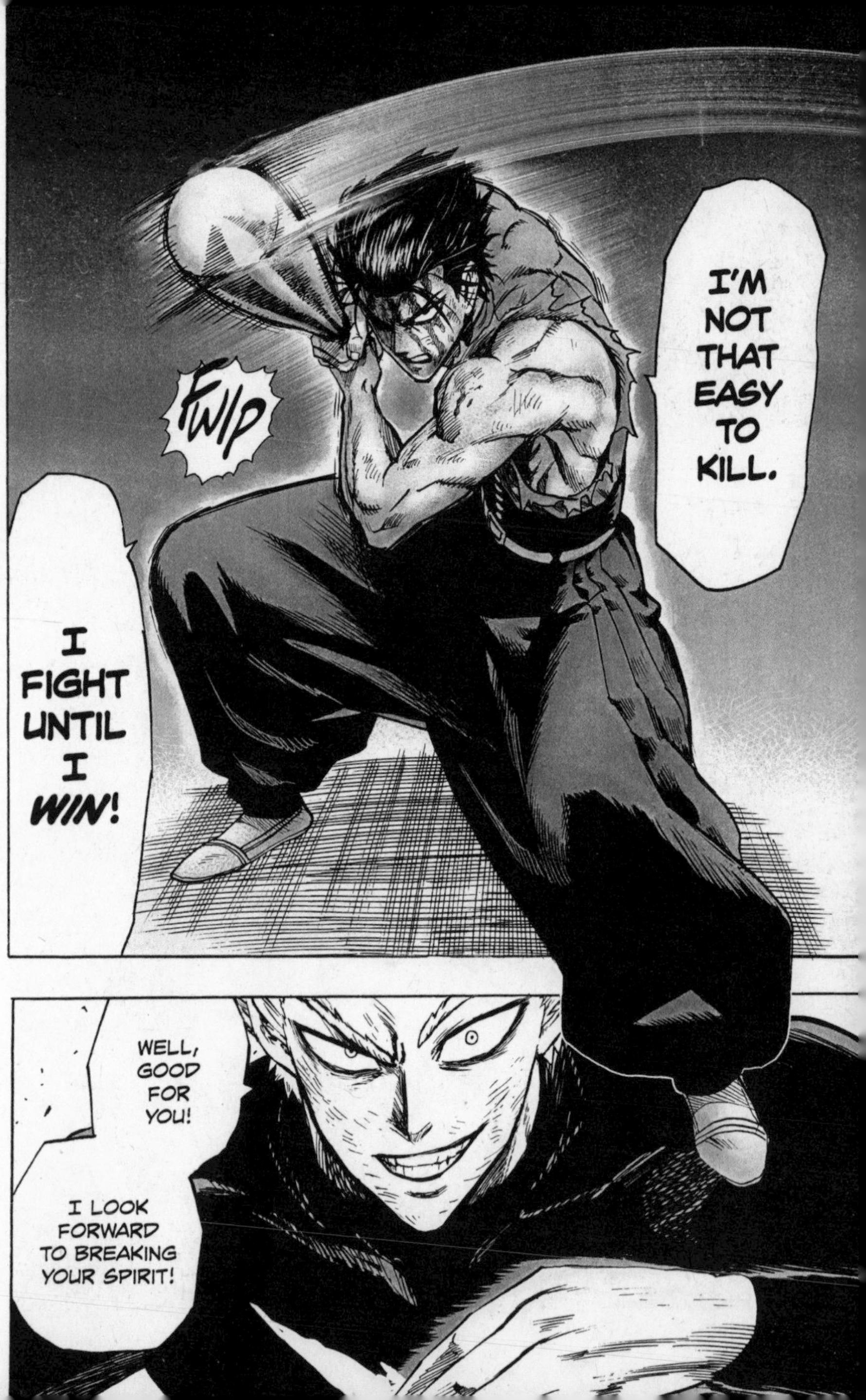
I'M NOT THAT EASY TO KILL.
FWIP
I FIGHT UNTIL I *WIN*!
WELL, GOOD FOR YOU!
I LOOK FORWARD TO BREAKING YOUR SPIRIT!

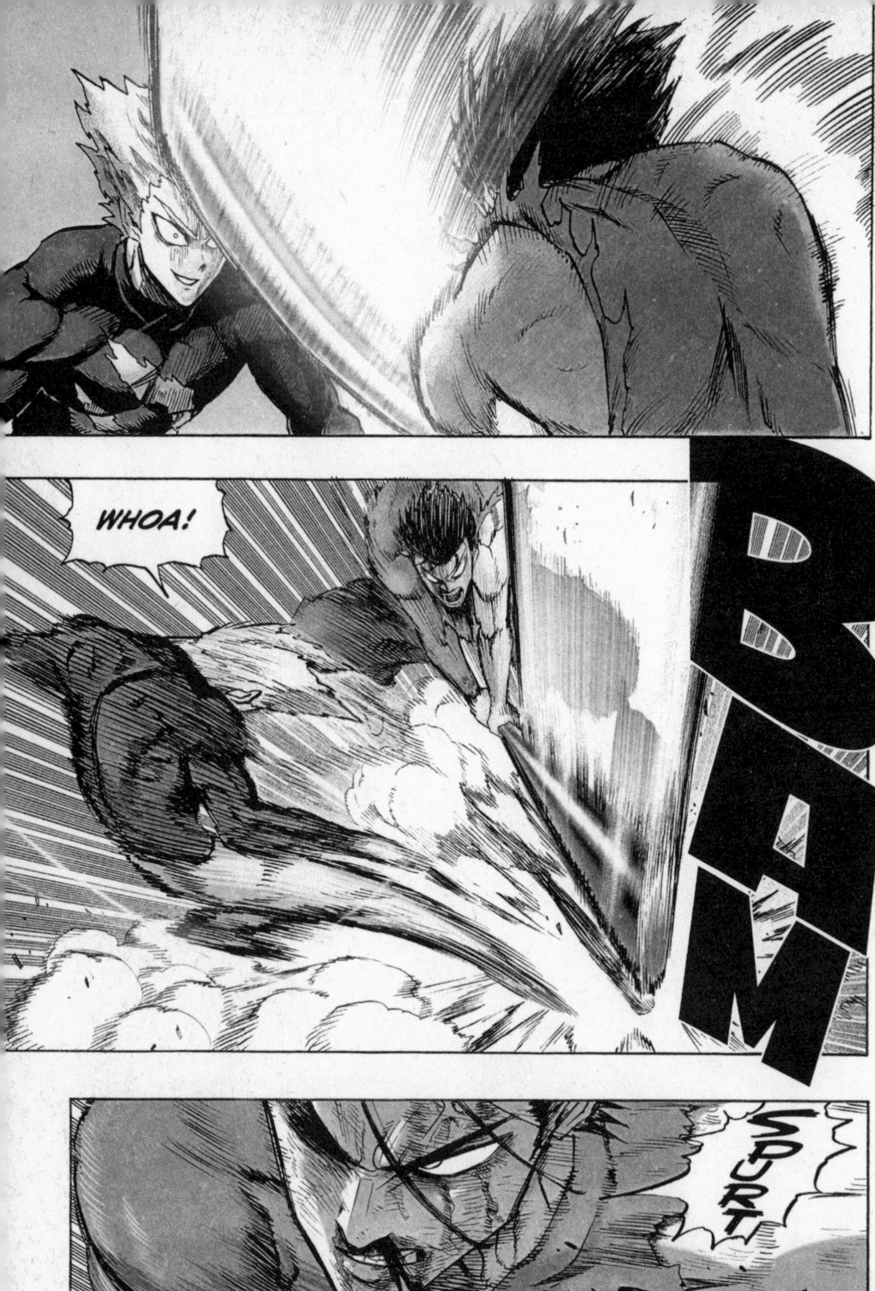
BAM
WHOA!
SPURT!

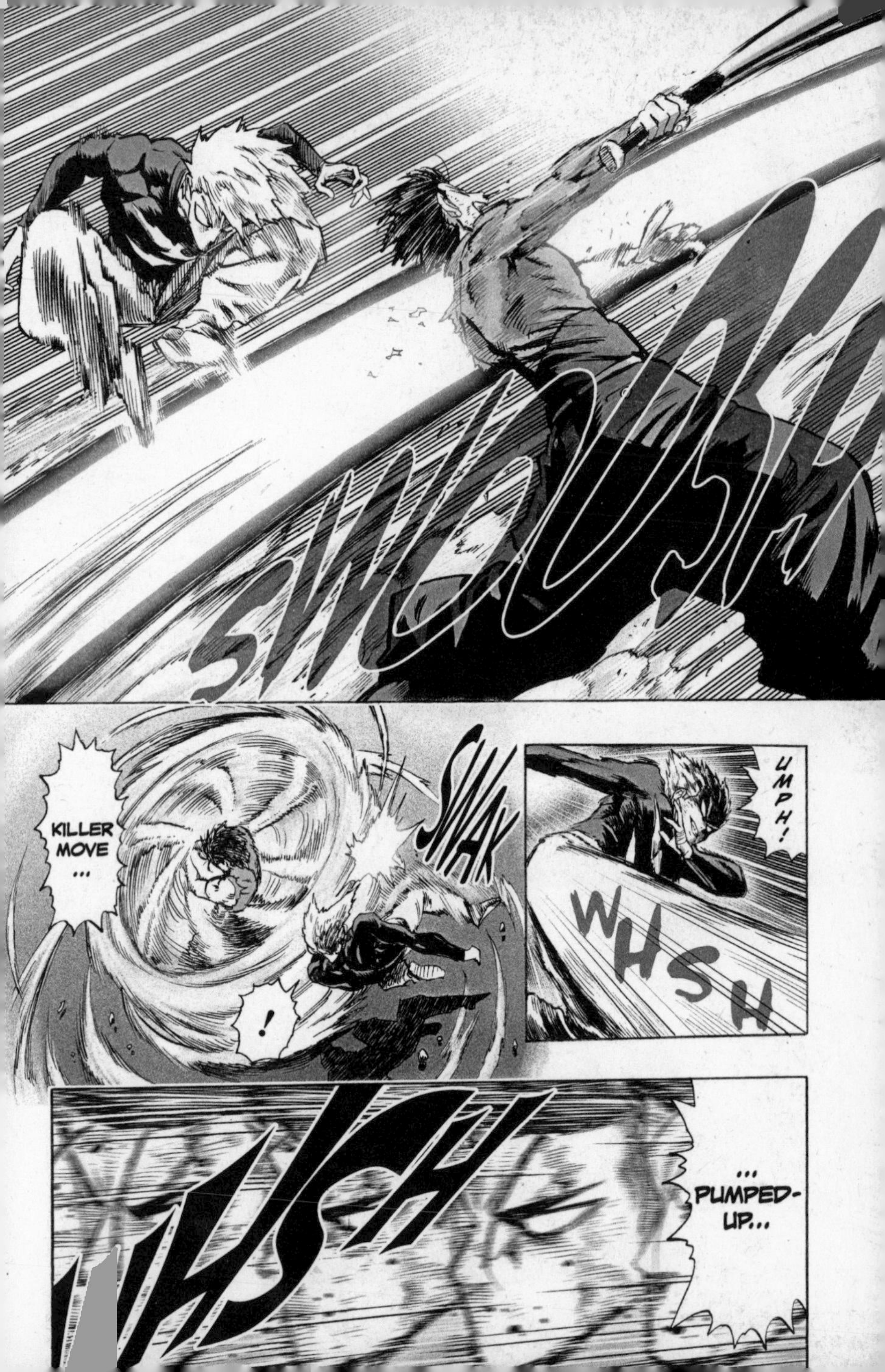
SWOOSH
UMPH!
WHSH
SWAK
KILLER MOVE ...
!
WHSH
... PUMPED-UP...

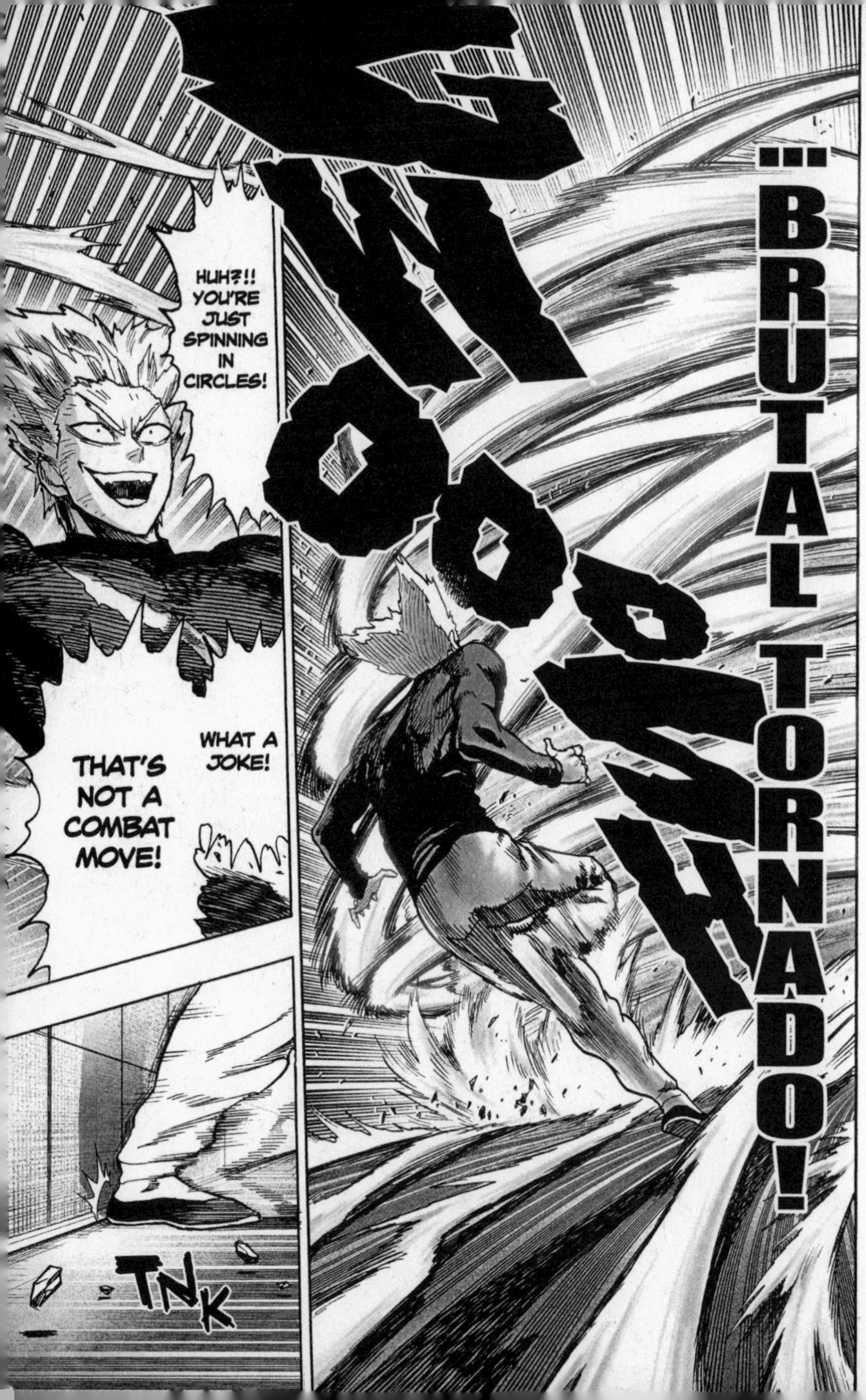

...BRUTAL TORNADO!
SWOOOSH
HUH?!! YOU'RE JUST SPINNING IN CIRCLES!
WHAT A JOKE!
THAT'S NOT A COMBAT MOVE!
TNK

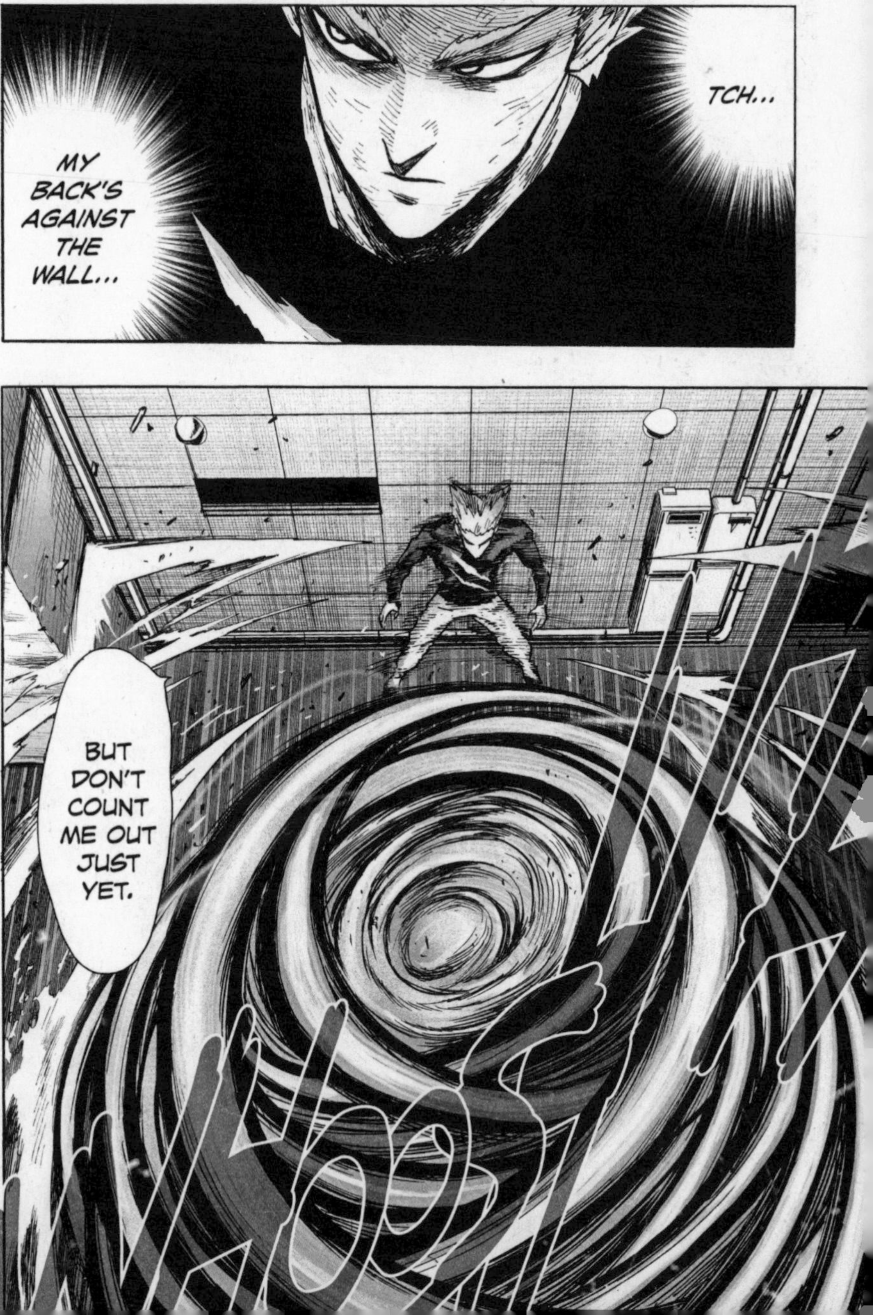
TCH...
MY BACK'S AGAINST THE WALL...
BUT DON'T COUNT ME OUT JUST YET.

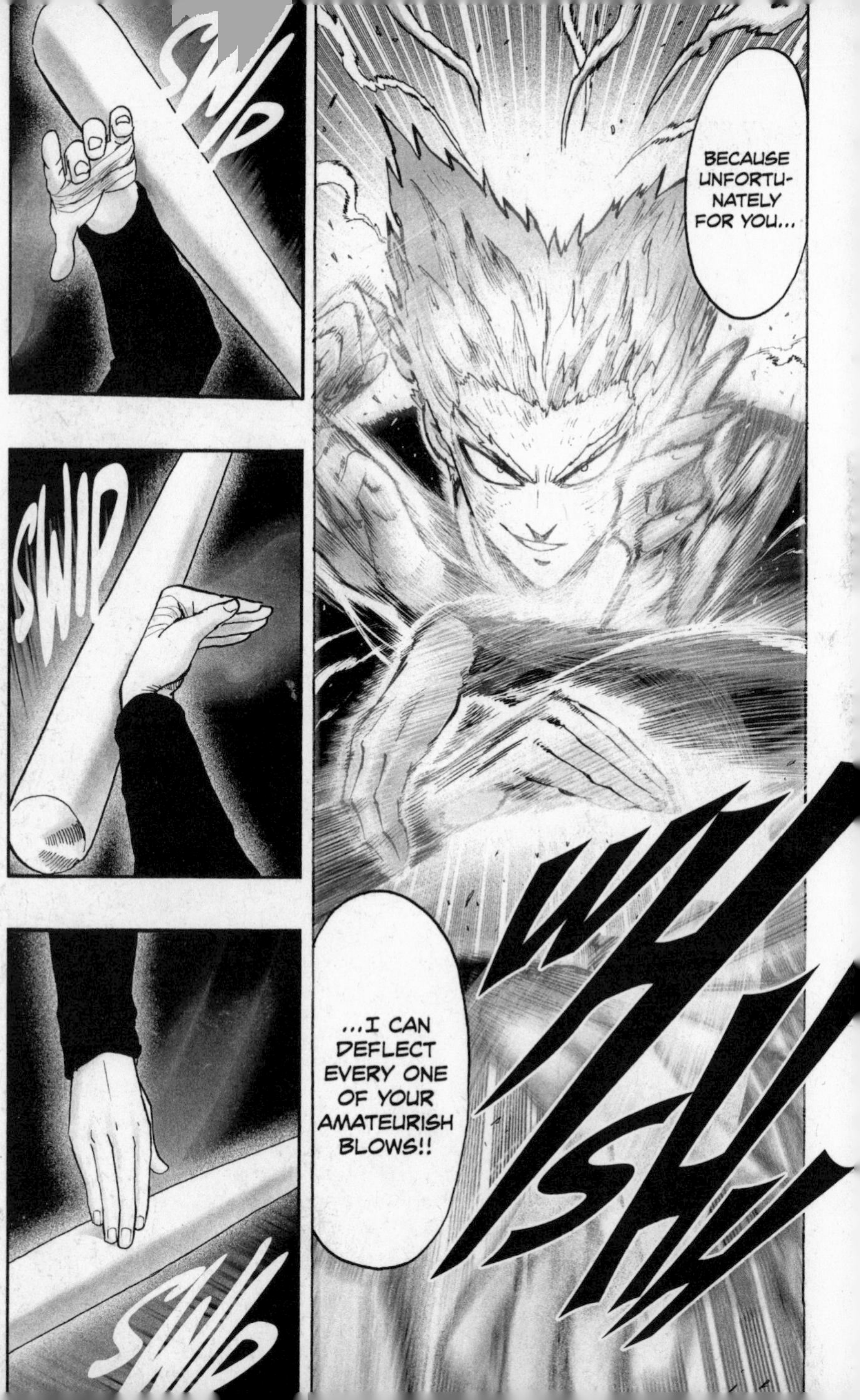
BECAUSE UNFORTU-NATELY FOR YOU...
...I CAN DEFLECT EVERY ONE OF YOUR AMATEURISH BLOWS!!
SWIP
SWIP
SWIP

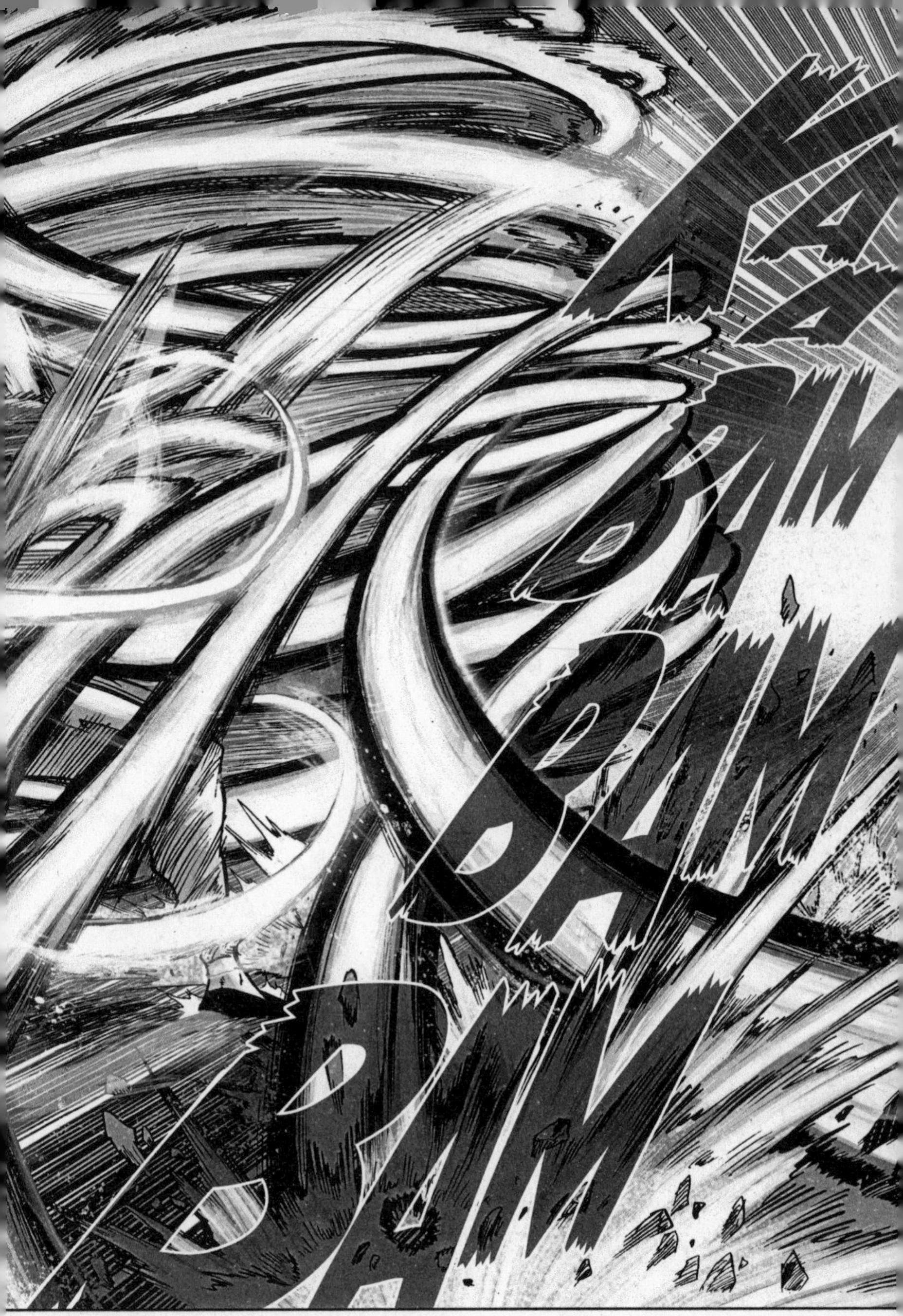
BAM BAM BAM

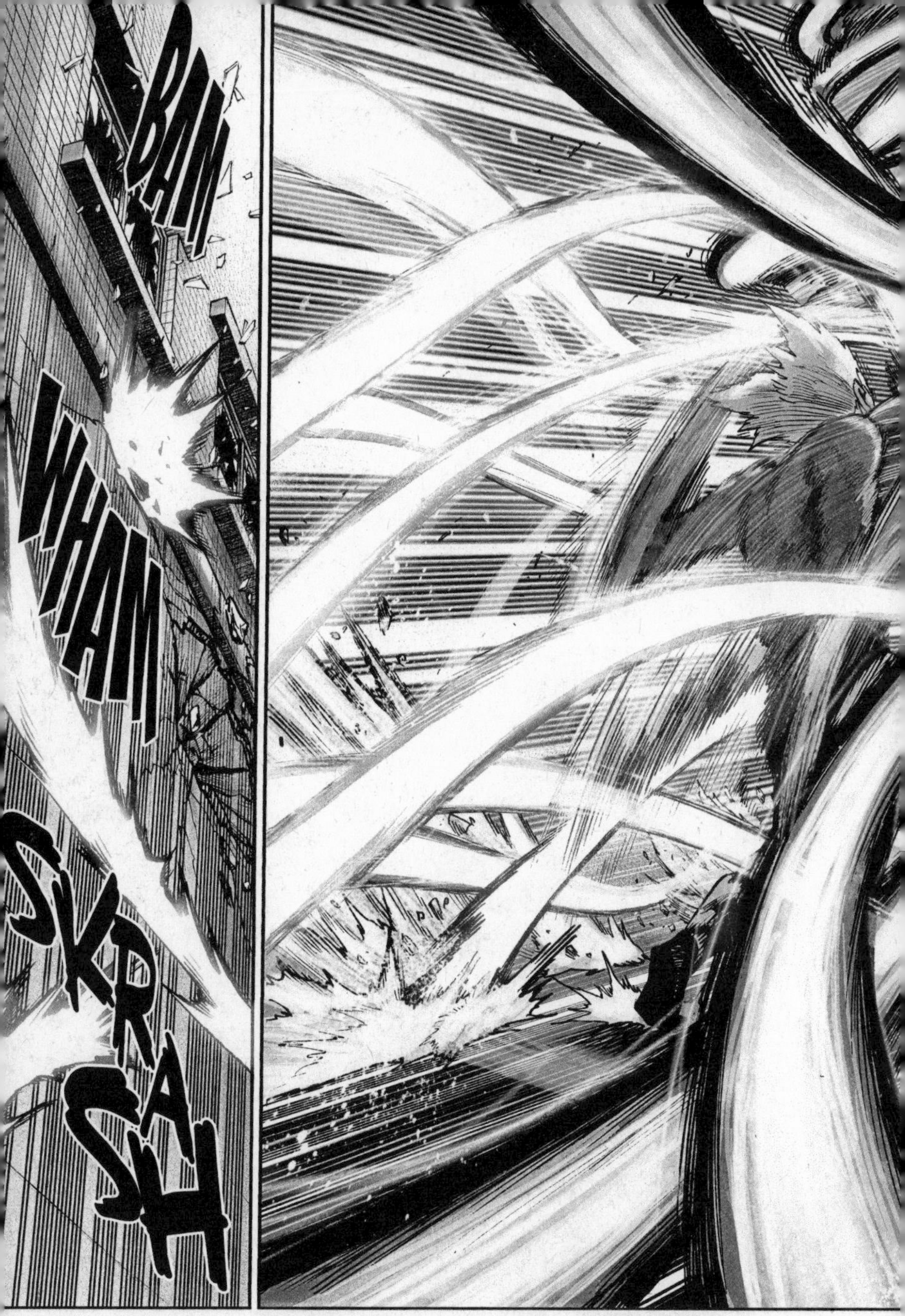
BAM
WHAM
SKRASH

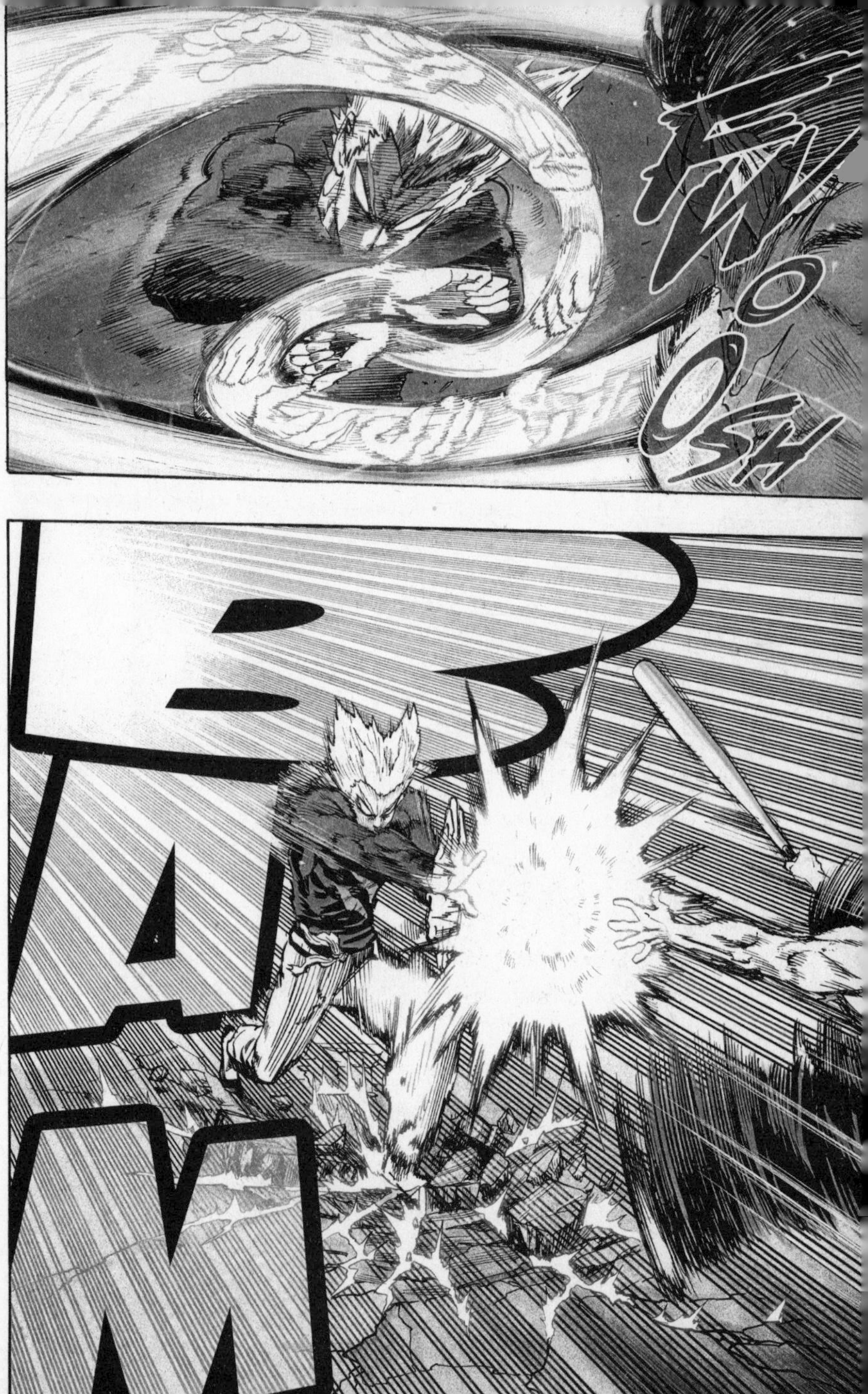
FWOOSH
BAM

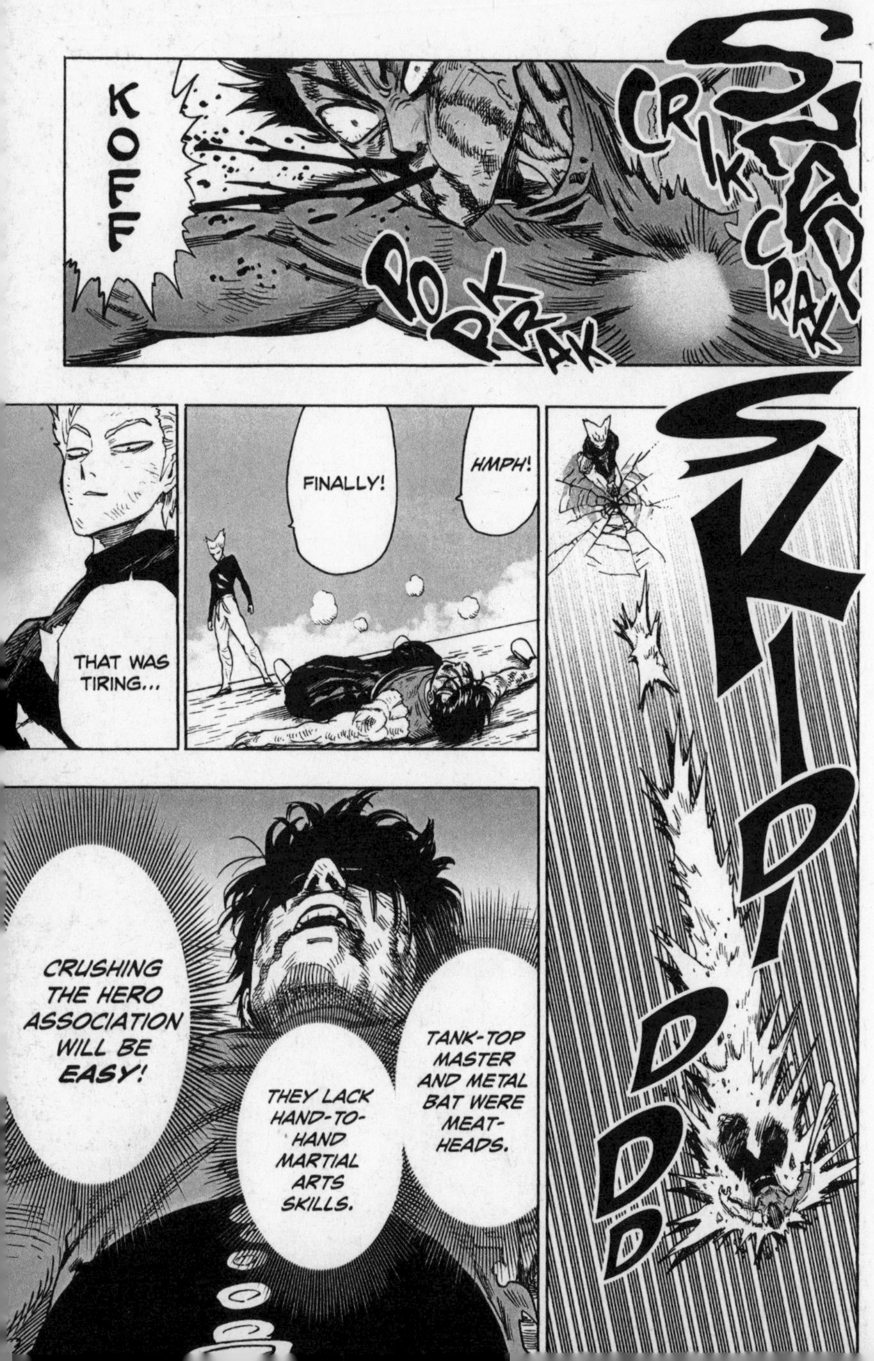
SNAP
CRIK
CRAK
CRAK
POK
PRAK
KOFF
SKIDDDD
HMPH!
FINALLY!
THAT WAS TIRING...
TANK-TOP MASTER AND METAL BAT WERE MEAT-HEADS.
THEY LACK HAND-TO-HAND MARTIAL ARTS SKILLS.
CRUSHING THE HERO ASSOCIATION WILL BE EASY!

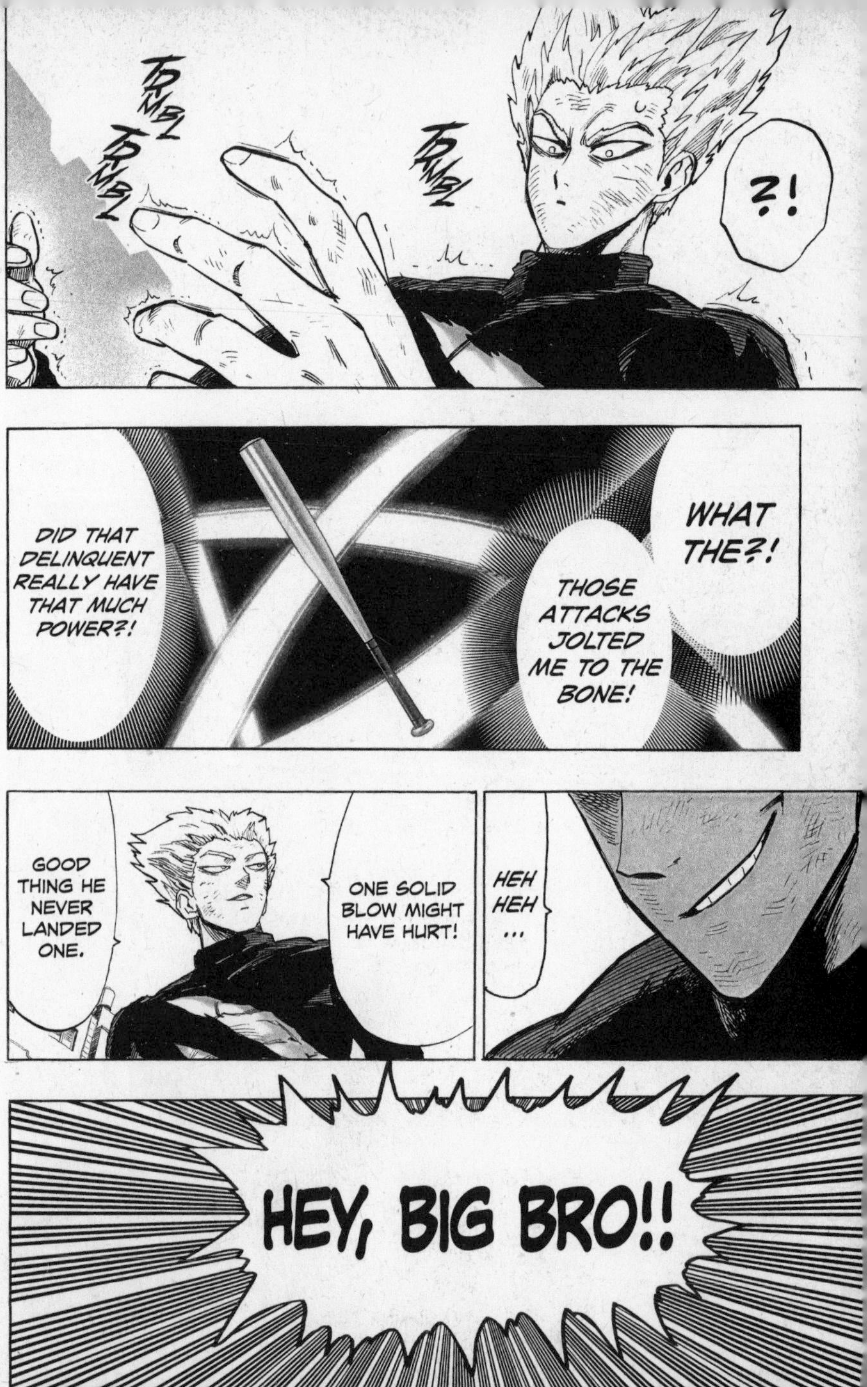
?!
TRMBL
TRMBL
TRMBL
WHAT THE?!
THOSE ATTACKS JOLTED ME TO THE BONE!
DID THAT DELINQUENT REALLY HAVE THAT MUCH POWER?!
HEH HEH ...
ONE SOLID BLOW MIGHT HAVE HURT!
GOOD THING HE NEVER LANDED ONE.
HEY, BIG BRO!!

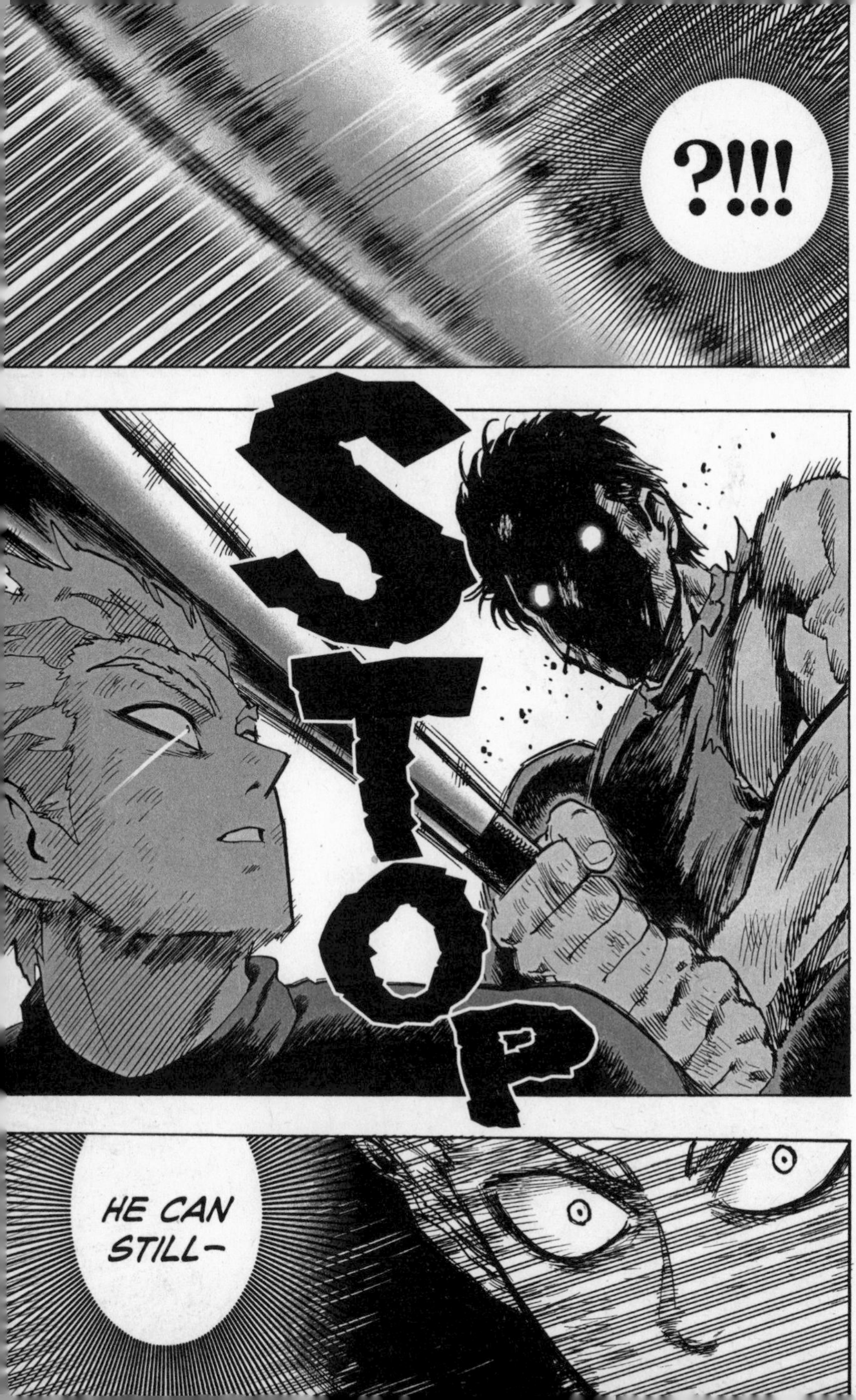
?!!!
STOP
HE CAN STILL-

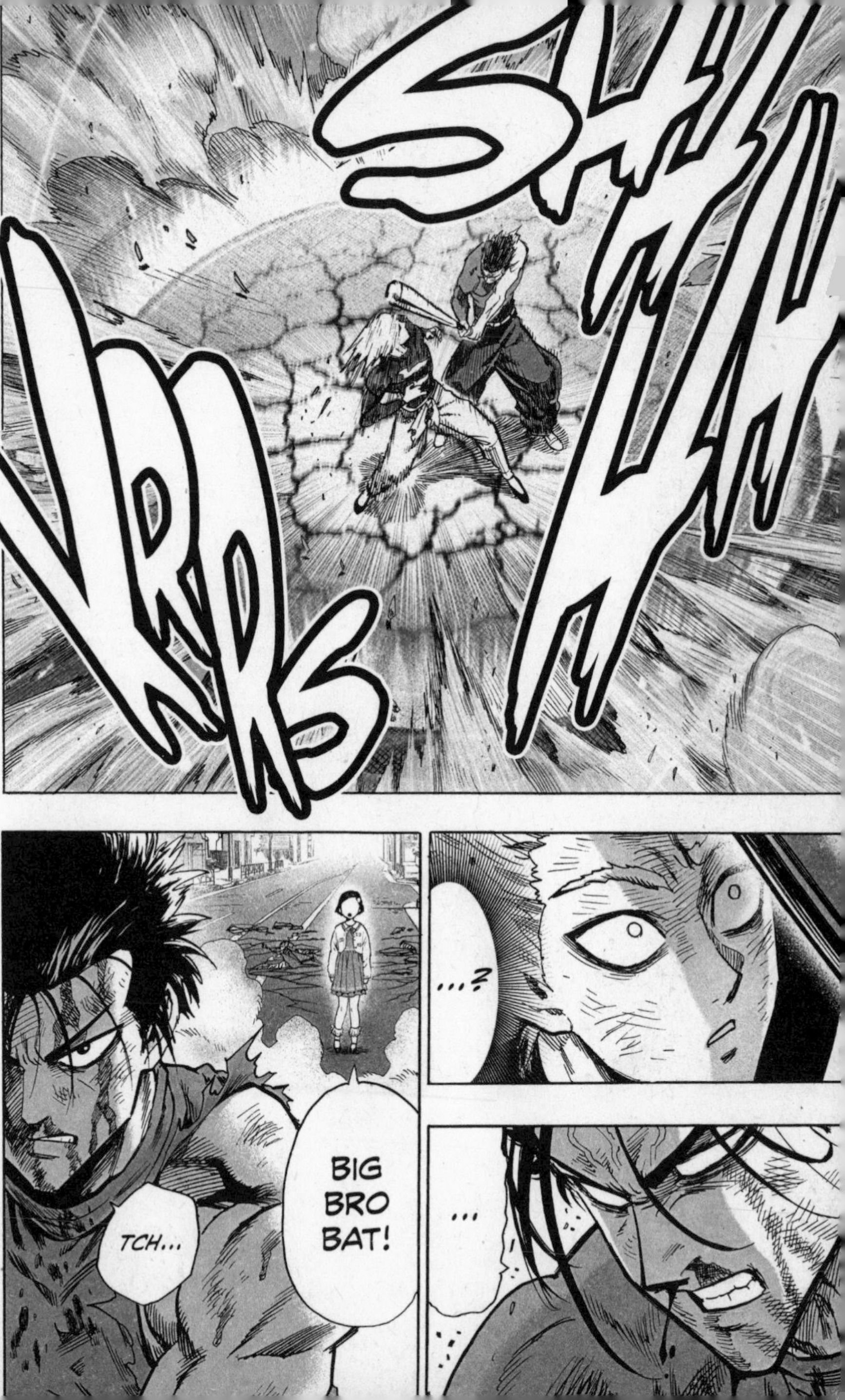
...?
...
BIG BRO BAT!
TCH...

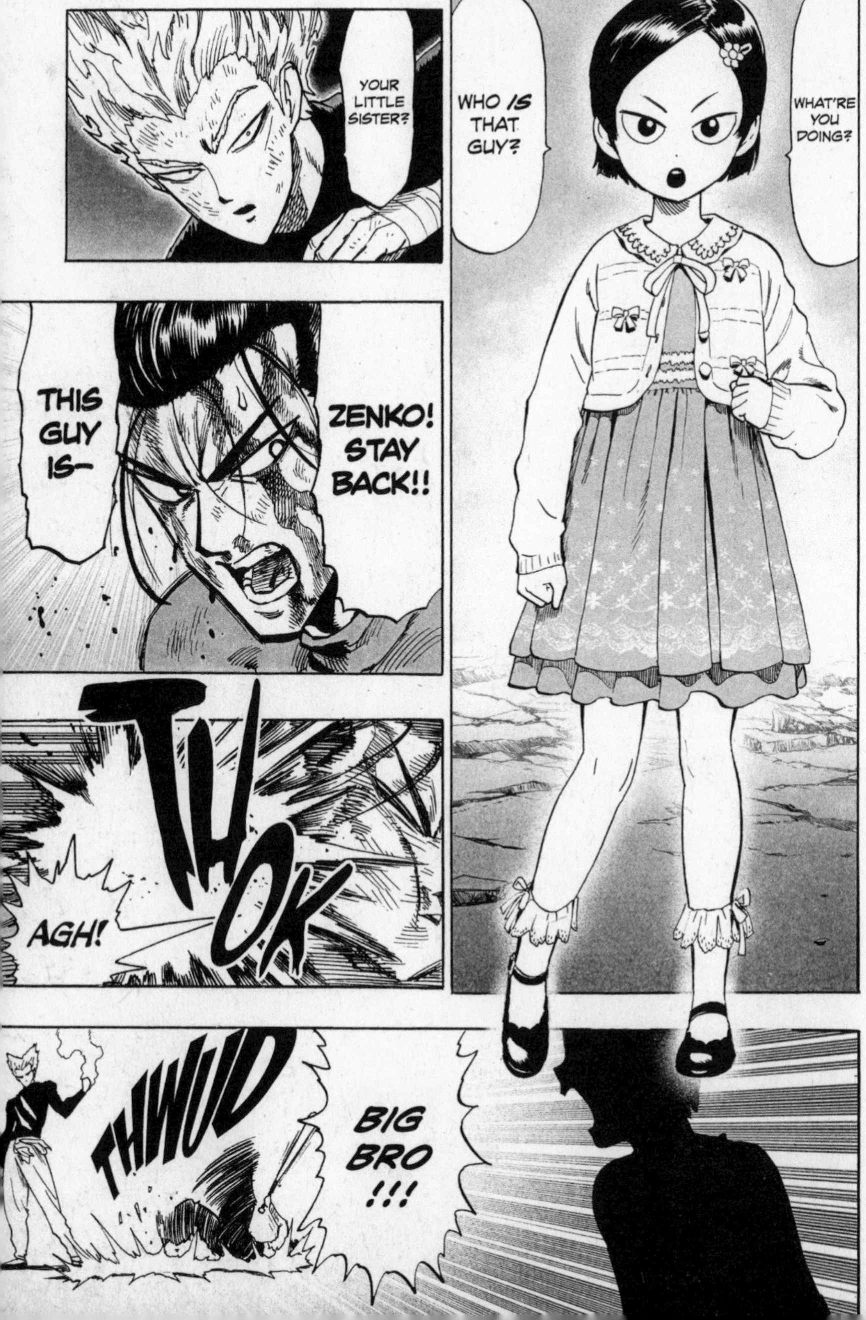
WHAT'RE YOU DOING?
WHO *IS* THAT GUY?
YOUR LITTLE SISTER?
ZENKO! STAY BACK!!
THIS GUY IS-
THWOK
AGH!
BIG BRO!!!
THWUD

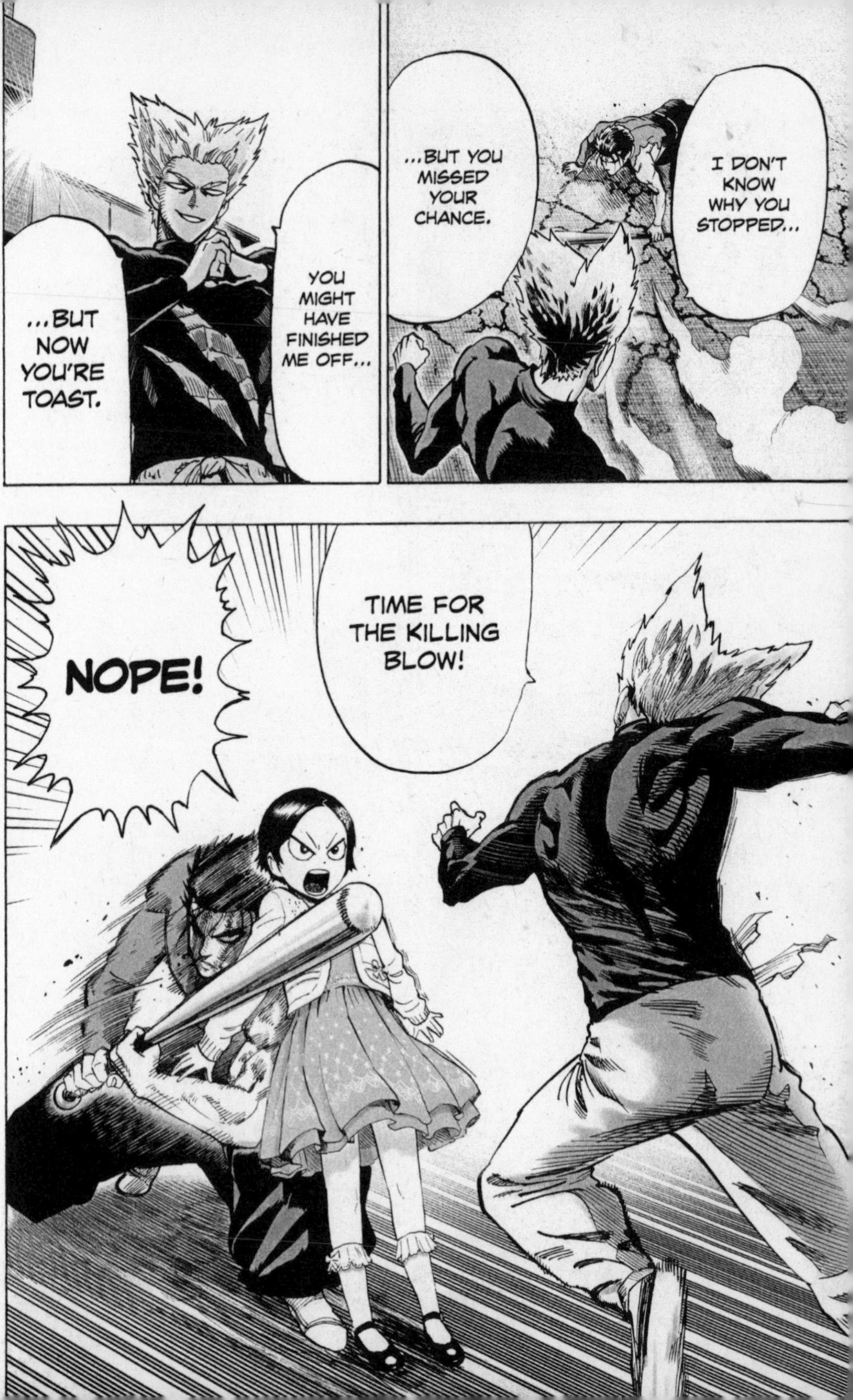
I DON'T KNOW WHY YOU STOPPED...
...BUT YOU MISSED YOUR CHANCE.
YOU MIGHT HAVE FINISHED ME OFF...
...BUT NOW YOU'RE TOAST.
TIME FOR THE KILLING BLOW!
NOPE!

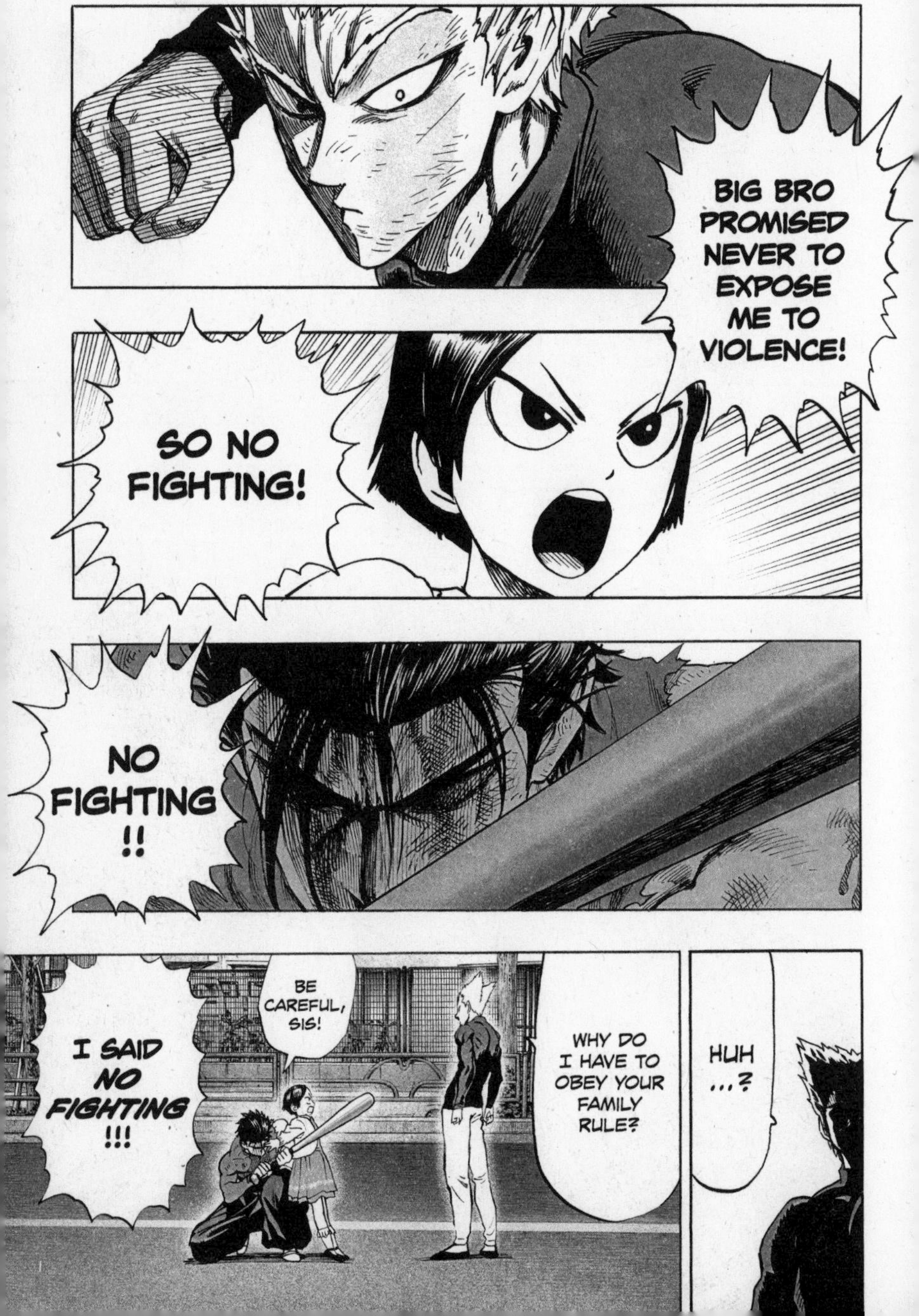
BIG BRO PROMISED NEVER TO EXPOSE ME TO VIOLENCE!
SO NO FIGHTING!
NO FIGHTING !!
HUH ...?
WHY DO I HAVE TO OBEY YOUR FAMILY RULE?
BE CAREFUL, SIS!
I SAID *NO FIGHTING* !!!

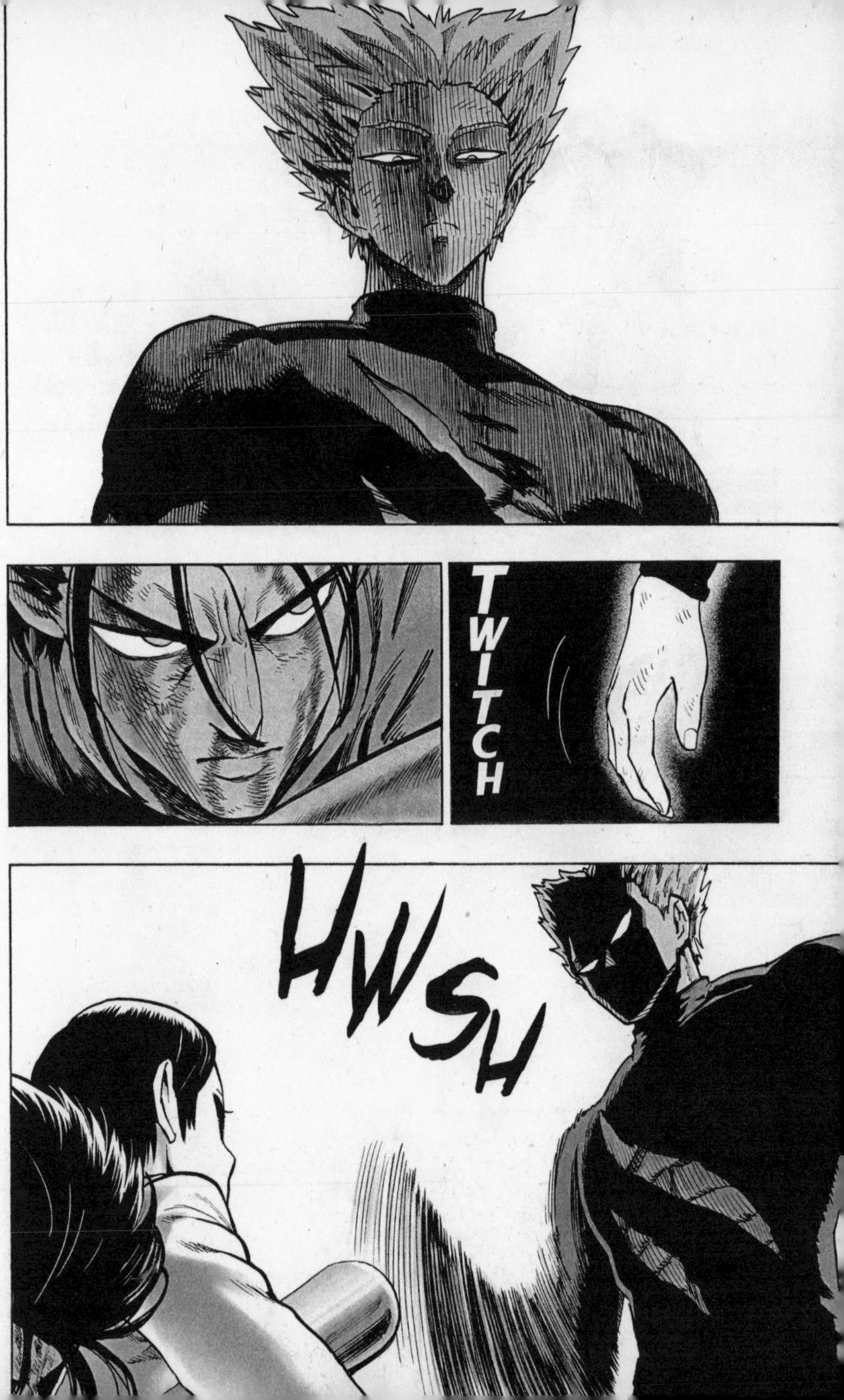
TWITCH
HWSH

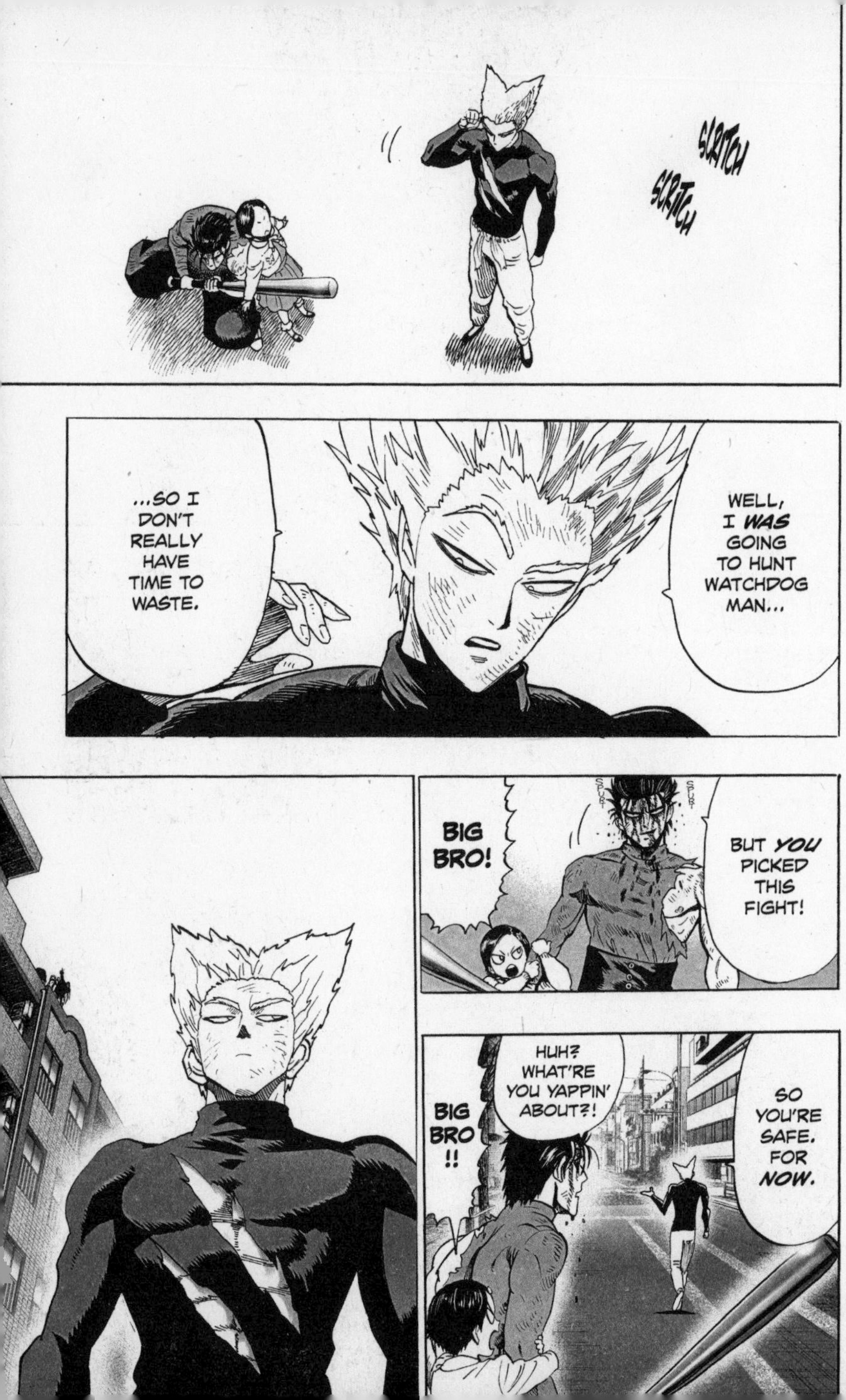
SCRITCH
SCRITCH
WELL, I *WAS* GOING TO HUNT WATCHDOG MAN...
...SO I DON'T REALLY HAVE TIME TO WASTE.
SPURT
SPURT
BUT *YOU* PICKED THIS FIGHT!
BIG BRO!
SO YOU'RE SAFE. FOR *NOW*.
HUH? WHAT'RE YOU YAPPIN' ABOUT?!
BIG BRO !!

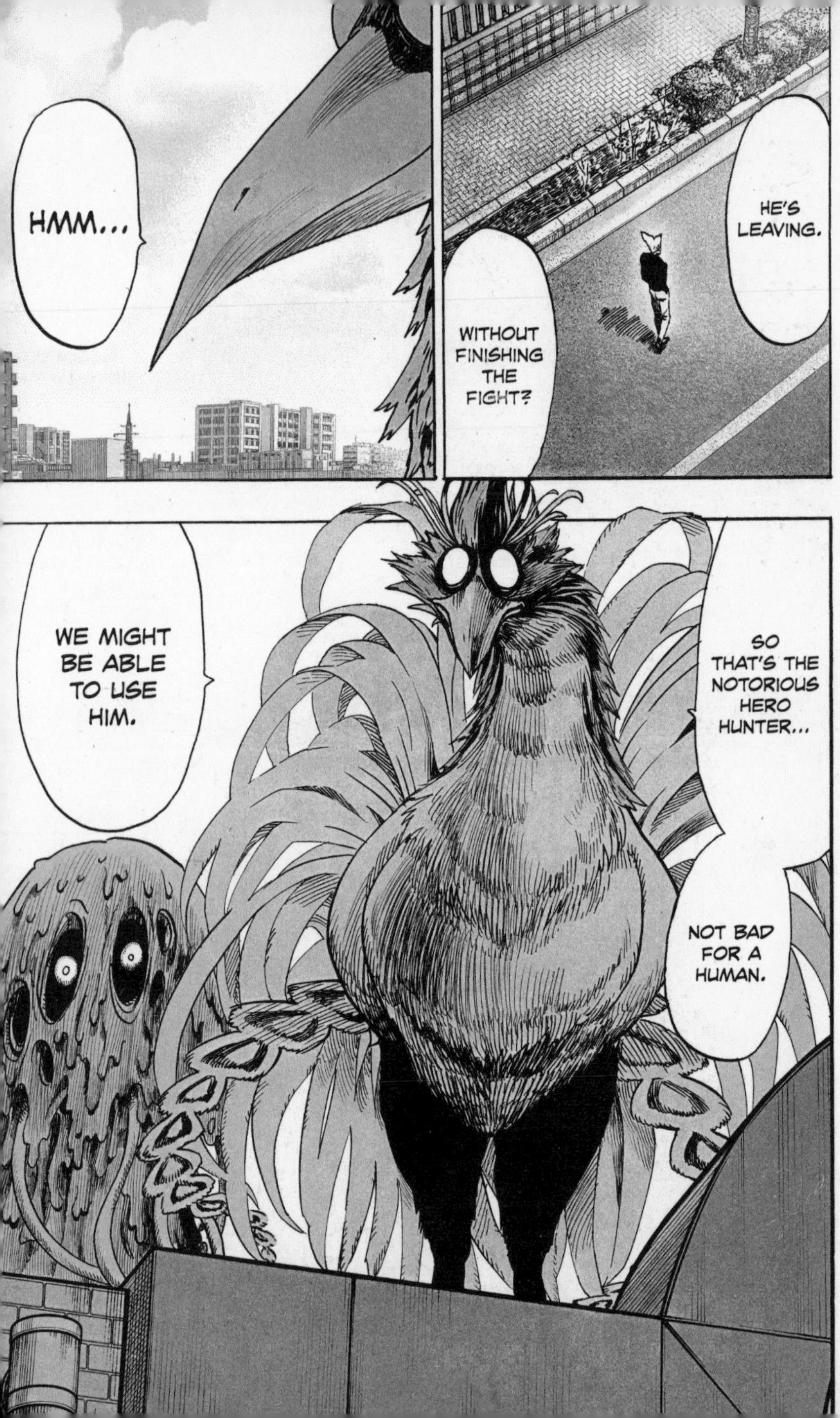
HE'S LEAVING.
WITHOUT FINISHING THE FIGHT?
HMM...
SO THAT'S THE NOTORIOUS HERO HUNTER...
NOT BAD FOR A HUMAN.
WE MIGHT BE ABLE TO USE HIM.

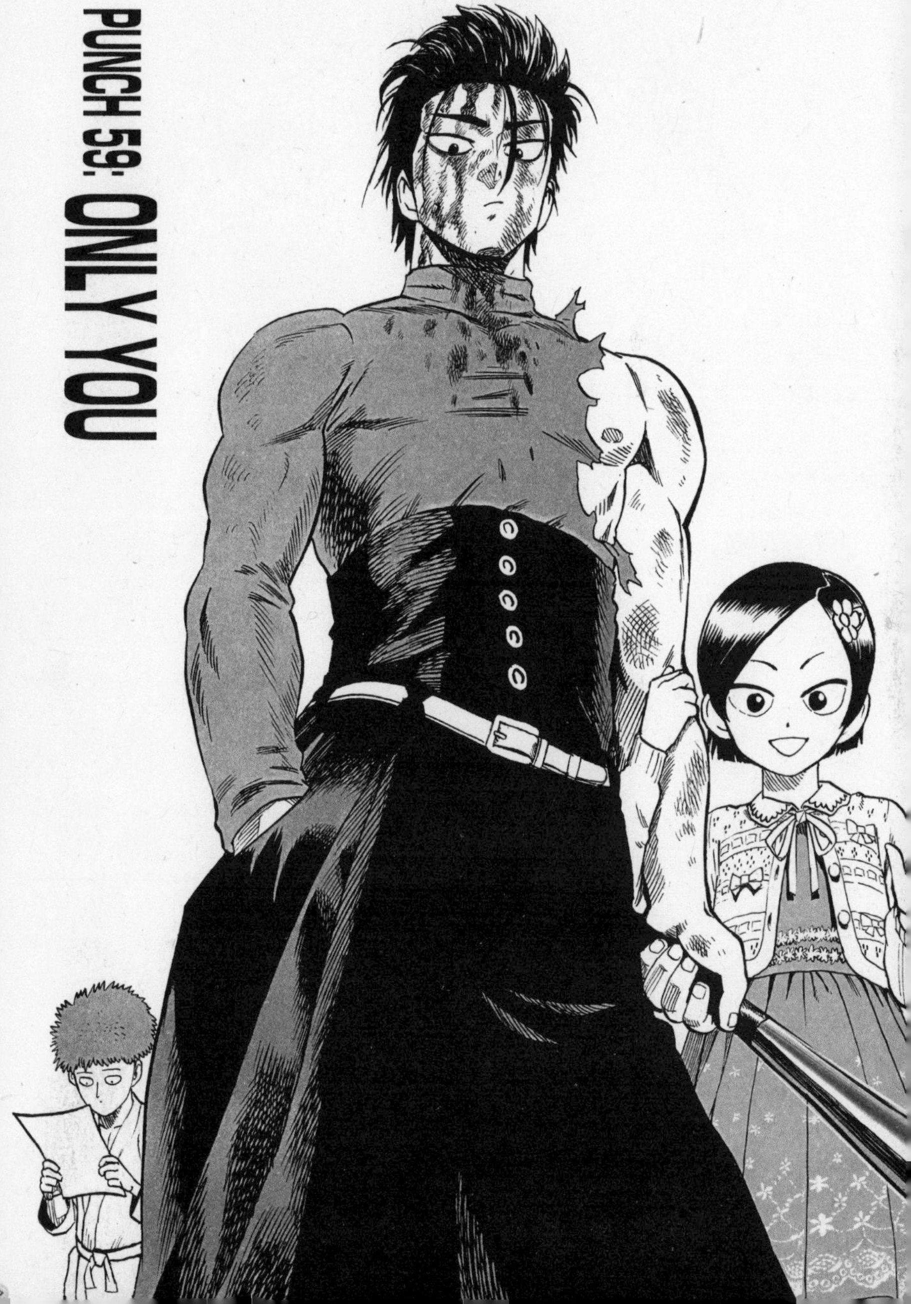
PUNCH 59: ONLY YOU

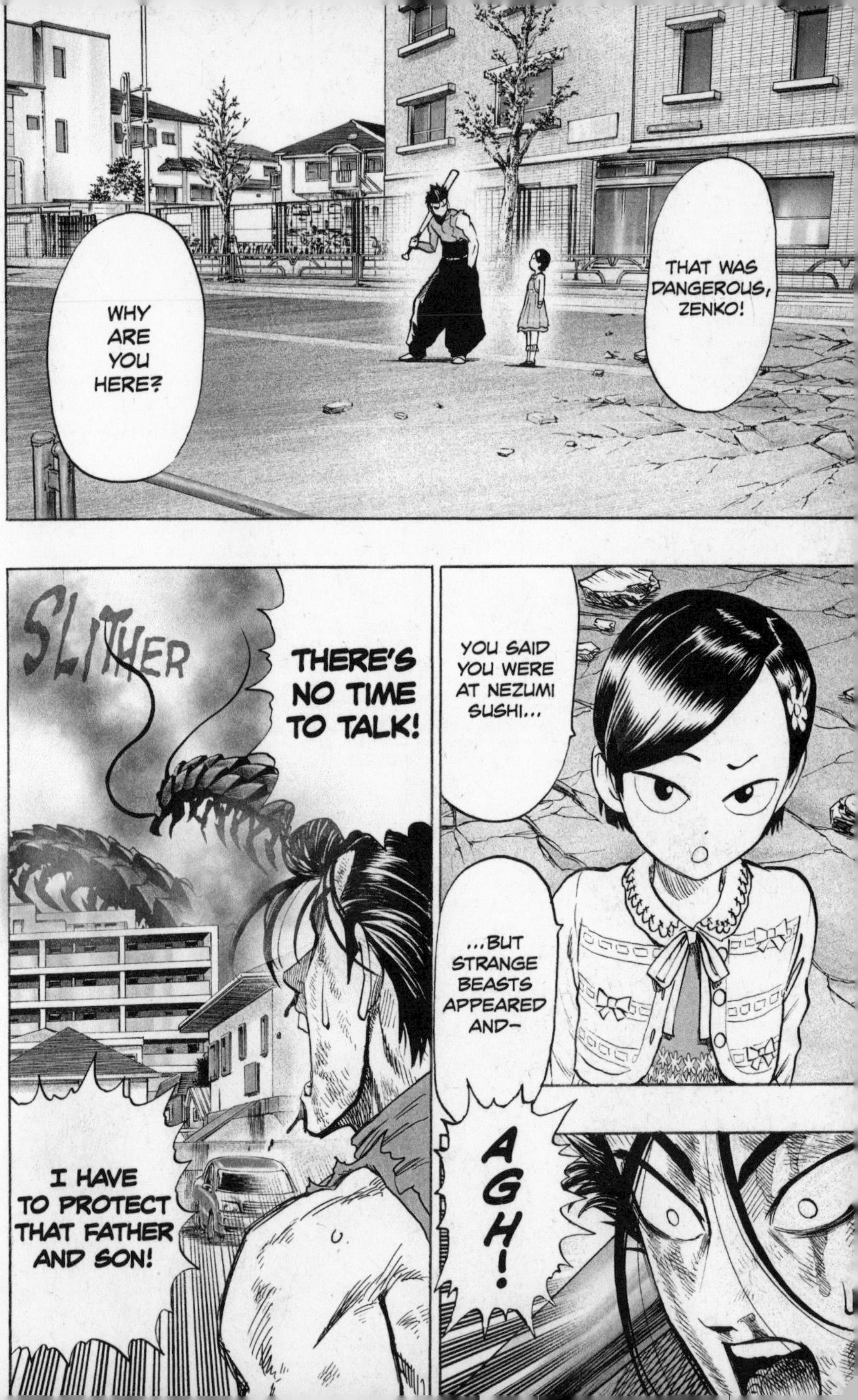
THAT WAS DANGEROUS, ZENKO!
WHY ARE YOU HERE?
YOU SAID YOU WERE AT NEZUMI SUSHI...
...BUT STRANGE BEASTS APPEARED AND—
AGH!
THERE'S NO TIME TO TALK!
SLITHER
I HAVE TO PROTECT THAT FATHER AND SON!

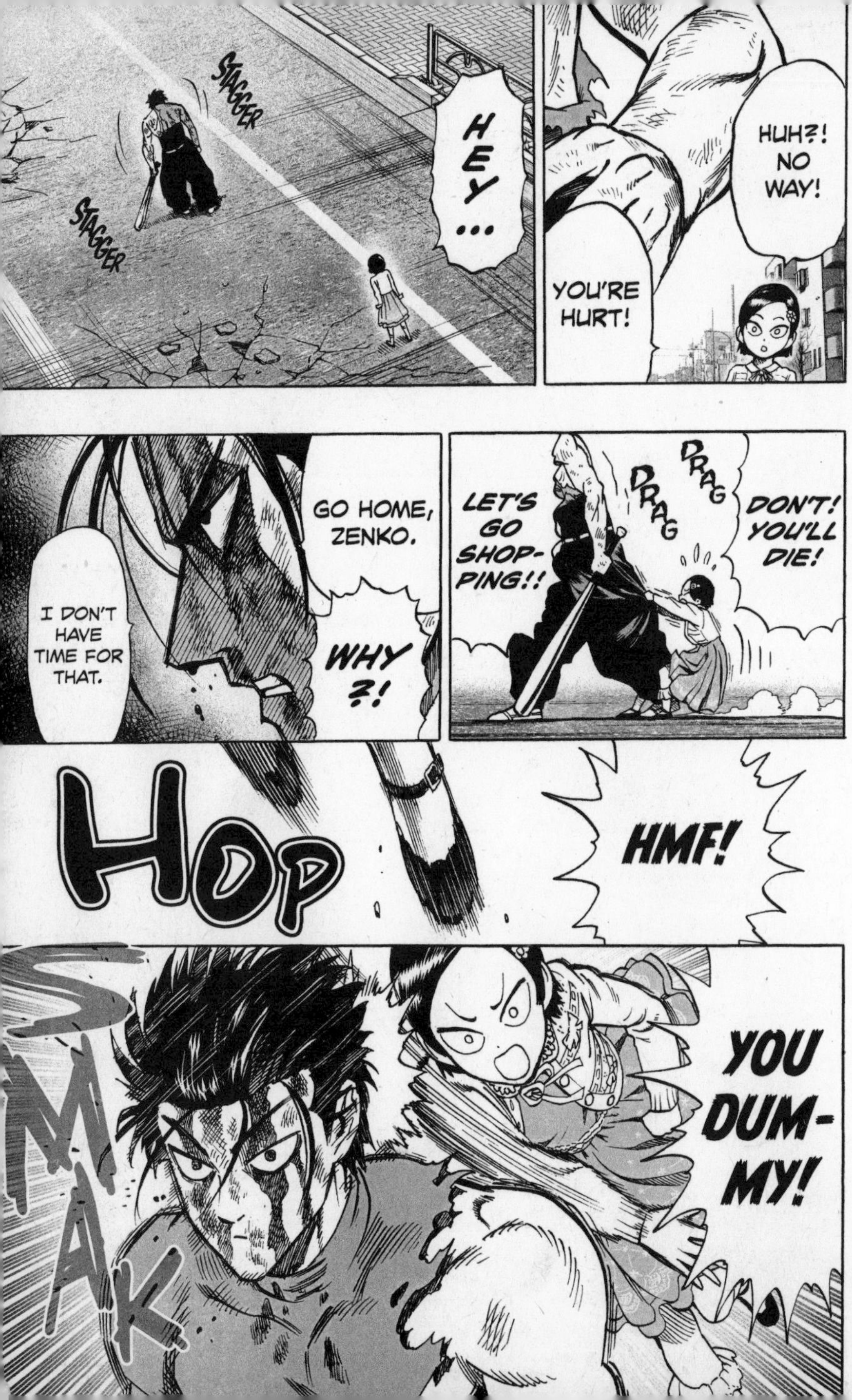
HUH?! NO WAY!
YOU'RE HURT!
HEY...
STAGGER
STAGGER
DRAG
DRAG
DON'T! YOU'LL DIE!
LET'S GO SHOP-PING!!
GO HOME, ZENKO.
WHY?!
I DON'T HAVE TIME FOR THAT.
HMF!
HOP
YOU DUM-MY!
SMAK

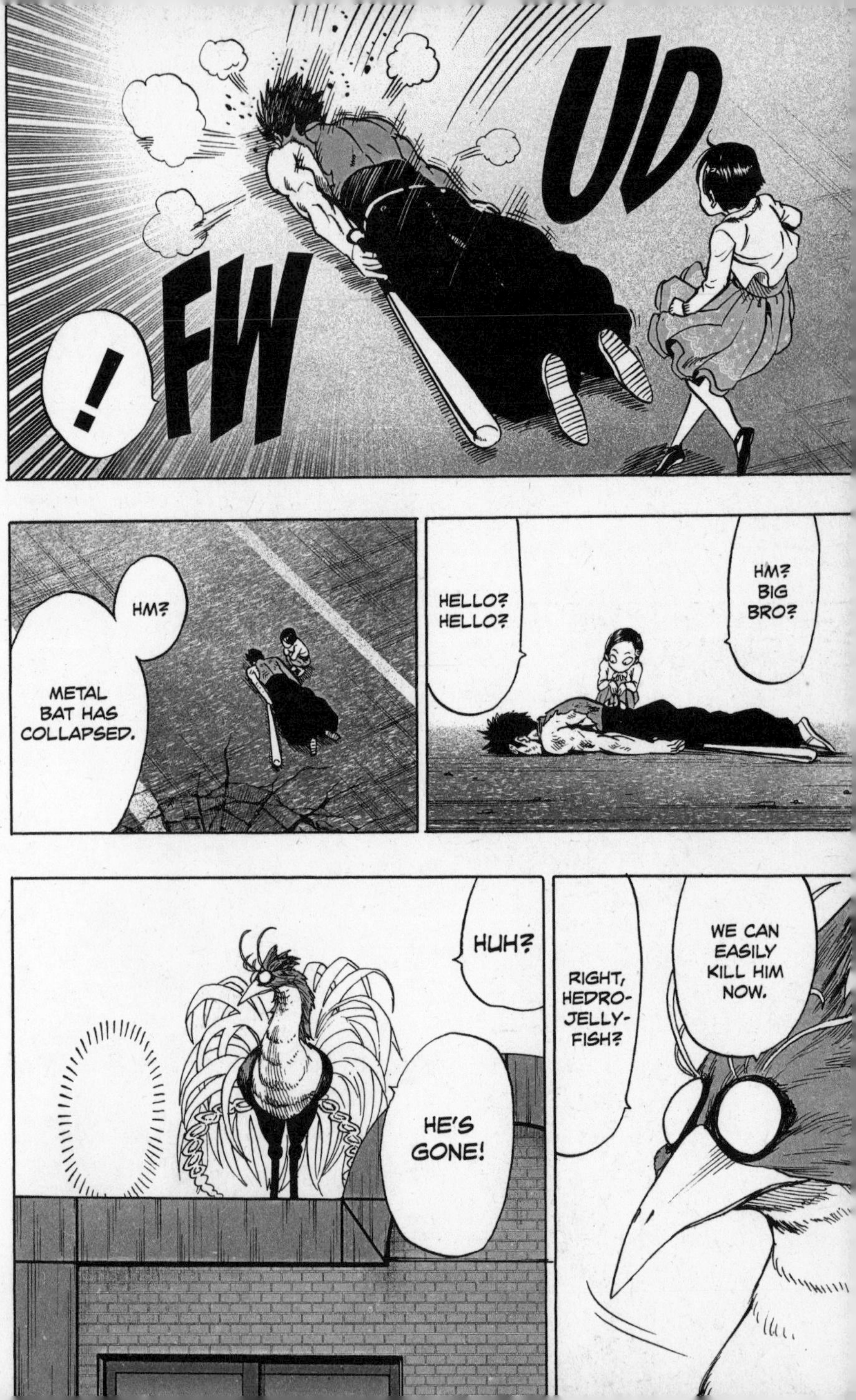
UD
!
FW
HM? BIG BRO?
HELLO? HELLO?
HM?
METAL BAT HAS COLLAPSED.
WE CAN EASILY KILL HIM NOW.
RIGHT, HEDRO-JELLY-FISH?
HUH?
HE'S GONE!

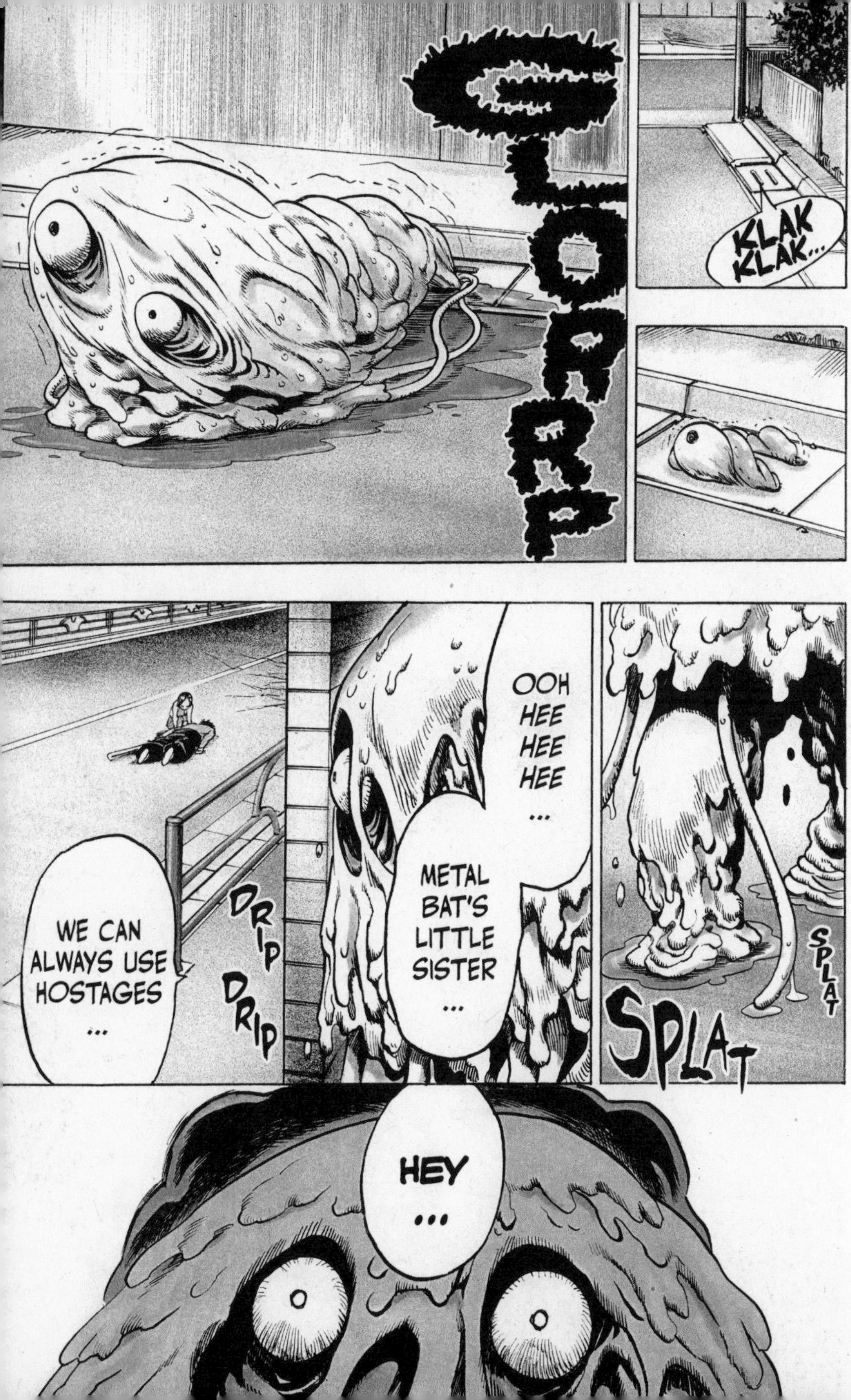
KLAK KLAK...
GLORRP
SPLAT
SPLAT
OOH HEE HEE HEE ...
METAL BAT'S LITTLE SISTER ...
DRIP DRIP
WE CAN ALWAYS USE HOSTAGES ...
HEY ...

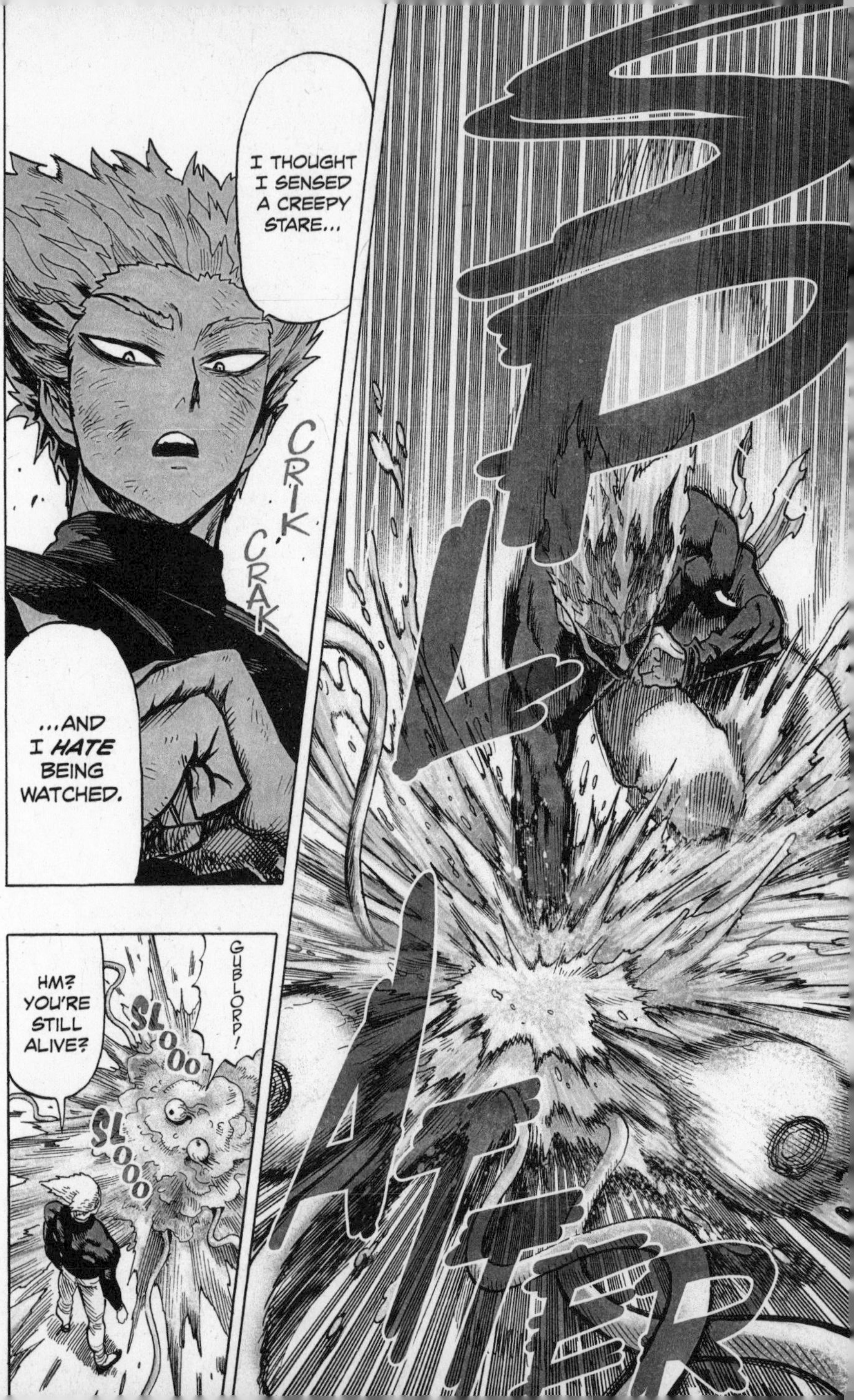
SPLATTER
I THOUGHT I SENSED A CREEPY STARE...
CRIK
CRAK
...AND I *HATE* BEING WATCHED.
GUBLORP!
HM? YOU'RE STILL ALIVE?
SLOOO
SLOOO

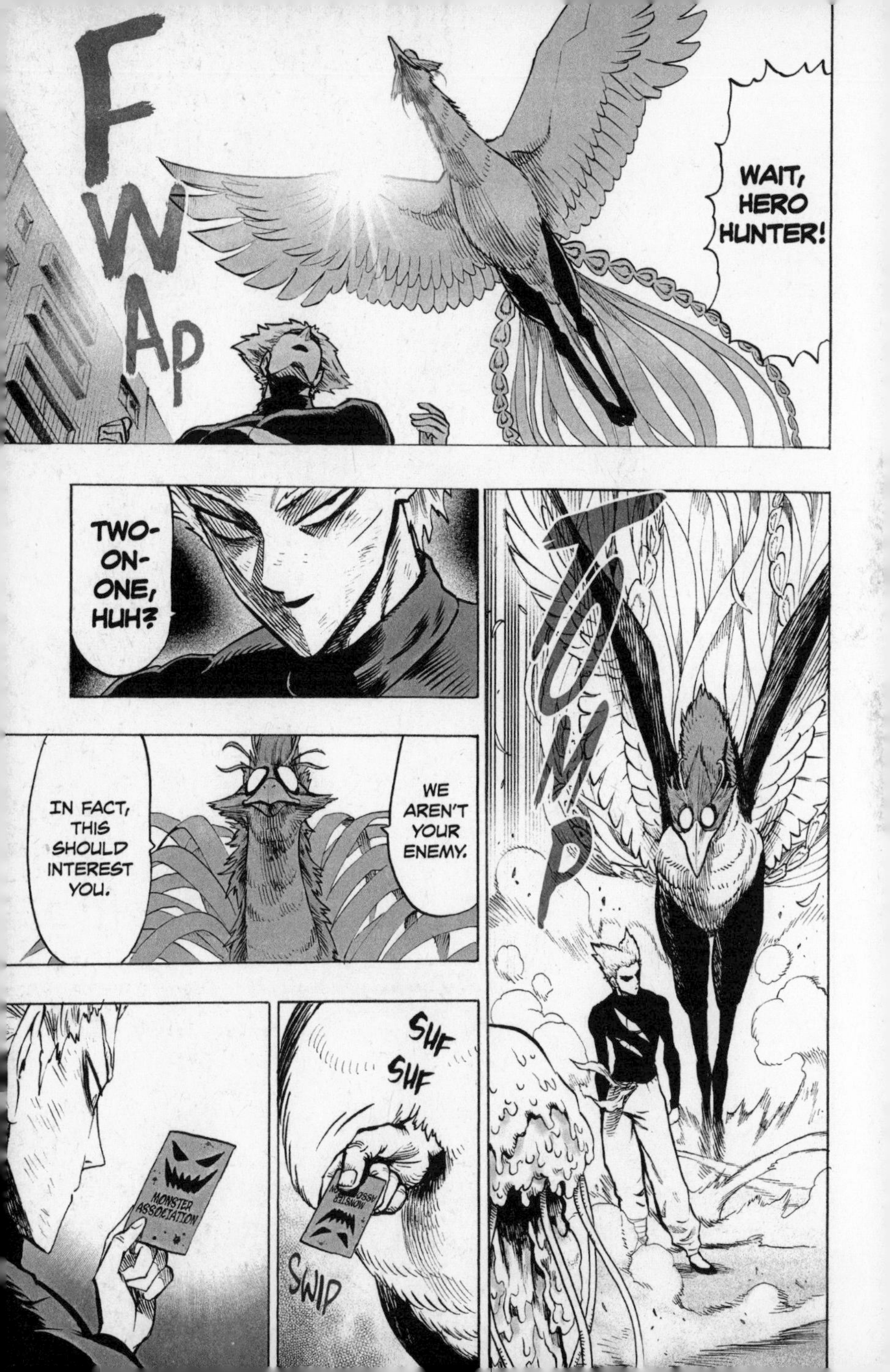
WAIT, HERO HUNTER!
FWAP
TWO-ON-ONE, HUH?
WE AREN'T YOUR ENEMY.
IN FACT, THIS SHOULD INTEREST YOU.
SUF SUF
MONSTER ASSOCIATION
SWIP
MONSTER ASSOCIATION

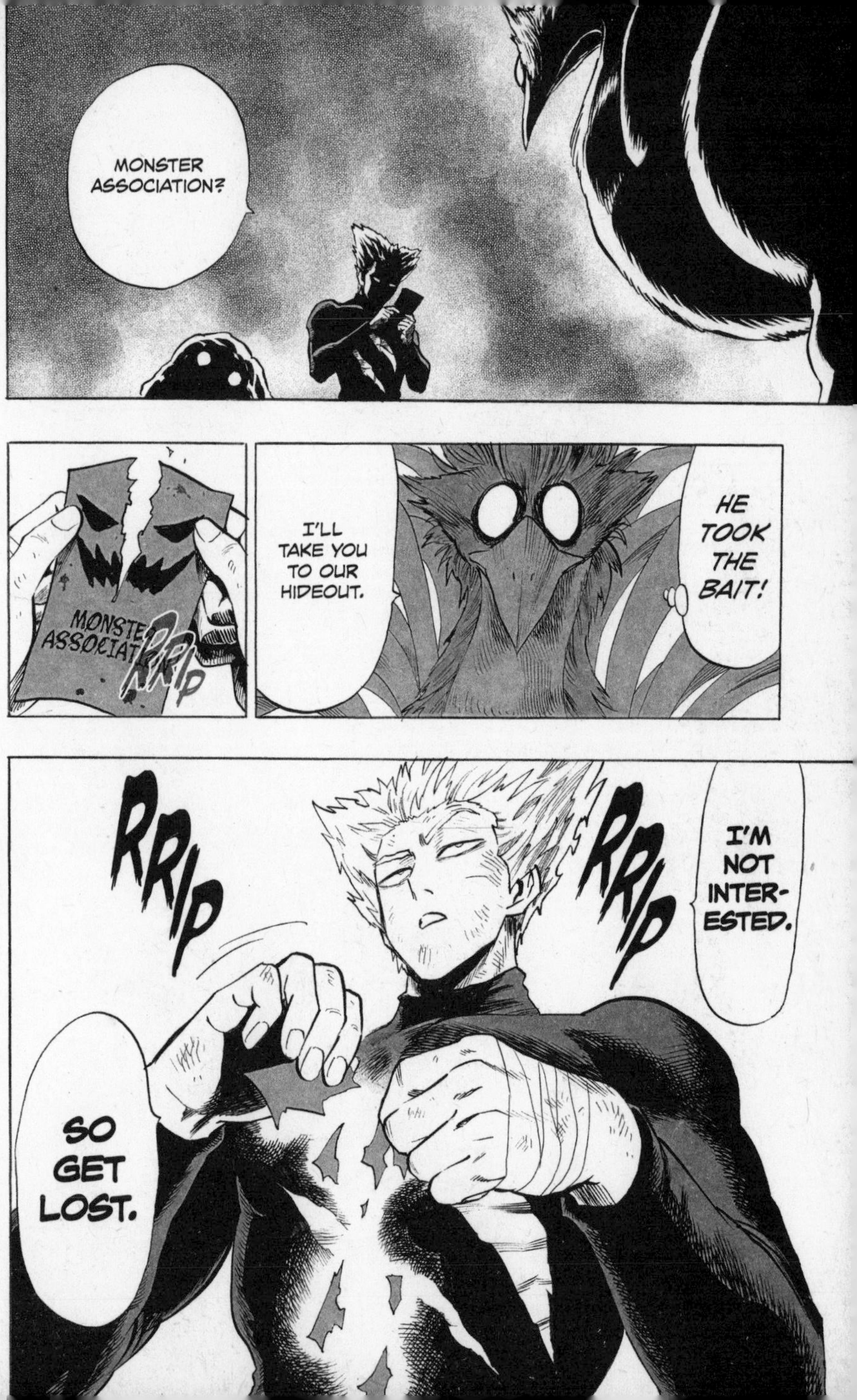
MONSTER ASSOCIATION?
HE TOOK THE BAIT!
I'LL TAKE YOU TO OUR HIDEOUT.
MONSTER ASSOCIATION
RRIP
RRIP
I'M NOT INTER-ESTED.
RRIP
SO GET LOST.

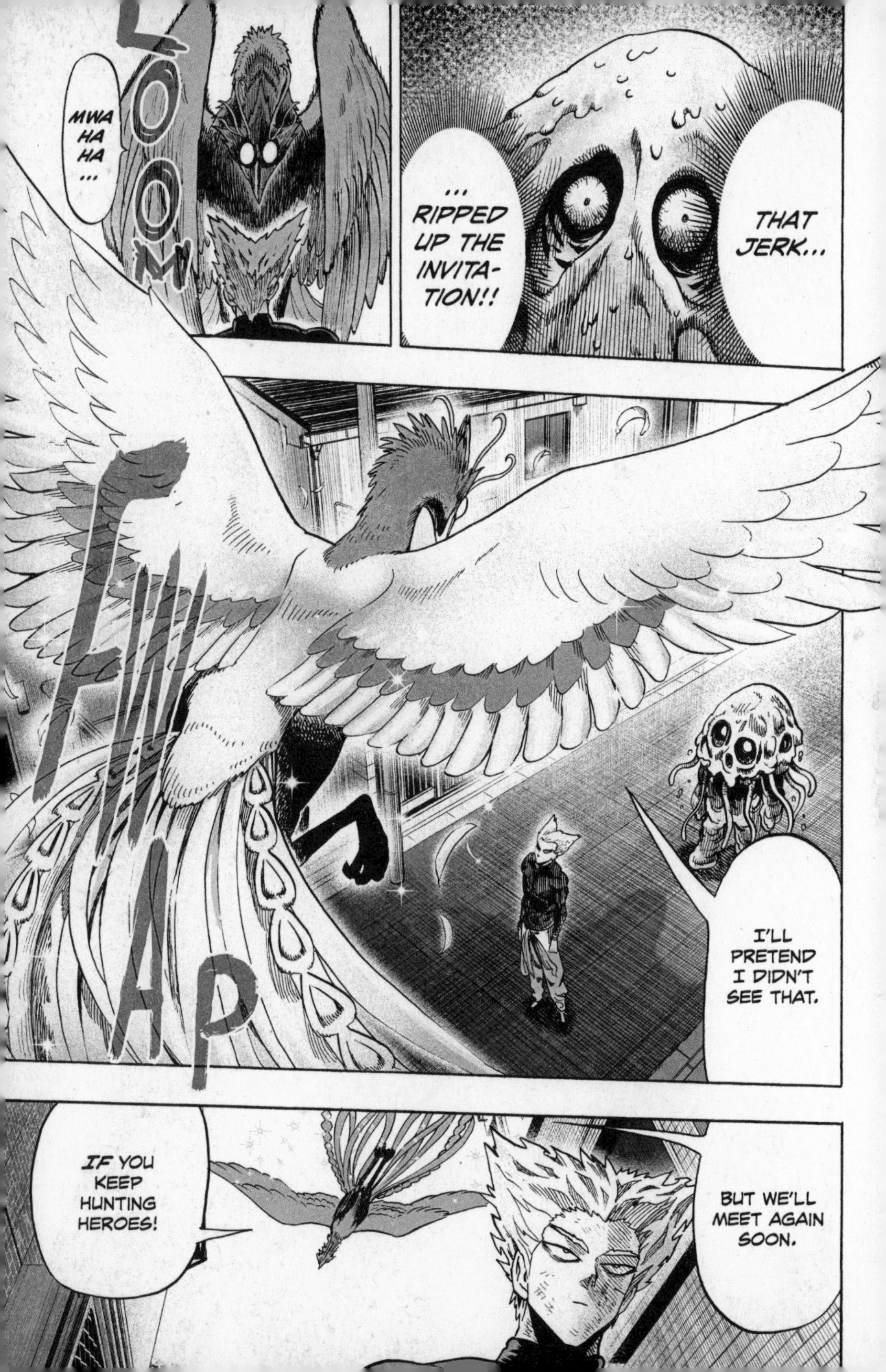
THAT JERK...
...RIPPED UP THE INVITATION!!
LOOOM
MWA HA HA...
FWAP
I'LL PRETEND I DIDN'T SEE THAT.
BUT WE'LL MEET AGAIN SOON.
IF YOU KEEP HUNTING HEROES!

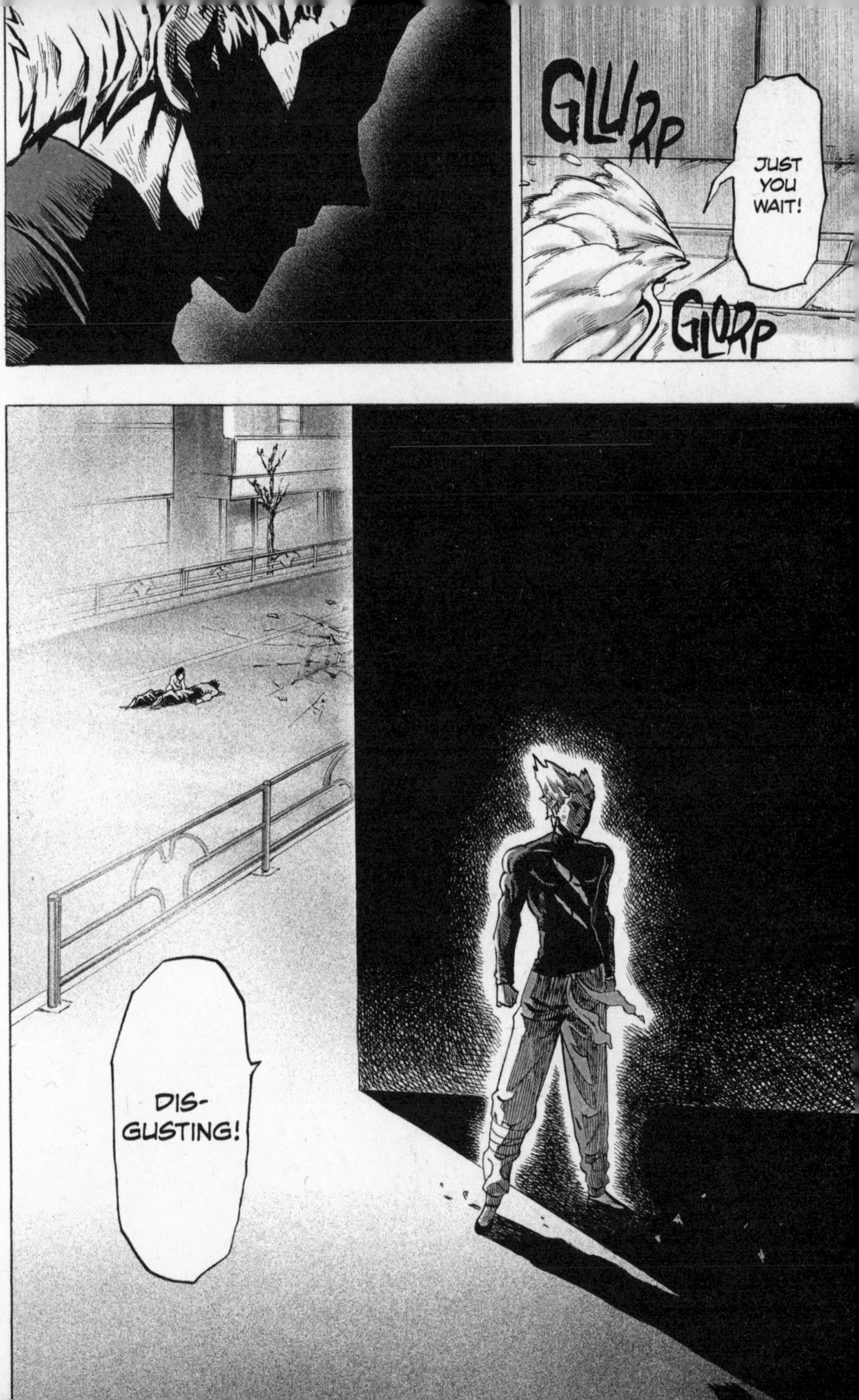
GLURP
JUST YOU WAIT!
GLORP
DIS-GUSTING!

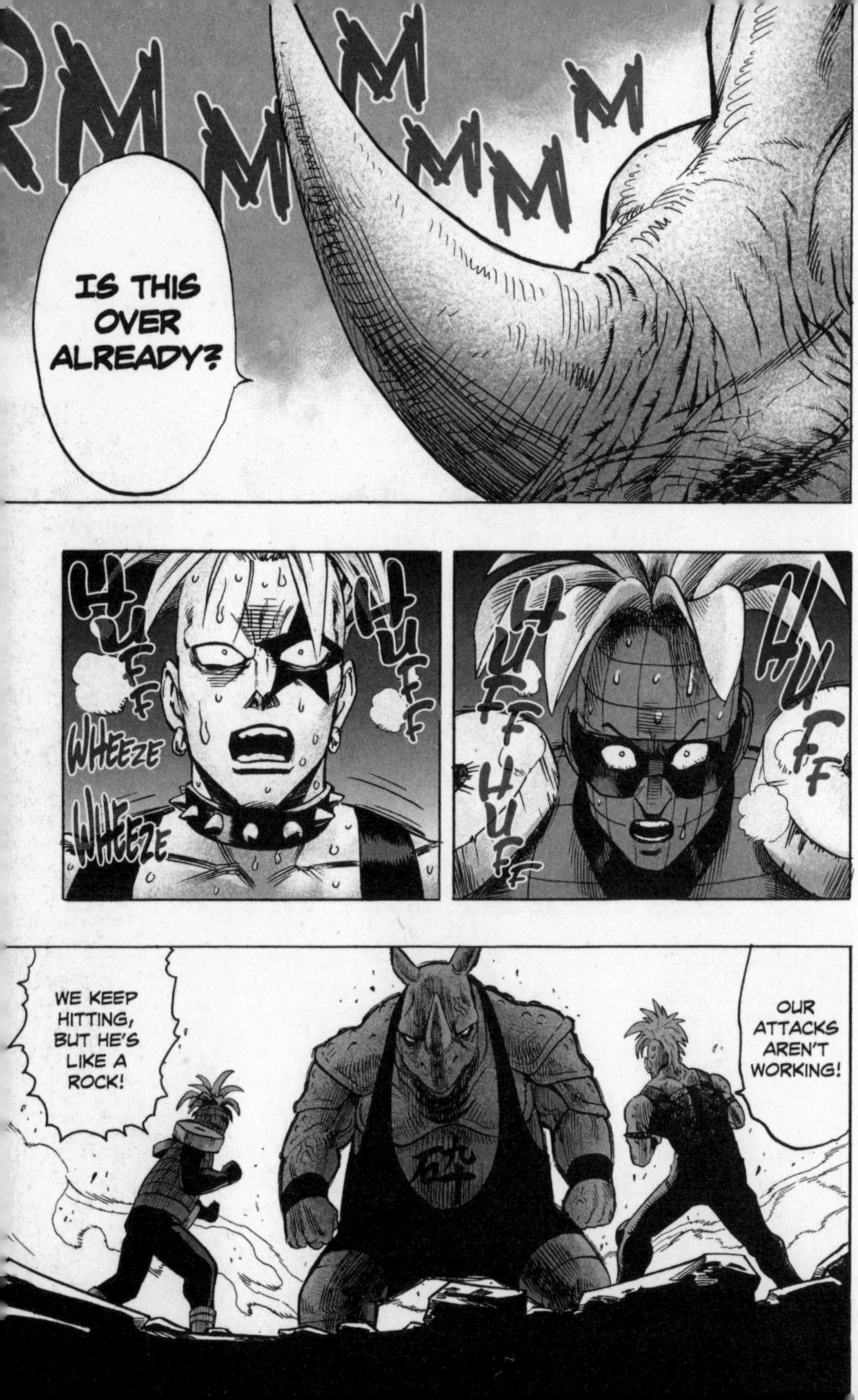
RMMMMMMMMMMM
IS THIS OVER ALREADY?
HUFF HUFF
HUFF
HUFF
HUFF
WHEEZE
WHEEZE
OUR ATTACKS AREN'T WORKING!
WE KEEP HITTING, BUT HE'S LIKE A ROCK!

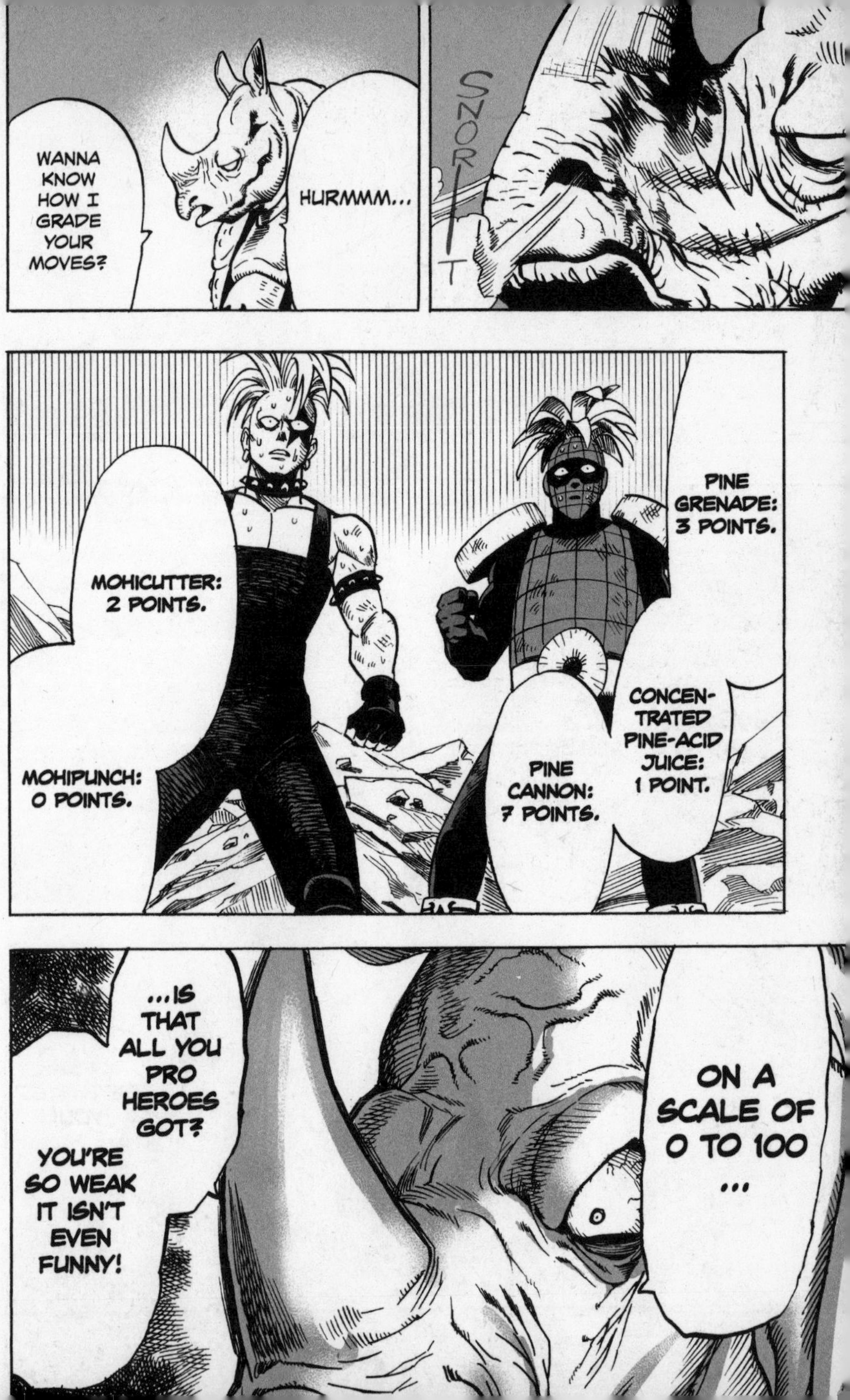
SNORT
HURMMM...
WANNA KNOW HOW I GRADE YOUR MOVES?
PINE GRENADE: 3 POINTS.
CONCENTRATED PINE-ACID JUICE: 1 POINT.
PINE CANNON: 7 POINTS.
MOHICUTTER: 2 POINTS.
MOHIPUNCH: 0 POINTS.
ON A SCALE OF 0 TO 100 ...
...IS THAT ALL YOU PRO HEROES GOT?
YOU'RE SO WEAK IT ISN'T EVEN FUNNY!

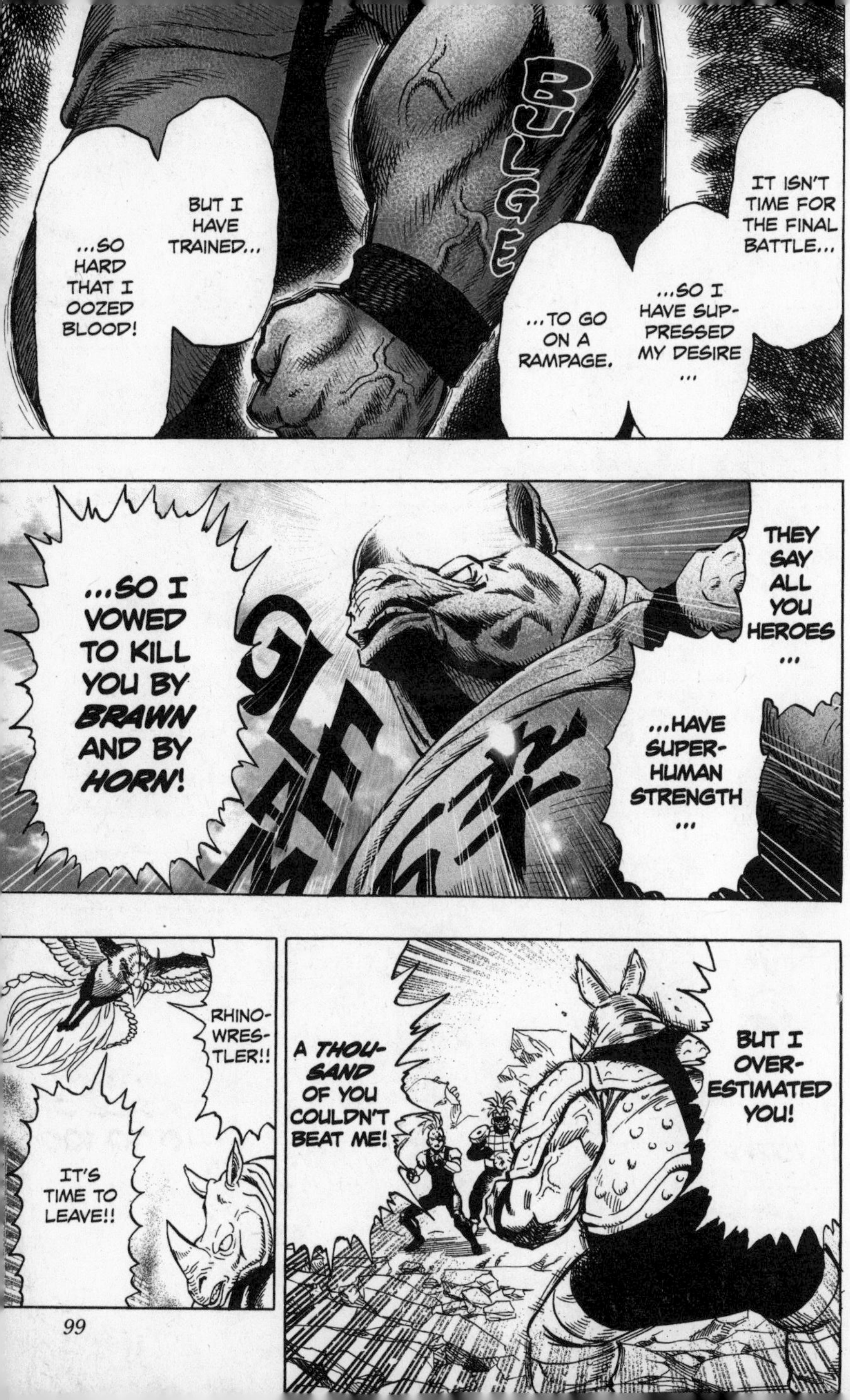
BULGE
IT ISN'T TIME FOR THE FINAL BATTLE...
...SO I HAVE SUP-PRESSED MY DESIRE...
...TO GO ON A RAMPAGE.
BUT I HAVE TRAINED...
...SO HARD THAT I OOZED BLOOD!
THEY SAY ALL YOU HEROES...
...HAVE SUPER-HUMAN STRENGTH...
...SO I VOWED TO KILL YOU BY *BRAWN* AND BY *HORN*!
BUT I OVER-ESTIMATED YOU!
A *THOU-SAND* OF YOU COULDN'T BEAT ME!
RHINO-WRES-TLER!!
IT'S TIME TO LEAVE!!

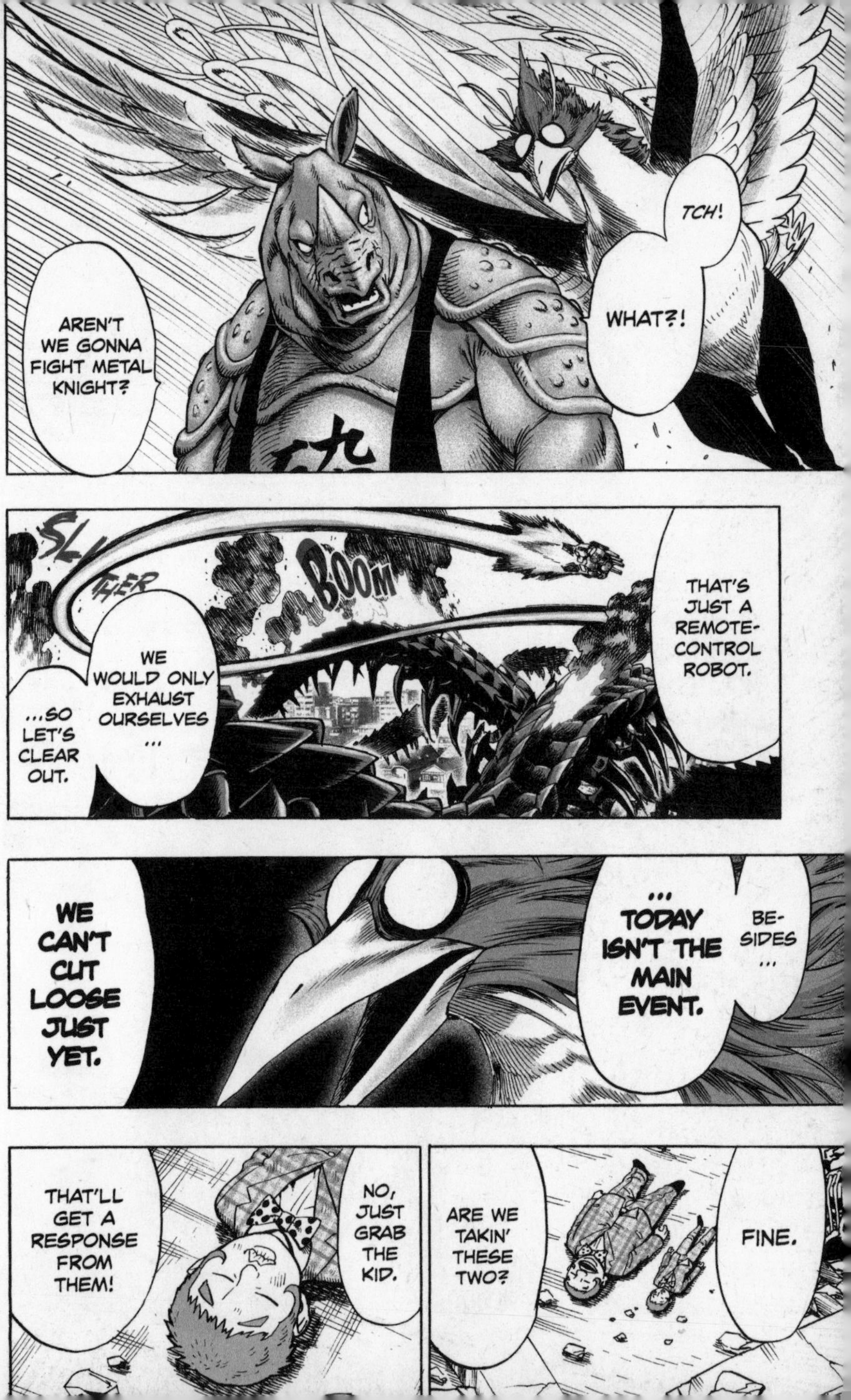
TCH!
WHAT?!
AREN'T WE GONNA FIGHT METAL KNIGHT?
THAT'S JUST A REMOTE-CONTROL ROBOT.
BOOM
SLITHER
WE WOULD ONLY EXHAUST OURSELVES...
...SO LET'S CLEAR OUT.
BE-SIDES...
...TODAY ISN'T THE MAIN EVENT.
WE CAN'T CUT LOOSE JUST YET.
FINE.
ARE WE TAKIN' THESE TWO?
NO, JUST GRAB THE KID.
THAT'LL GET A RESPONSE FROM THEM!

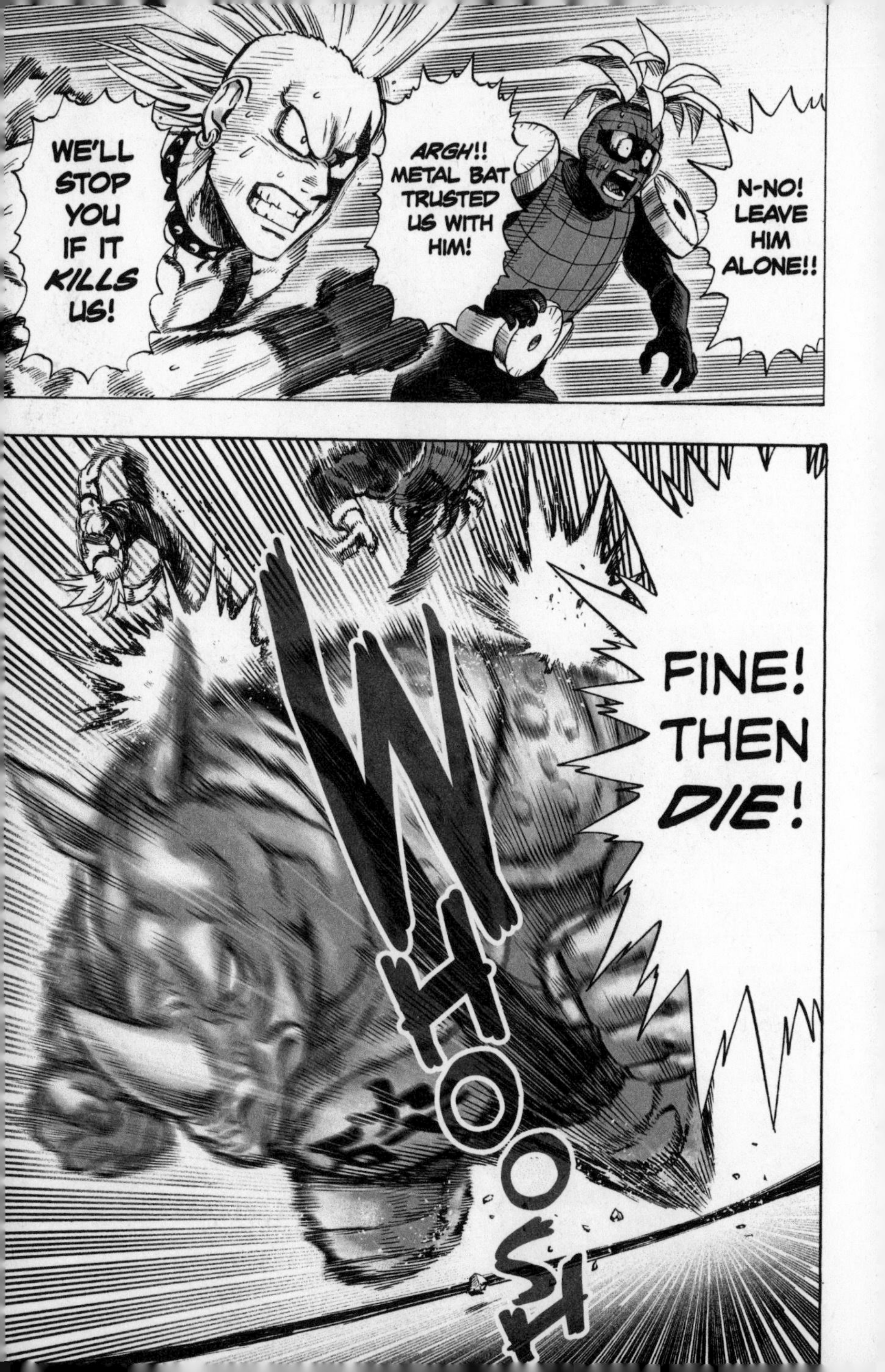
N-NO! LEAVE HIM ALONE!!
ARGH!! METAL BAT TRUSTED US WITH HIM!
WE'LL STOP YOU IF IT KILLS US!
FINE! THEN DIE!
WHOOOSH

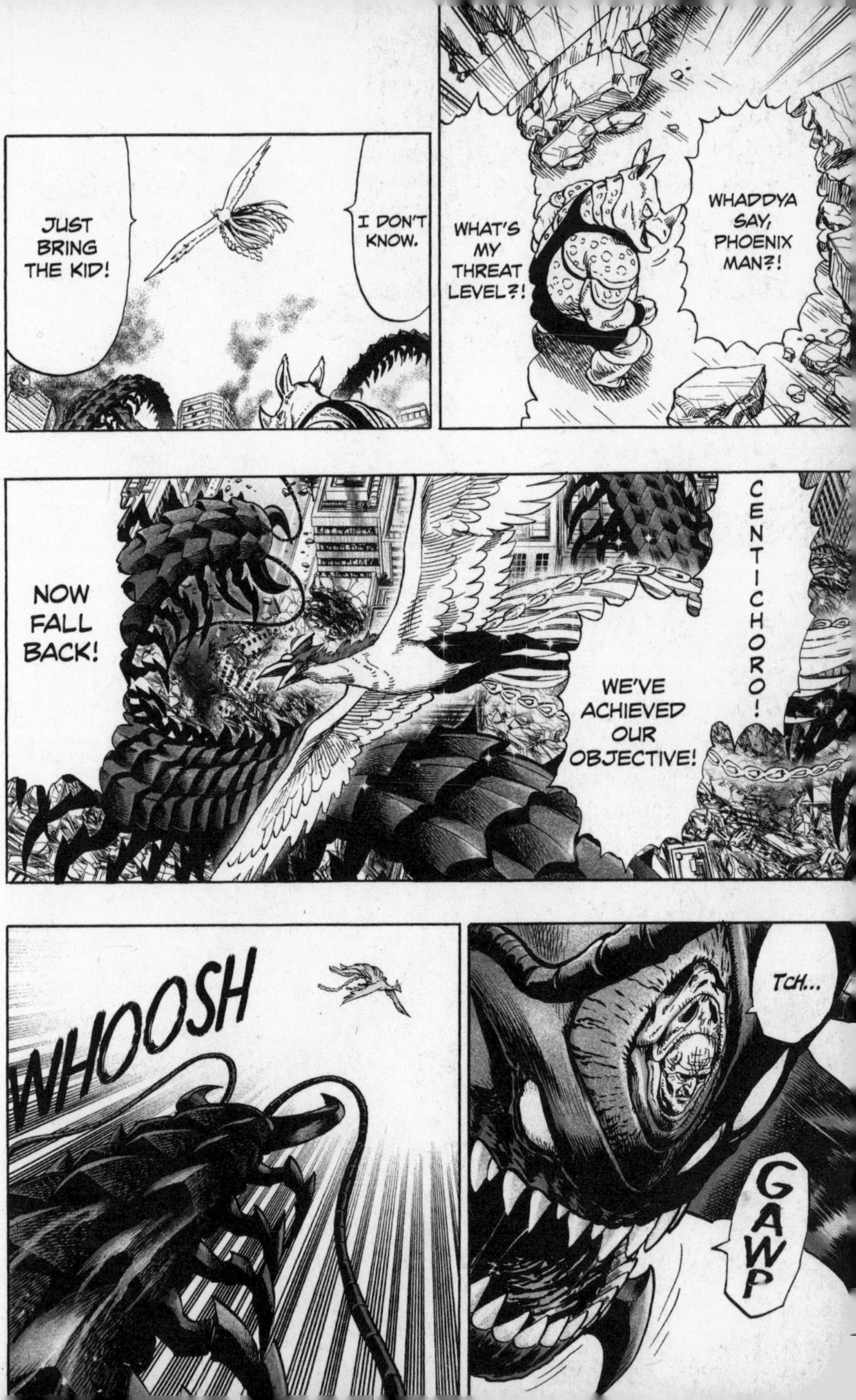
WHADDYA SAY, PHOENIX MAN?!
WHAT'S MY THREAT LEVEL?!
I DON'T KNOW.
JUST BRING THE KID!
CENTICHORO!
WE'VE ACHIEVED OUR OBJECTIVE!
NOW FALL BACK!
TCH...
GAWP
WHOOSH

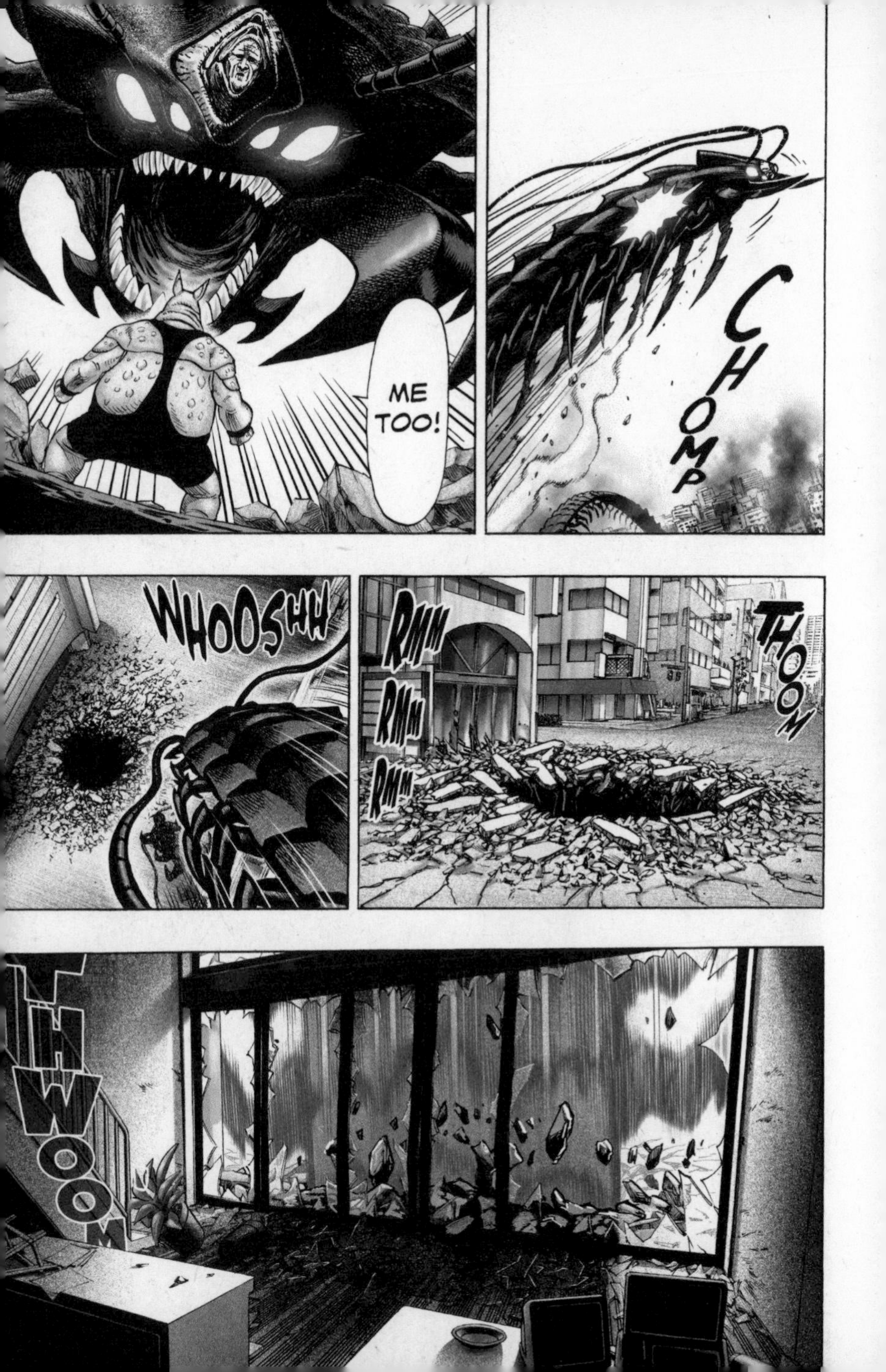
CHOMP
ME TOO!
THOOM
RMM RMM RMM
WHOOSHH
THWOOM

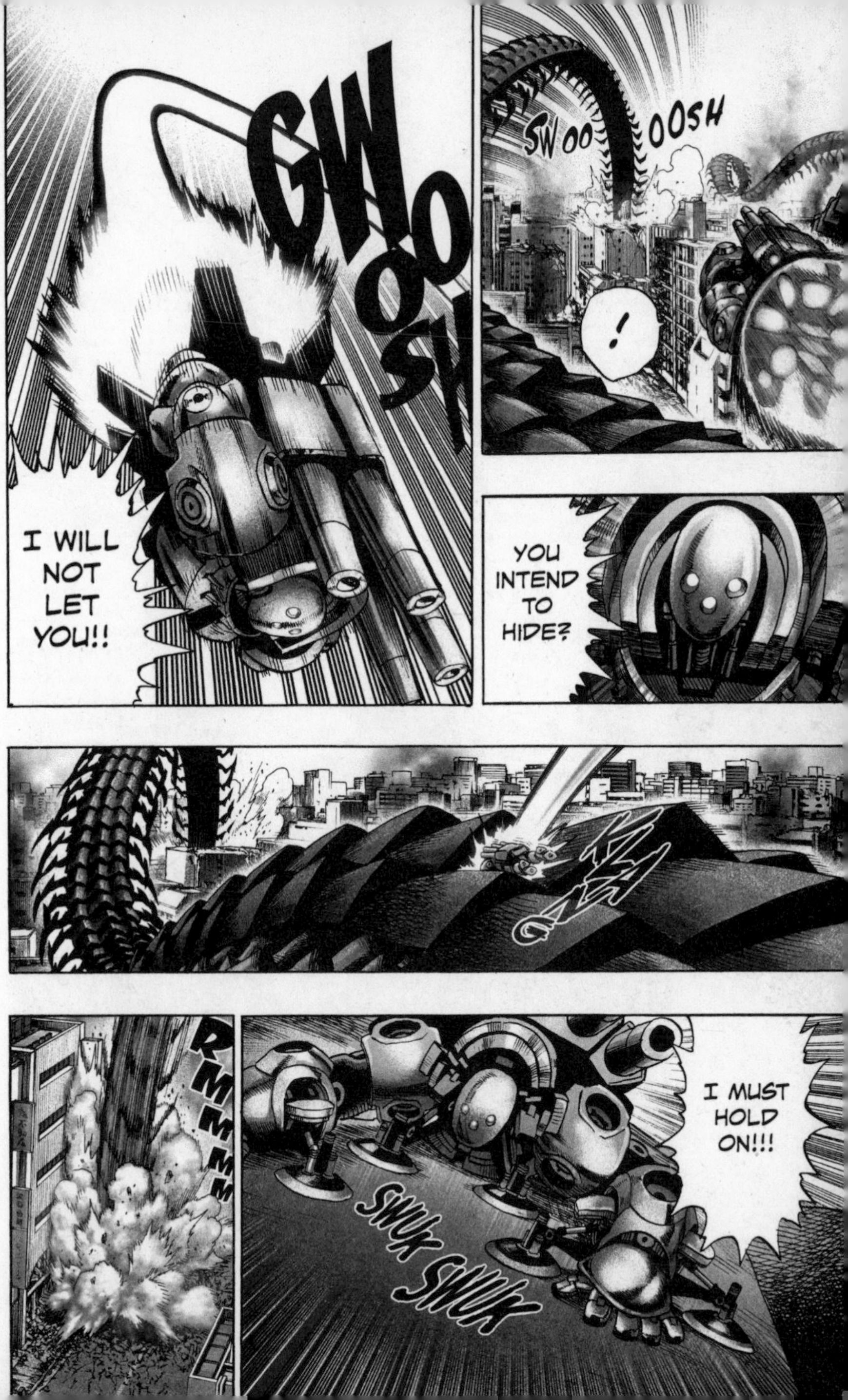
SWOOOOSH
!
YOU INTEND TO HIDE?
GWOOSH
I WILL NOT LET YOU!!
I MUST HOLD ON!!!
SWUK SWUK
RMMMMM

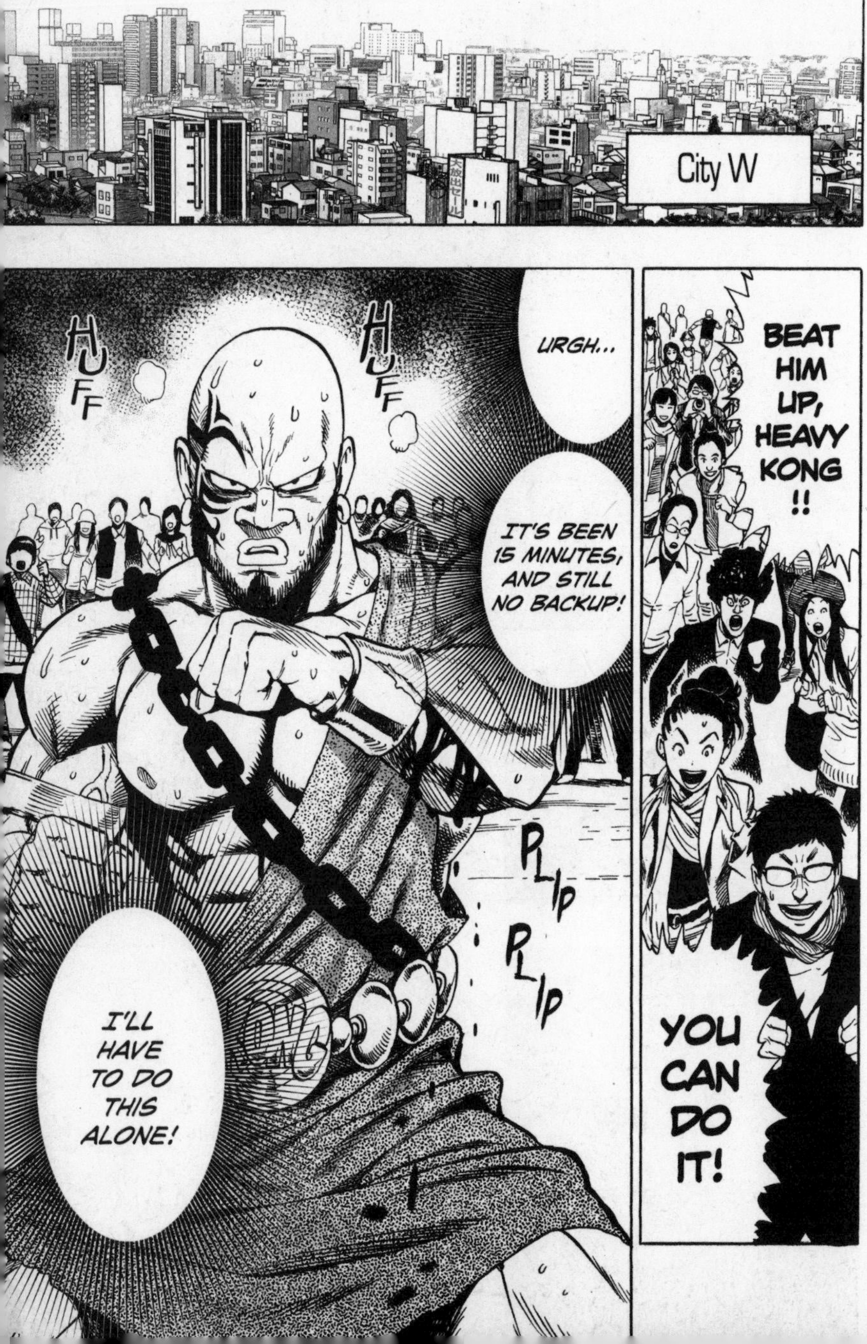
City W
BEAT HIM UP, HEAVY KONG!!
YOU CAN DO IT!
HUFF
HUFF
URGH...
IT'S BEEN 15 MINUTES, AND STILL NO BACKUP!
PLIP
PLIP
I'LL HAVE TO DO THIS ALONE!

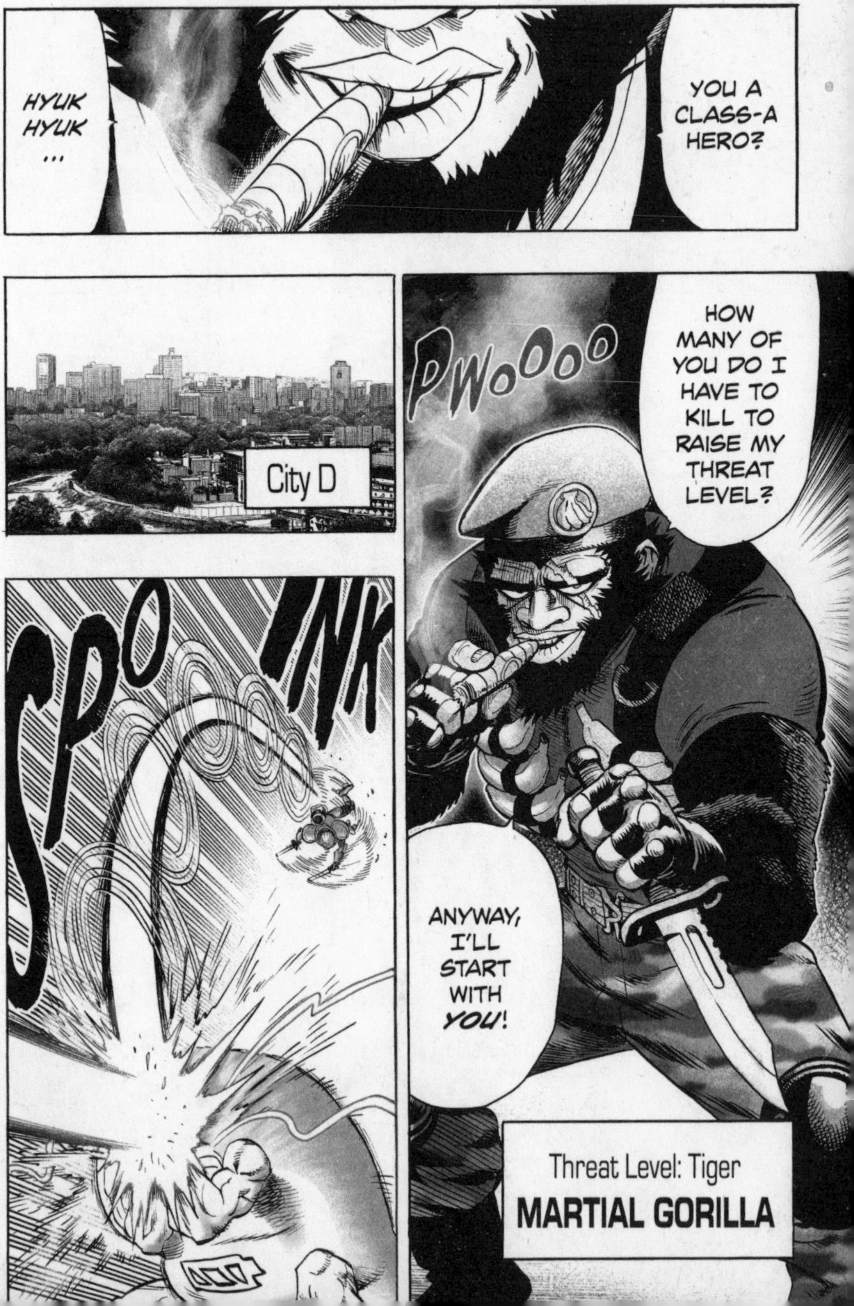
YOU A CLASS-A HERO?
HYUK HYUK ...
HOW MANY OF YOU DO I HAVE TO KILL TO RAISE MY THREAT LEVEL?
PWOOOO
ANYWAY, I'LL START WITH YOU!
Threat Level: Tiger
MARTIAL GORILLA
City D
SPOINK

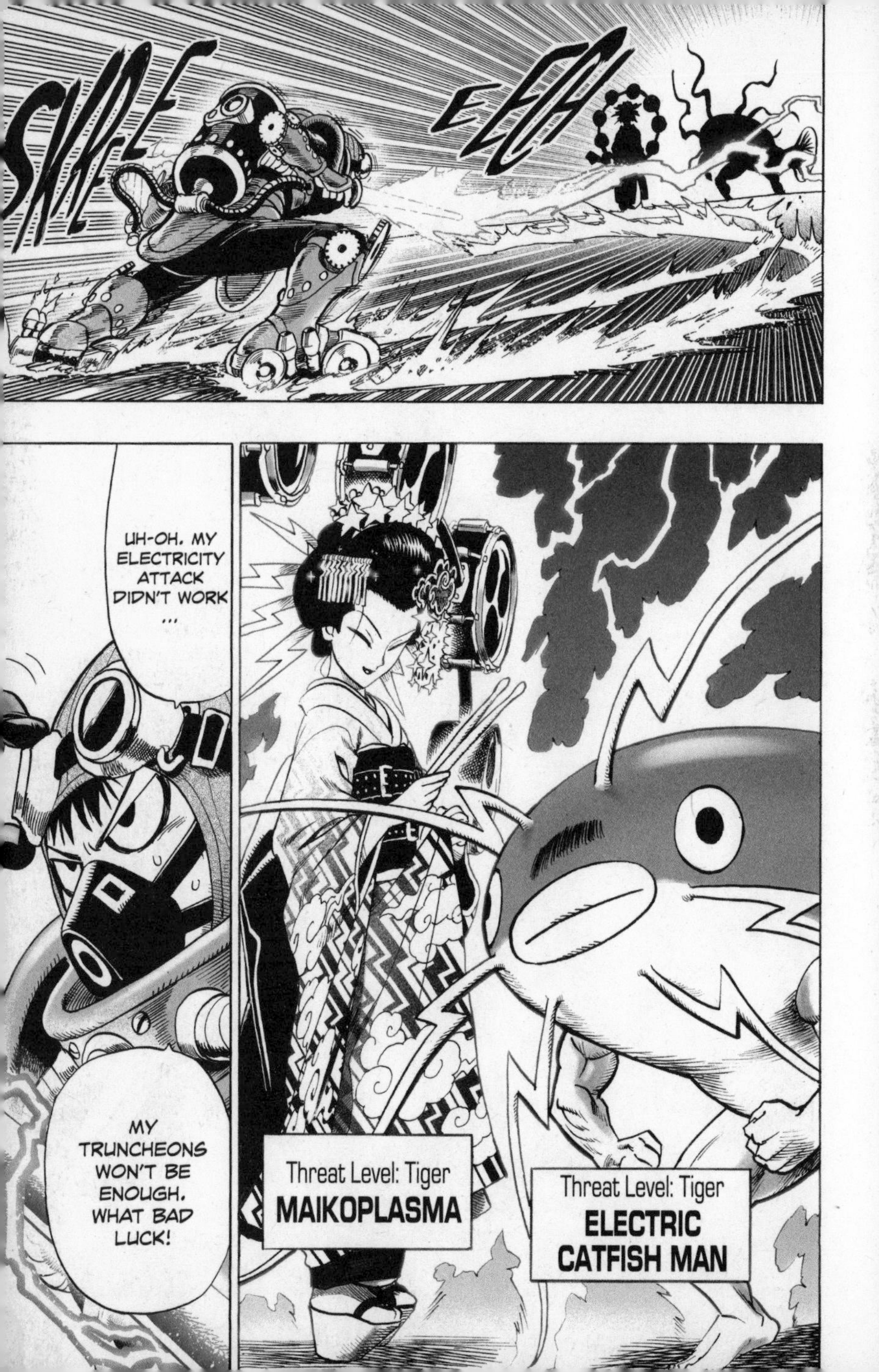
Threat Level: Tiger
ELECTRIC CATFISH MAN
Threat Level: Tiger
MAIKOPLASMA
UH-OH. MY ELECTRICITY ATTACK DIDN'T WORK ...
MY TRUNCHEONS WON'T BE ENOUGH. WHAT BAD LUCK!

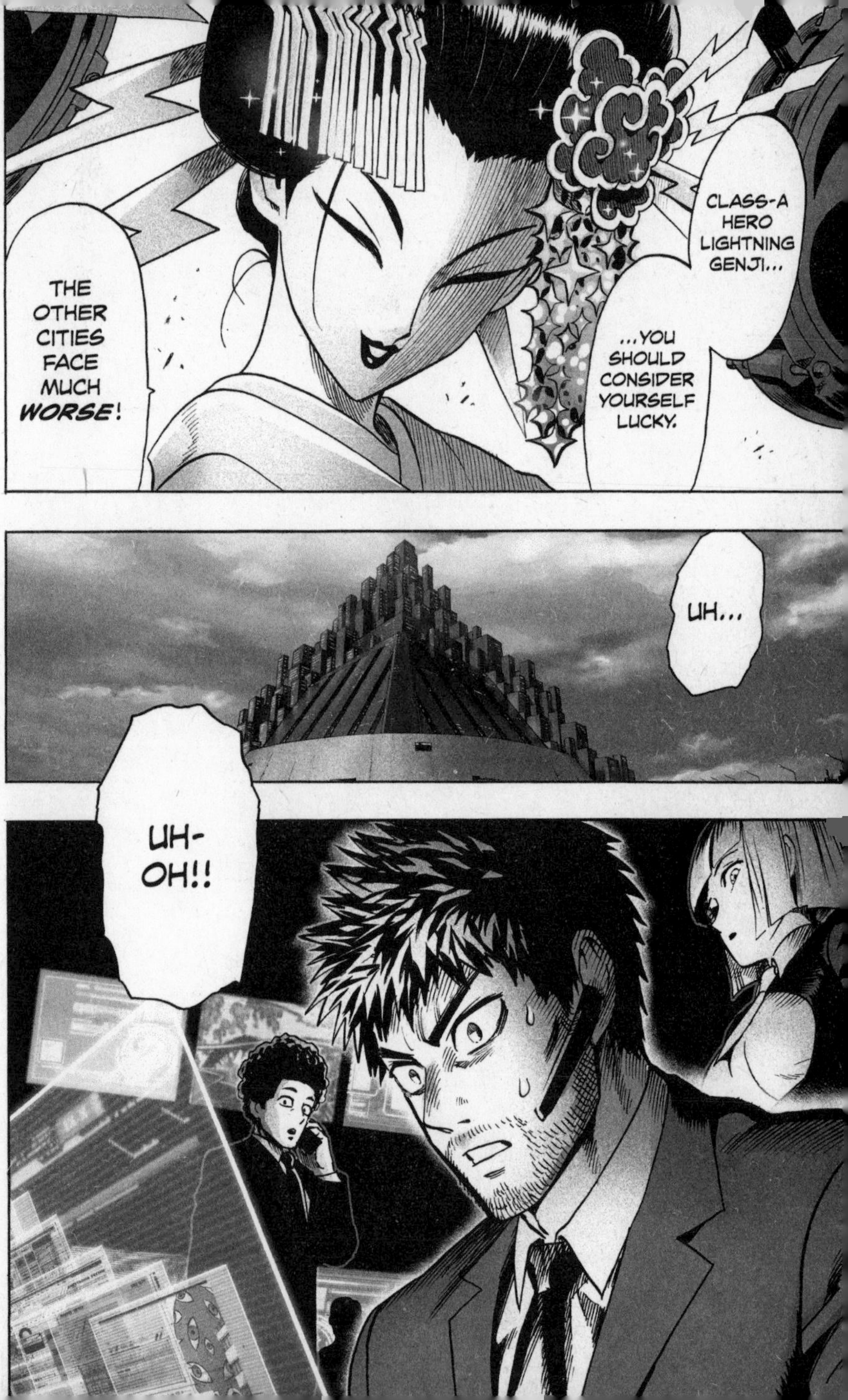
CLASS-A HERO LIGHTNING GENJI...
...YOU SHOULD CONSIDER YOURSELF LUCKY.
THE OTHER CITIES FACE MUCH WORSE!
UH...
UH-OH!!

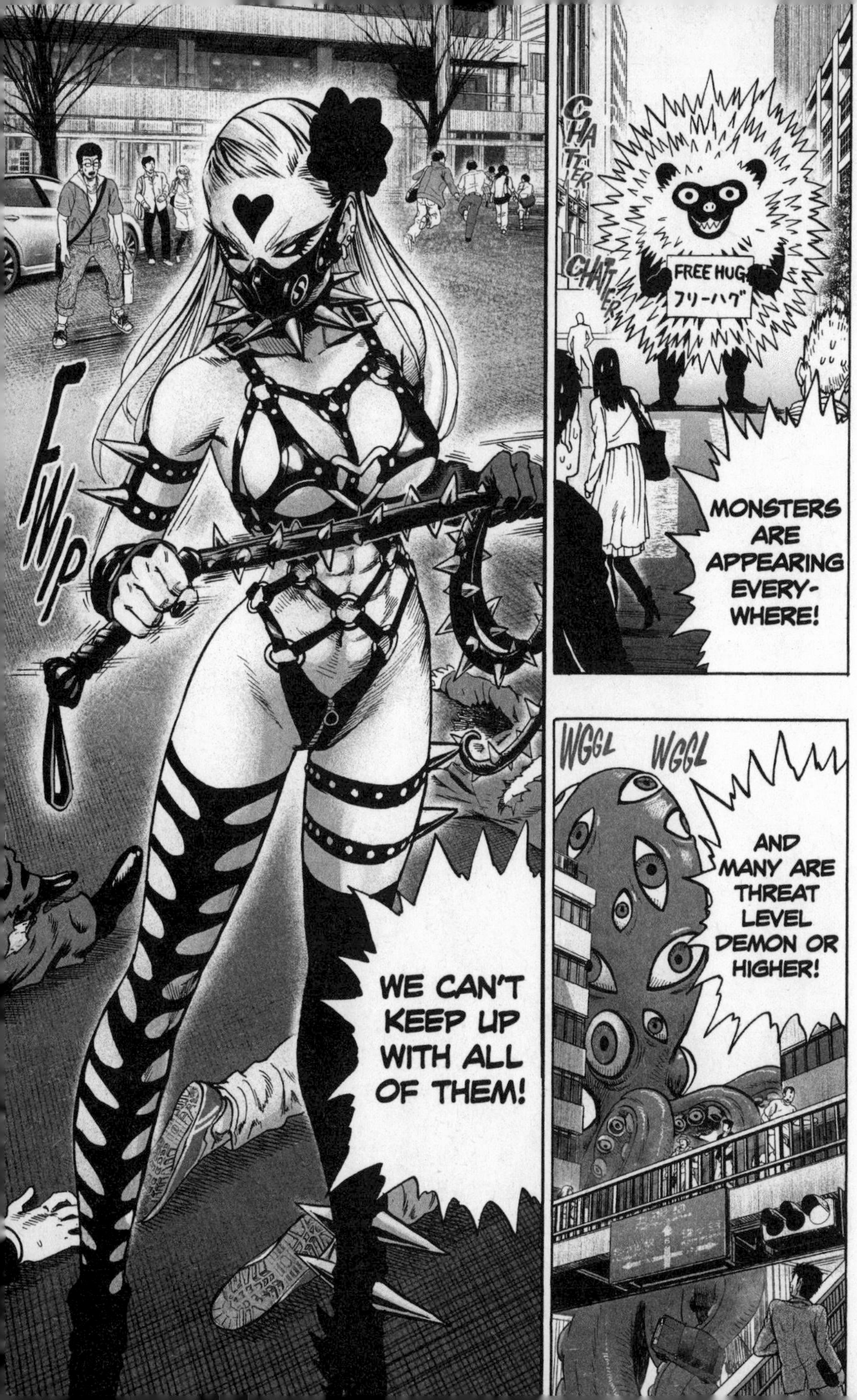
CHATTER
CHATTER
FREE HUG
フリーハグ
MONSTERS ARE APPEARING EVERY-WHERE!
WGGL
WGGL
AND MANY ARE THREAT LEVEL DEMON OR HIGHER!
FWIP
WE CAN'T KEEP UP WITH ALL OF THEM!

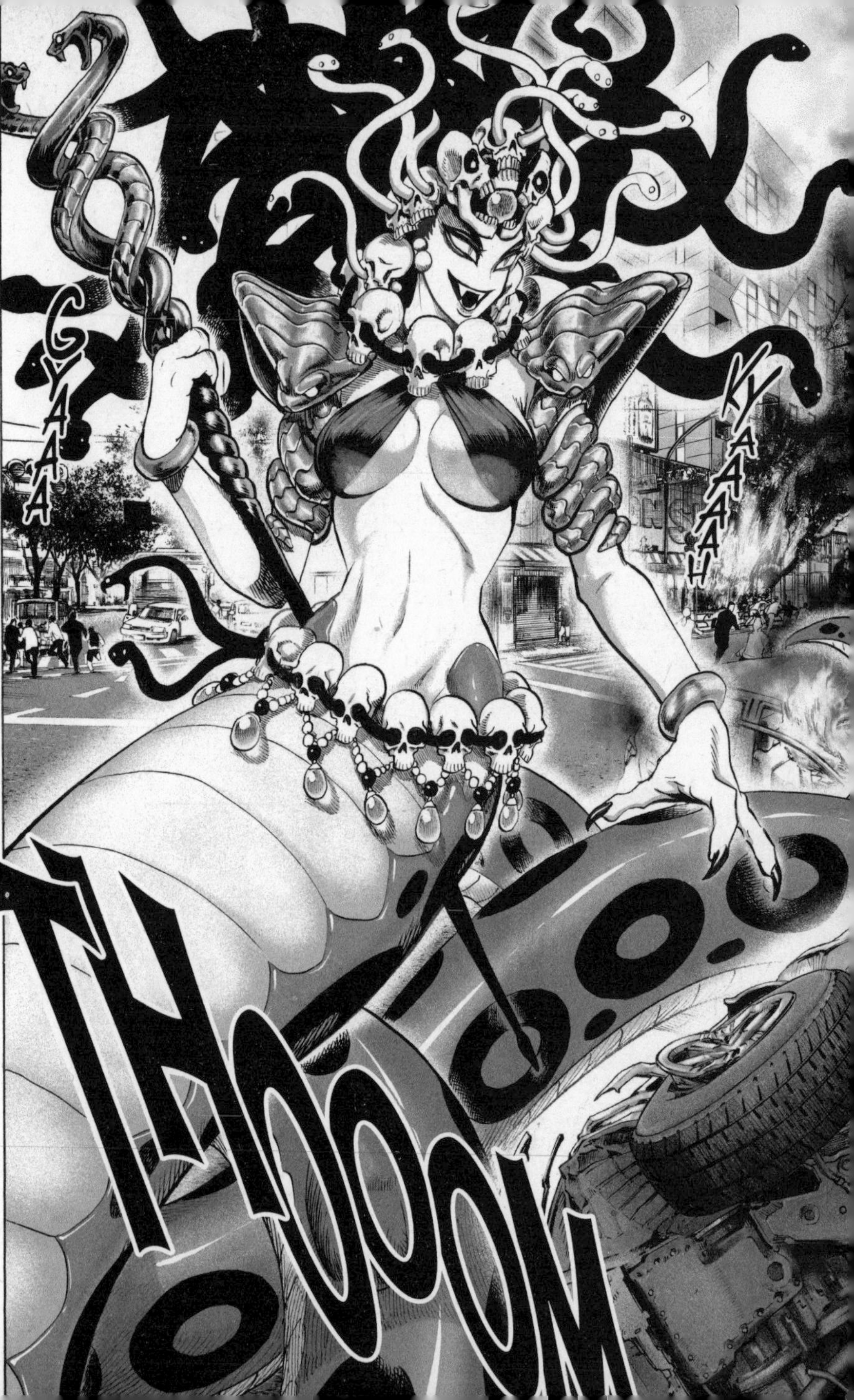
KYAAAAAH
GYAAAA
THOOOOOM

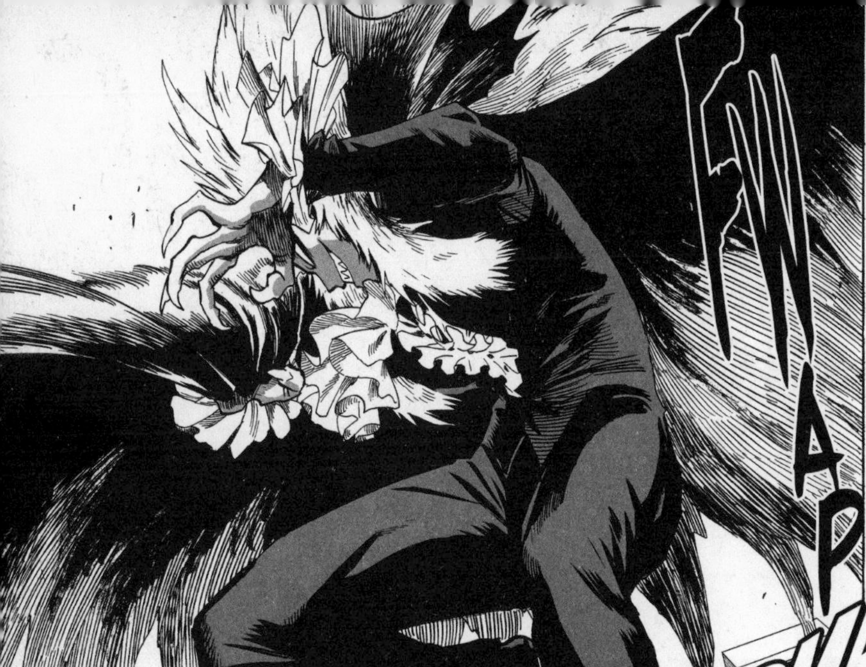
FWAP
RMBL RMBL
RMBL RMBL
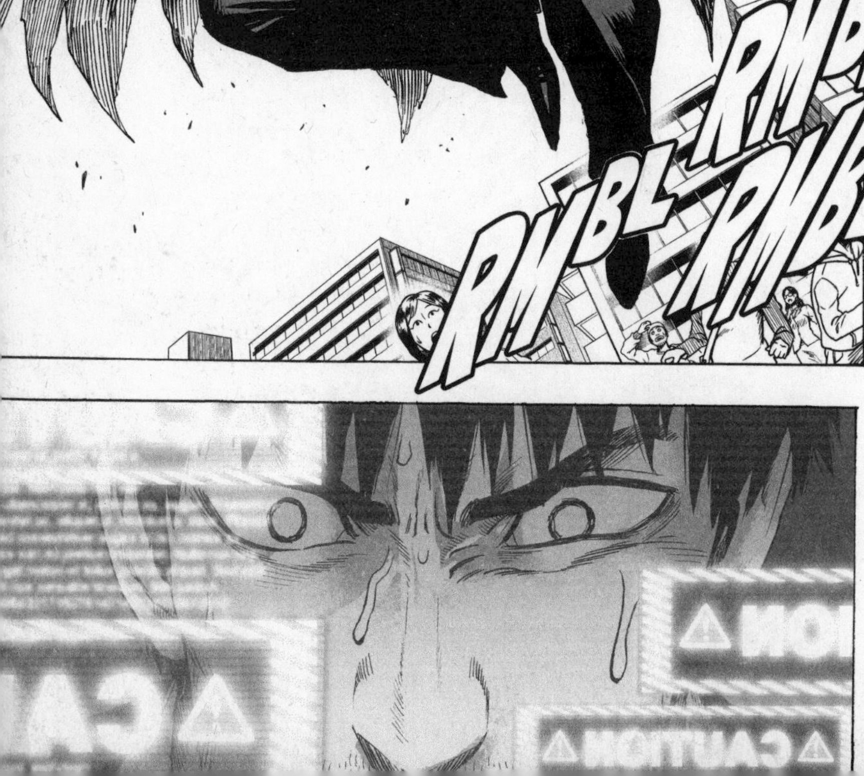

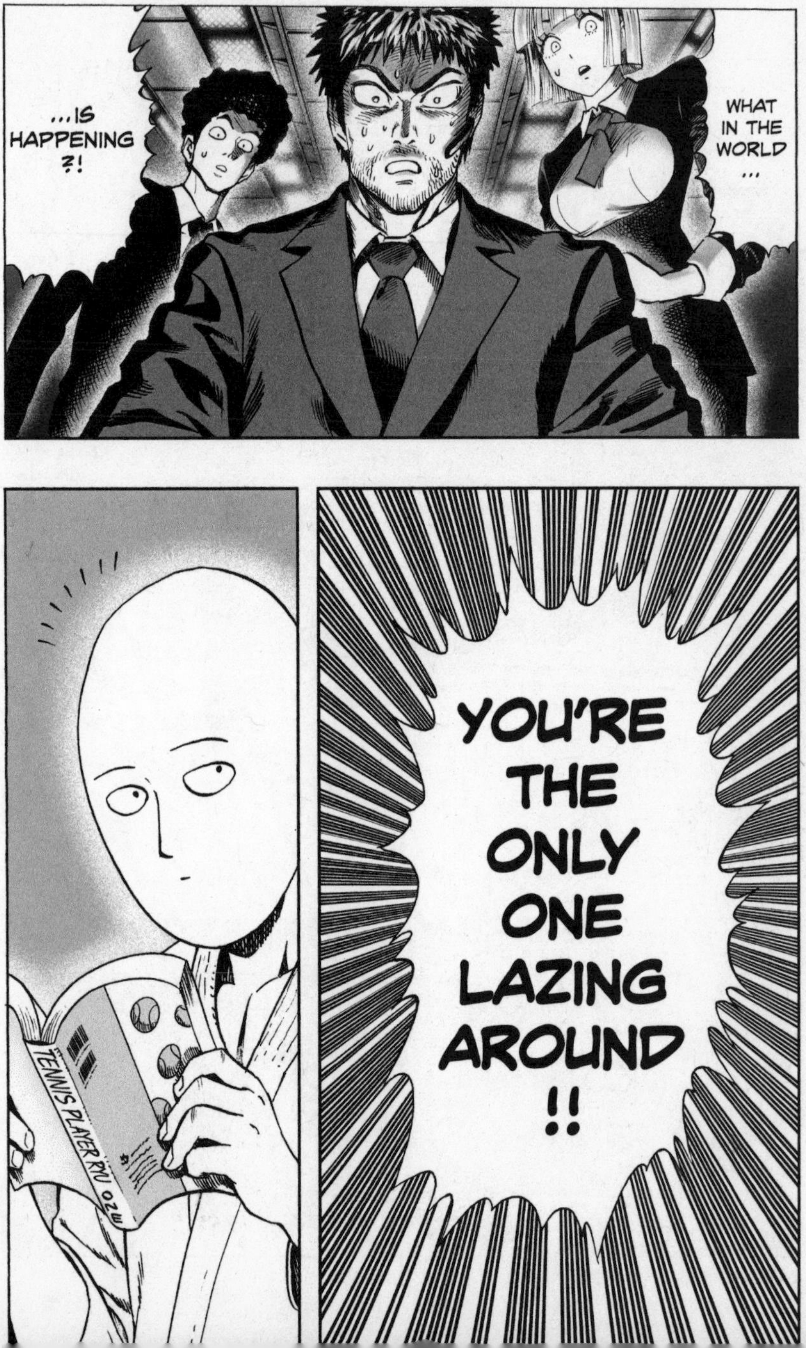
WHAT IN THE WORLD ...
...IS HAPPENING ?!
YOU'RE THE ONLY ONE LAZING AROUND !!
TENNIS PLAYER RYU

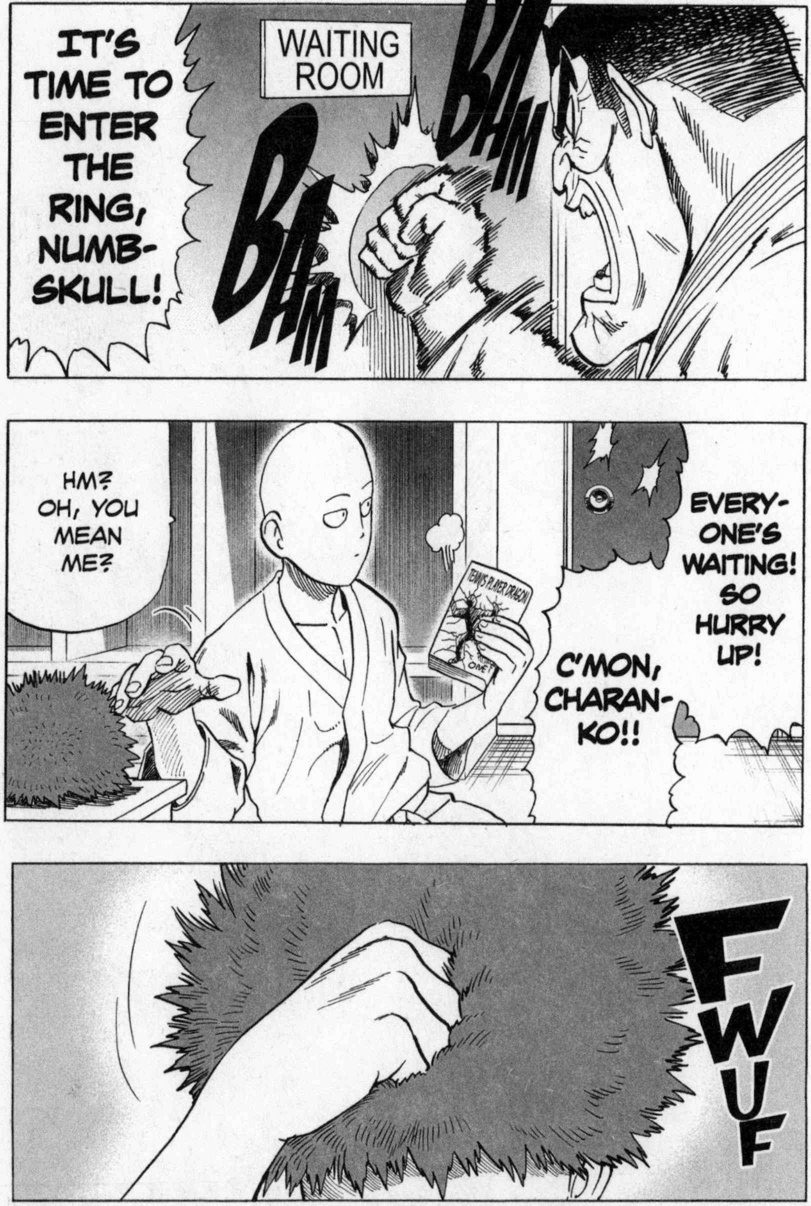
BAM
WAITING ROOM
IT'S TIME TO ENTER THE RING, NUMB-SKULL!
BAM
EVERY-ONE'S WAITING! SO HURRY UP!
C'MON, CHARAN-KO!!
TENNIS PLAYER DRAGON
ONE
HM? OH, YOU MEAN ME?
FWUF

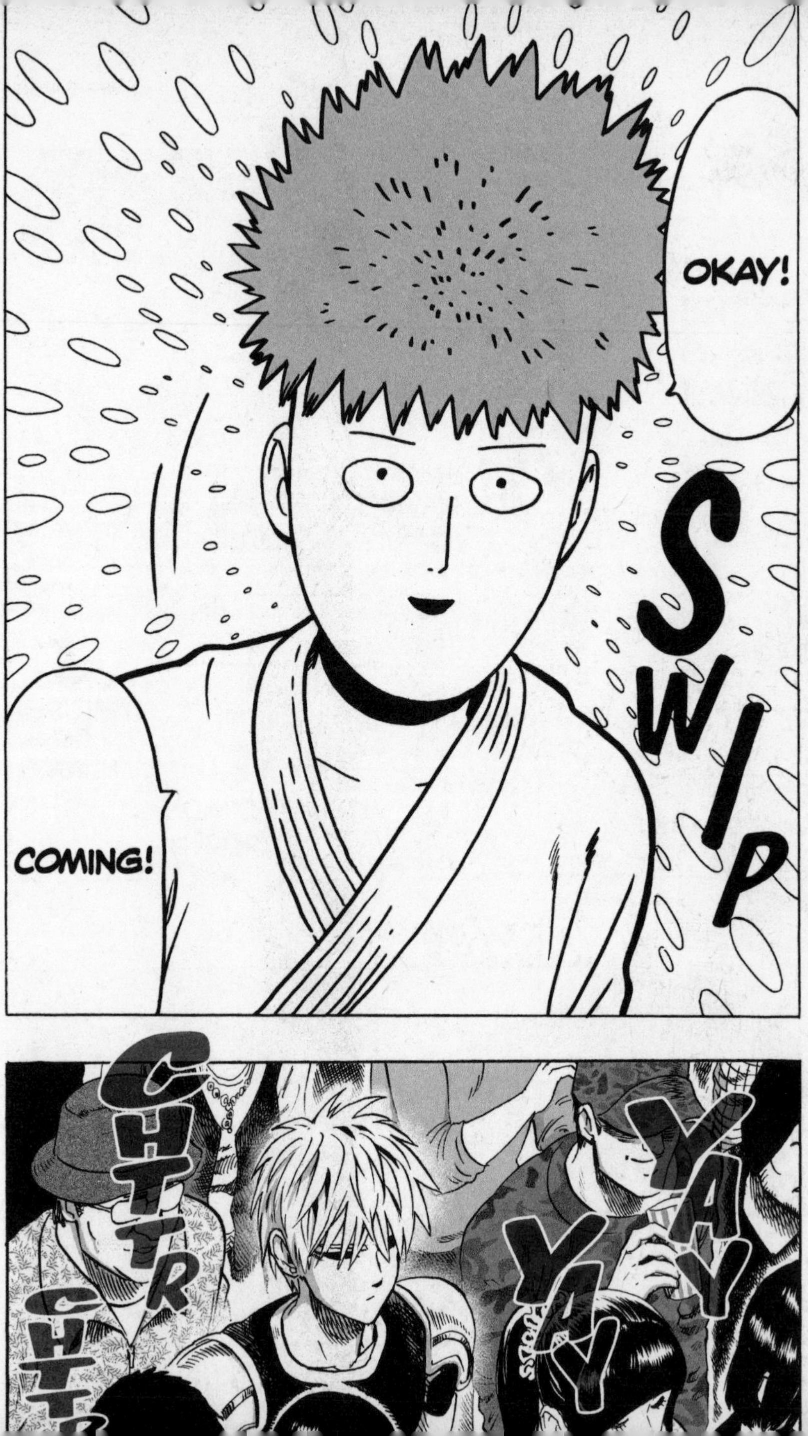
OKAY!
SWIP
COMING!
YAY
YAY
CHTTR

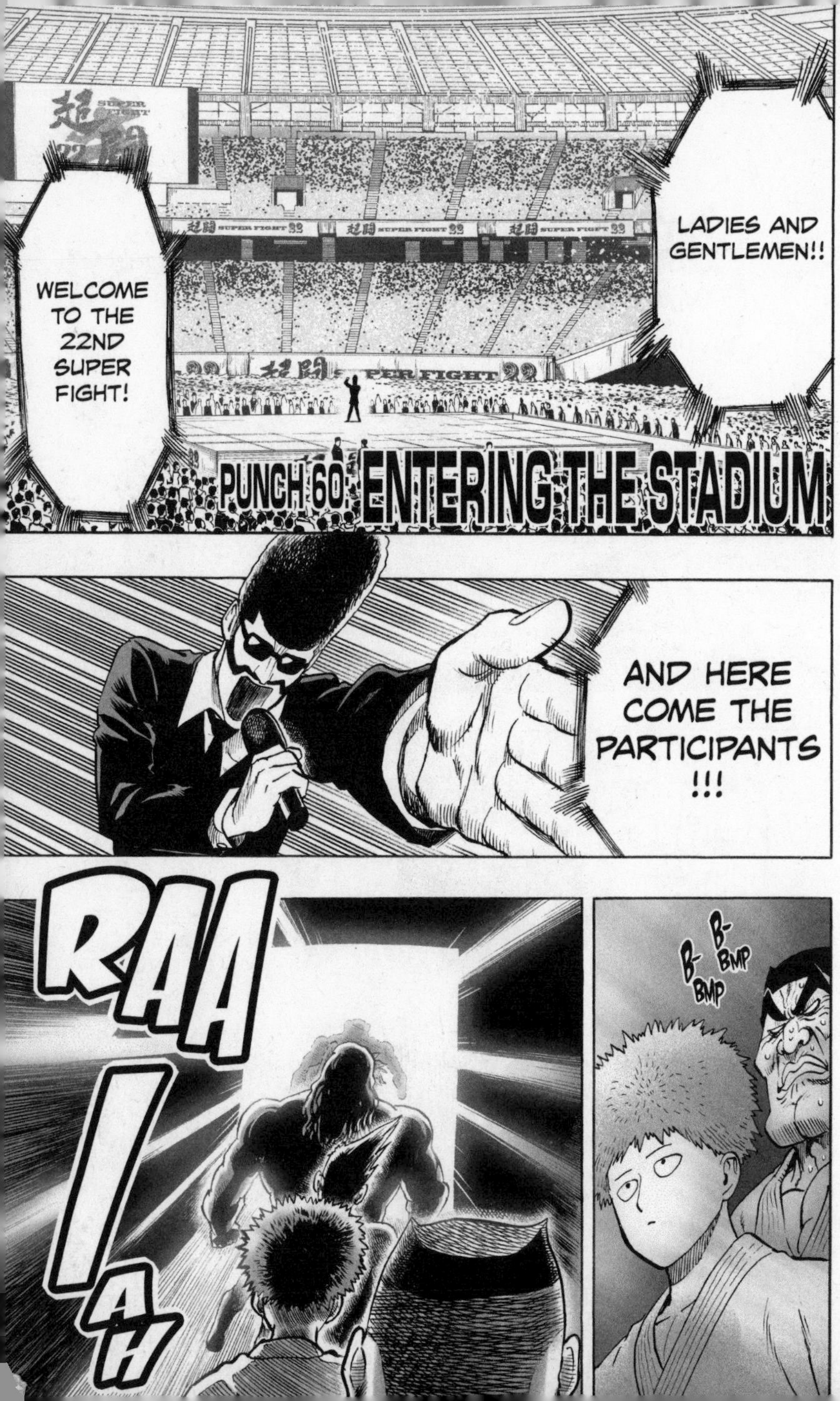
LADIES AND GENTLEMEN!!
WELCOME TO THE 22ND SUPER FIGHT!
PUNCH 60: ENTERING THE STADIUM
AND HERE COME THE PARTICIPANTS !!!
B-BMP B-BMP
RAAIAH

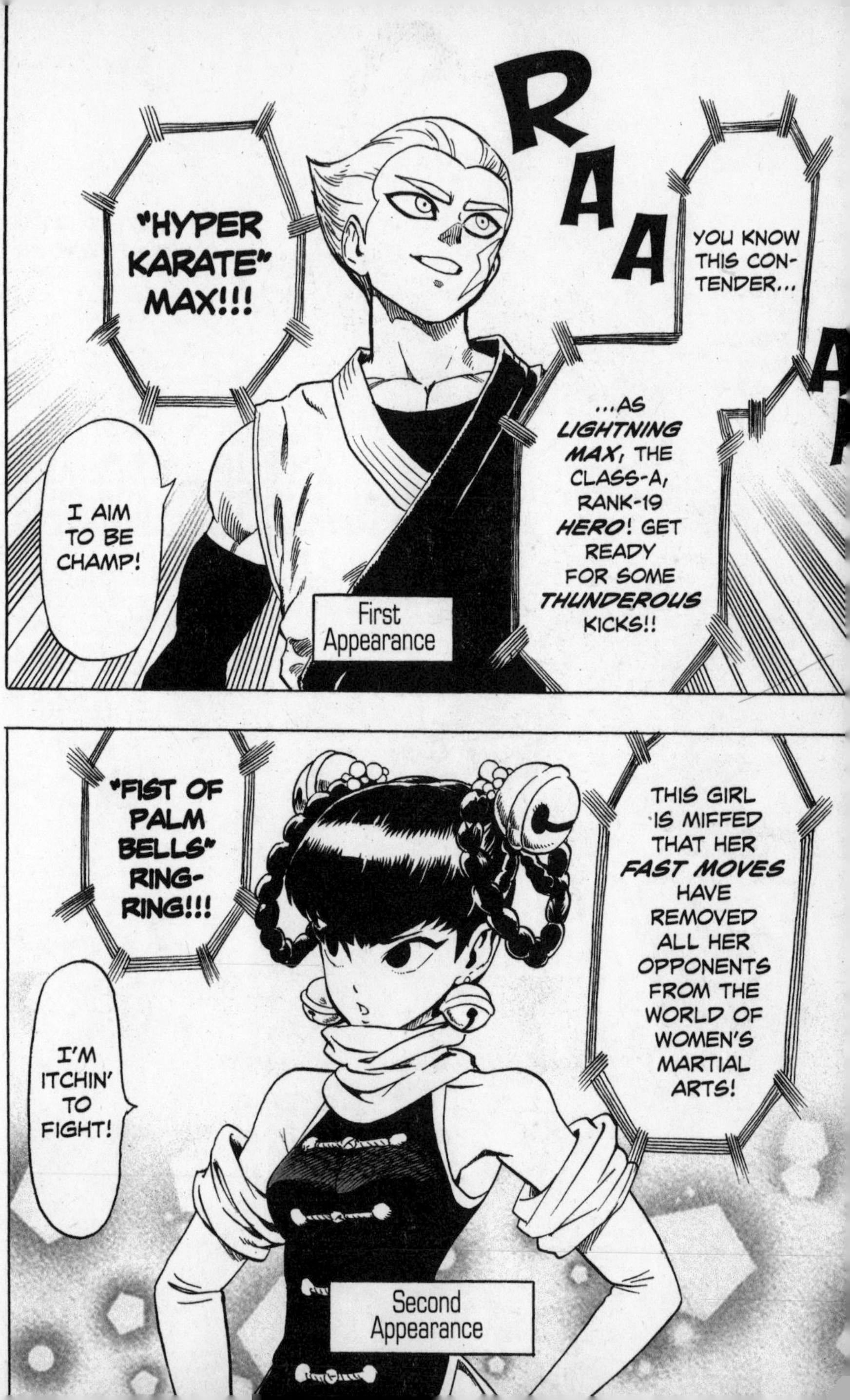
RAAA
YOU KNOW THIS CONTENDER...
"HYPER KARATE" MAX!!!
...AS *LIGHTNING MAX*, THE CLASS-A, RANK-19 *HERO*! GET READY FOR SOME *THUNDEROUS* KICKS!!
I AIM TO BE CHAMP!
First Appearance
THIS GIRL IS MIFFED THAT HER *FAST MOVES* HAVE REMOVED ALL HER OPPONENTS FROM THE WORLD OF WOMEN'S MARTIAL ARTS!
"FIST OF PALM BELLS" RING-RING!!!
I'M ITCHIN' TO FIGHT!
Second Appearance

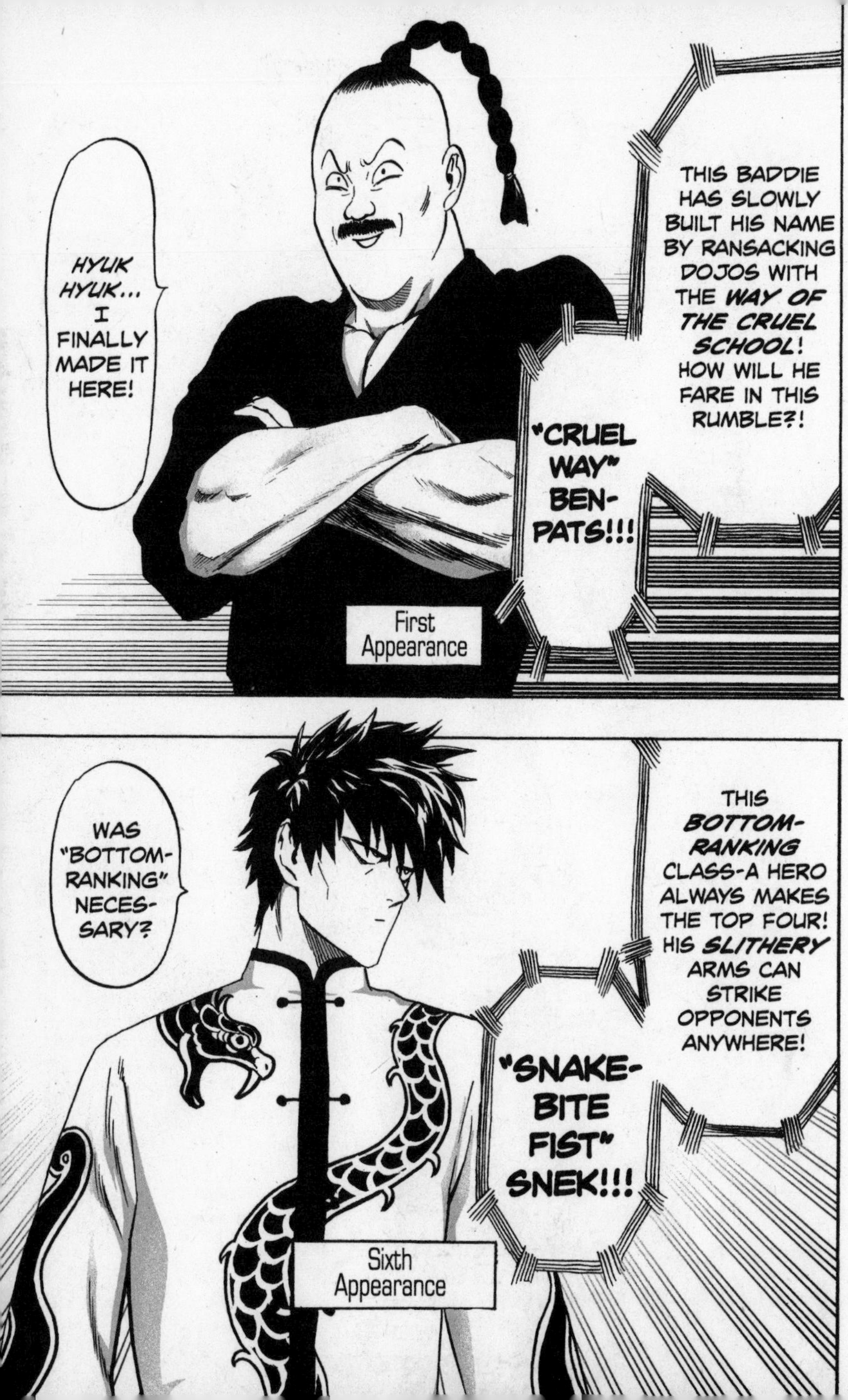
THIS BADDIE HAS SLOWLY BUILT HIS NAME BY RANSACKING DOJOS WITH THE WAY OF THE CRUEL SCHOOL! HOW WILL HE FARE IN THIS RUMBLE?!
"CRUEL WAY" BEN-PATS!!!
HYUK HYUK... I FINALLY MADE IT HERE!
First Appearance
THIS BOTTOM-RANKING CLASS-A HERO ALWAYS MAKES THE TOP FOUR! HIS SLITHERY ARMS CAN STRIKE OPPONENTS ANYWHERE!
"SNAKE-BITE FIST" SNEK!!!
WAS "BOTTOM-RANKING" NECES-SARY?
Sixth Appearance

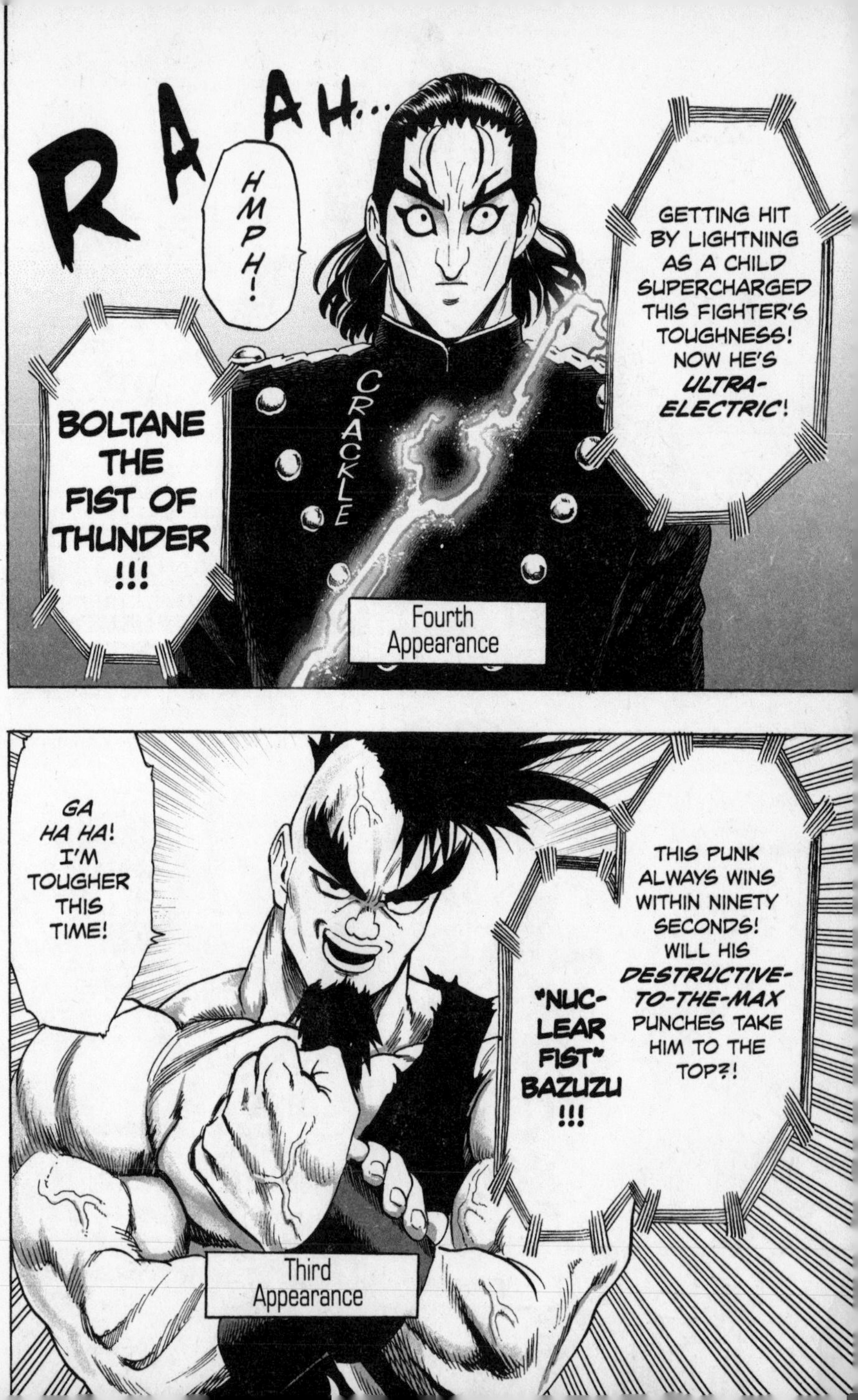
GETTING HIT BY LIGHTNING AS A CHILD SUPERCHARGED THIS FIGHTER'S TOUGHNESS! NOW HE'S *ULTRA-ELECTRIC*!
HMPH!
RAAH...
CRACKLE
BOLTANE THE FIST OF THUNDER !!!
Fourth Appearance
THIS PUNK ALWAYS WINS WITHIN NINETY SECONDS! WILL HIS *DESTRUCTIVE-TO-THE-MAX* PUNCHES TAKE HIM TO THE TOP?!
"NUC-LEAR FIST" BAZUZU !!!
GA HA HA! I'M TOUGHER THIS TIME!
Third Appearance

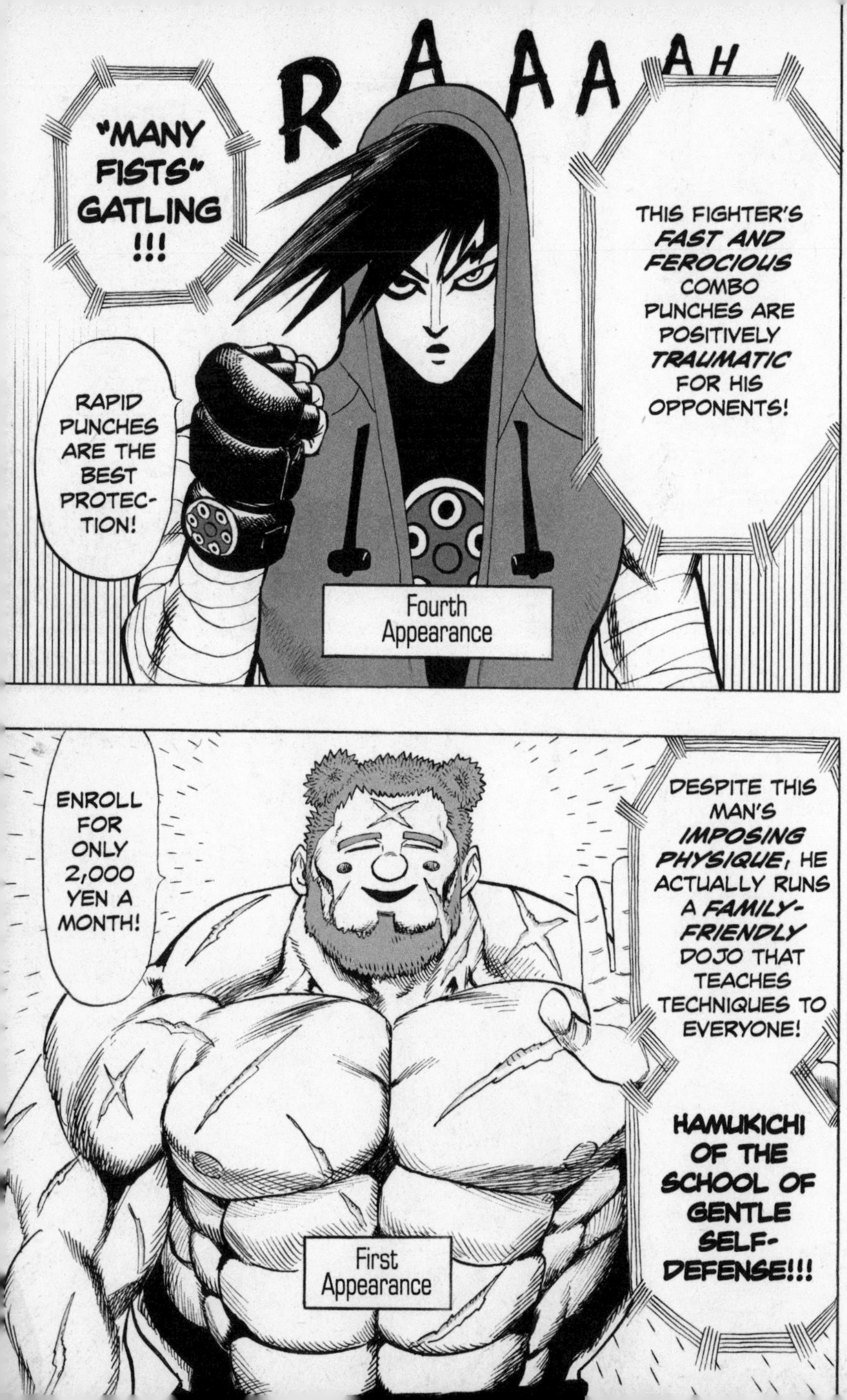
RAAAAAH
THIS FIGHTER'S FAST AND FEROCIOUS COMBO PUNCHES ARE POSITIVELY TRAUMATIC FOR HIS OPPONENTS!
"MANY FISTS" GATLING !!!
RAPID PUNCHES ARE THE BEST PROTEC- TION!
Fourth Appearance
DESPITE THIS MAN'S IMPOSING PHYSIQUE, HE ACTUALLY RUNS A FAMILY- FRIENDLY DOJO THAT TEACHES TECHNIQUES TO EVERYONE!
ENROLL FOR ONLY 2,000 YEN A MONTH!
HAMUKICHI OF THE SCHOOL OF GENTLE SELF- DEFENSE!!!
First Appearance

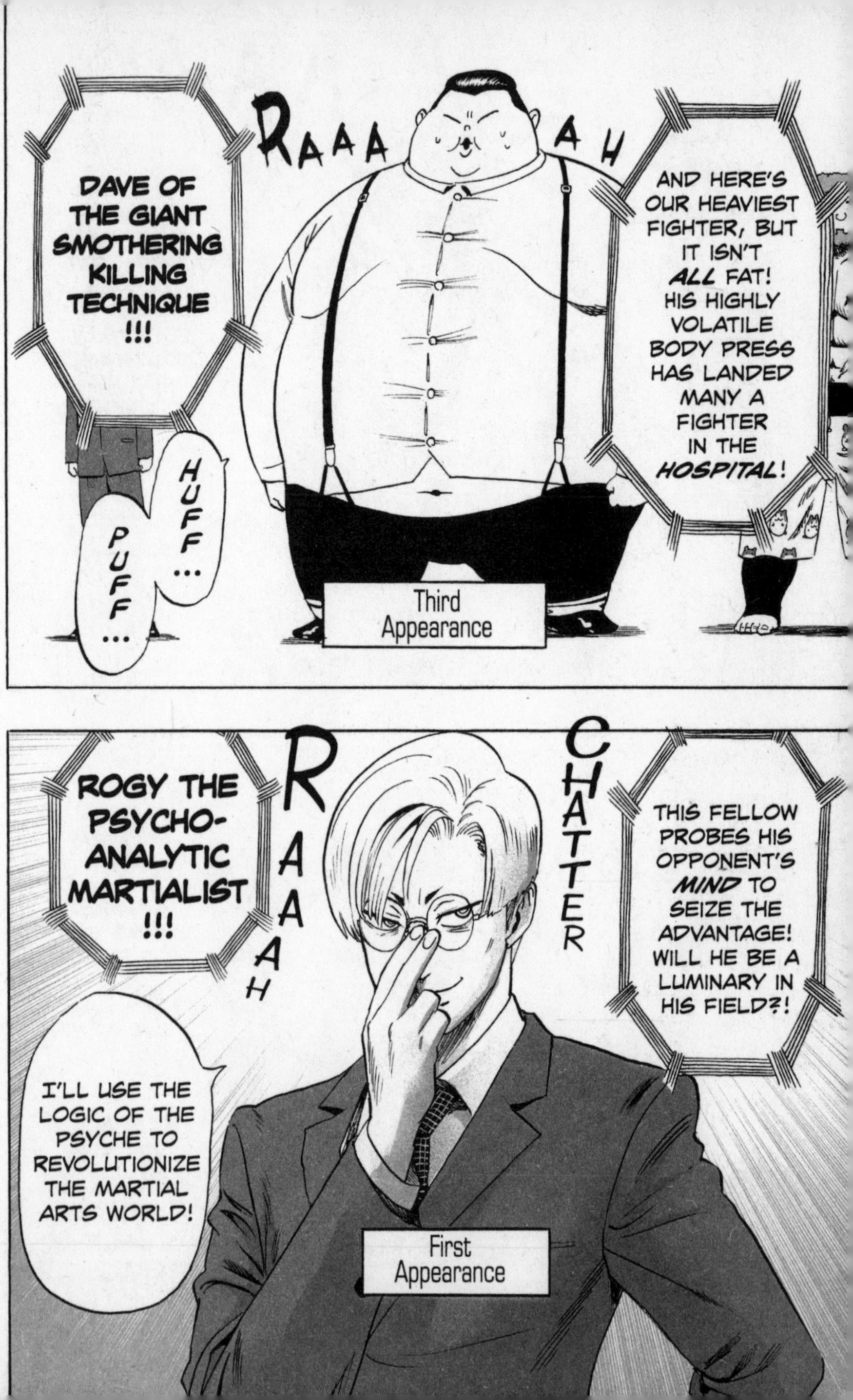
AND HERE'S OUR HEAVIEST FIGHTER, BUT IT ISN'T *ALL* FAT! HIS HIGHLY VOLATILE BODY PRESS HAS LANDED MANY A FIGHTER IN THE *HOSPITAL*!
RAAAAH
DAVE OF THE GIANT SMOTHERING KILLING TECHNIQUE!!!
HUFF...
PUFF...
Third Appearance
CHATTER
THIS FELLOW PROBES HIS OPPONENT'S *MIND* TO SEIZE THE ADVANTAGE! WILL HE BE A LUMINARY IN HIS FIELD?!
RAAAAH
ROGY THE PSYCHO-ANALYTIC MARTIALIST!!!
I'LL USE THE LOGIC OF THE PSYCHE TO REVOLUTIONIZE THE MARTIAL ARTS WORLD!
First Appearance

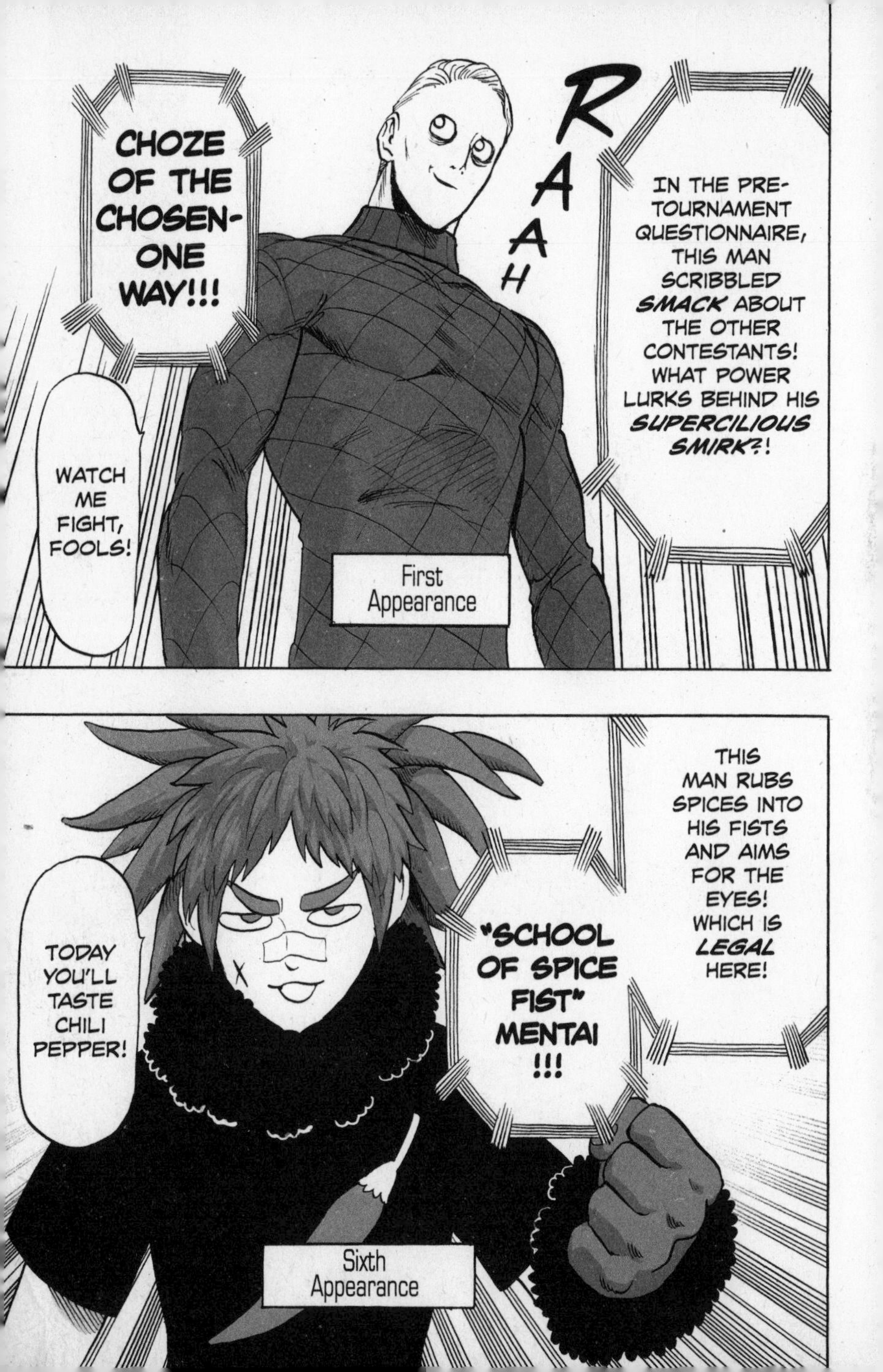
RAAH
IN THE PRE-TOURNAMENT QUESTIONNAIRE, THIS MAN SCRIBBLED SMACK ABOUT THE OTHER CONTESTANTS! WHAT POWER LURKS BEHIND HIS SUPERCILIOUS SMIRK?!
CHOZE OF THE CHOSEN-ONE WAY!!!
WATCH ME FIGHT, FOOLS!
First Appearance
THIS MAN RUBS SPICES INTO HIS FISTS AND AIMS FOR THE EYES! WHICH IS LEGAL HERE!
"SCHOOL OF SPICE FIST" MENTAI !!!
TODAY YOU'LL TASTE CHILI PEPPER!
Sixth Appearance

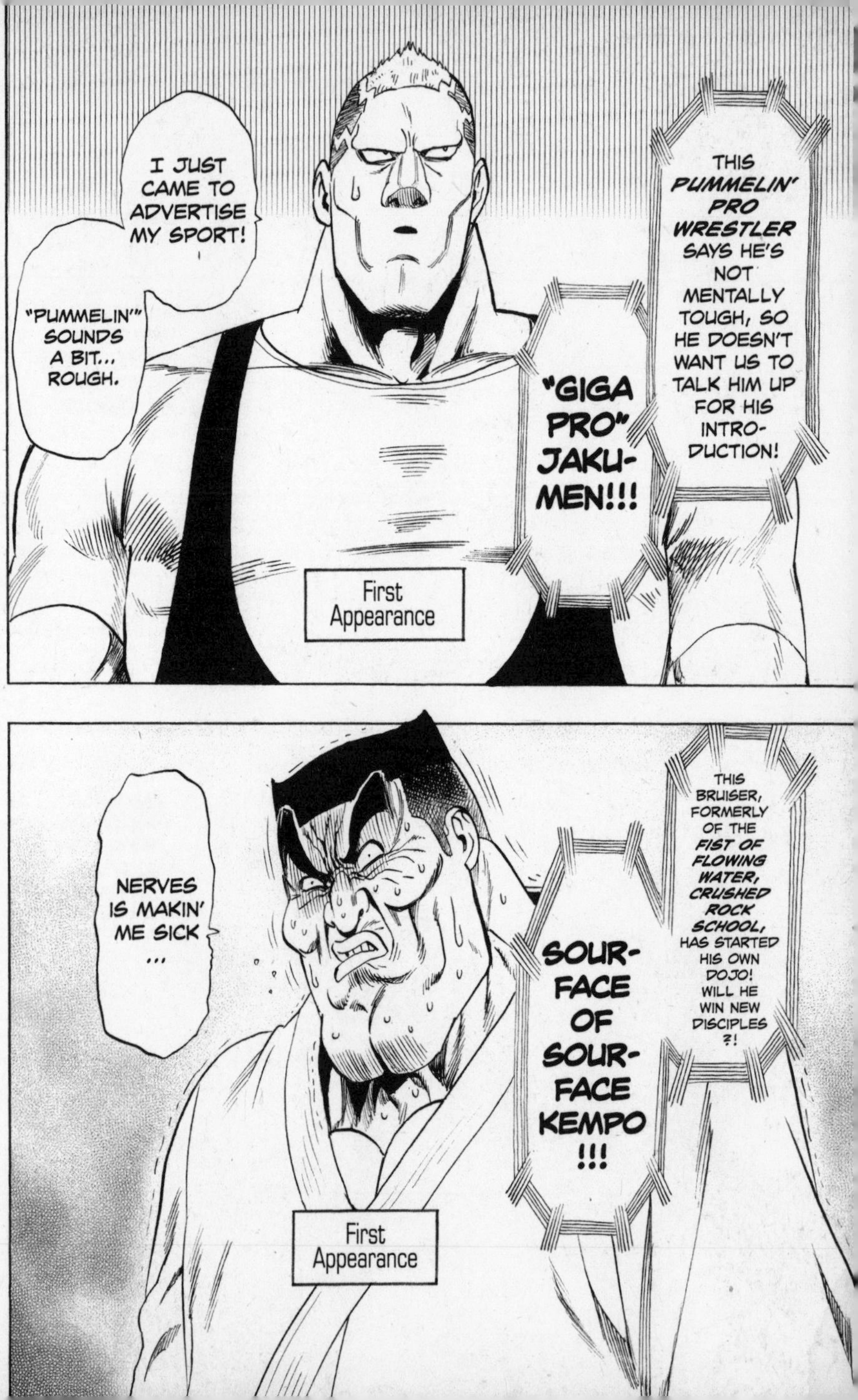
THIS *PUMMELIN' PRO WRESTLER* SAYS HE'S NOT MENTALLY TOUGH, SO HE DOESN'T WANT US TO TALK HIM UP FOR HIS INTRO-DUCTION!
"GIGA PRO" JAKU-MEN!!!
I JUST CAME TO ADVERTISE MY SPORT!
"PUMMELIN'" SOUNDS A BIT... ROUGH.
First Appearance
THIS BRUISER, FORMERLY OF THE *FIST OF FLOWING WATER, CRUSHED ROCK SCHOOL,* HAS STARTED HIS OWN DOJO! WILL HE WIN NEW DISCIPLES ?!
SOUR-FACE OF SOUR-FACE KEMPO !!!
NERVES IS MAKIN' ME SICK ...
First Appearance

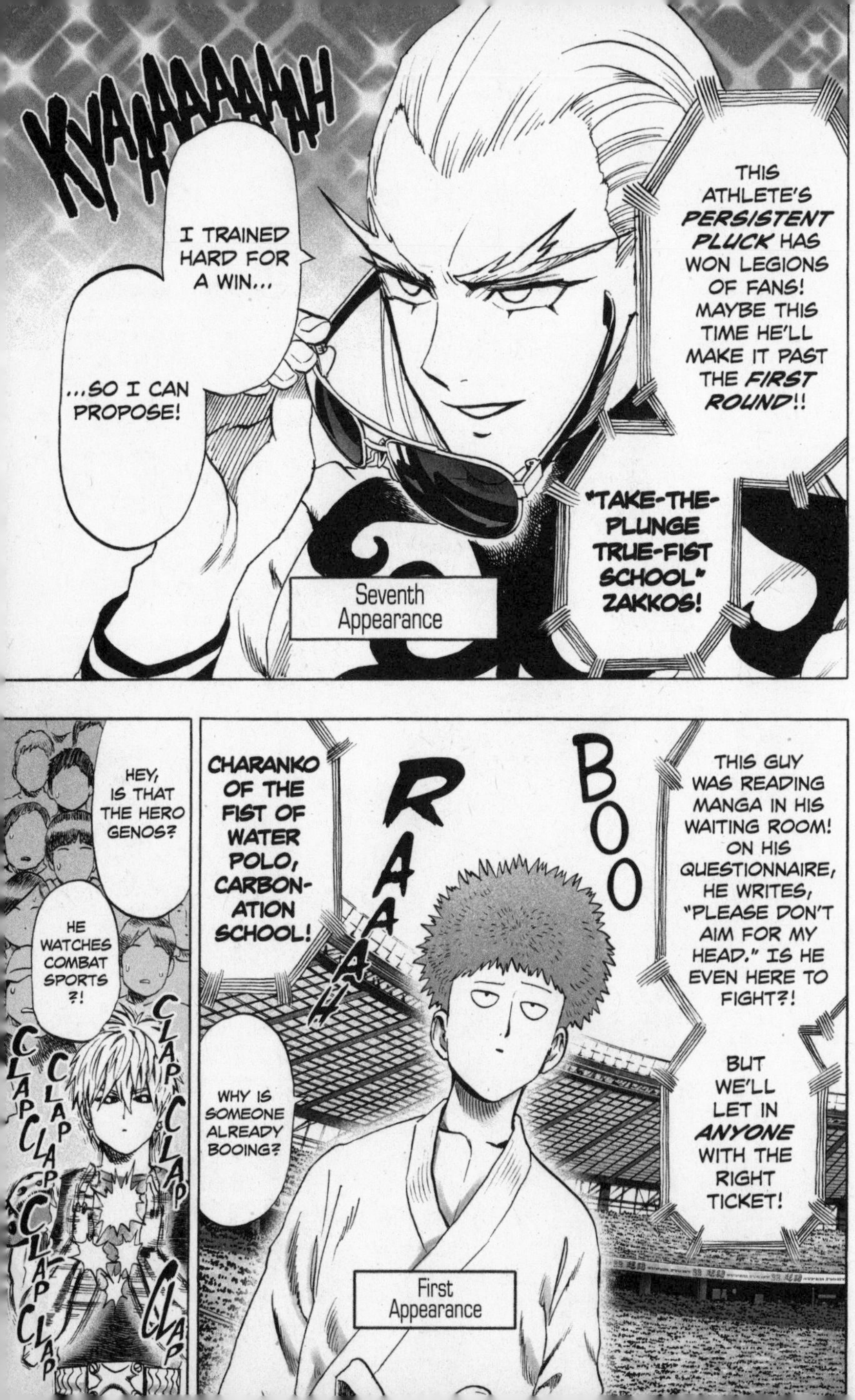

THIS ATHLETE'S *PERSISTENT PLUCK* HAS WON LEGIONS OF FANS! MAYBE THIS TIME HE'LL MAKE IT PAST THE *FIRST ROUND*!!
KYAAAAAAAAH
I TRAINED HARD FOR A WIN...
"TAKE-THE-PLUNGE TRUE-FIST SCHOOL" ZAKKOS!
...SO I CAN PROPOSE!
Seventh Appearance
THIS GUY WAS READING MANGA IN HIS WAITING ROOM! ON HIS QUESTIONNAIRE, HE WRITES, "PLEASE DON'T AIM FOR MY HEAD." IS HE EVEN HERE TO FIGHT?!
BOO
RAAAH
CHARANKO OF THE FIST OF WATER POLO, CARBON-ATION SCHOOL!
BUT WE'LL LET IN *ANYONE* WITH THE RIGHT TICKET!
WHY IS SOMEONE ALREADY BOOING?
First Appearance
HEY, IS THAT THE HERO GENOS?
HE WATCHES COMBAT SPORTS?!
CLAP CLAP CLAP
CLAP CLAP CLAP
CLAP CLAP CLAP
CLAP CLAP

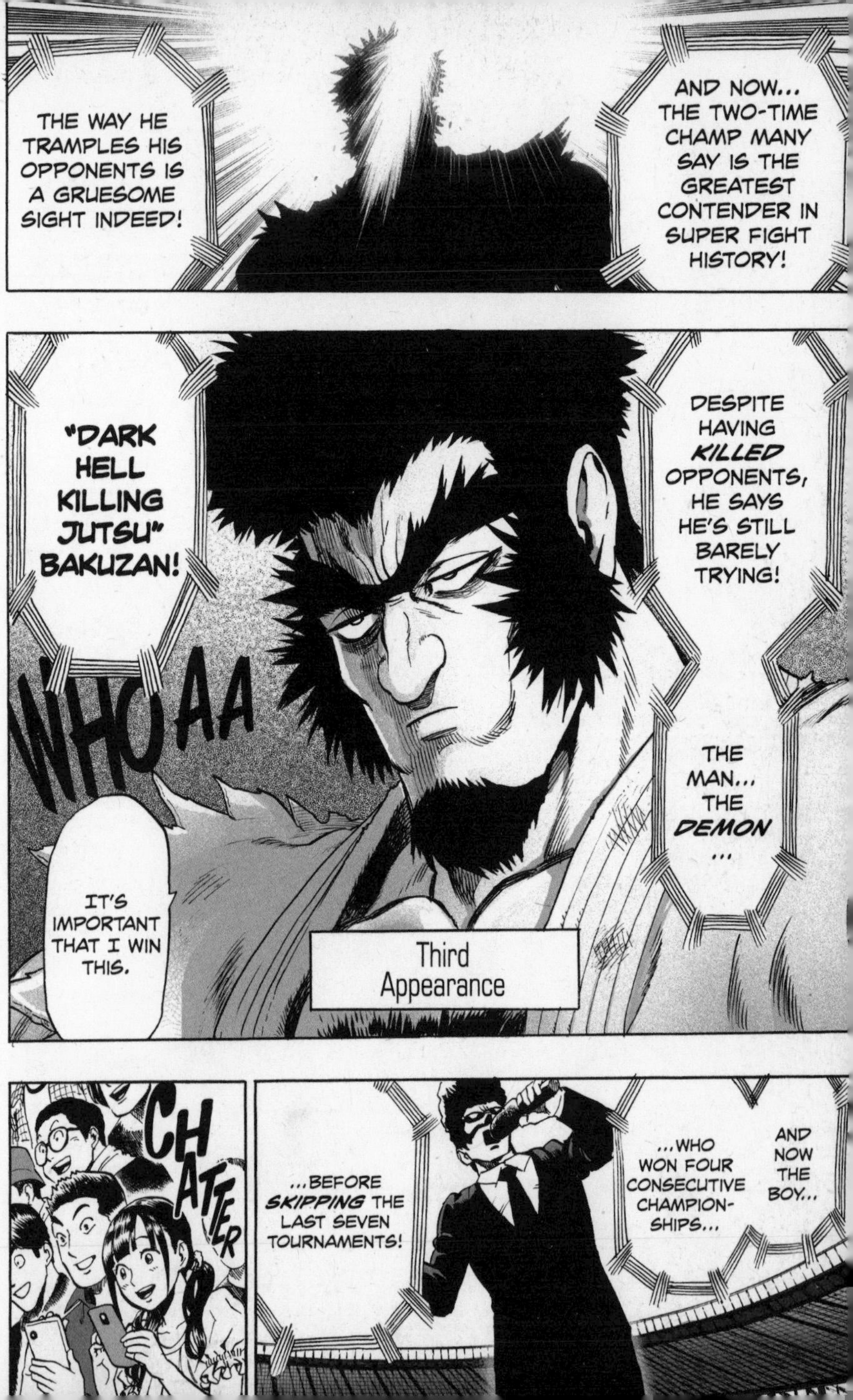
AND NOW... THE TWO-TIME CHAMP MANY SAY IS THE GREATEST CONTENDER IN SUPER FIGHT HISTORY!
THE WAY HE TRAMPLES HIS OPPONENTS IS A GRUESOME SIGHT INDEED!
DESPITE HAVING KILLED OPPONENTS, HE SAYS HE'S STILL BARELY TRYING!
THE MAN... THE DEMON...
"DARK HELL KILLING JUTSU" BAKUZAN!
WHOAA
IT'S IMPORTANT THAT I WIN THIS.
Third Appearance
AND NOW THE BOY...
...WHO WON FOUR CONSECUTIVE CHAMPION-SHIPS...
...BEFORE SKIPPING THE LAST SEVEN TOURNAMENTS!
CHATTER

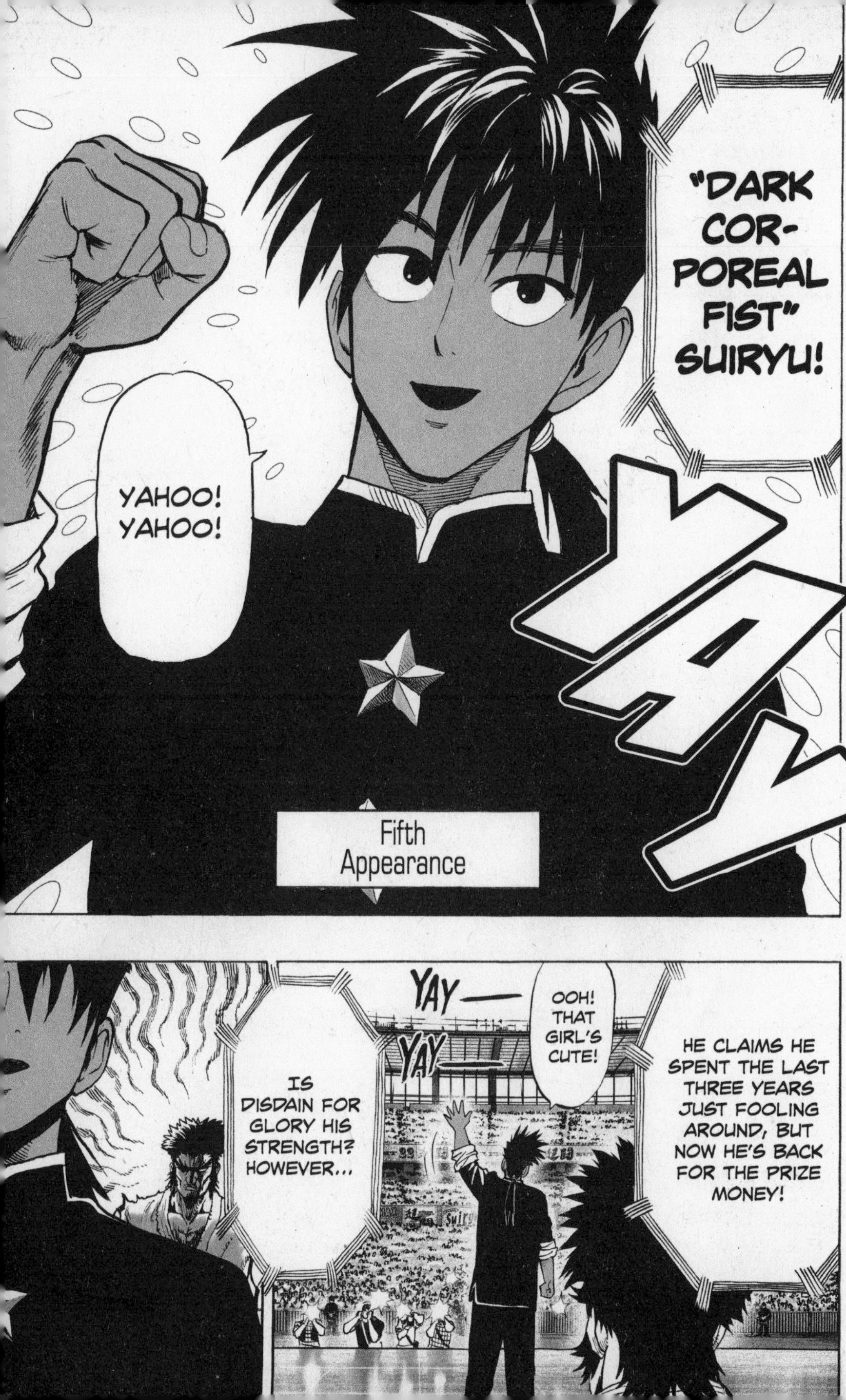
"DARK COR-POREAL FIST" SUIRYU!
YAY
YAHOO! YAHOO!
Fifth Appearance
HE CLAIMS HE SPENT THE LAST THREE YEARS JUST FOOLING AROUND, BUT NOW HE'S BACK FOR THE PRIZE MONEY!
OOH! THAT GIRL'S CUTE!
YAY—
YAY—
IS DISDAIN FOR GLORY HIS STRENGTH? HOWEVER...

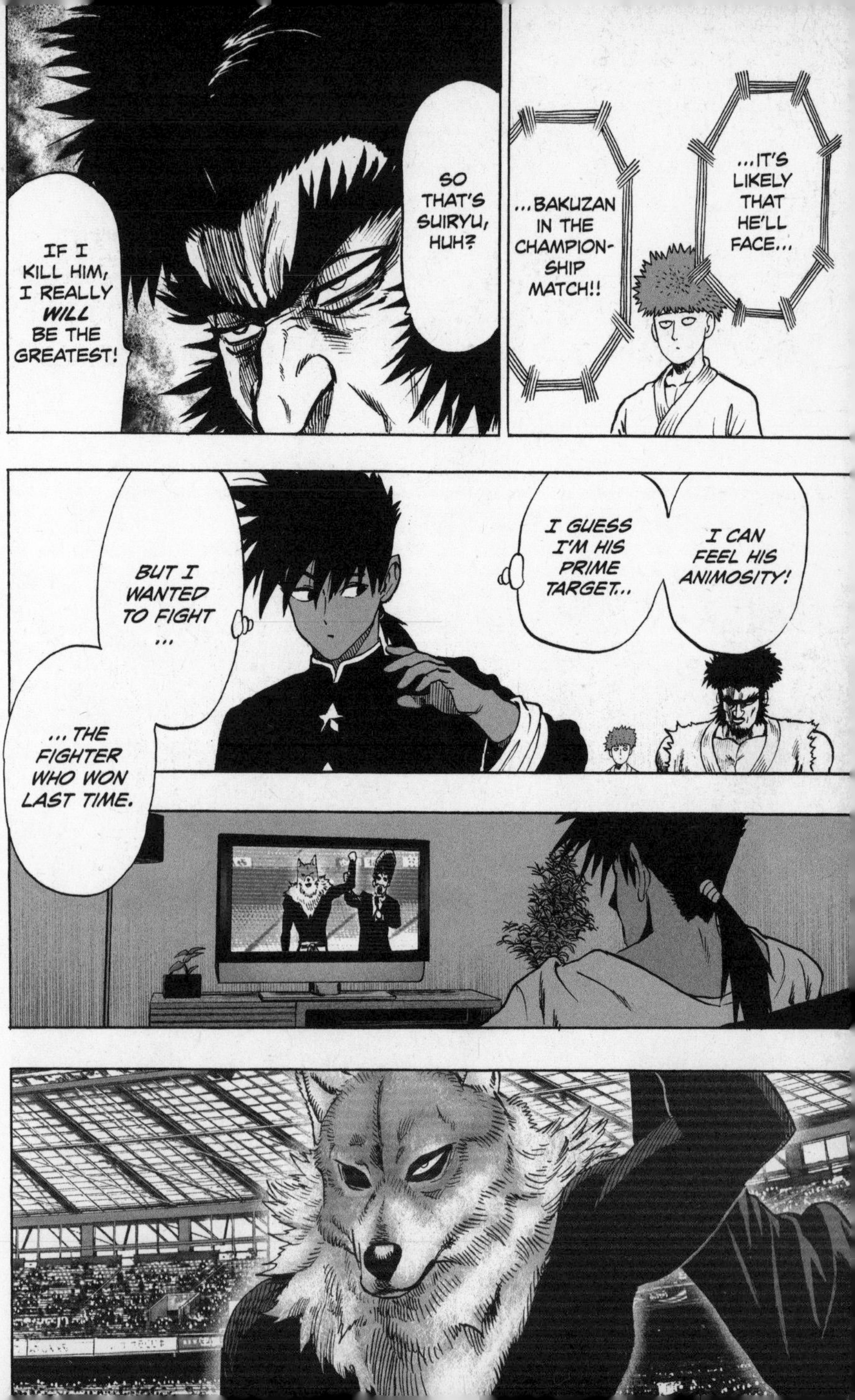
...IT'S LIKELY THAT HE'LL FACE...
...BAKUZAN IN THE CHAMPION-SHIP MATCH!!
SO THAT'S SUIRYU, HUH?
IF I KILL HIM, I REALLY *WILL* BE THE GREATEST!
I CAN FEEL HIS ANIMOSITY!
I GUESS I'M HIS PRIME TARGET...
BUT I WANTED TO FIGHT ...
...THE FIGHTER WHO WON LAST TIME.

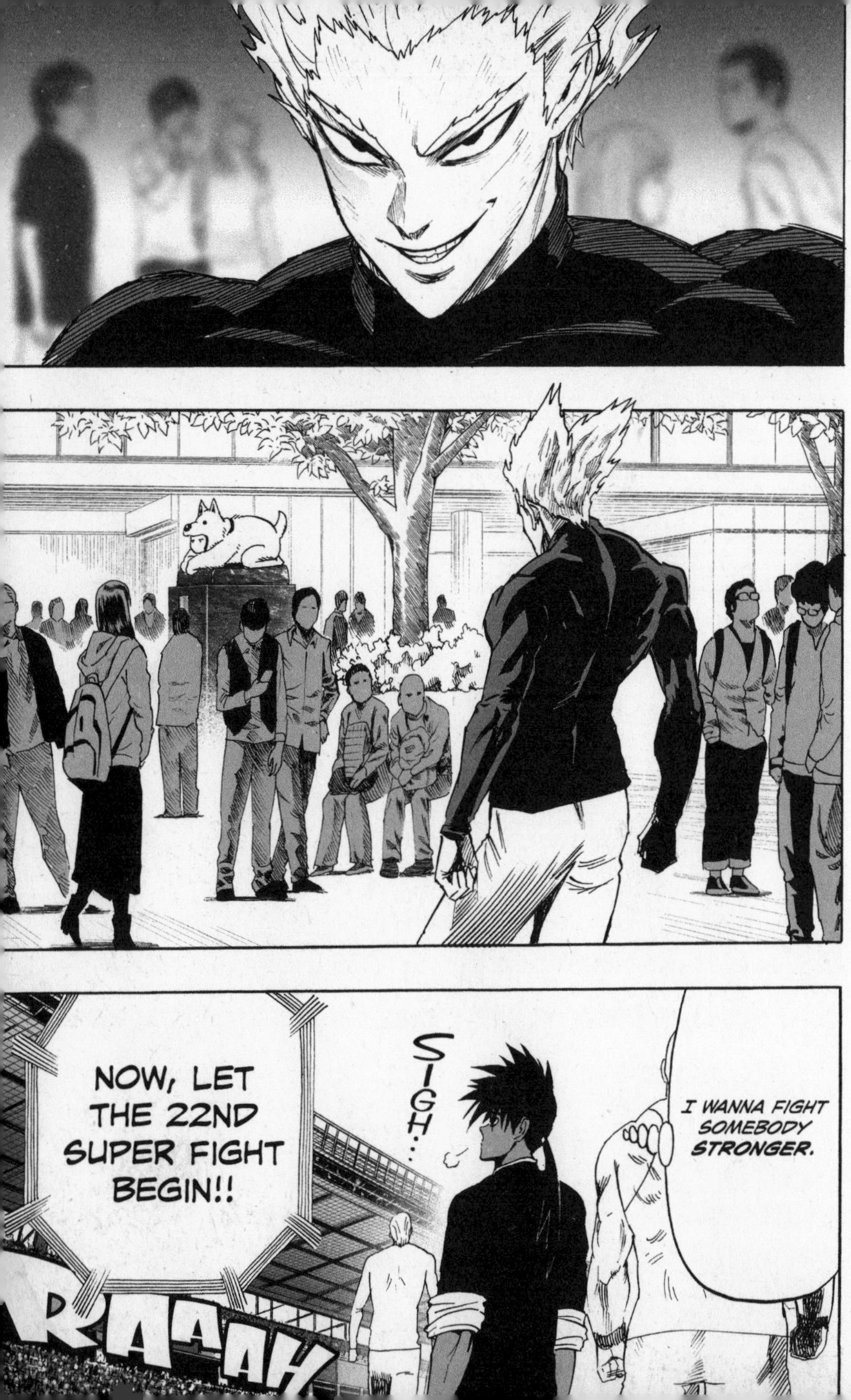
I WANNA FIGHT SOMEBODY STRONGER.
SIGH...
NOW, LET THE 22ND SUPER FIGHT BEGIN!!
RAAAH

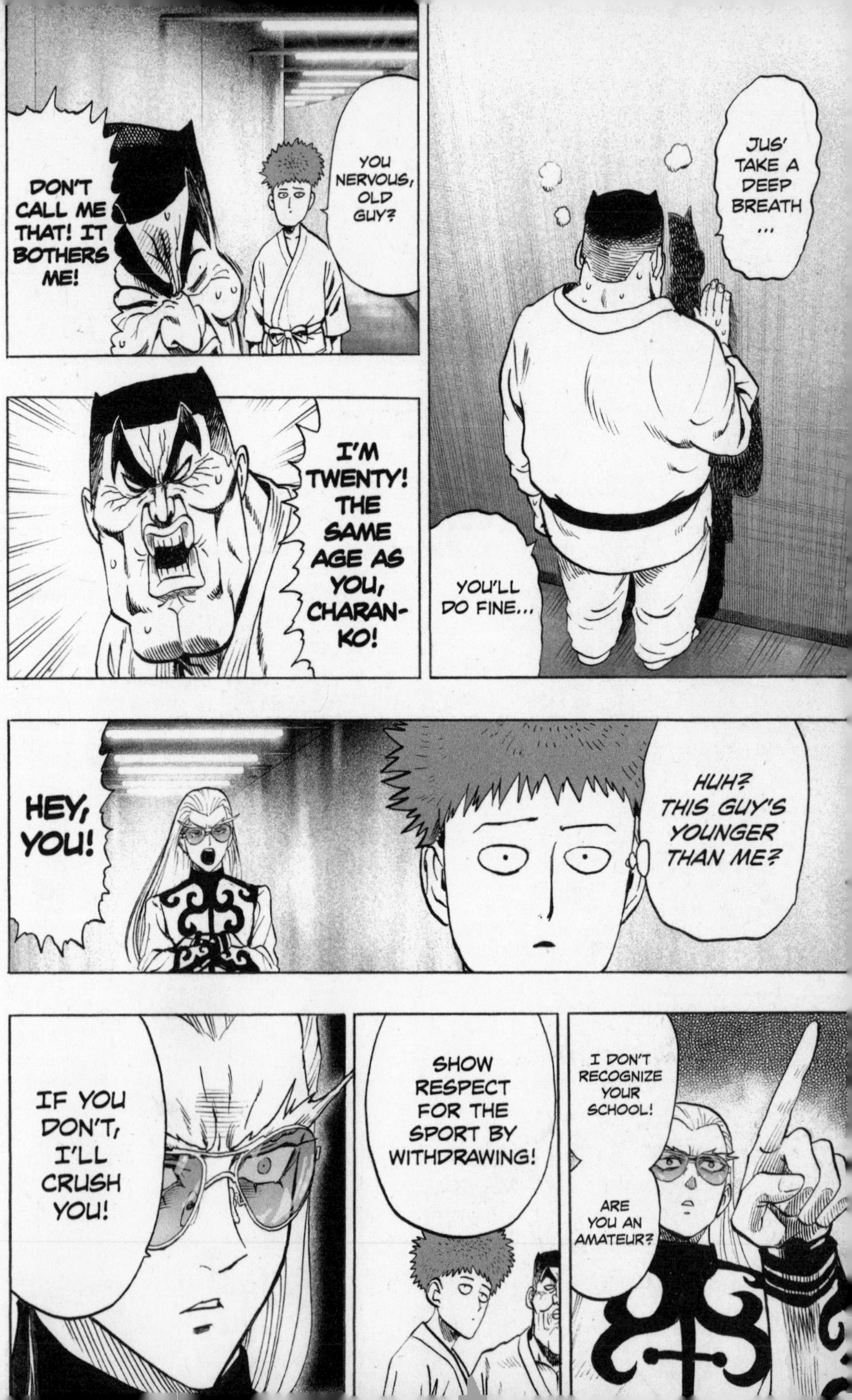
JUS' TAKE A DEEP BREATH ...
YOU'LL DO FINE...
YOU NERVOUS, OLD GUY?
DON'T CALL ME THAT! IT BOTHERS ME!
I'M TWENTY! THE SAME AGE AS YOU, CHARANKO!
HUH? THIS GUY'S YOUNGER THAN ME?
HEY, YOU!
I DON'T RECOGNIZE YOUR SCHOOL!
ARE YOU AN AMATEUR?
SHOW RESPECT FOR THE SPORT BY WITHDRAWING!
IF YOU DON'T, I'LL CRUSH YOU!

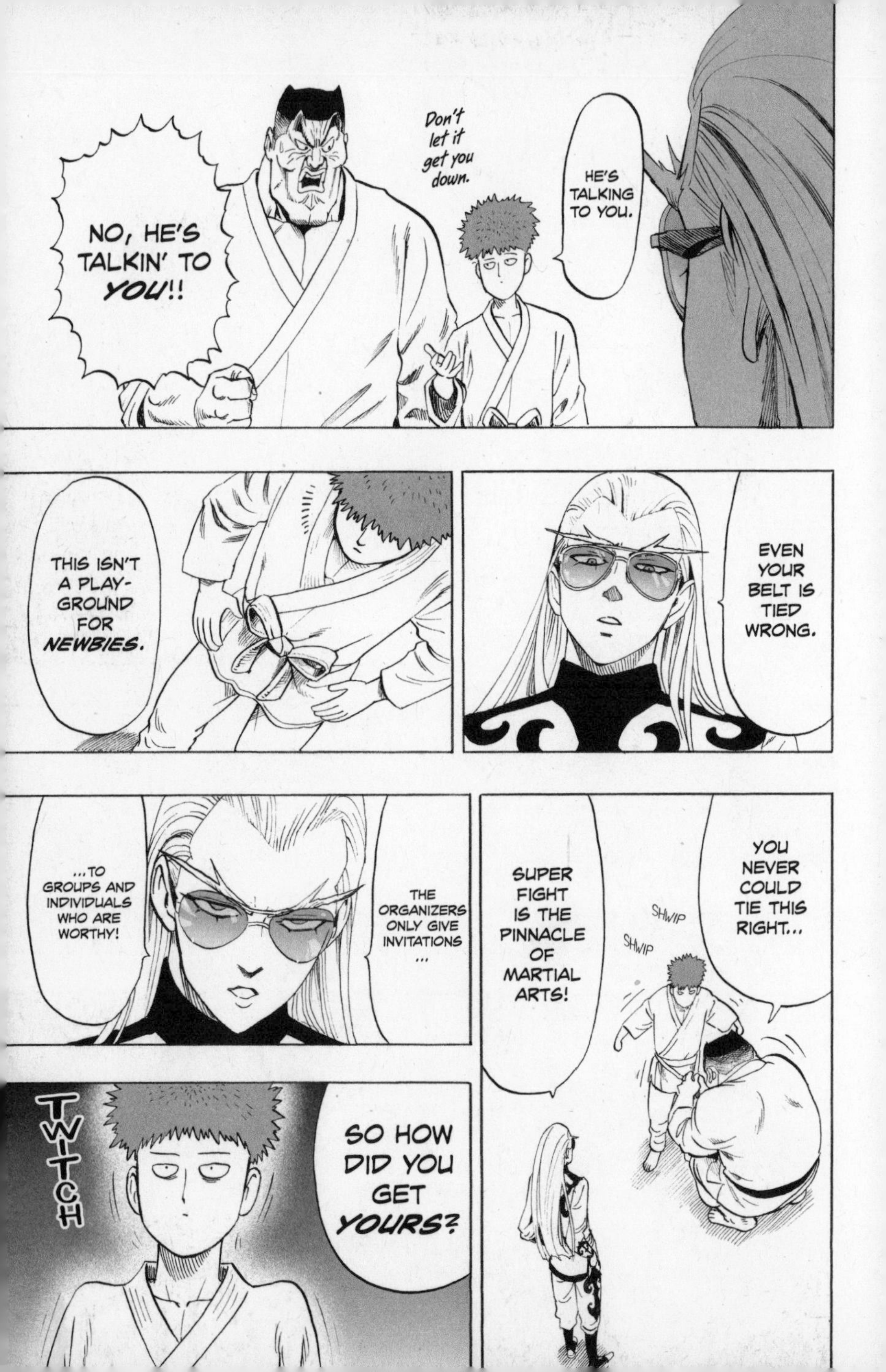
HE'S TALKING TO YOU.
Don't let it get you down.
NO, HE'S TALKIN' TO YOU!!
EVEN YOUR BELT IS TIED WRONG.
THIS ISN'T A PLAY-GROUND FOR NEWBIES.
YOU NEVER COULD TIE THIS RIGHT...
SHWIP
SHWIP
SUPER FIGHT IS THE PINNACLE OF MARTIAL ARTS!
THE ORGANIZERS ONLY GIVE INVITATIONS ...
...TO GROUPS AND INDIVIDUALS WHO ARE WORTHY!
SO HOW DID YOU GET YOURS?
TWITCH

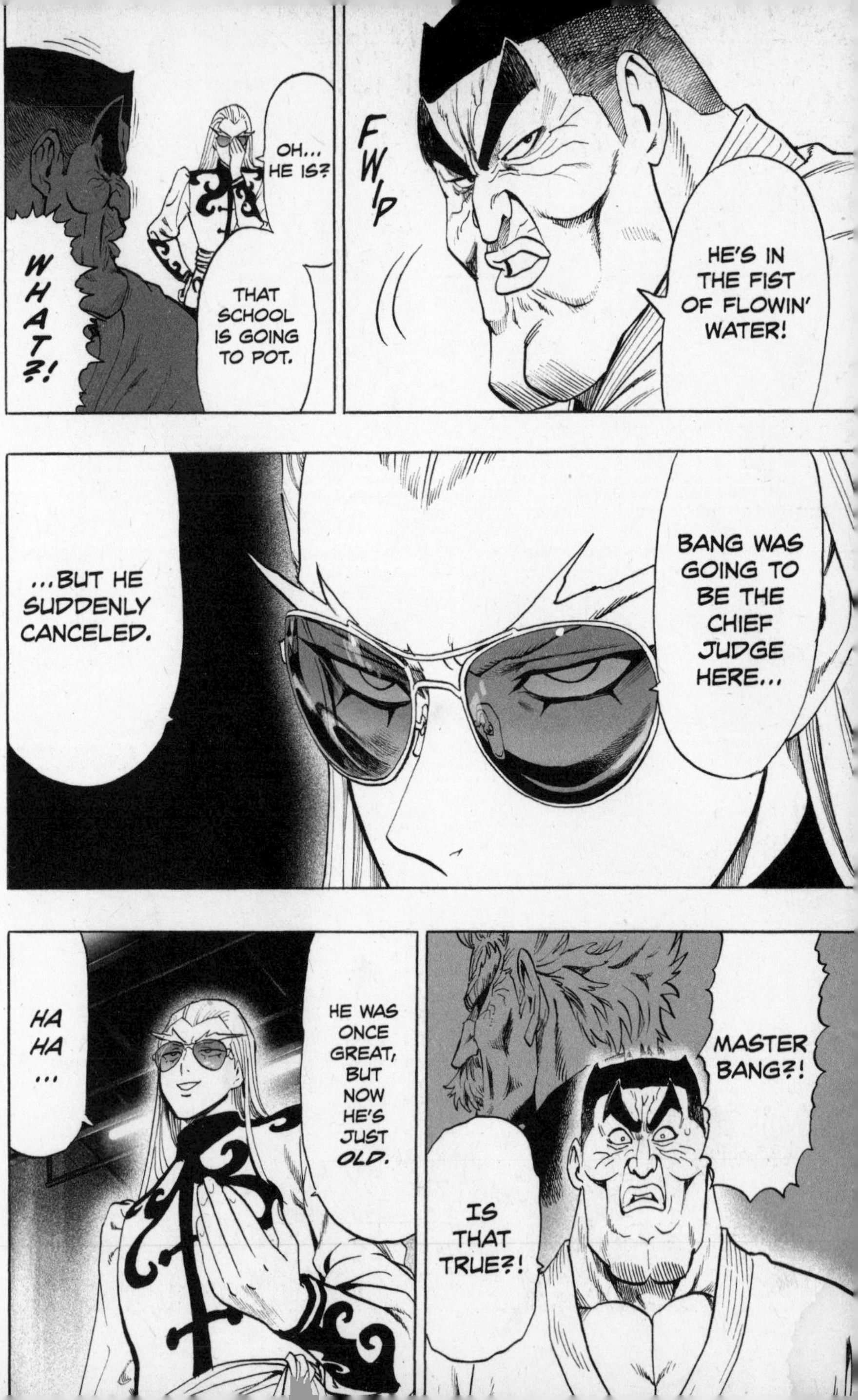
FWIP
HE'S IN THE FIST OF FLOWIN' WATER!
OH... HE IS?
THAT SCHOOL IS GOING TO POT.
WHAT?!
BANG WAS GOING TO BE THE CHIEF JUDGE HERE...
...BUT HE SUDDENLY CANCELED.
MASTER BANG?!
IS THAT TRUE?!
HE WAS ONCE GREAT, BUT NOW HE'S JUST OLD.
HA HA...

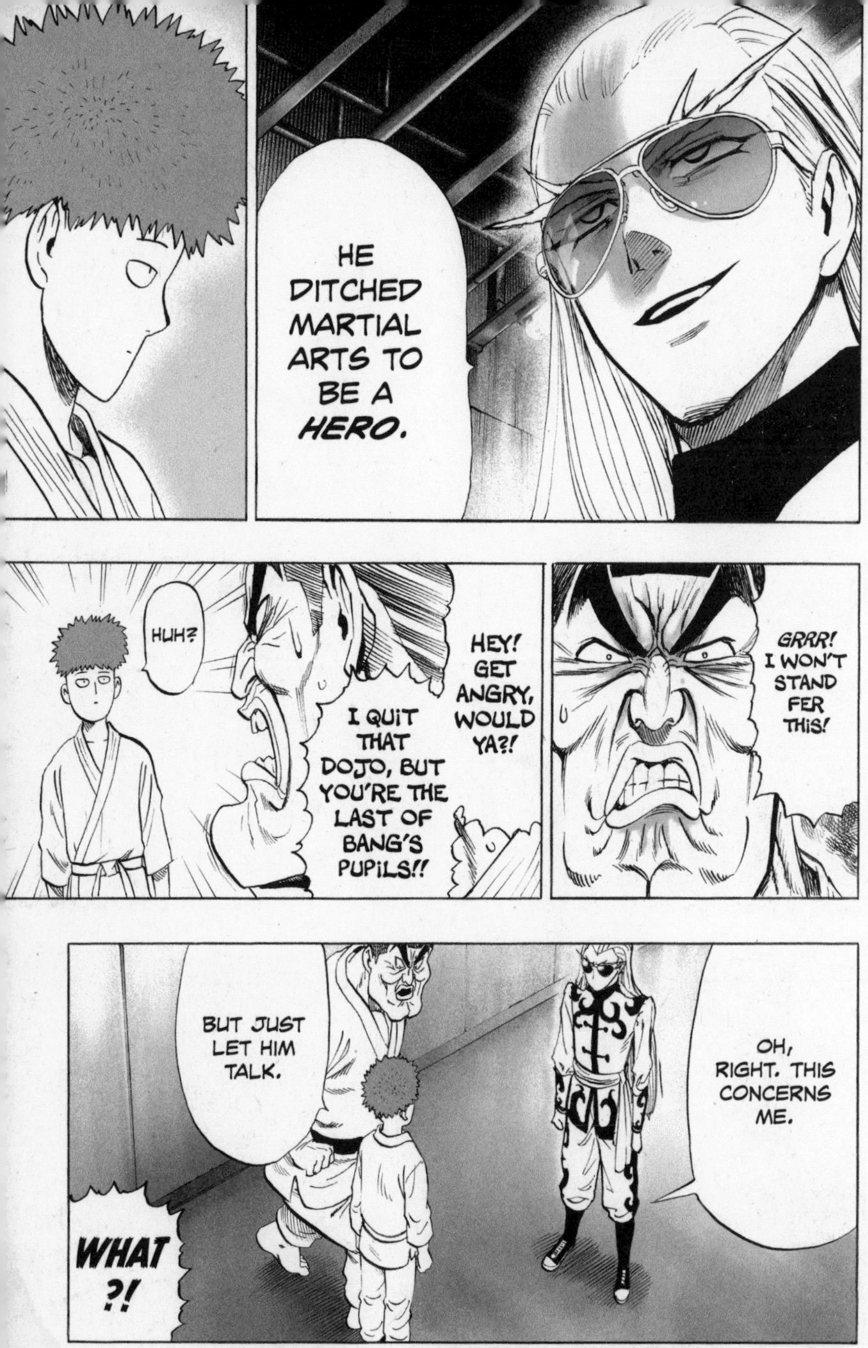
HE DITCHED MARTIAL ARTS TO BE A HERO.
GRRR! I WON'T STAND FER THIS!
HEY! GET ANGRY, WOULD YA?!
HUH?
I QUIT THAT DOJO, BUT YOU'RE THE LAST OF BANG'S PUPILS!!
OH, RIGHT. THIS CONCERNS ME.
BUT JUST LET HIM TALK.
WHAT?!

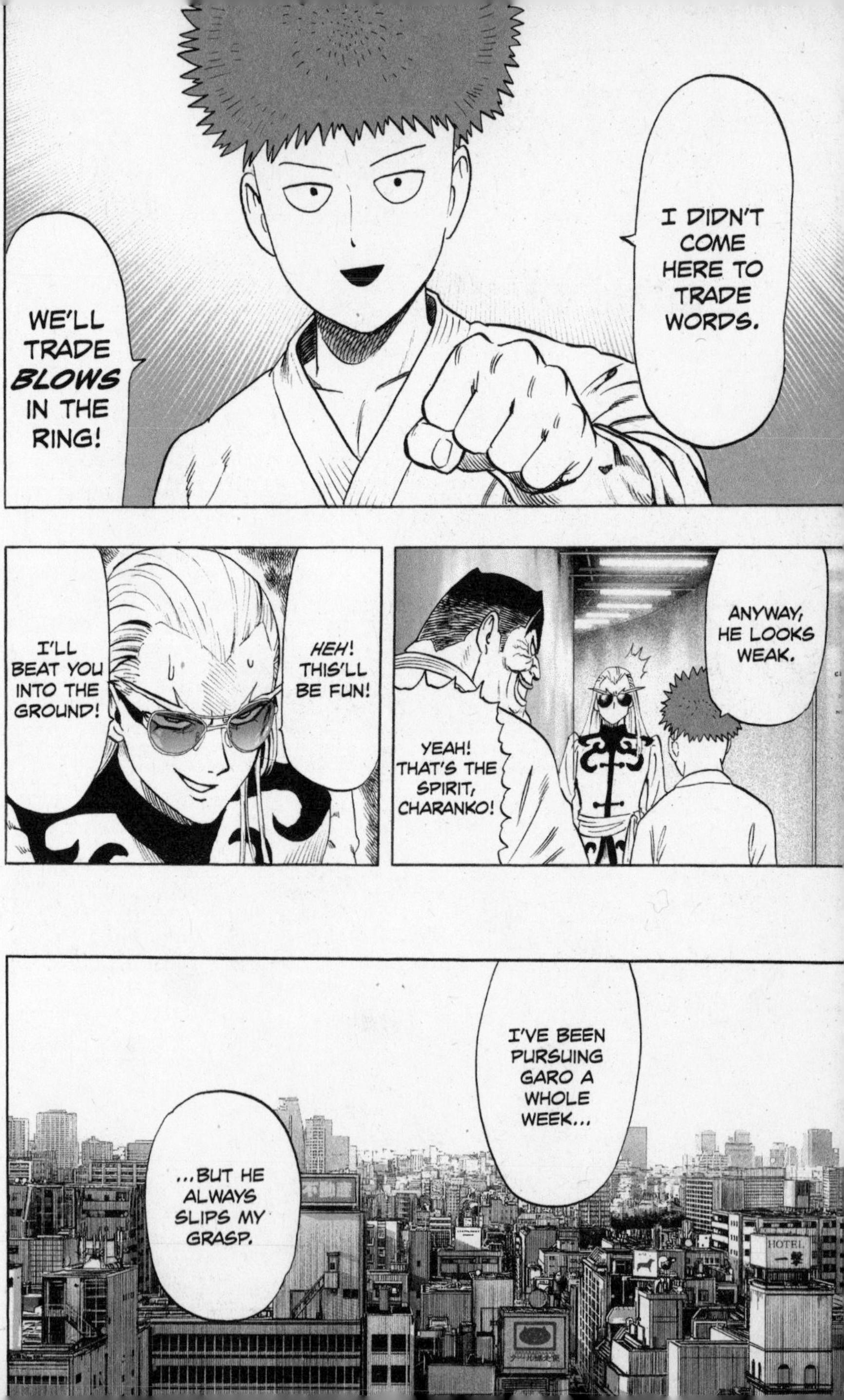
I DIDN'T COME HERE TO TRADE WORDS.
WE'LL TRADE *BLOWS* IN THE RING!
ANYWAY, HE LOOKS WEAK.
YEAH! THAT'S THE SPIRIT, CHARANKO!
HEH! THIS'LL BE FUN!
I'LL BEAT YOU INTO THE GROUND!
I'VE BEEN PURSUING GARO A WHOLE WEEK...
...BUT HE ALWAYS SLIPS MY GRASP.
HOTEL

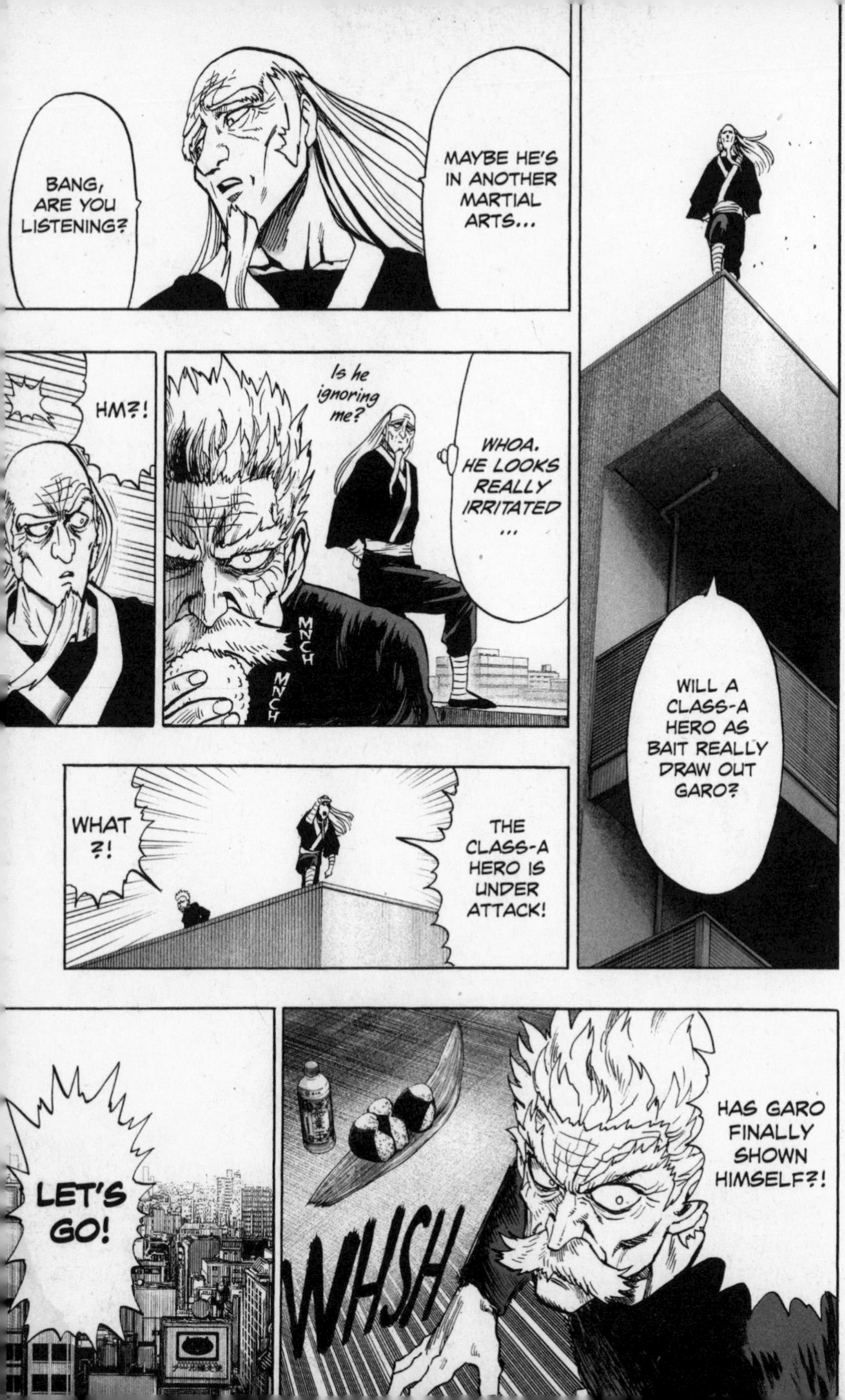
WILL A CLASS-A HERO AS BAIT REALLY DRAW OUT GARO?
MAYBE HE'S IN ANOTHER MARTIAL ARTS...
BANG, ARE YOU LISTENING?
WHOA. HE LOOKS REALLY IRRITATED...
Is he ignoring me?
MNCH
MNCH
HM?!
THE CLASS-A HERO IS UNDER ATTACK!
WHAT?!
HAS GARO FINALLY SHOWN HIMSELF?!
WHSH
LET'S GO!

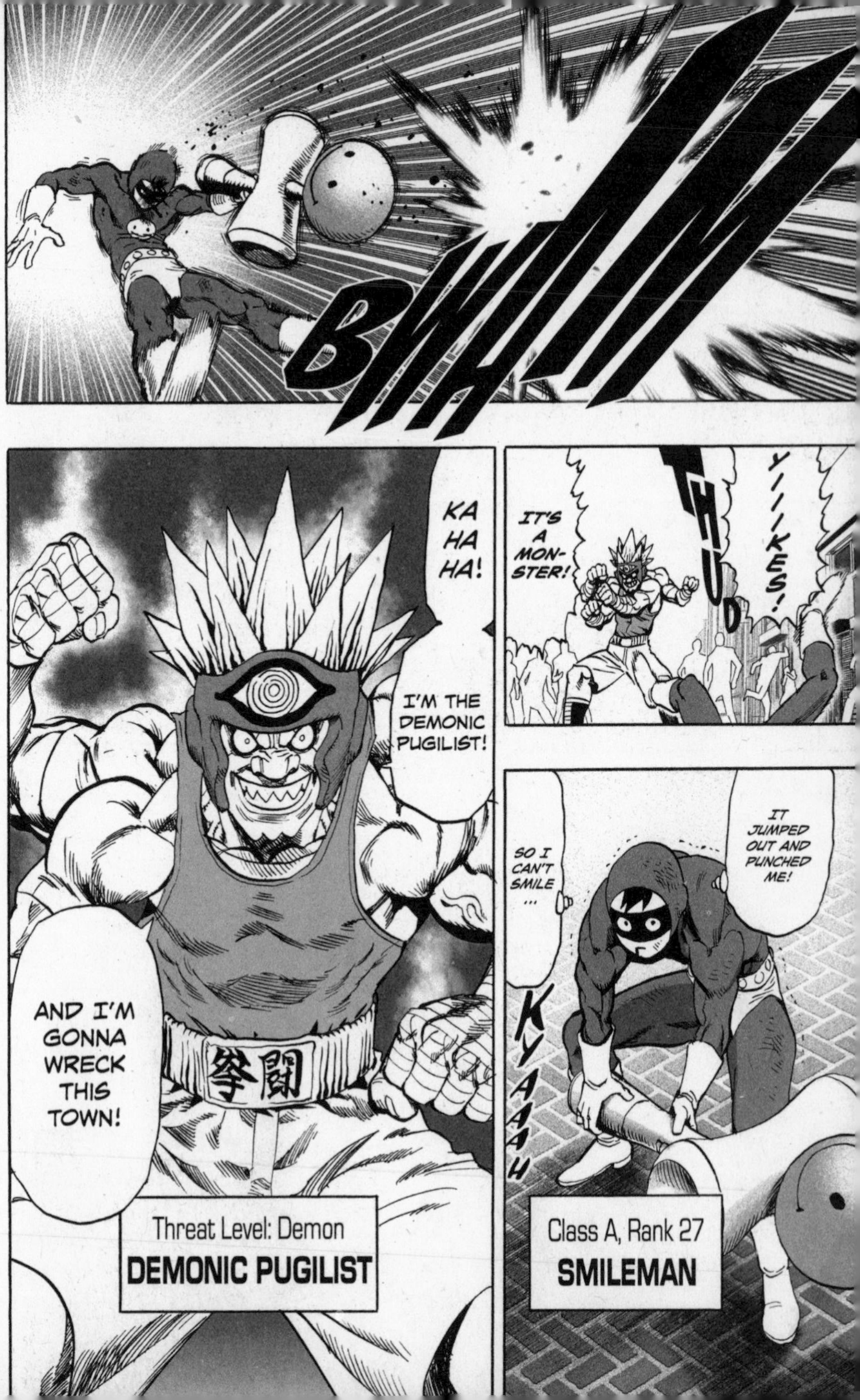
BWHM
YIIIKES!
THUD
IT'S A MONSTER!
IT JUMPED OUT AND PUNCHED ME!
SO I CAN'T SMILE...
KYAAAAH
Class A, Rank 27
SMILEMAN
KA HA HA!
I'M THE DEMONIC PUGILIST!
AND I'M GONNA WRECK THIS TOWN!
拳闘
Threat Level: Demon
DEMONIC PUGILIST

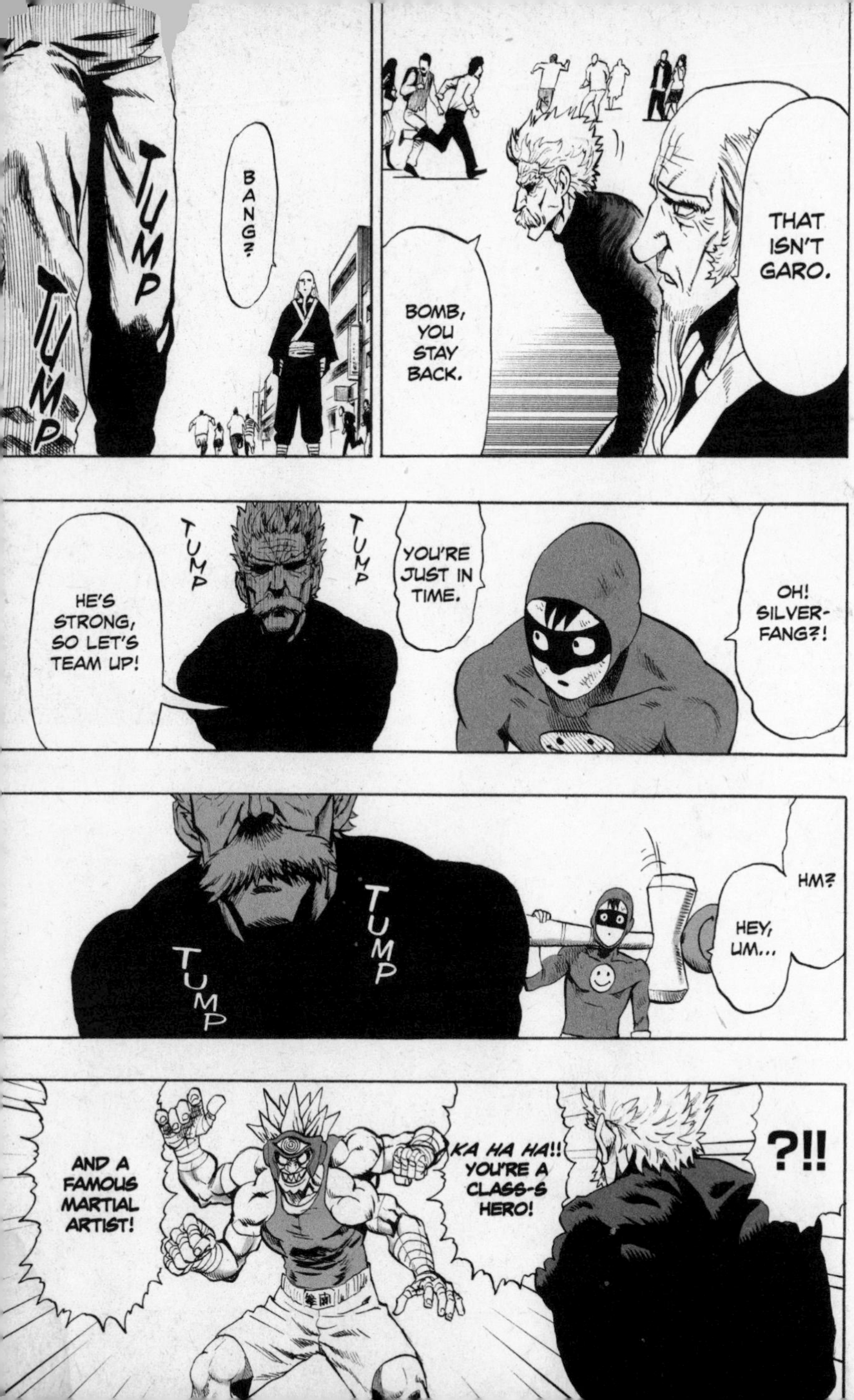
THAT ISN'T GARO.
BOMB, YOU STAY BACK.
BANG?
TUMP
TUMP
TUMP
OH! SILVER-FANG?!
YOU'RE JUST IN TIME.
TUMP
TUMP
HE'S STRONG, SO LET'S TEAM UP!
HM?
HEY, UM...
TUMP
TUMP
?!!
KA HA HA!! YOU'RE A CLASS-S HERO!
AND A FAMOUS MARTIAL ARTIST!

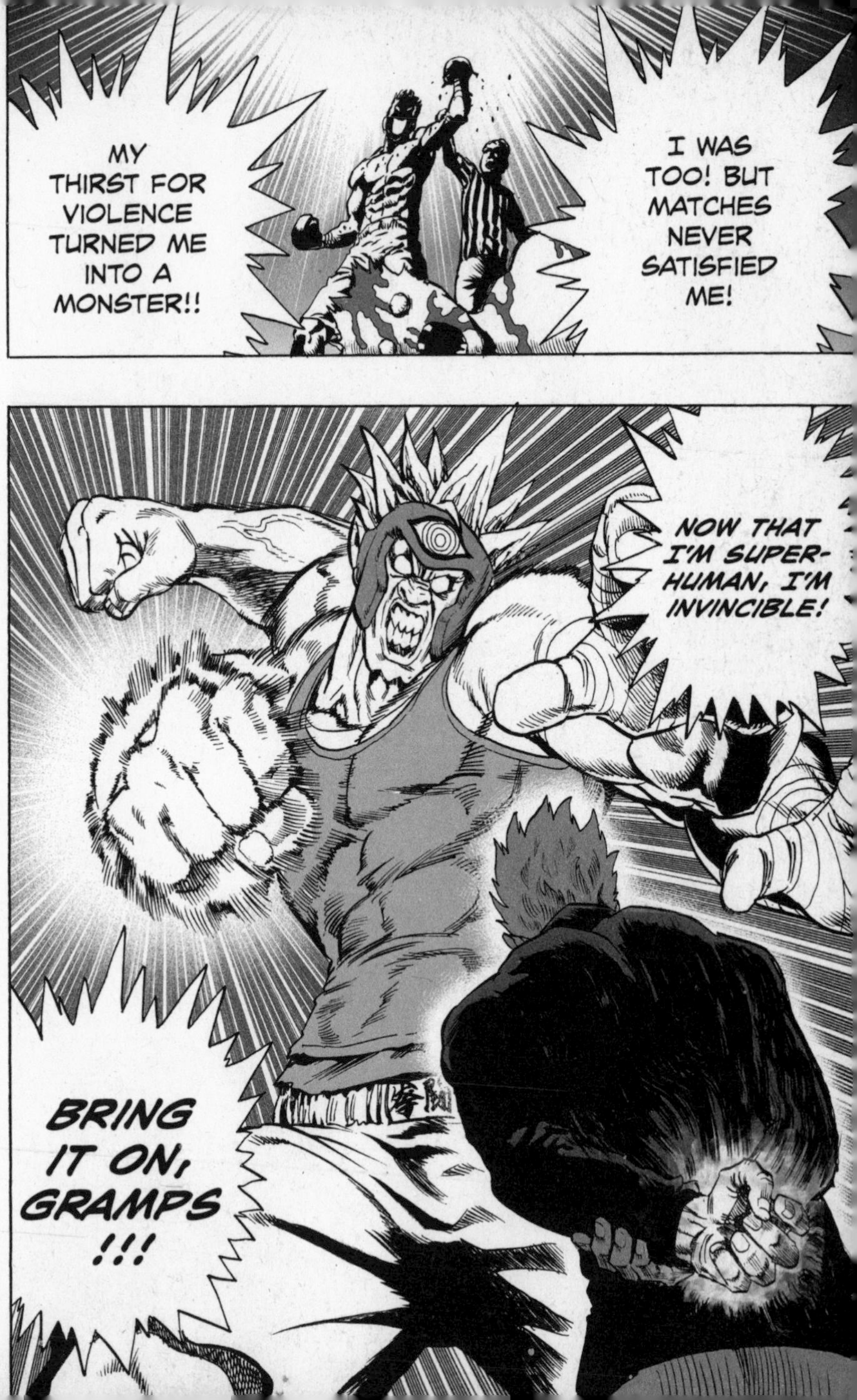
I WAS TOO! BUT MATCHES NEVER SATISFIED ME!
MY THIRST FOR VIOLENCE TURNED ME INTO A MONSTER!!
NOW THAT I'M SUPER-HUMAN, I'M INVINCIBLE!
BRING IT ON, GRAMPS !!!

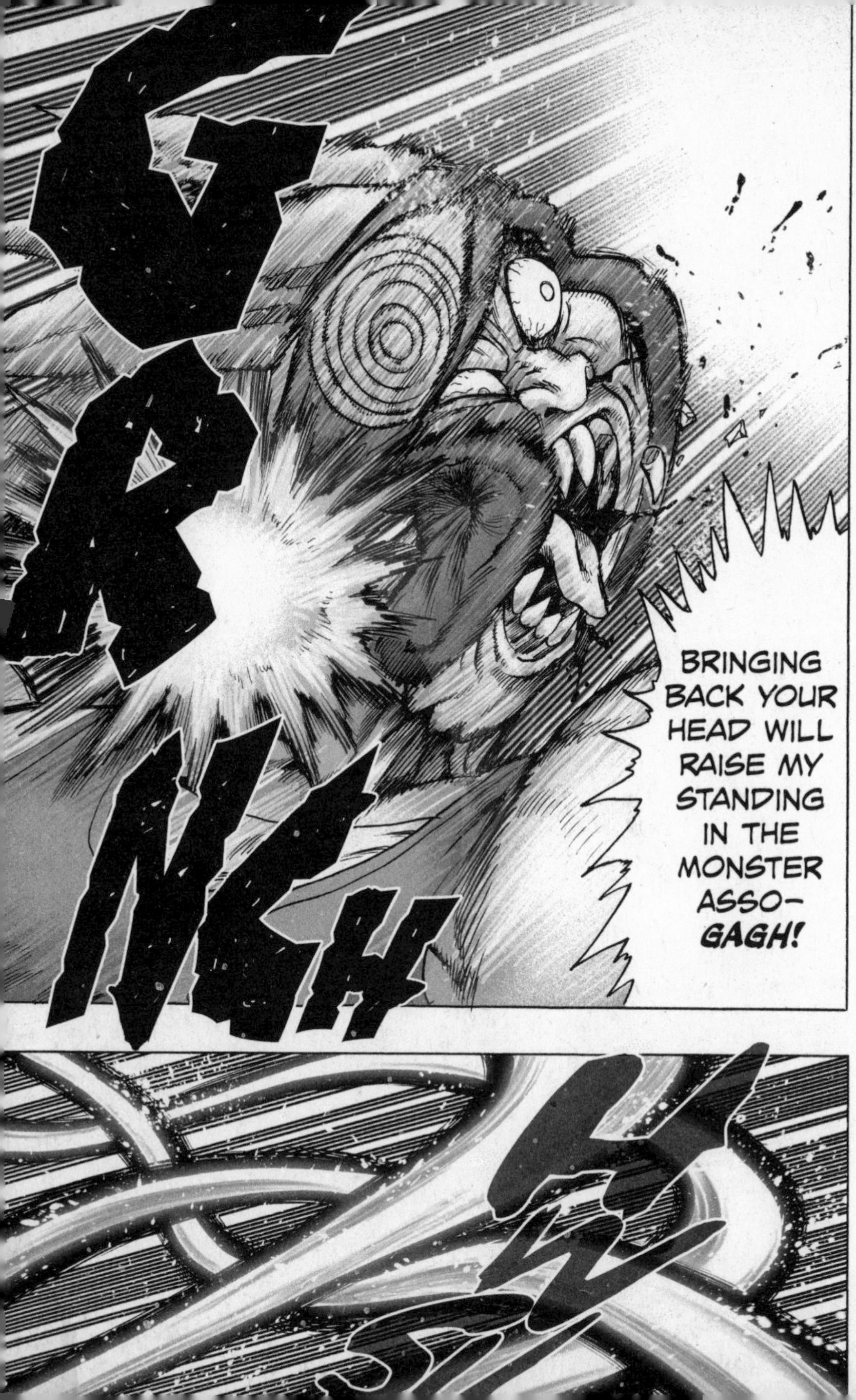
BRINGING BACK YOUR HEAD WILL RAISE MY STANDING IN THE MONSTER ASSO- GAGH!

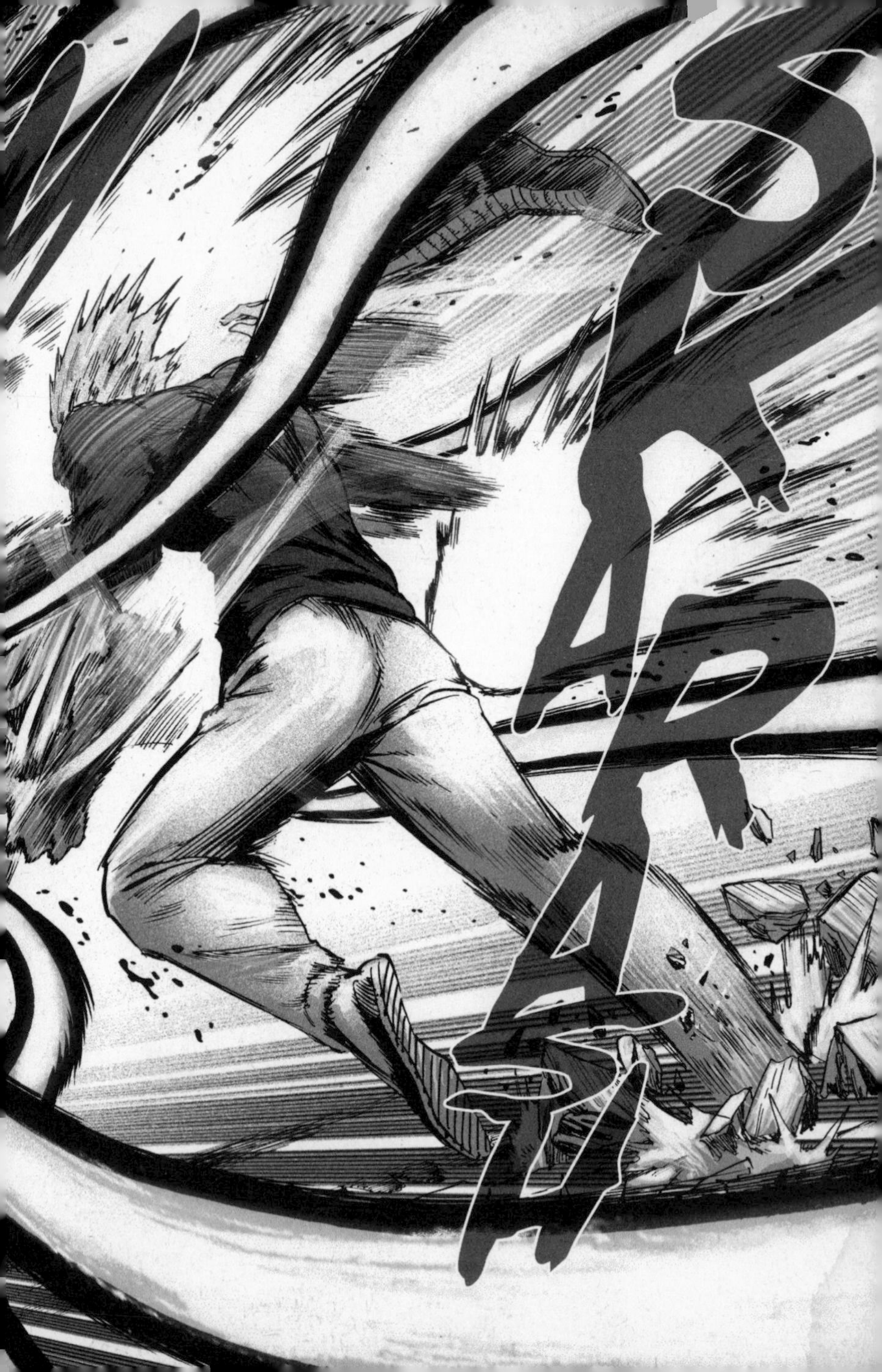

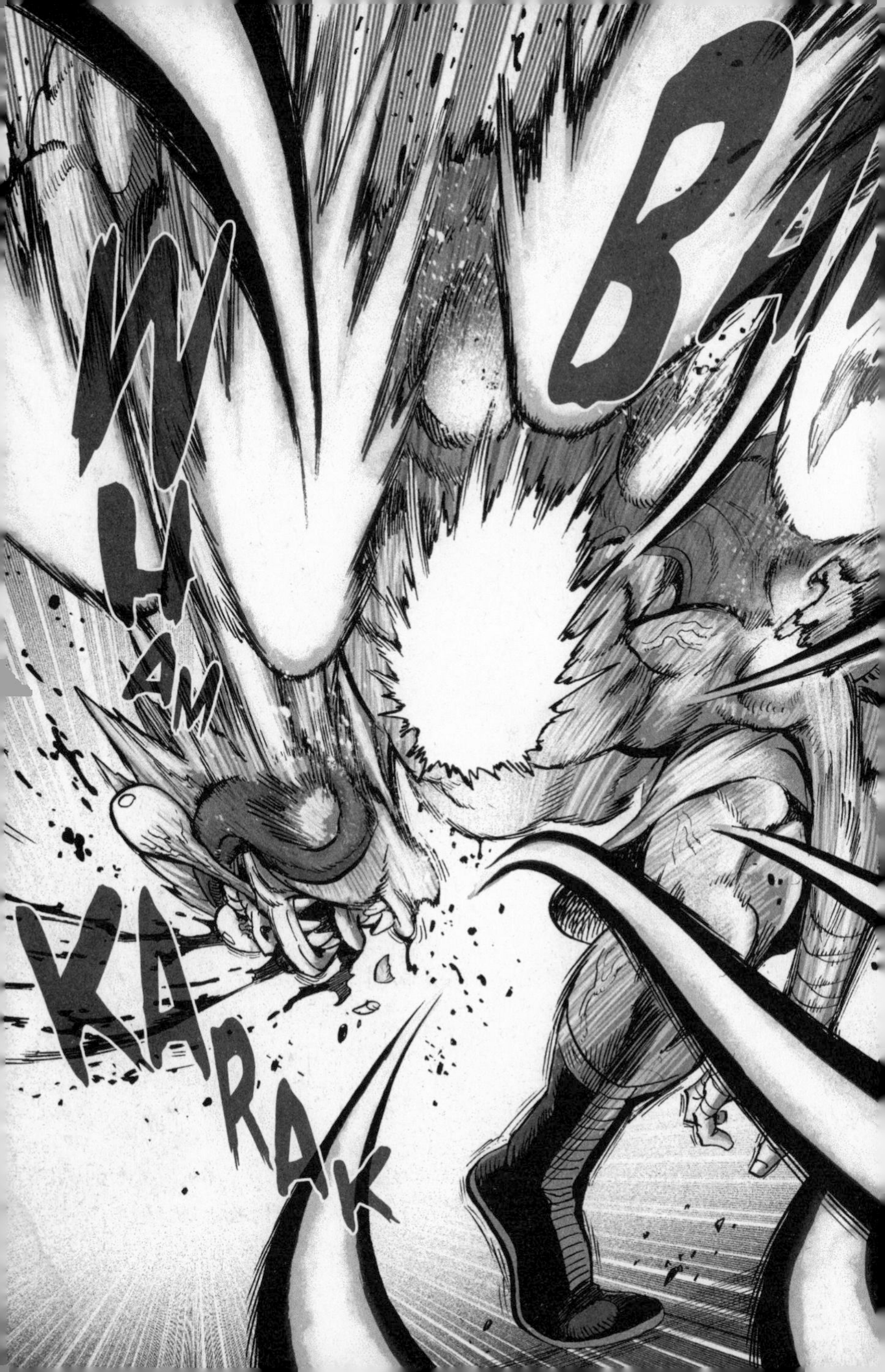
BA
WHAM
KARAK

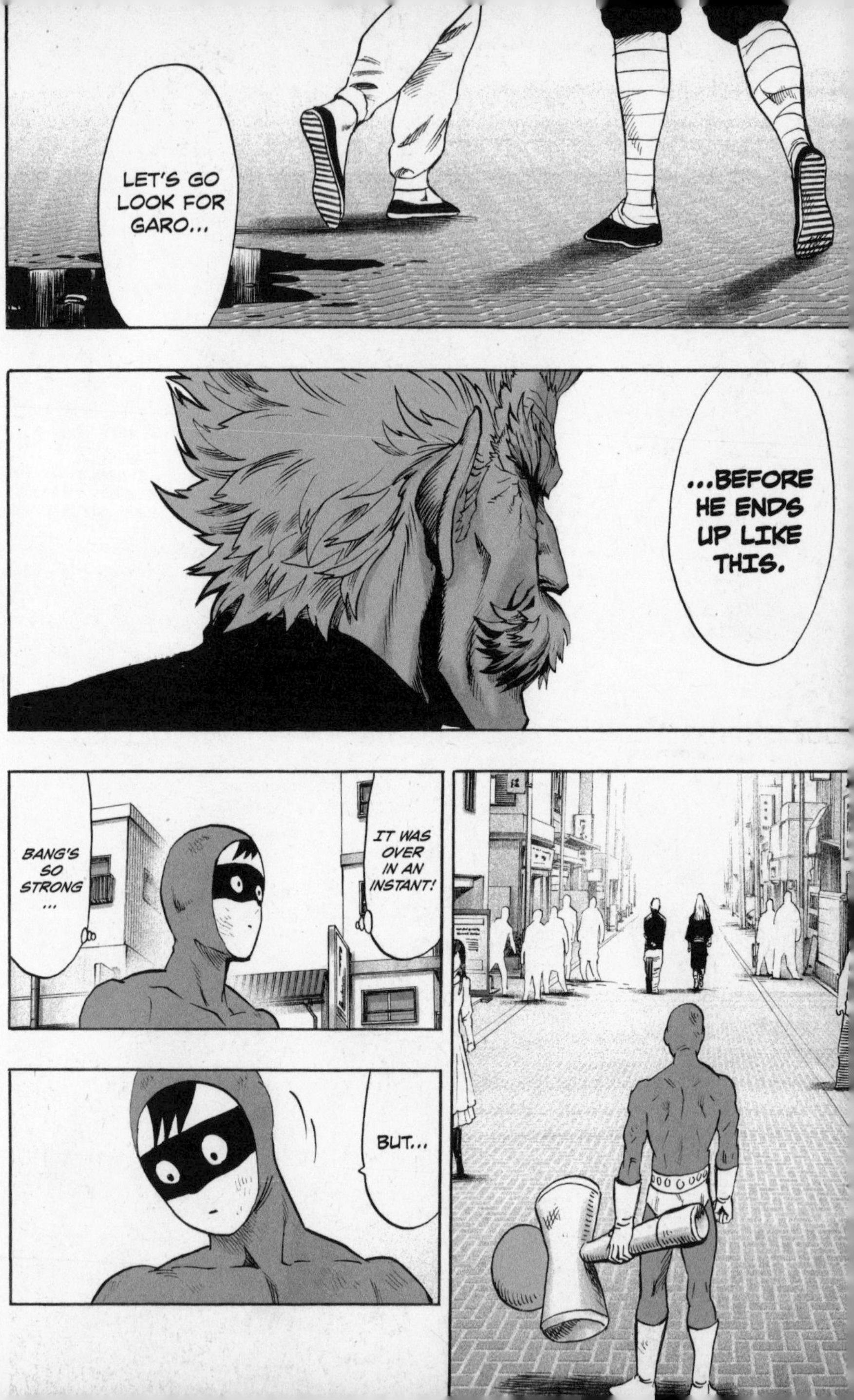
LET'S GO LOOK FOR GARO...
...BEFORE HE ENDS UP LIKE THIS.
IT WAS OVER IN AN INSTANT!
BANG'S SO STRONG ...
BUT...

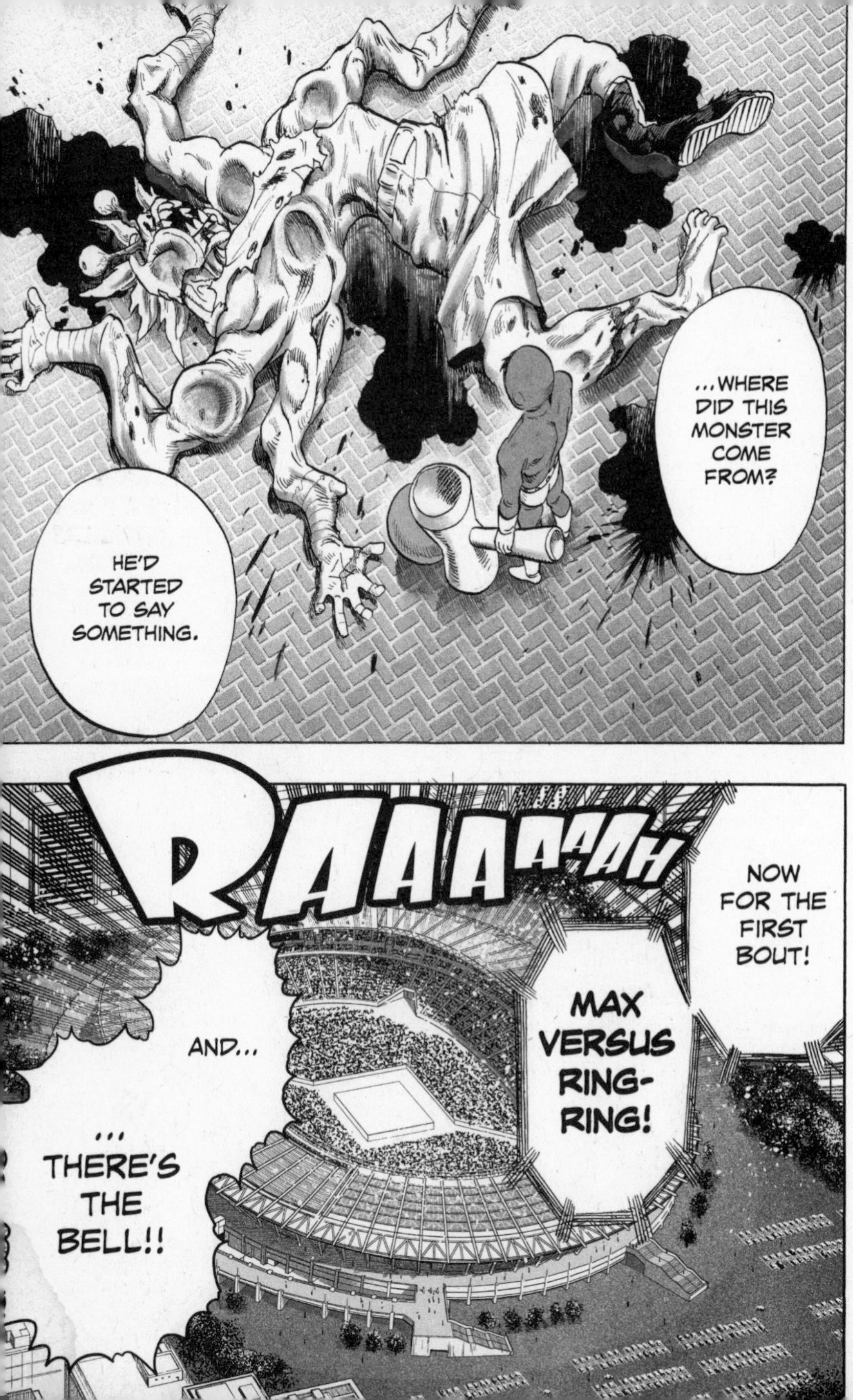
...WHERE DID THIS MONSTER COME FROM?
HE'D STARTED TO SAY SOMETHING.
RAAAAAAH
NOW FOR THE FIRST BOUT!
MAX VERSUS RING-RING!
AND...
...THERE'S THE BELL!!

PUNCH 61: DARK HORSE

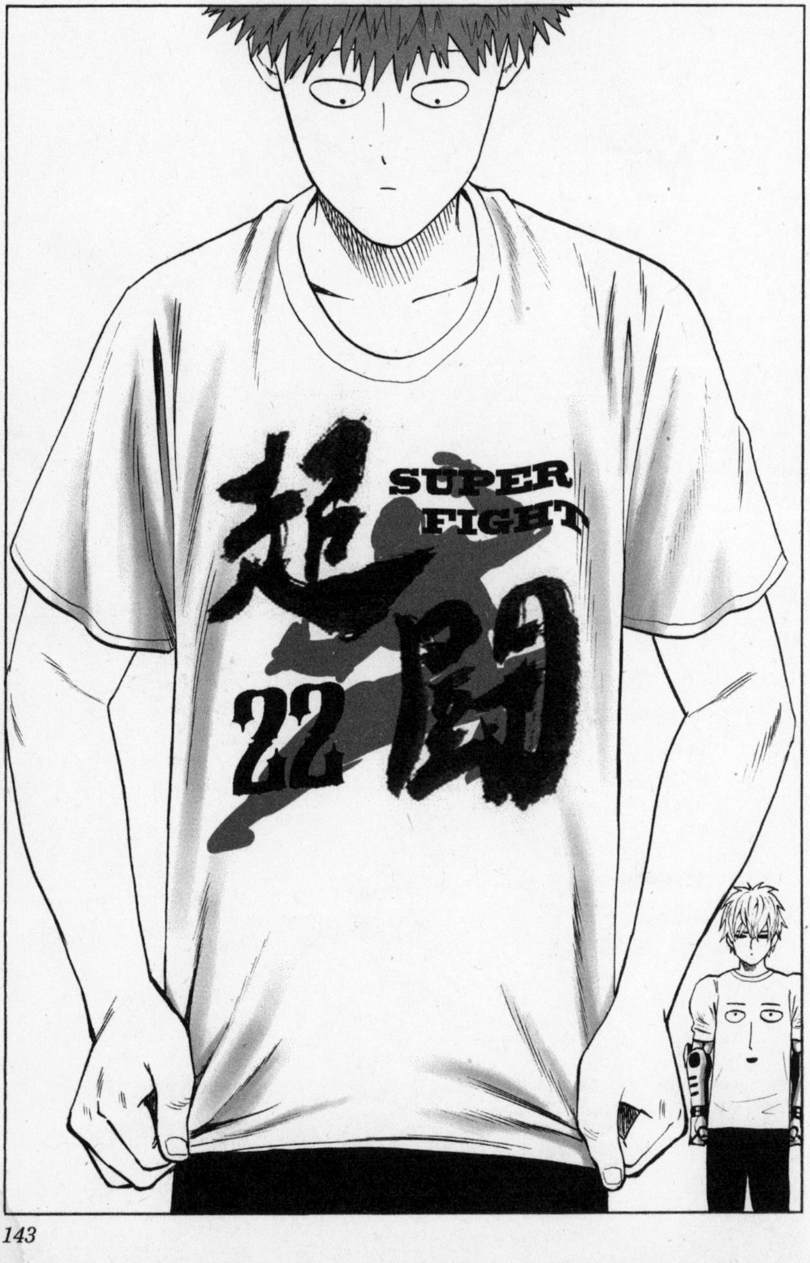

超闘
SUPER FIGHT
22

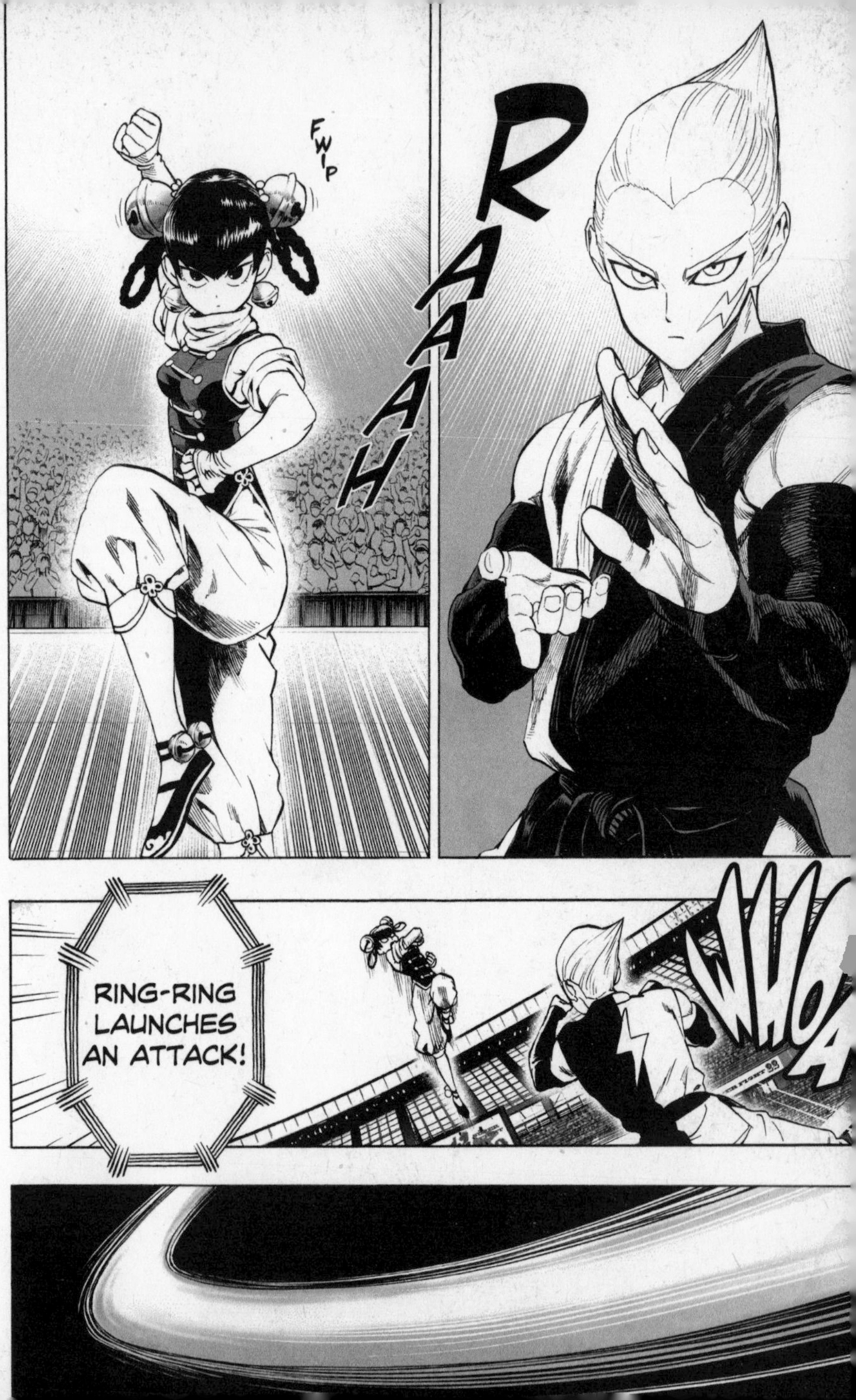
RAAAAH
FWIP
WHOA
RING-RING LAUNCHES AN ATTACK!

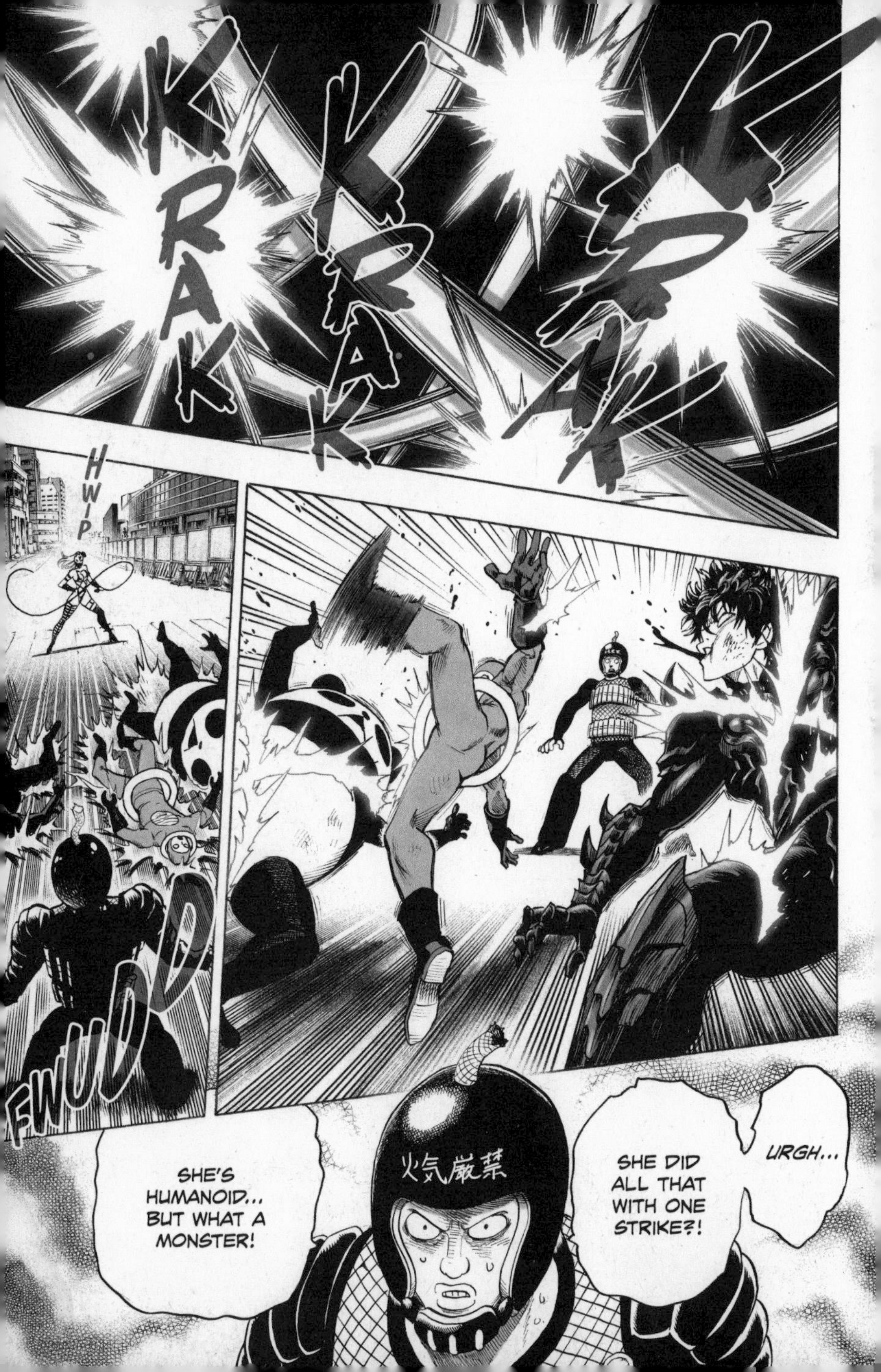
KRAK
KRAK
KRAK
HWIP
FWUD
URGH...
SHE DID ALL THAT WITH ONE STRIKE?!
火気厳禁
SHE'S HUMANOID... BUT WHAT A MONSTER!

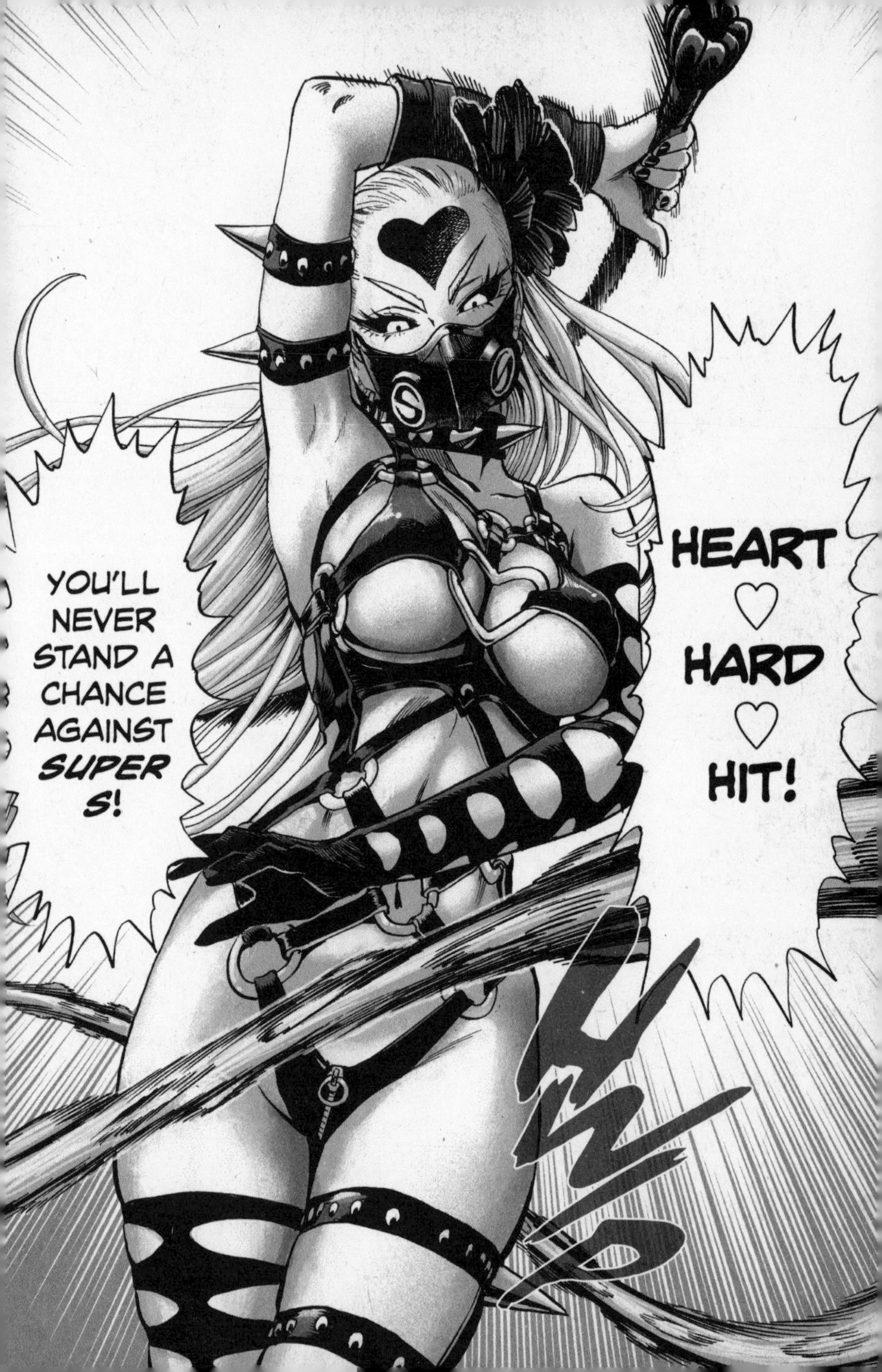
HEART ♡ HARD ♡ HIT!
YOU'LL NEVER STAND A CHANCE AGAINST *SUPER S*!

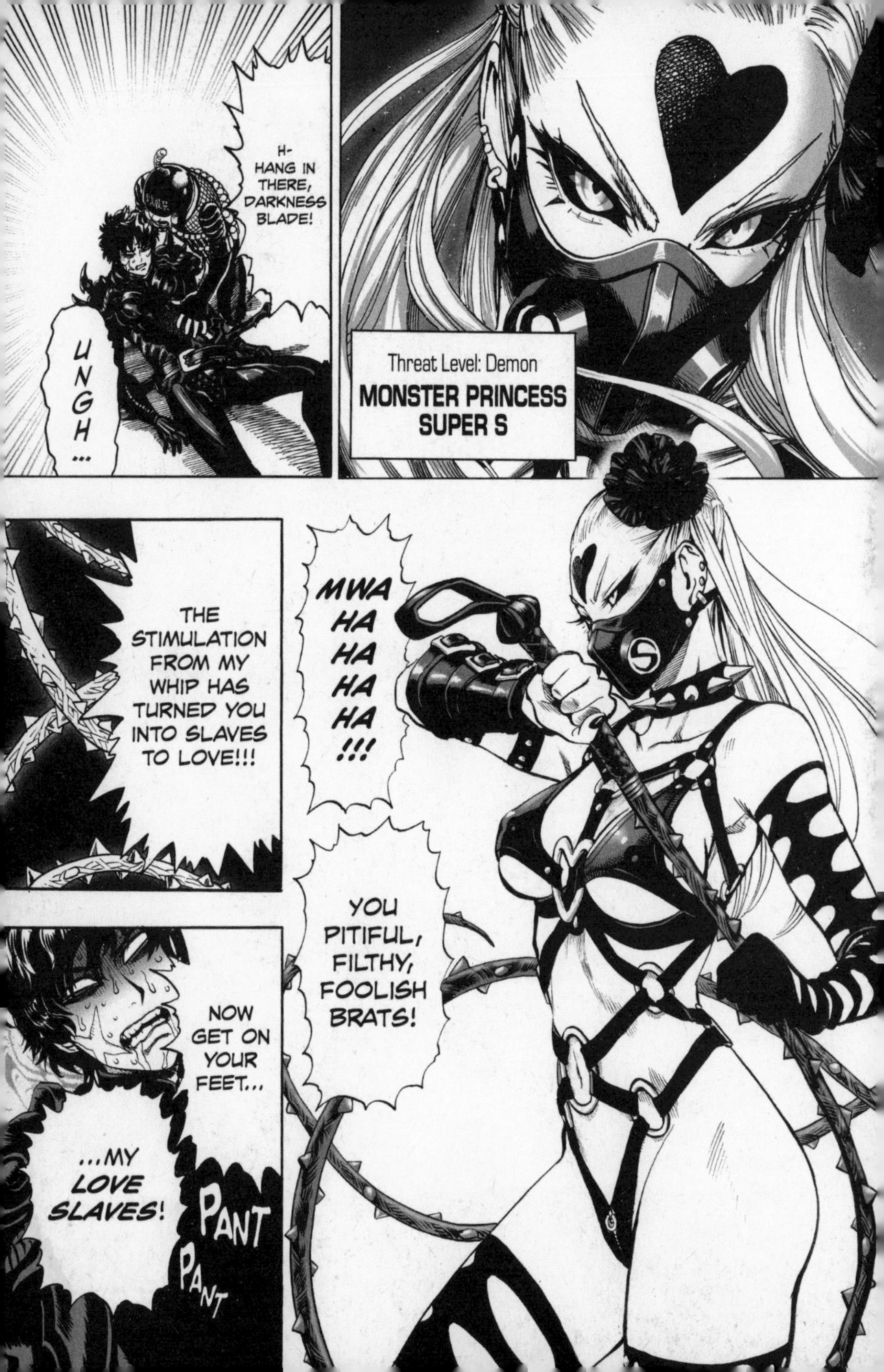
Threat Level: Demon
MONSTER PRINCESS SUPER S
H- HANG IN THERE, DARKNESS BLADE!
UNGH...
MWA HA HA HA HA!!!
YOU PITIFUL, FILTHY, FOOLISH BRATS!
THE STIMULATION FROM MY WHIP HAS TURNED YOU INTO SLAVES TO LOVE!!!
NOW GET ON YOUR FEET...
...MY LOVE SLAVES!
PANT
PANT

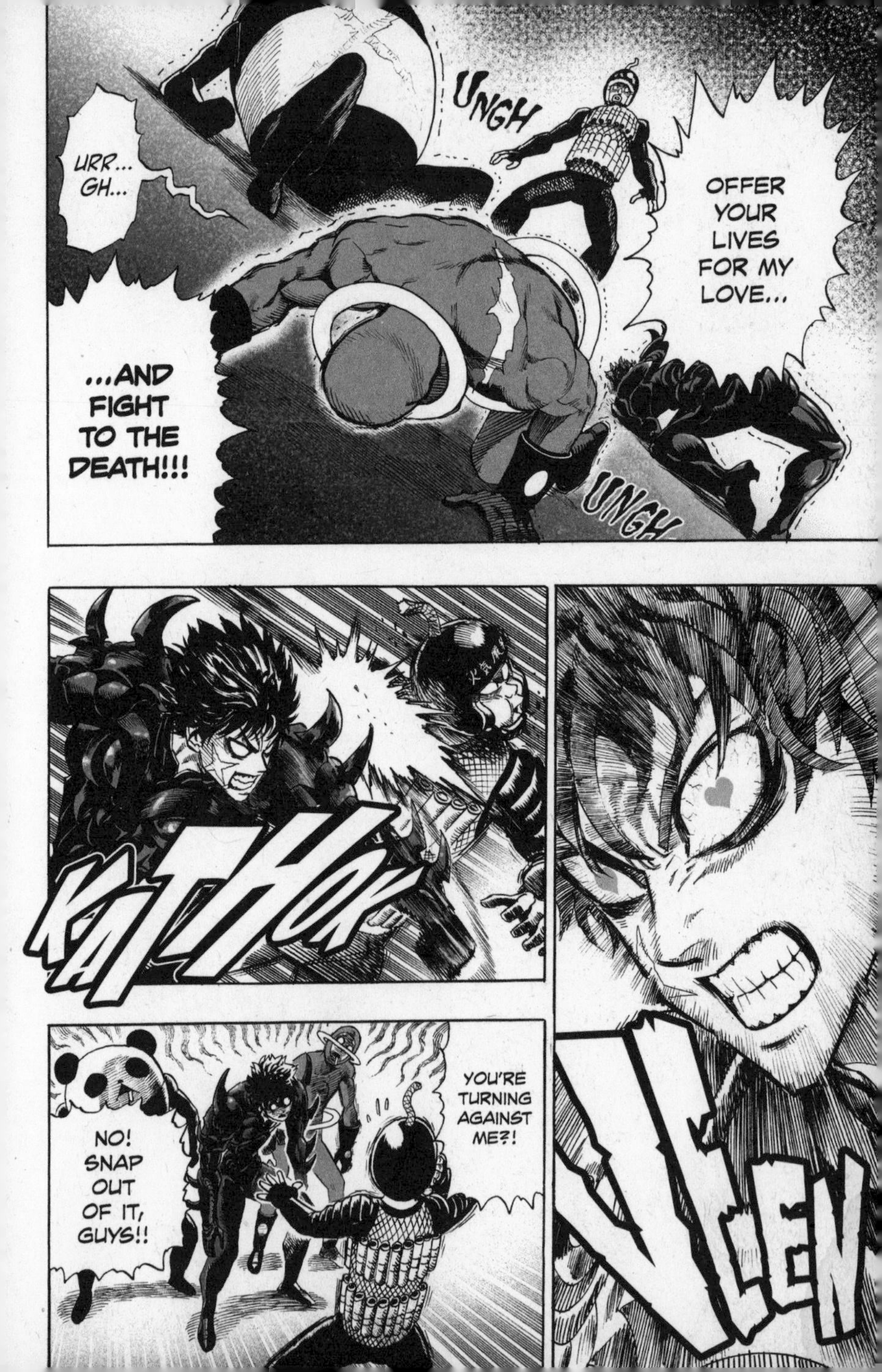

OFFER YOUR LIVES FOR MY LOVE...
UNGH
URR... GH...
...AND FIGHT TO THE DEATH!!!
UNGH
KATHOK
YOU'RE TURNING AGAINST ME?!
NO! SNAP OUT OF IT, GUYS!!

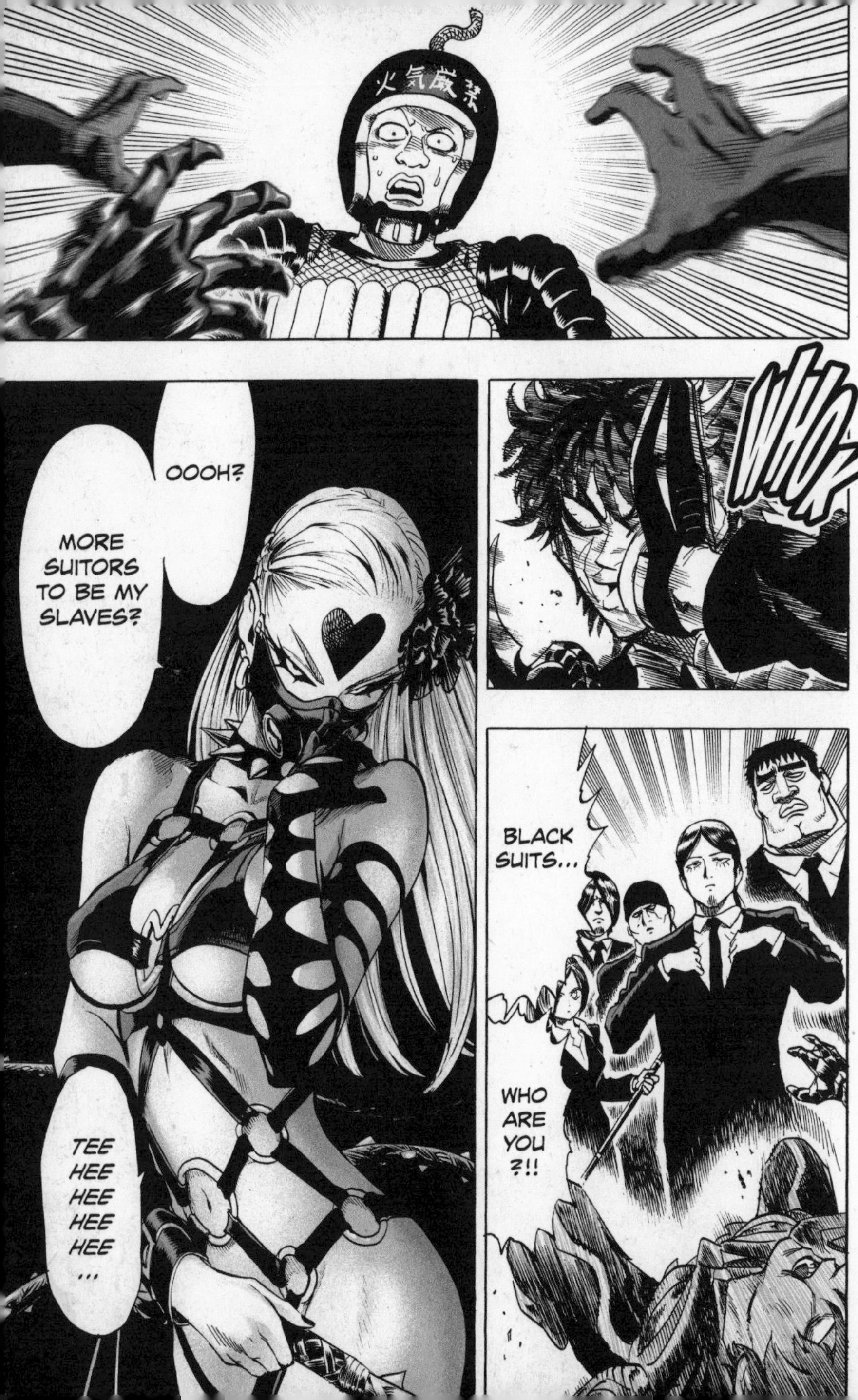
火気厳禁
WHOK
BLACK SUITS...
WHO ARE YOU ?!!
OOOH?
MORE SUITORS TO BE MY SLAVES?
TEE HEE HEE HEE HEE ...

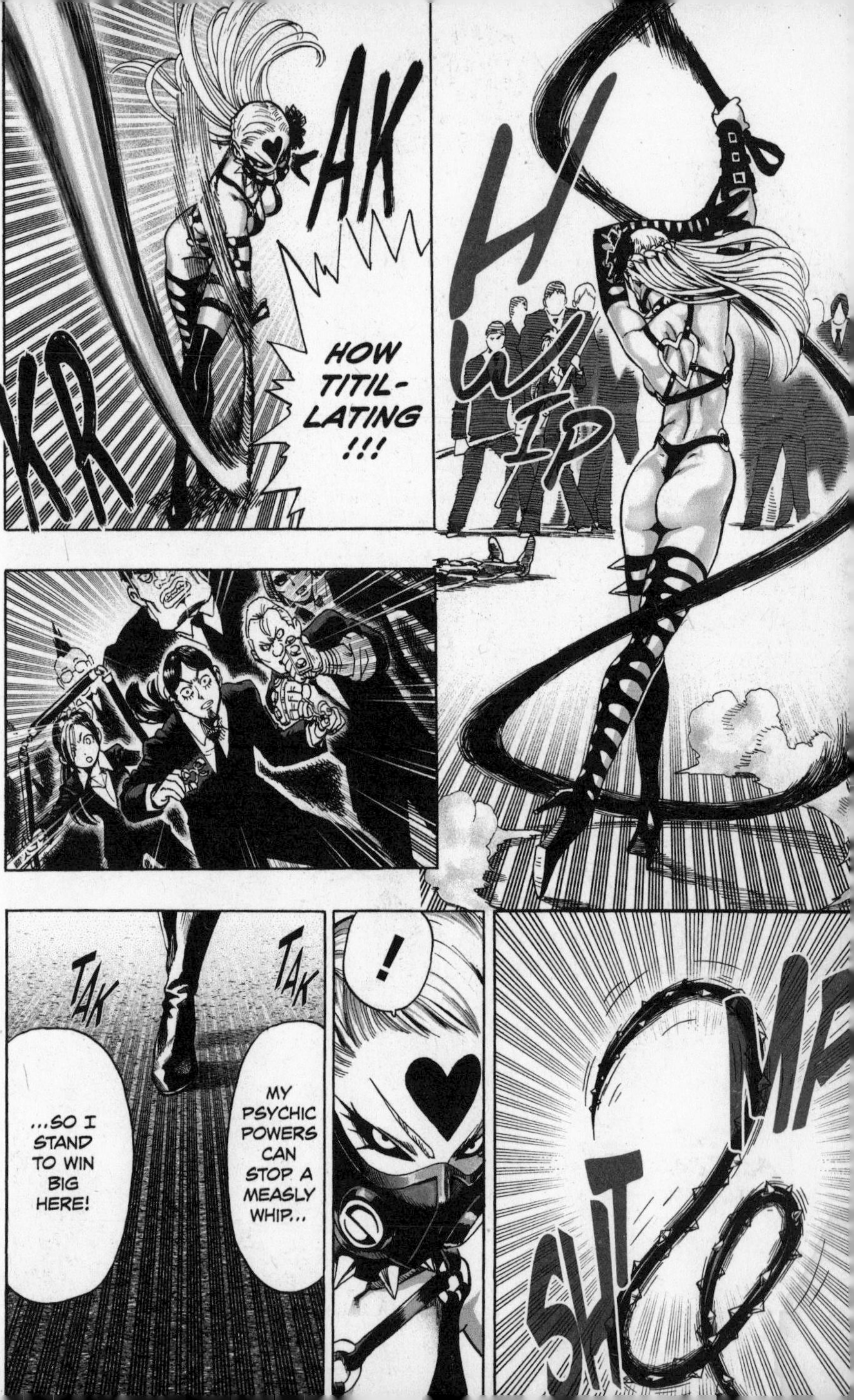
WHIP
KRAK
HOW TITIL-LATING !!!
!
MY PSYCHIC POWERS CAN STOP A MEASLY WHIP...
TAK TAK
...SO I STAND TO WIN BIG HERE!

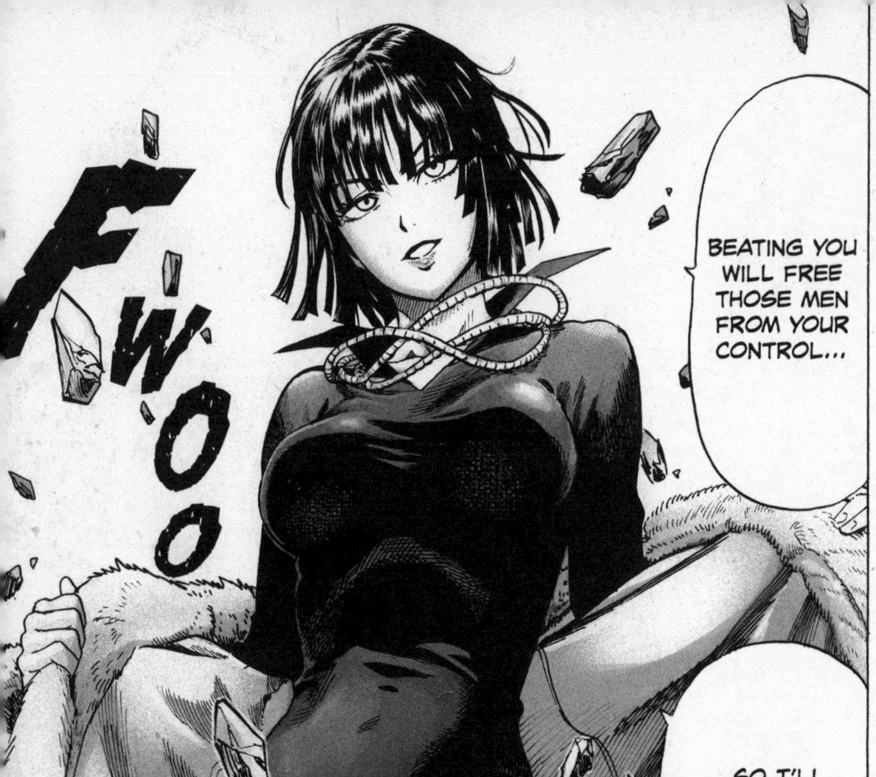
BEATING YOU WILL FREE THOSE MEN FROM YOUR CONTROL...
FWOOO
...SO I'LL SCORE A HEROIC DEED *AND* PUT THEM IN MY DEBT!

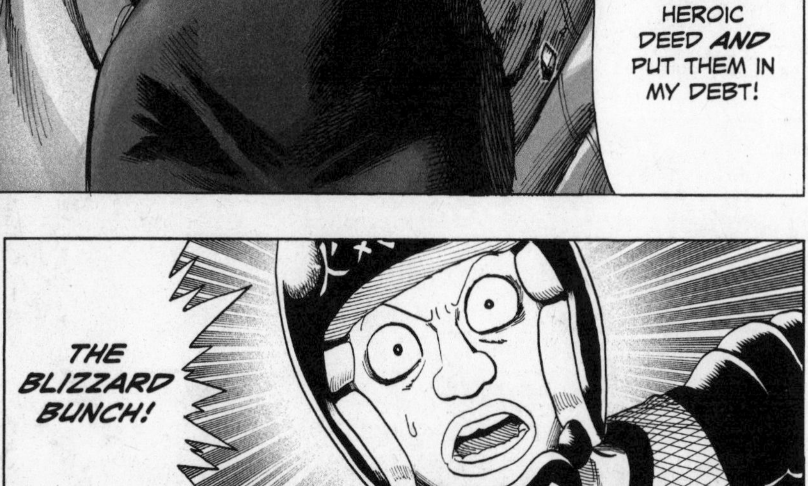
THE BLIZZARD BUNCH!

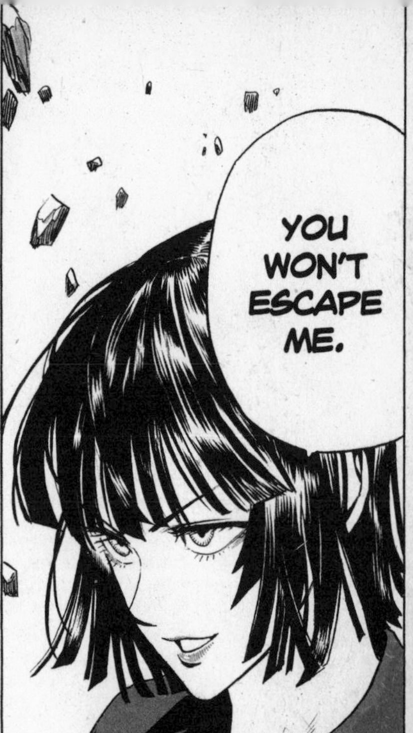
YOU WON'T ESCAPE ME.

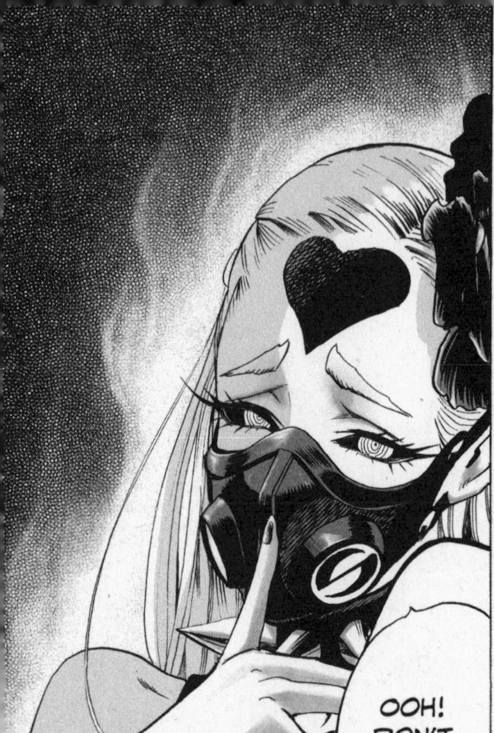
OOH! DON'T TICKLE MY SADISM!
I MIGHT GET TOO EXCITED AND KILL YOU!

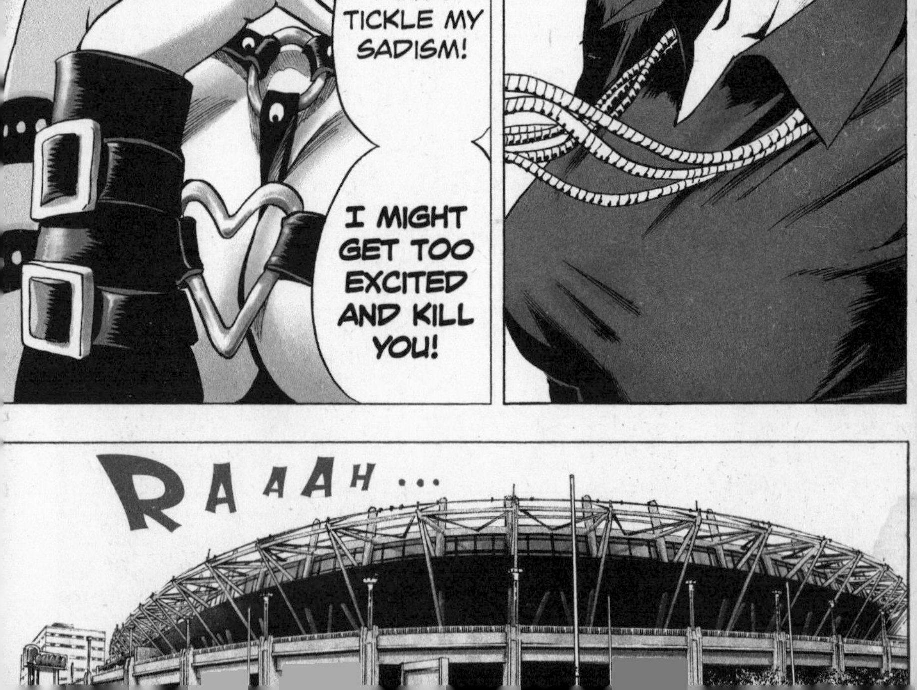
RAAAH ...

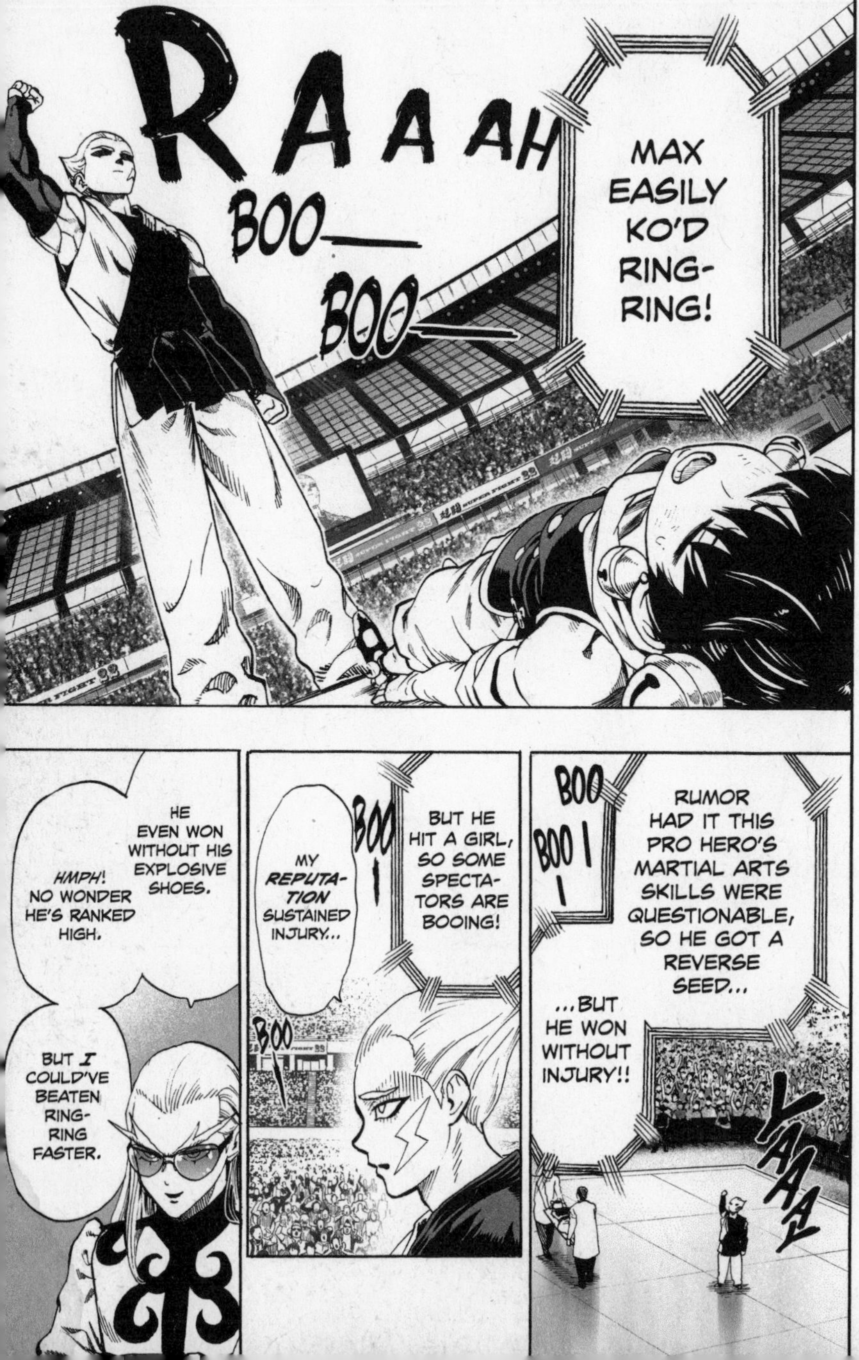
MAX EASILY KO'D RING-RING!
RAAAH
BOO—
BOO—
BOO
BOO
RUMOR HAD IT THIS PRO HERO'S MARTIAL ARTS SKILLS WERE QUESTIONABLE, SO HE GOT A REVERSE SEED...
...BUT HE WON WITHOUT INJURY!!
YAAAY
BUT HE HIT A GIRL, SO SOME SPECTATORS ARE BOOING!
BOO
MY *REPUTATION* SUSTAINED INJURY...
BOO
HE EVEN WON WITHOUT HIS EXPLOSIVE SHOES.
HMPH! NO WONDER HE'S RANKED HIGH.
BUT *I* COULD'VE BEATEN RING-RING FASTER.

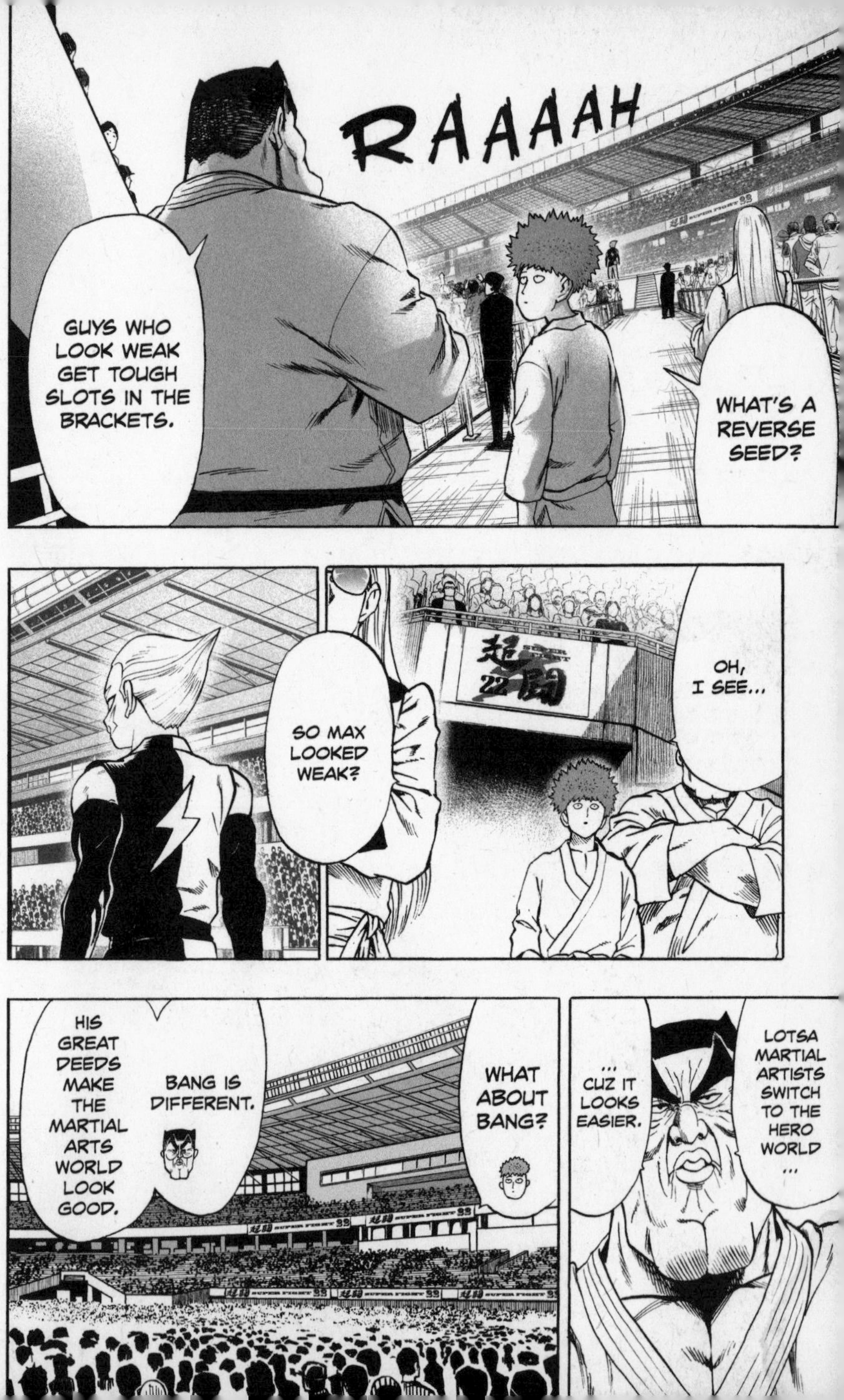
RAAAAH
WHAT'S A REVERSE SEED?
GUYS WHO LOOK WEAK GET TOUGH SLOTS IN THE BRACKETS.
OH, I SEE...
SO MAX LOOKED WEAK?
LOTSA MARTIAL ARTISTS SWITCH TO THE HERO WORLD ...
... CUZ IT LOOKS EASIER.
WHAT ABOUT BANG?
BANG IS DIFFERENT.
HIS GREAT DEEDS MAKE THE MARTIAL ARTS WORLD LOOK GOOD.

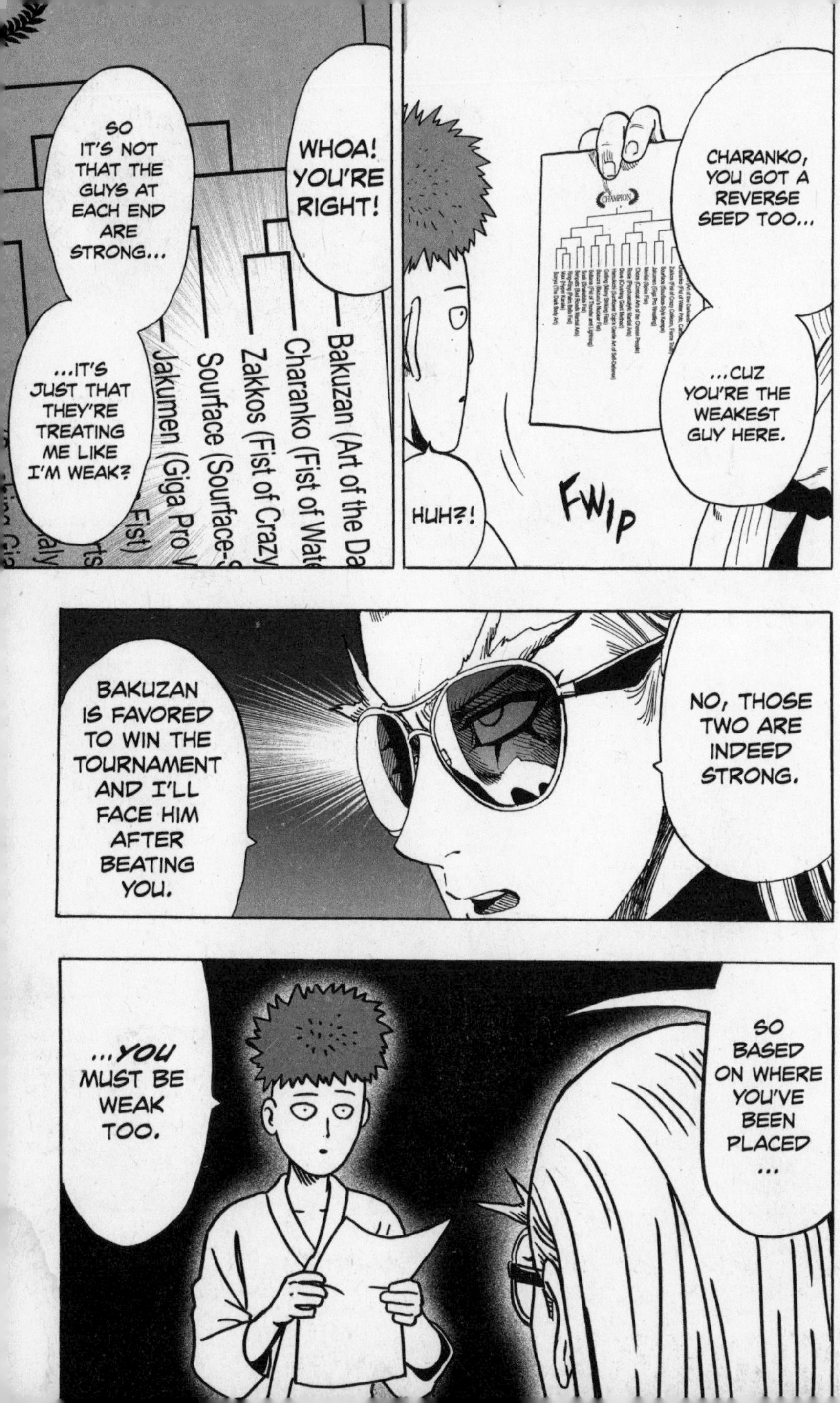
CHARANKO, YOU GOT A REVERSE SEED TOO...
...CUZ YOU'RE THE WEAKEST GUY HERE.
FWIP
HUH?!
WHOA! YOU'RE RIGHT!
SO IT'S NOT THAT THE GUYS AT EACH END ARE STRONG...
...IT'S JUST THAT THEY'RE TREATING ME LIKE I'M WEAK?
Bakuzan (Art of the Da
Charanko (Fist of Wate
Zakkos (Fist of Crazy
Sourface (Sourface-S
NO, THOSE TWO ARE INDEED STRONG.
BAKUZAN IS FAVORED TO WIN THE TOURNAMENT AND I'LL FACE HIM AFTER BEATING YOU.
SO BASED ON WHERE YOU'VE BEEN PLACED...
...*YOU* MUST BE WEAK TOO.

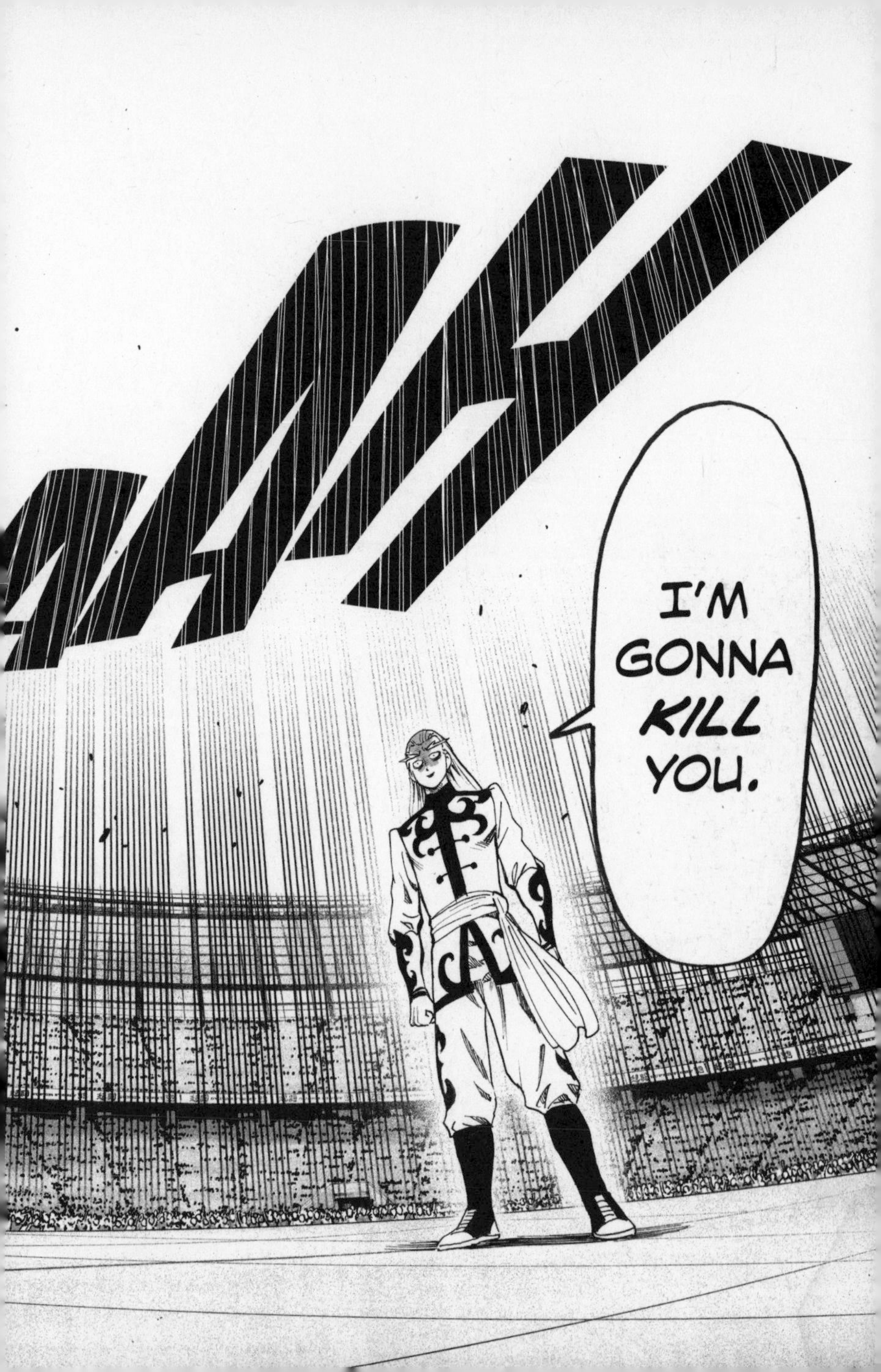
I'M GONNA KILL YOU.

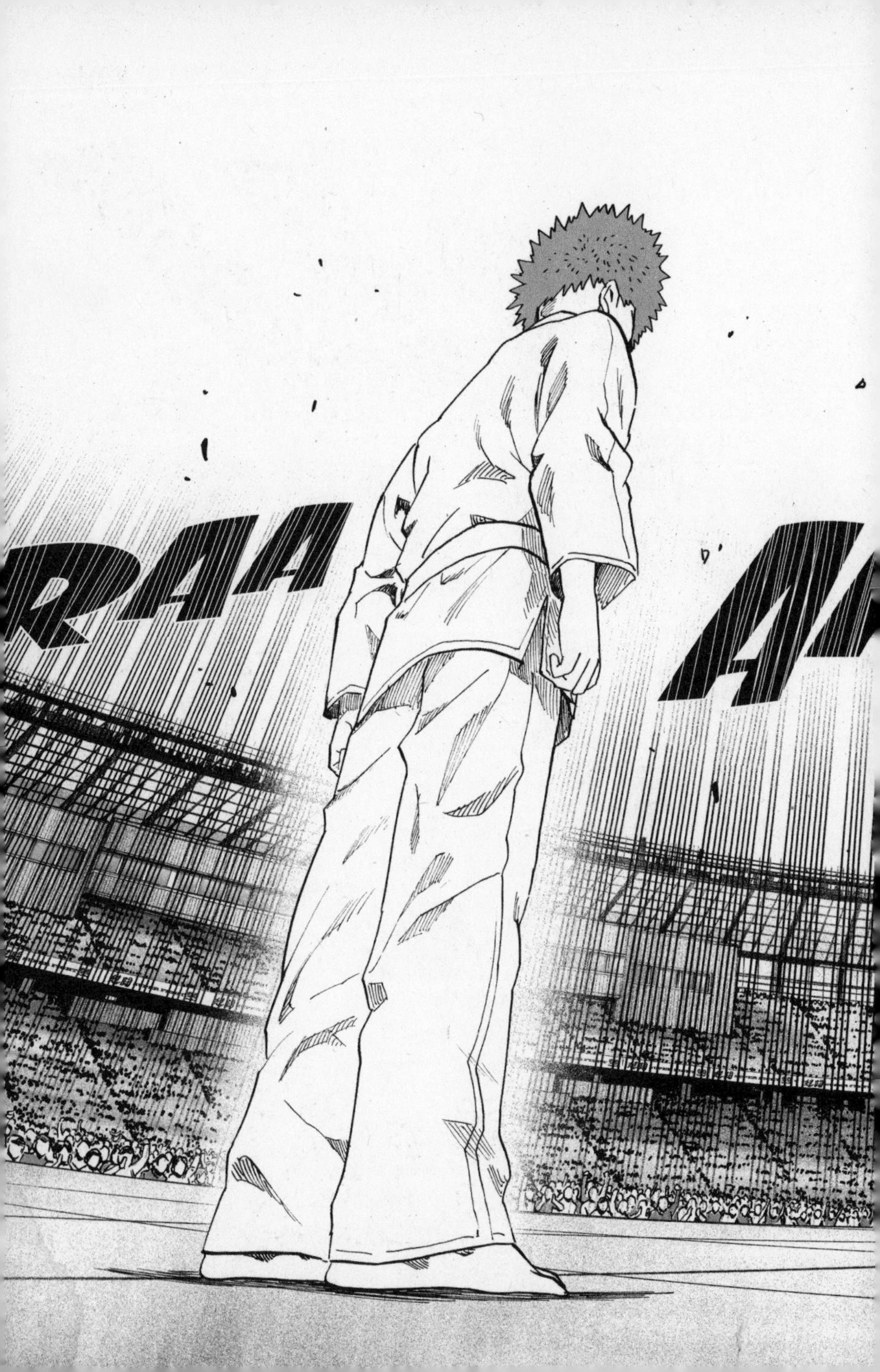
RAAA
AA

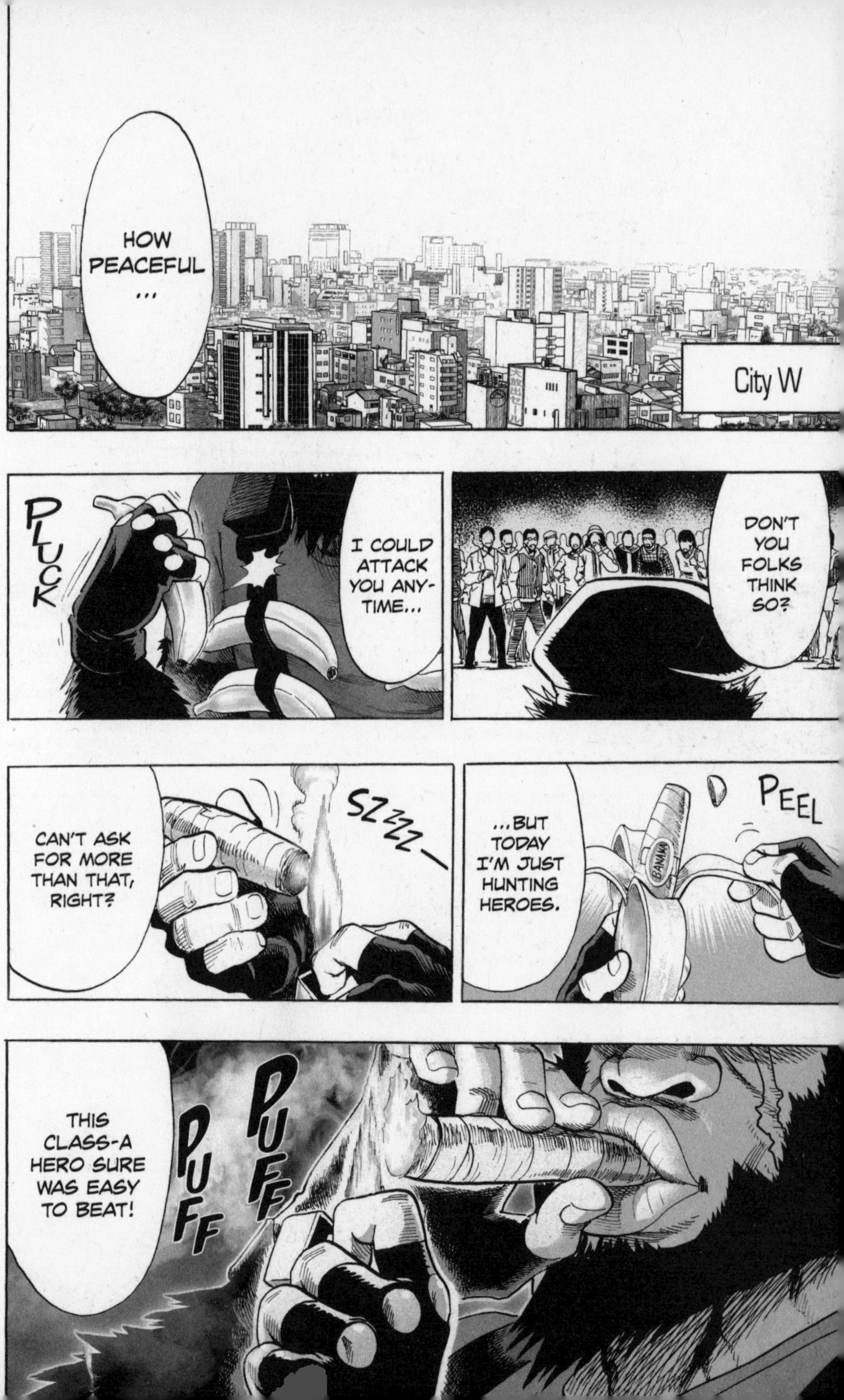
City W
HOW PEACEFUL ...
DON'T YOU FOLKS THINK SO?
I COULD ATTACK YOU ANY-TIME...
PLUCK
PEEL
...BUT TODAY I'M JUST HUNTING HEROES.
BANANA
SZZZZ-
CAN'T ASK FOR MORE THAN THAT, RIGHT?
PUFF
PUFF
THIS CLASS-A HERO SURE WAS EASY TO BEAT!

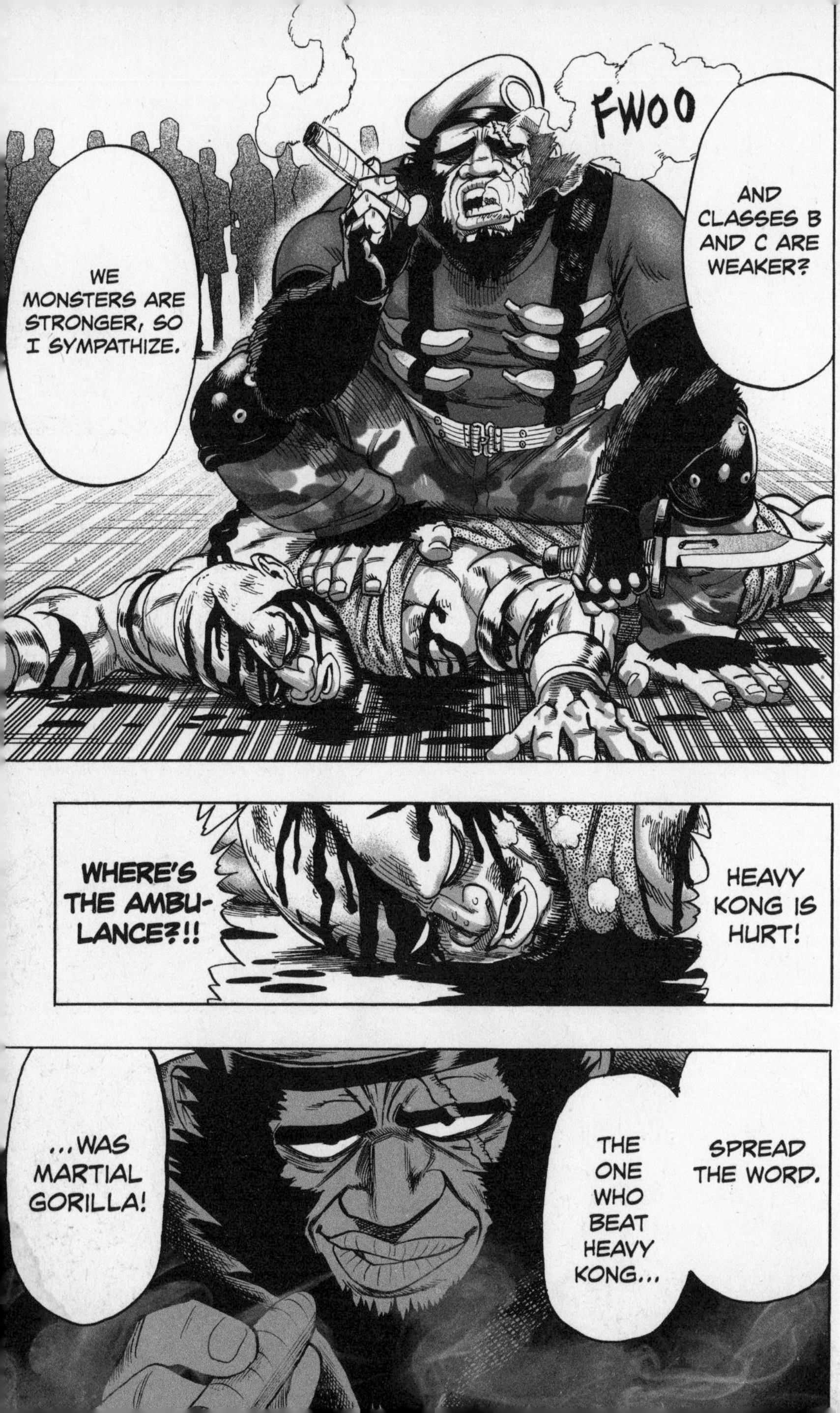
AND CLASSES B AND C ARE WEAKER?
FWOO
WE MONSTERS ARE STRONGER, SO I SYMPATHIZE.
HEAVY KONG IS HURT!
WHERE'S THE AMBULANCE?!!
SPREAD THE WORD.
THE ONE WHO BEAT HEAVY KONG...
...WAS MARTIAL GORILLA!

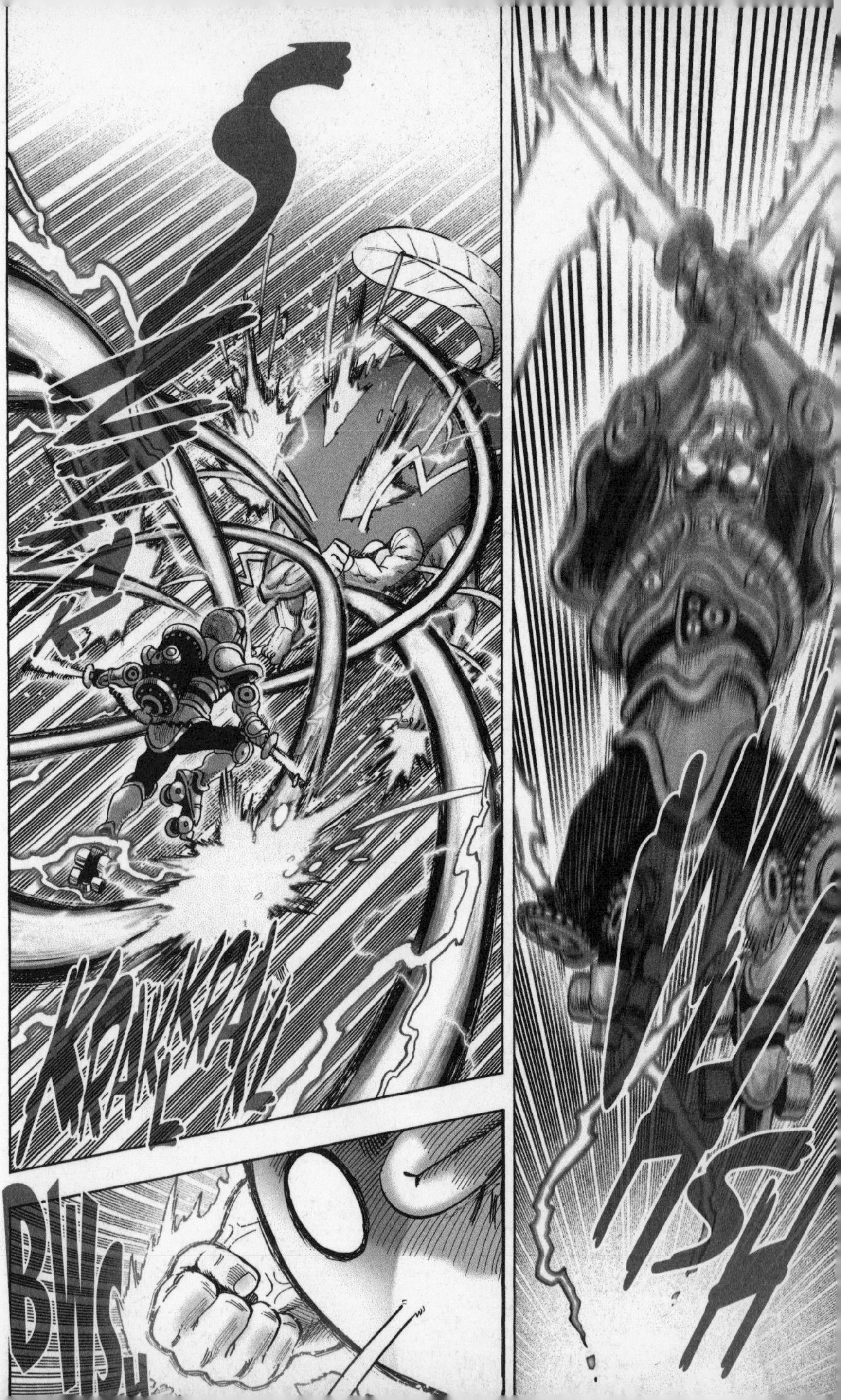
BWSH

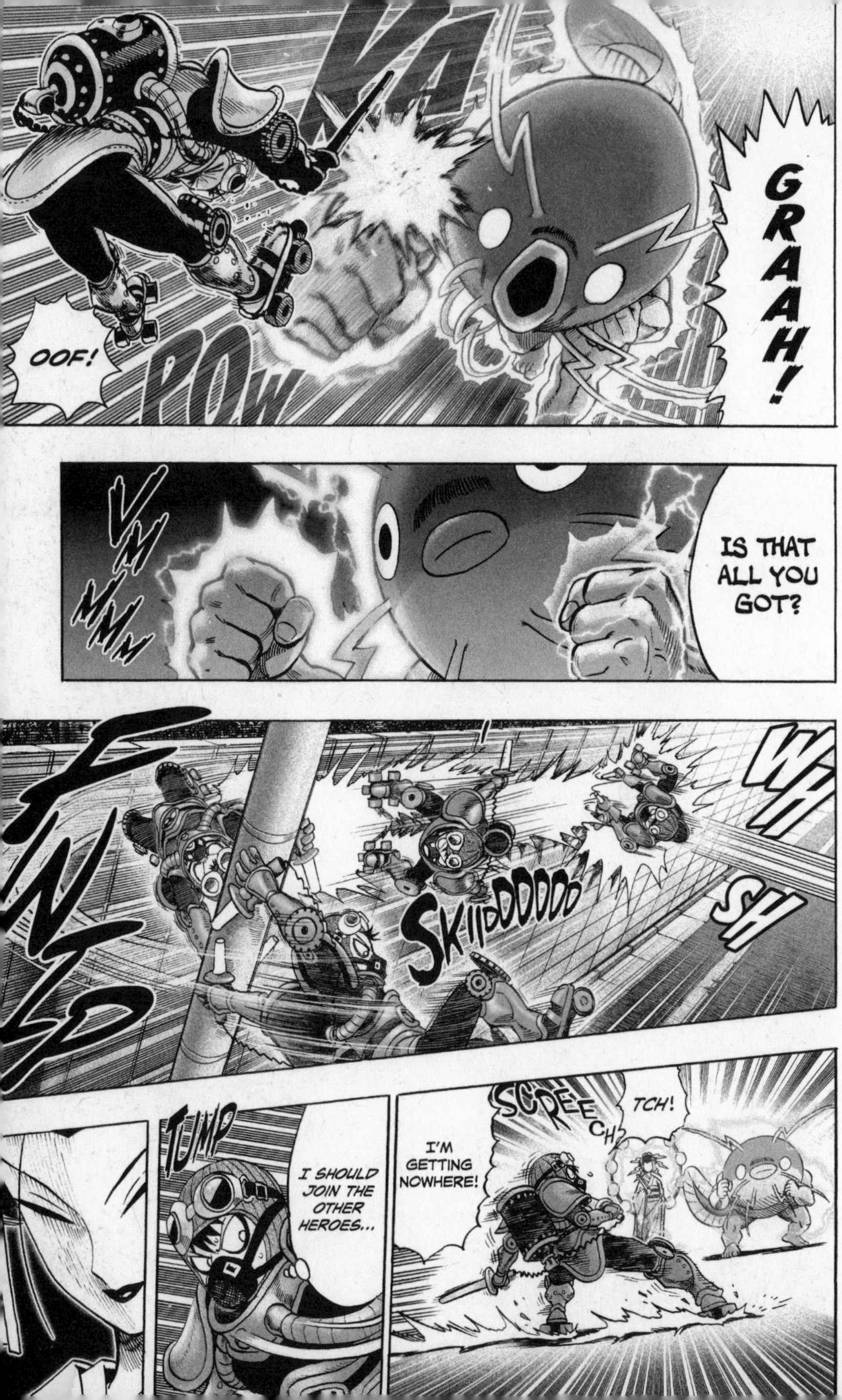
GRAAH!
KA
POW
OOF!
IS THAT ALL YOU GOT?
VMMMM
WH
SH
SKIDDDDDD
TCH!
SCREEECH
I'M GETTING NOWHERE!
TUMP
I SHOULD JOIN THE OTHER HEROES...

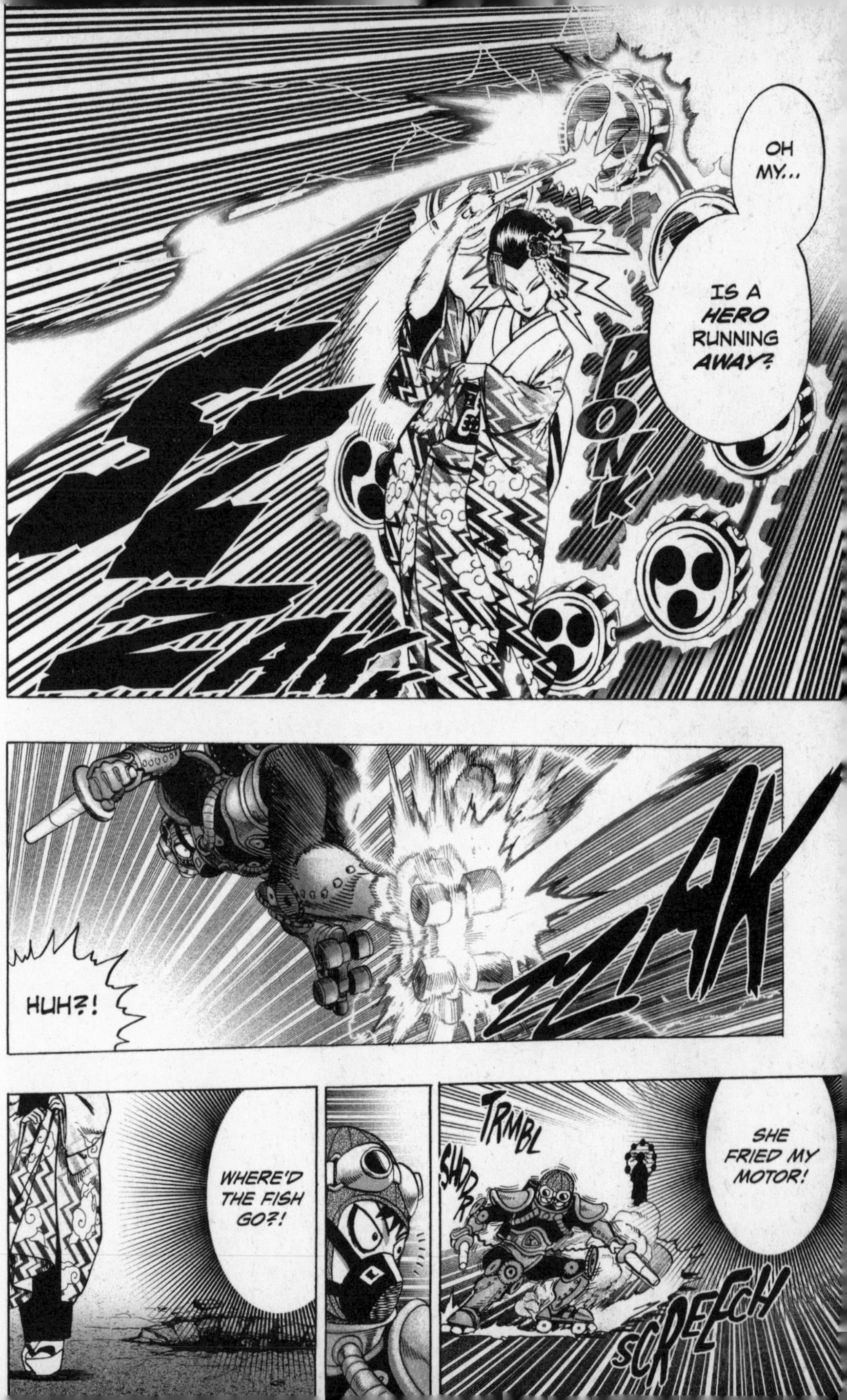
POW
OH MY...
IS A HERO RUNNING AWAY?!
ZAK
ZAK
HUH?!
SHE FRIED MY MOTOR!
TRMBL
SHDDR
SCREECH
WHERE'D THE FISH GO?!

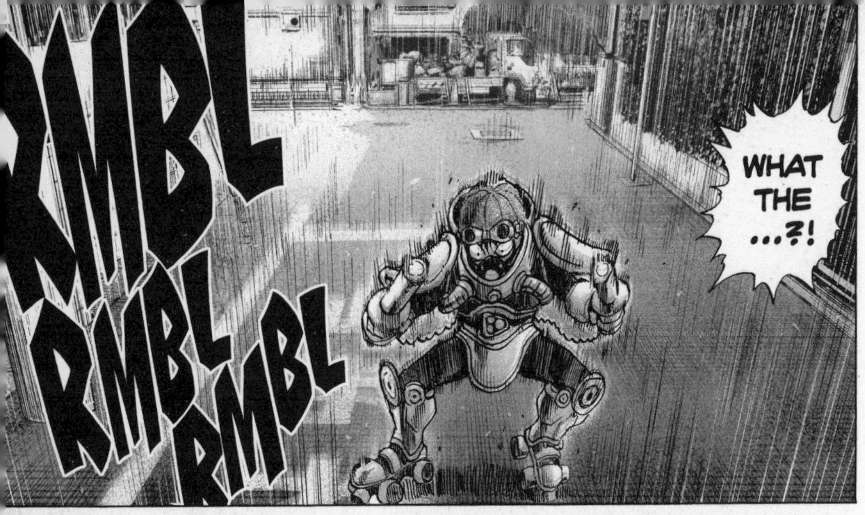
WHAT THE ...?!
RMBL RMBL RMBL

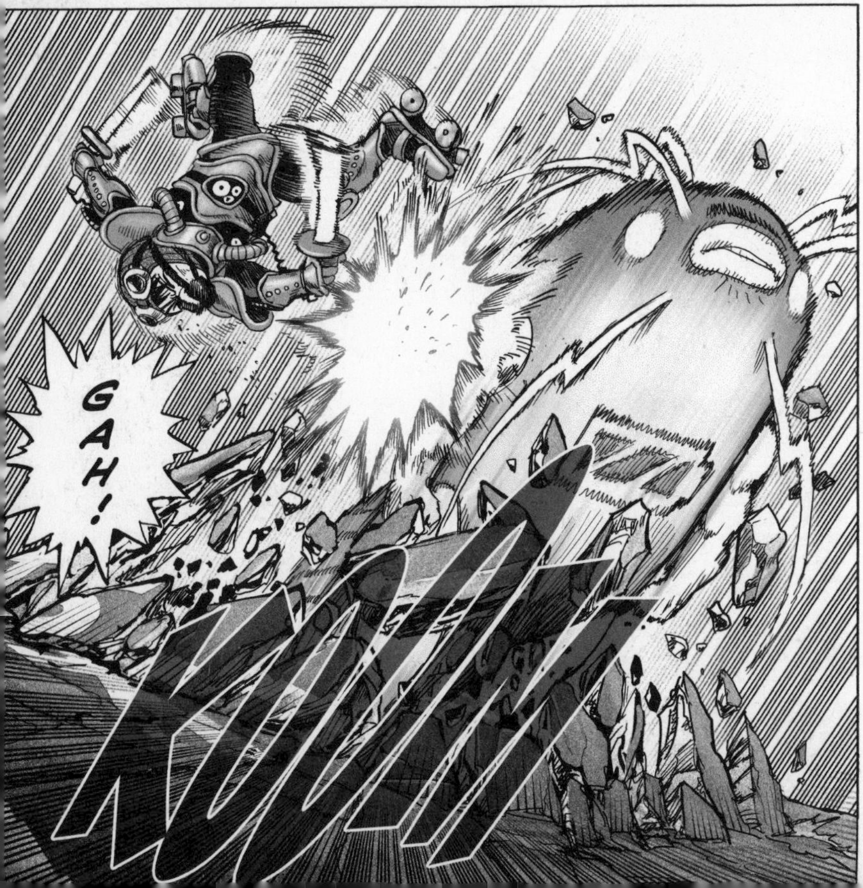
GAH!

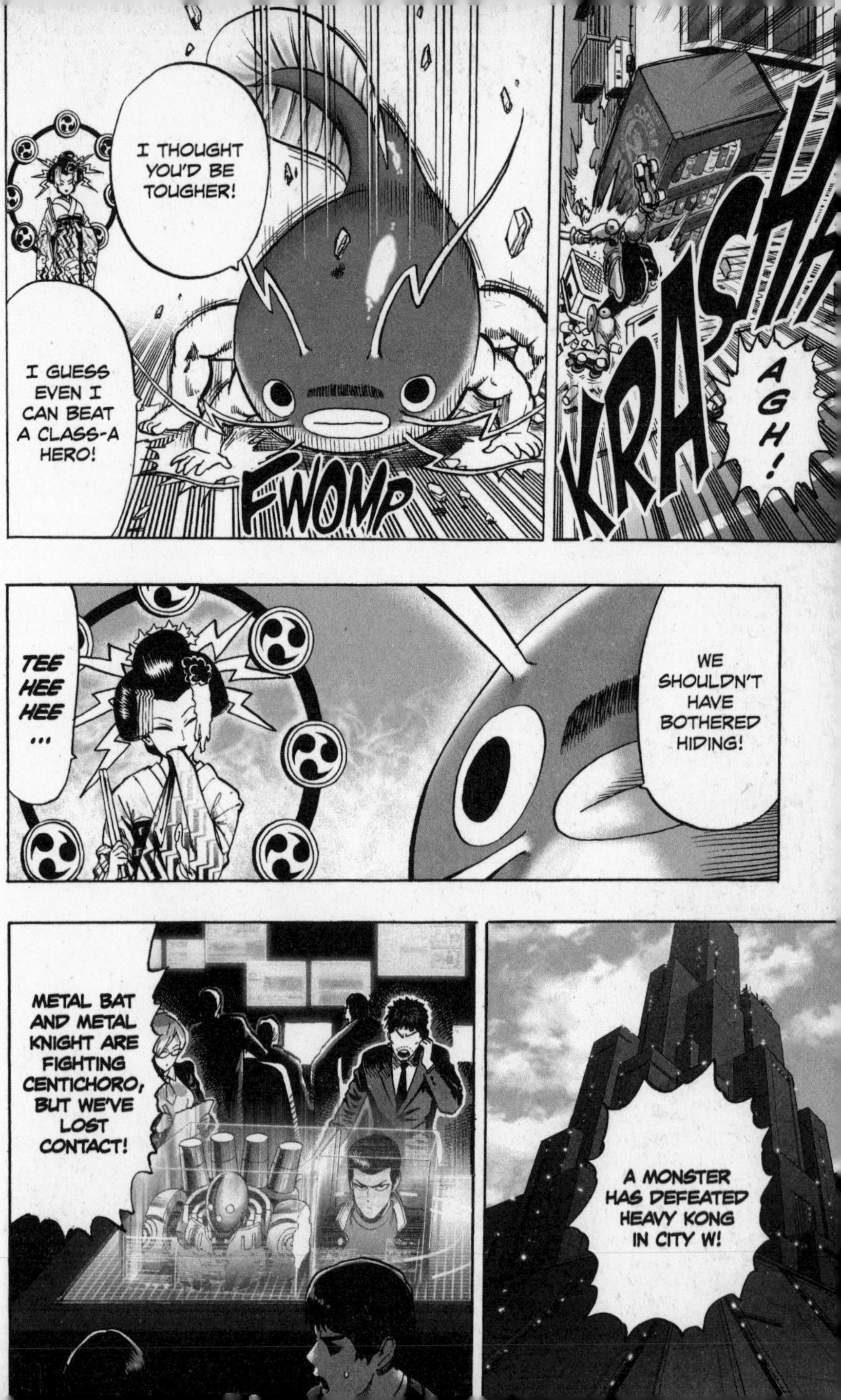
KRASH
AGH!
I THOUGHT YOU'D BE TOUGHER!
I GUESS EVEN I CAN BEAT A CLASS-A HERO!
FWOMP
WE SHOULDN'T HAVE BOTHERED HIDING!
TEE HEE HEE...
A MONSTER HAS DEFEATED HEAVY KONG IN CITY W!
METAL BAT AND METAL KNIGHT ARE FIGHTING CENTICHORO, BUT WE'VE LOST CONTACT!

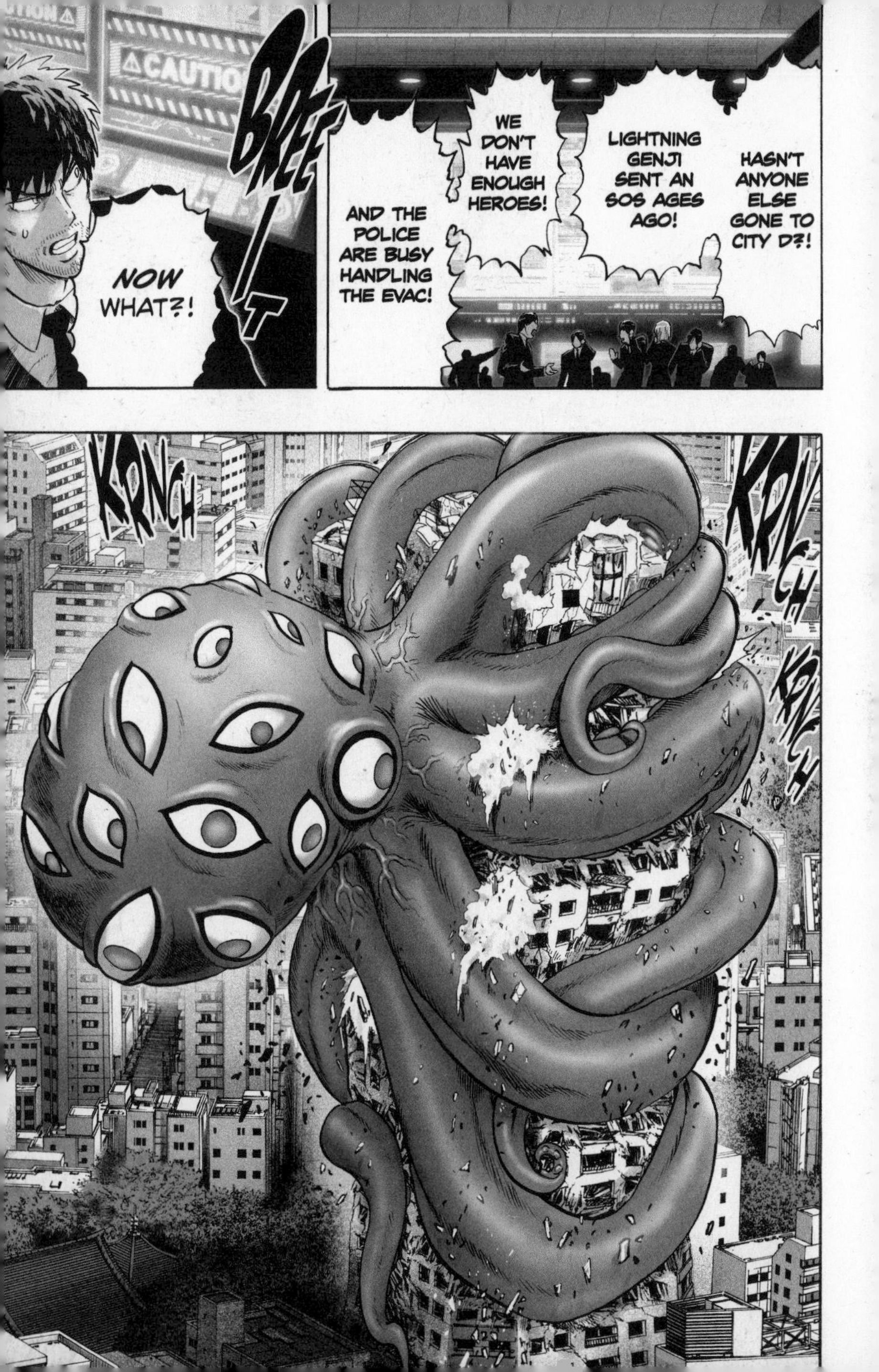
HASN'T ANYONE ELSE GONE TO CITY D?!
LIGHTNING GENJI SENT AN SOS AGES AGO!
WE DON'T HAVE ENOUGH HEROES!
AND THE POLICE ARE BUSY HANDLING THE EVAC!
CAUTION
NOW WHAT?!
KRNCH
KRNCH
KRNCH
KRNCH

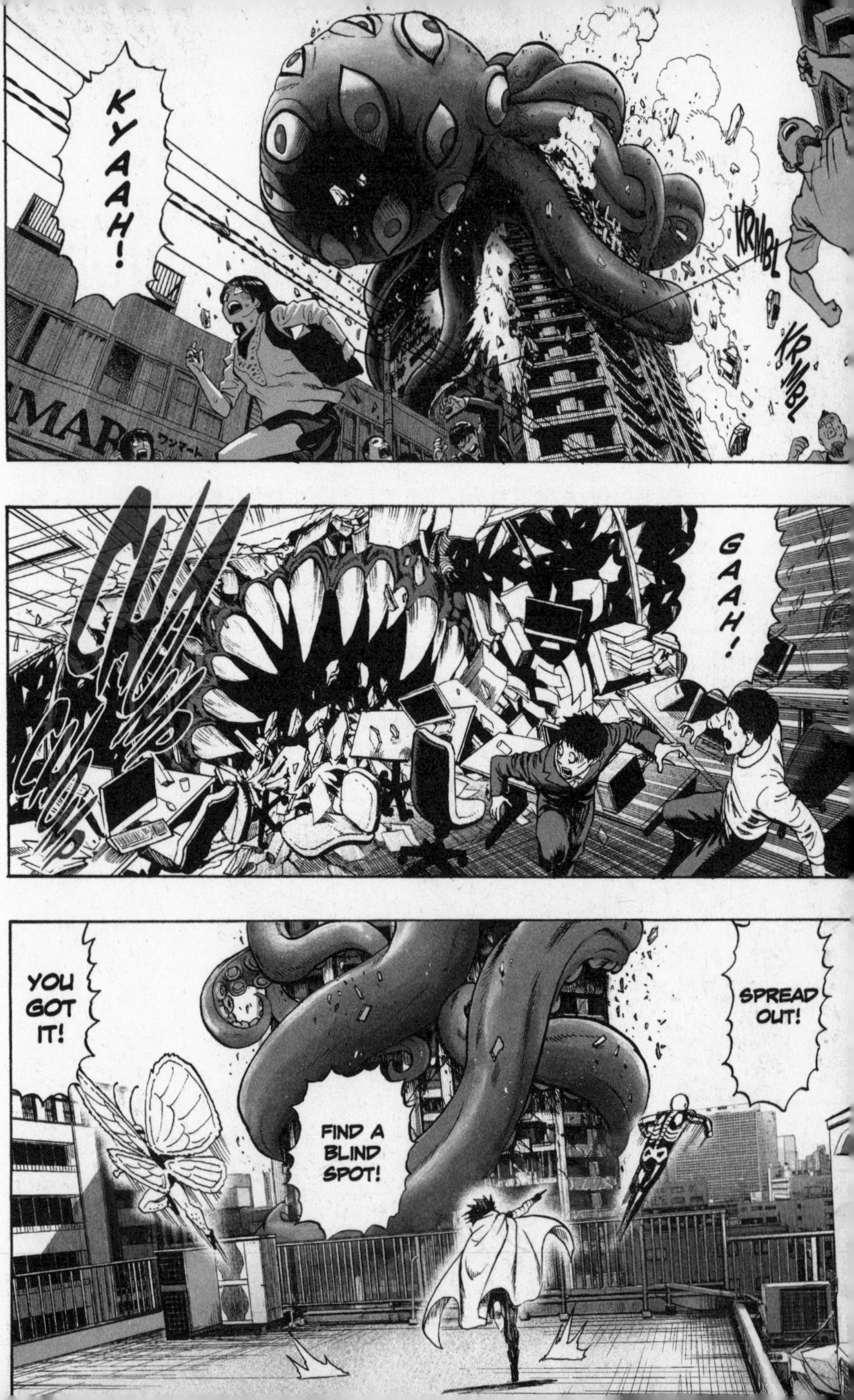
KRMBL
KRMBL
KYAAAH!
GAAAH!
SPREAD OUT!
FIND A BLIND SPOT!
YOU GOT IT!

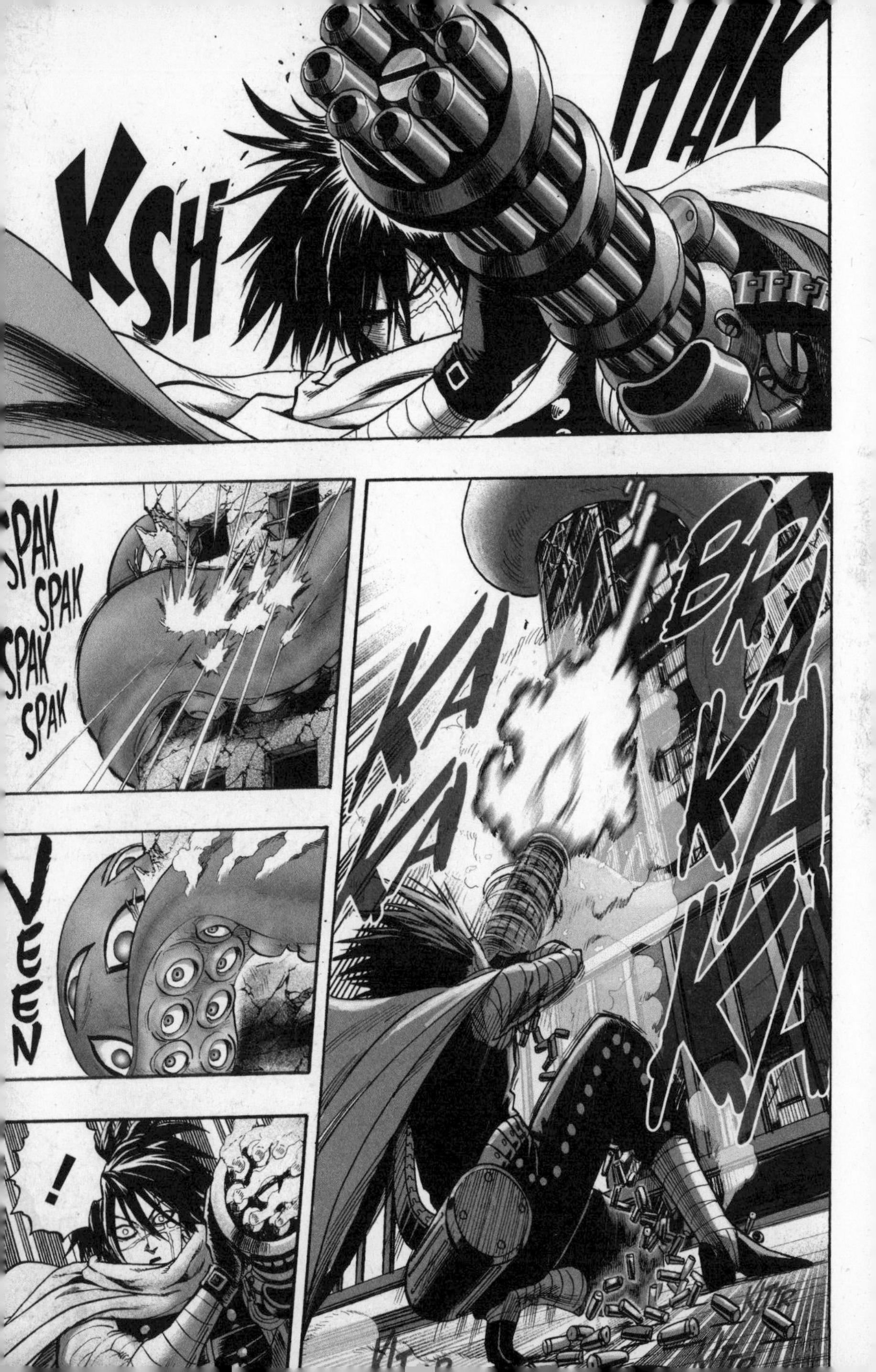
HAK
KSH
BRAKAKAKA
KAKA
SPAK SPAK SPAK SPAK
VEEEN
!

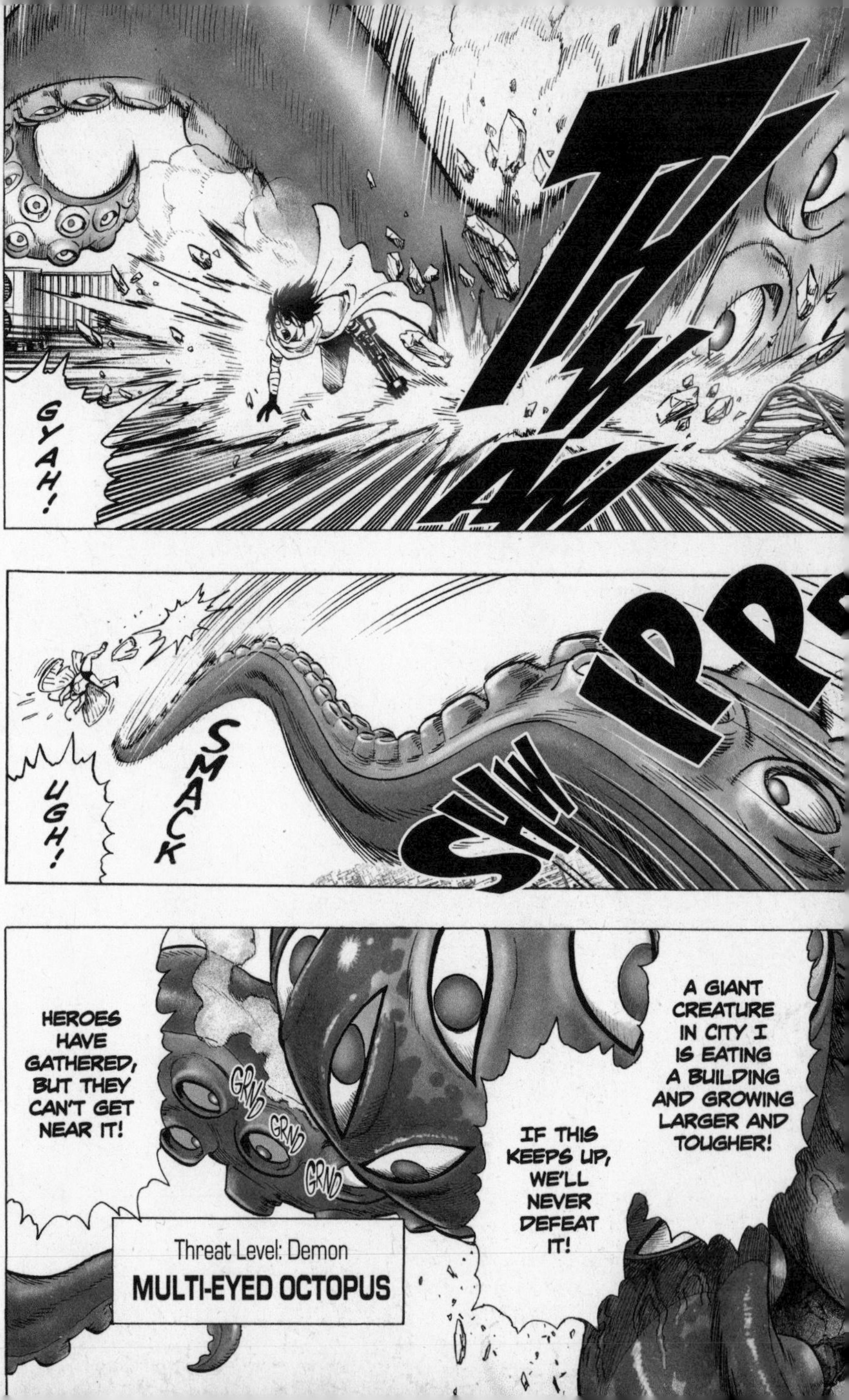
THWAM
GYAH!
SHWIPP
SMACK
UGH!
A GIANT CREATURE IN CITY I IS EATING A BUILDING AND GROWING LARGER AND TOUGHER!
IF THIS KEEPS UP, WE'LL NEVER DEFEAT IT!
HEROES HAVE GATHERED, BUT THEY CAN'T GET NEAR IT!
GRND
GRND
GRND
Threat Level: Demon
MULTI-EYED OCTOPUS

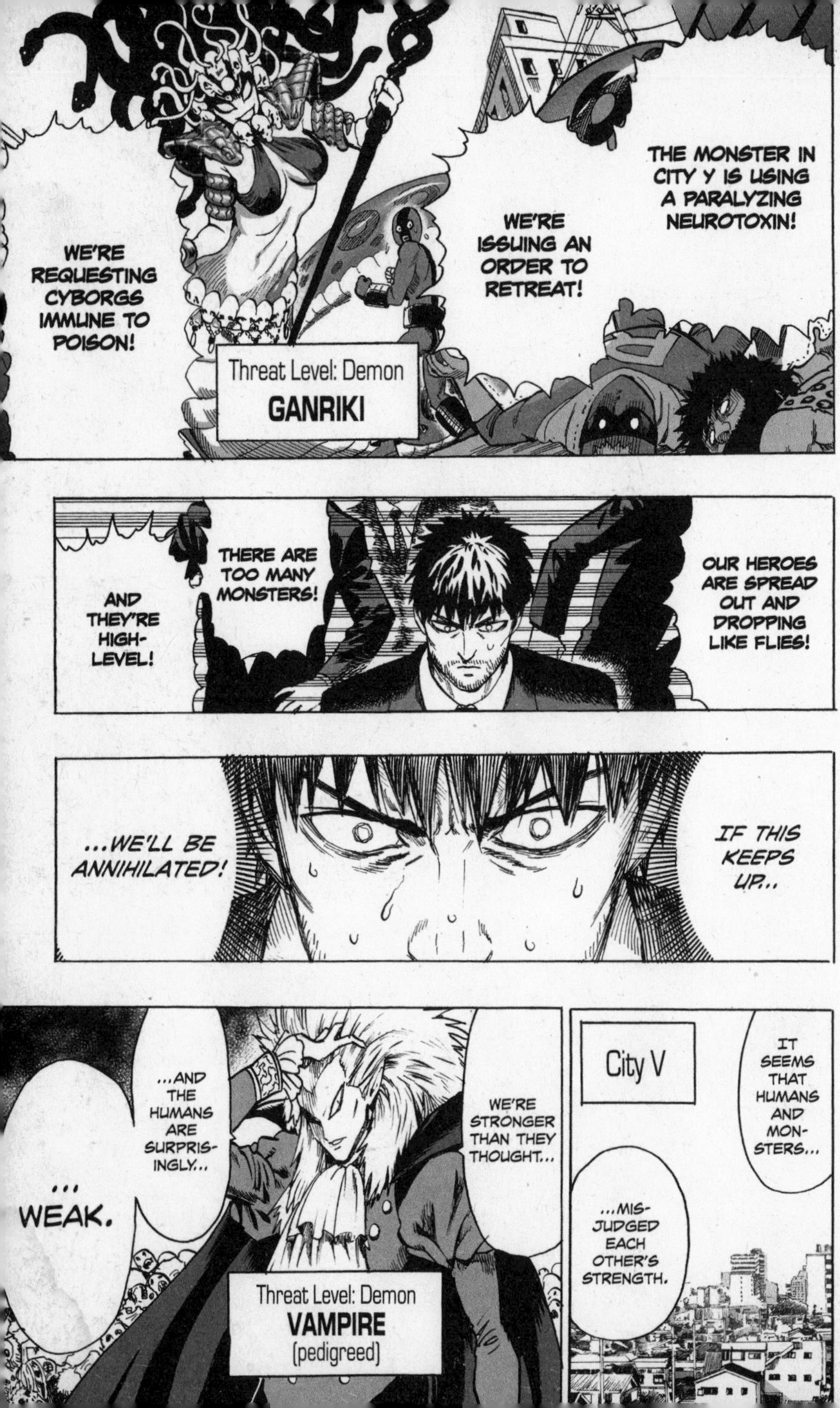
THE MONSTER IN CITY Y IS USING A PARALYZING NEUROTOXIN!
WE'RE ISSUING AN ORDER TO RETREAT!
WE'RE REQUESTING CYBORGS IMMUNE TO POISON!
Threat Level: Demon
GANRIKI
OUR HEROES ARE SPREAD OUT AND DROPPING LIKE FLIES!
THERE ARE TOO MANY MONSTERS!
AND THEY'RE HIGH-LEVEL!
IF THIS KEEPS UP...
...WE'LL BE ANNIHILATED!
City V
IT SEEMS THAT HUMANS AND MON-STERS...
...MIS-JUDGED EACH OTHER'S STRENGTH.
WE'RE STRONGER THAN THEY THOUGHT...
...AND THE HUMANS ARE SURPRIS-INGLY...
...WEAK.
Threat Level: Demon
VAMPIRE
(pedigreed)

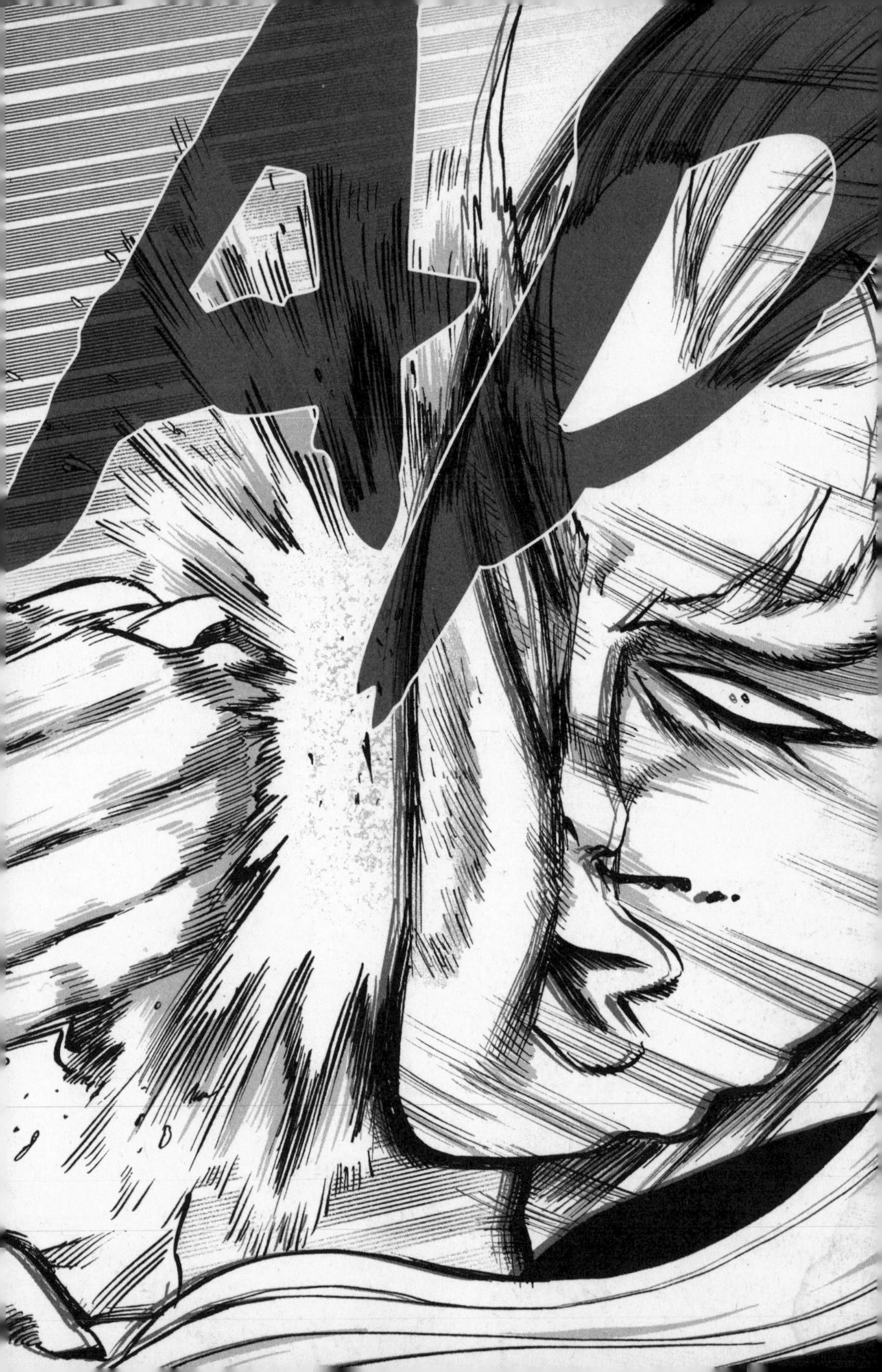

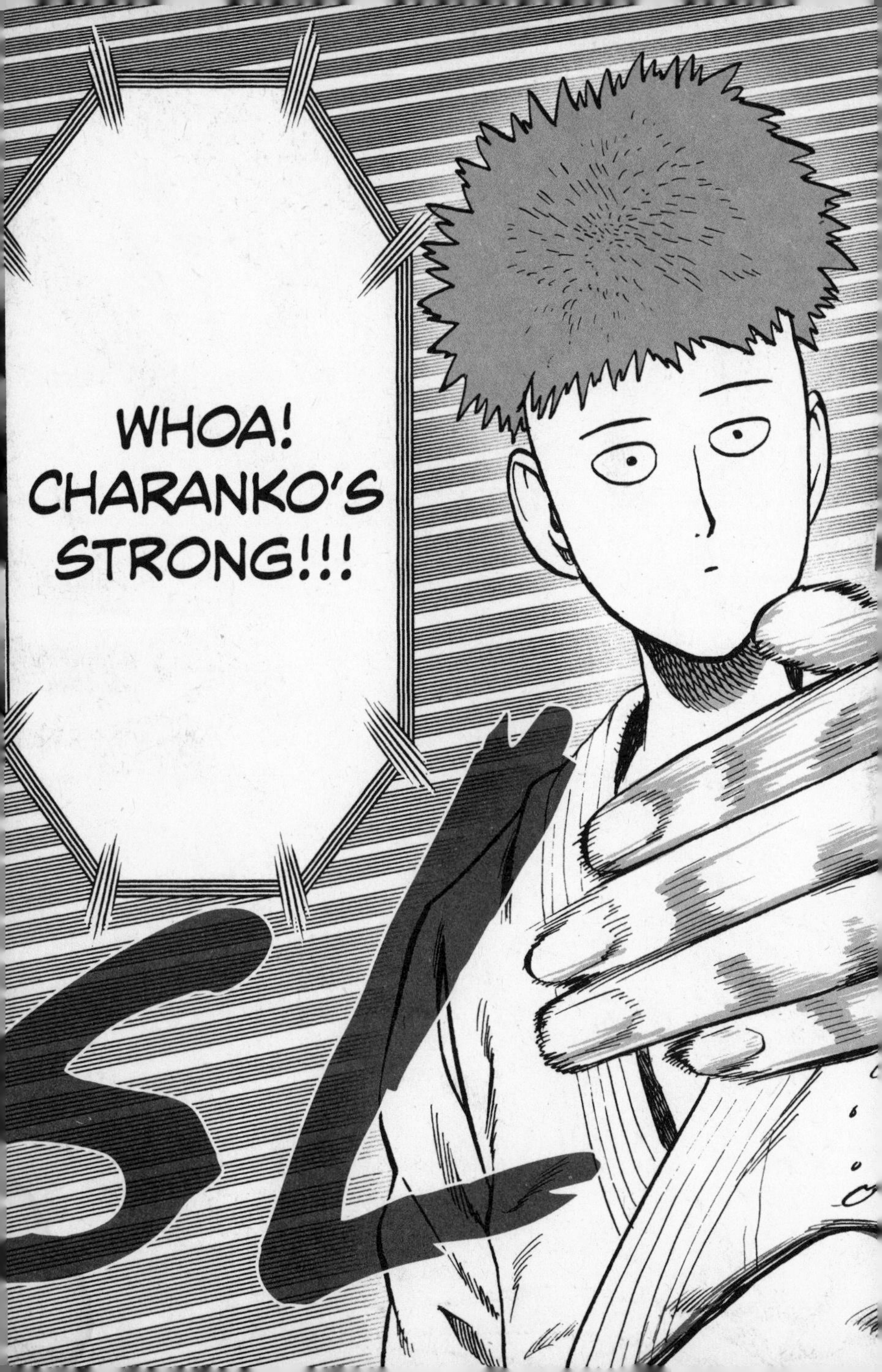
WHOA! CHARANKO'S STRONG!!!

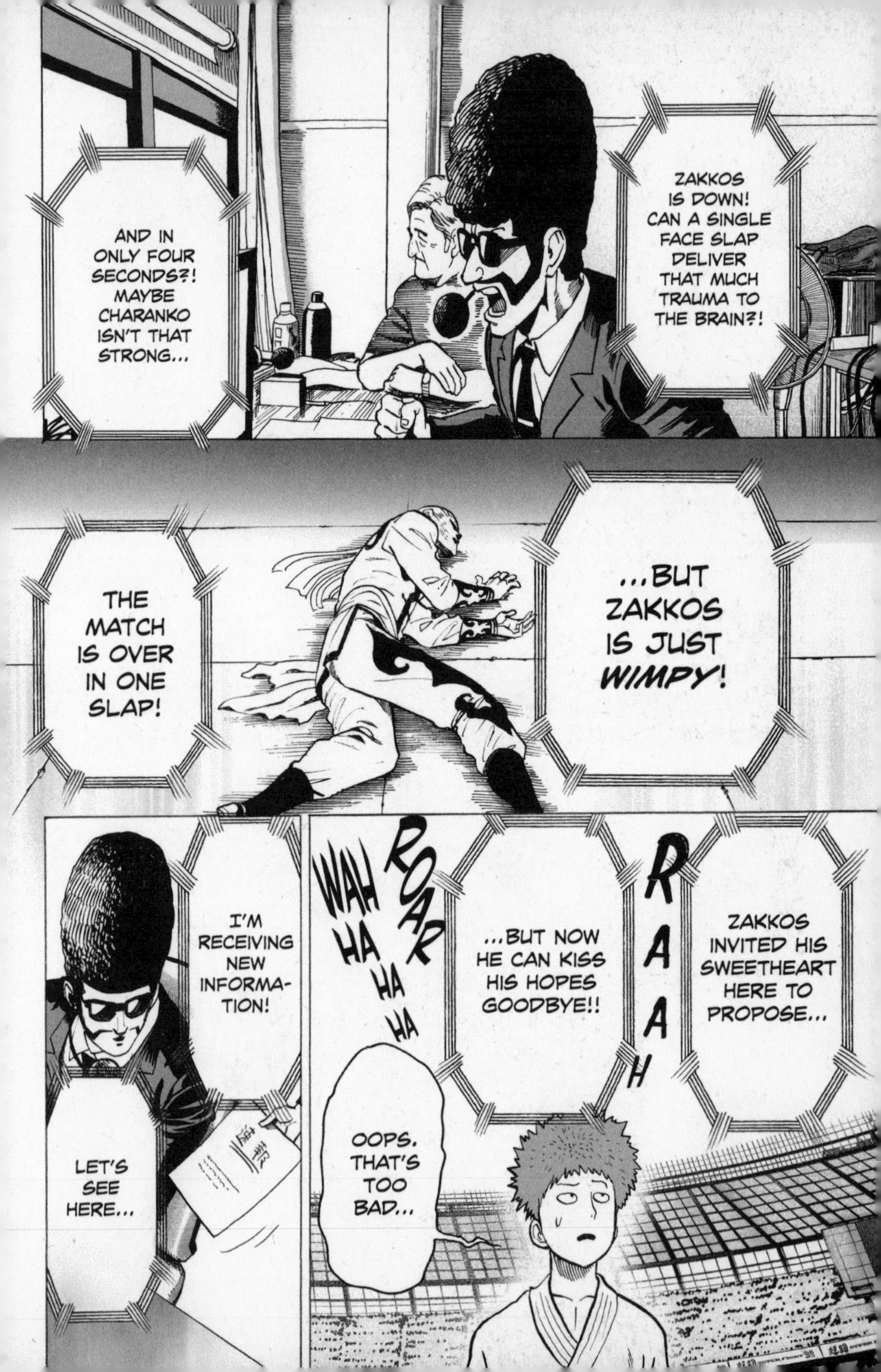
ZAKKOS IS DOWN! CAN A SINGLE FACE SLAP DELIVER THAT MUCH TRAUMA TO THE BRAIN?!
AND IN ONLY FOUR SECONDS?! MAYBE CHARANKO ISN'T THAT STRONG...
...BUT ZAKKOS IS JUST *WIMPY*!
THE MATCH IS OVER IN ONE SLAP!
ZAKKOS INVITED HIS SWEETHEART HERE TO PROPOSE...
RAAAH
...BUT NOW HE CAN KISS HIS HOPES GOODBYE!!
ROAR
WAH HA HA HA HA
OOPS. THAT'S TOO BAD...
I'M RECEIVING NEW INFORMATION!
LET'S SEE HERE...

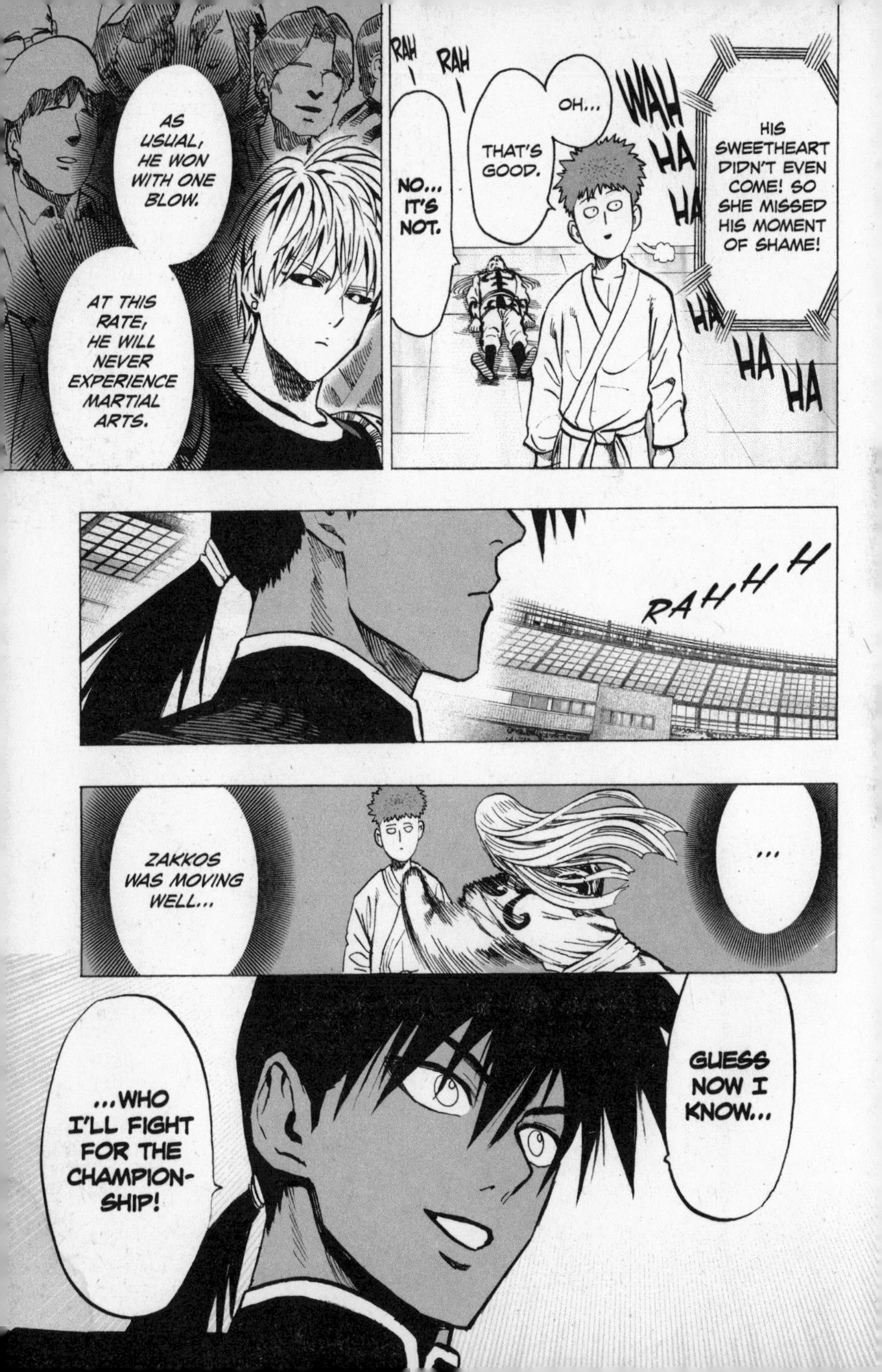
HIS SWEETHEART DIDN'T EVEN COME! SO SHE MISSED HIS MOMENT OF SHAME!
WAH HA HA HA HA HA HA
OH...
THAT'S GOOD.
RAH RAH
NO... IT'S NOT.
AS USUAL, HE WON WITH ONE BLOW.
AT THIS RATE, HE WILL NEVER EXPERIENCE MARTIAL ARTS.
RAHHH
...
ZAKKOS WAS MOVING WELL...
GUESS NOW I KNOW...
...WHO I'LL FIGHT FOR THE CHAMPION-SHIP!

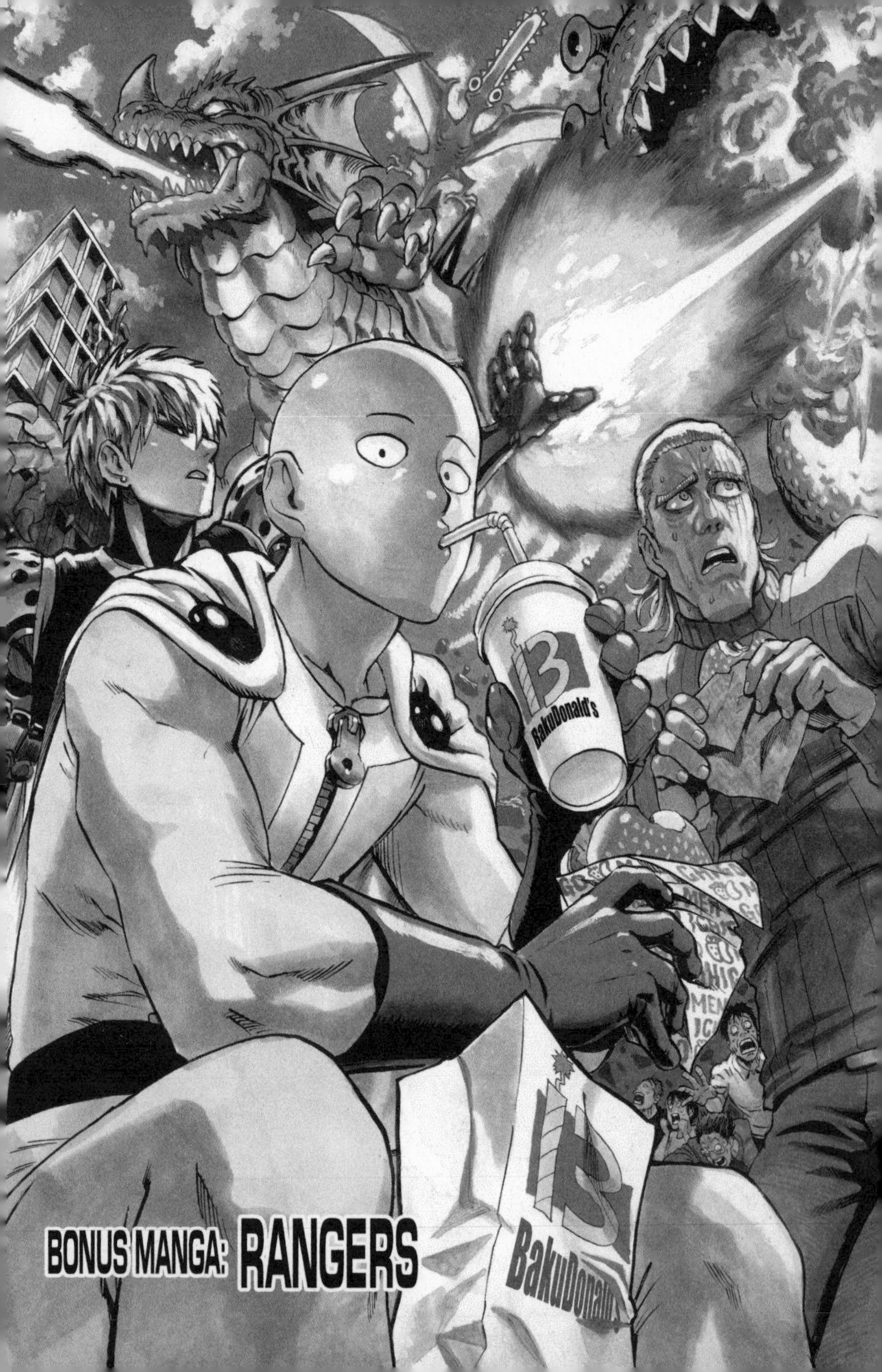
BakuDonald's
BONUS MANGA: RANGERS
BakuDonald's

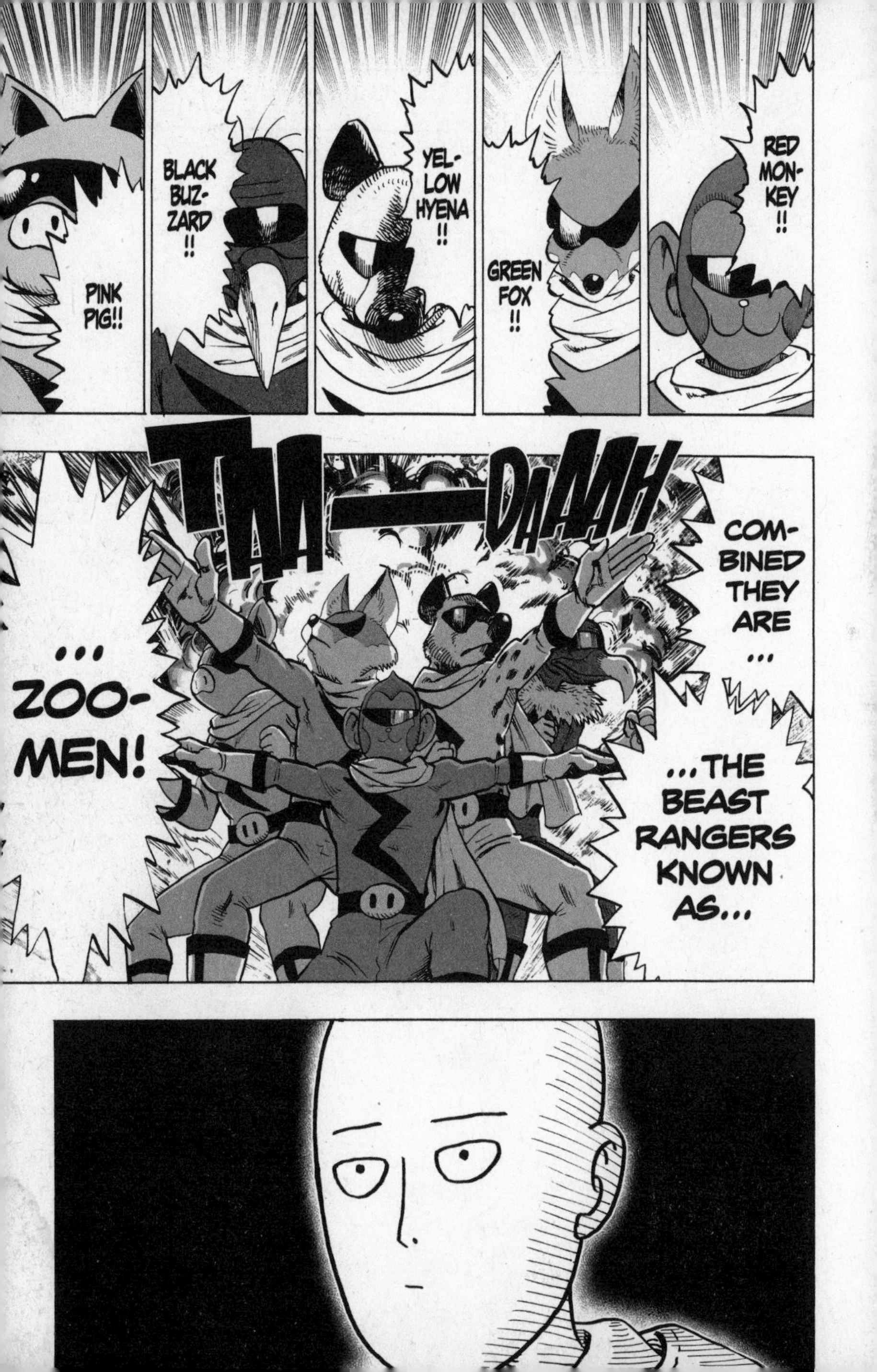
RED MON-KEY !!
GREEN FOX !!
YEL-LOW HYENA !!
BLACK BUZ-ZARD !!
PINK PIG!!
COM-BINED THEY ARE ...
...THE BEAST RANGERS KNOWN AS...
TAA—DAAAH
... ZOO-MEN!

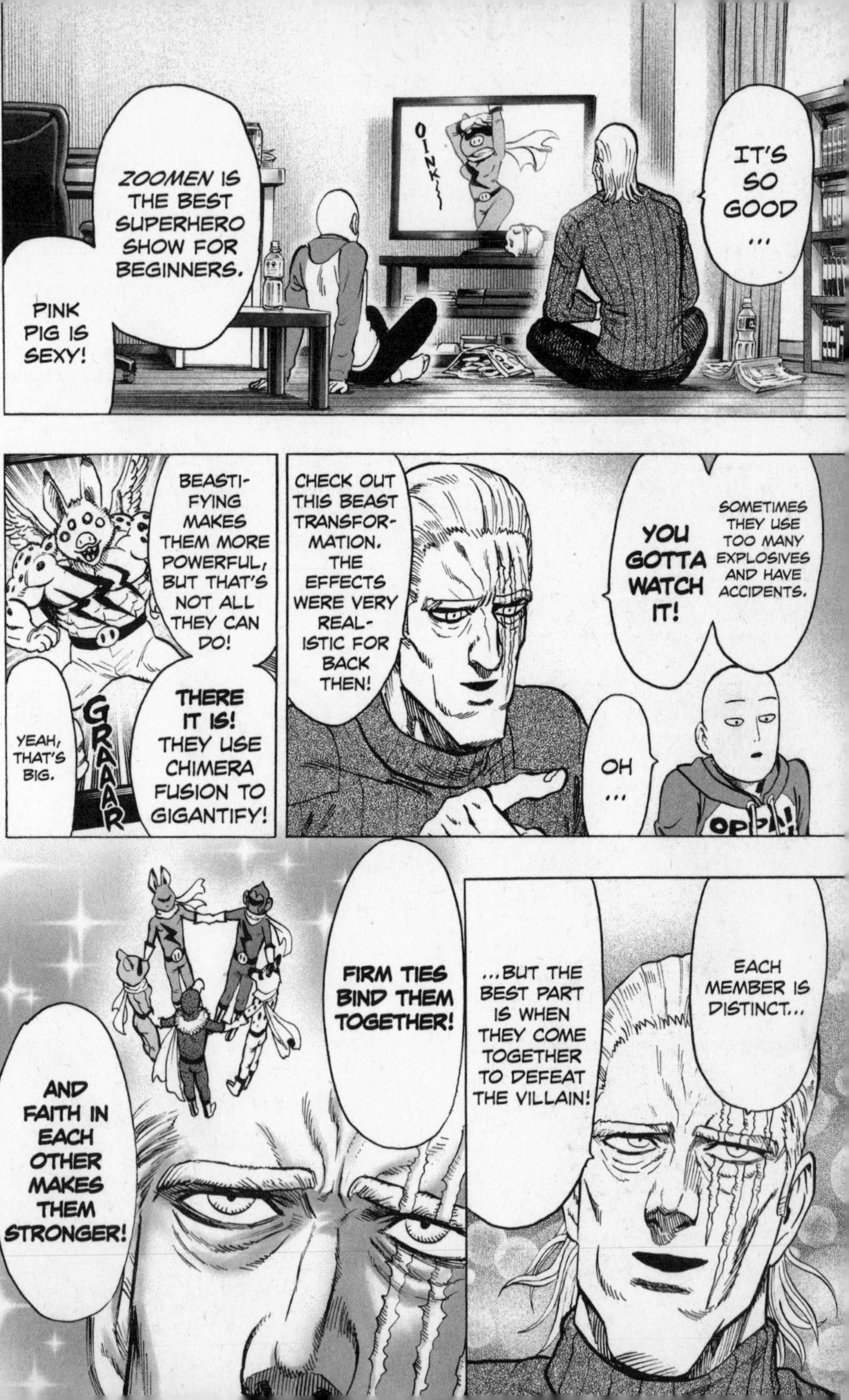
IT'S SO GOOD ...
OINK~
ZOOMEN IS THE BEST SUPERHERO SHOW FOR BEGINNERS.
PINK PIG IS SEXY!
SOMETIMES THEY USE TOO MANY EXPLOSIVES AND HAVE ACCIDENTS.
YOU GOTTA WATCH IT!
CHECK OUT THIS BEAST TRANSFORMATION. THE EFFECTS WERE VERY REALISTIC FOR BACK THEN!
OH ...
BEASTIFYING MAKES THEM MORE POWERFUL, BUT THAT'S NOT ALL THEY CAN DO!
THERE IT IS! THEY USE CHIMERA FUSION TO GIGANTIFY!
GRAAAR
YEAH, THAT'S BIG.
EACH MEMBER IS DISTINCT...
...BUT THE BEST PART IS WHEN THEY COME TOGETHER TO DEFEAT THE VILLAIN!
FIRM TIES BIND THEM TOGETHER!
AND FAITH IN EACH OTHER MAKES THEM STRONGER!

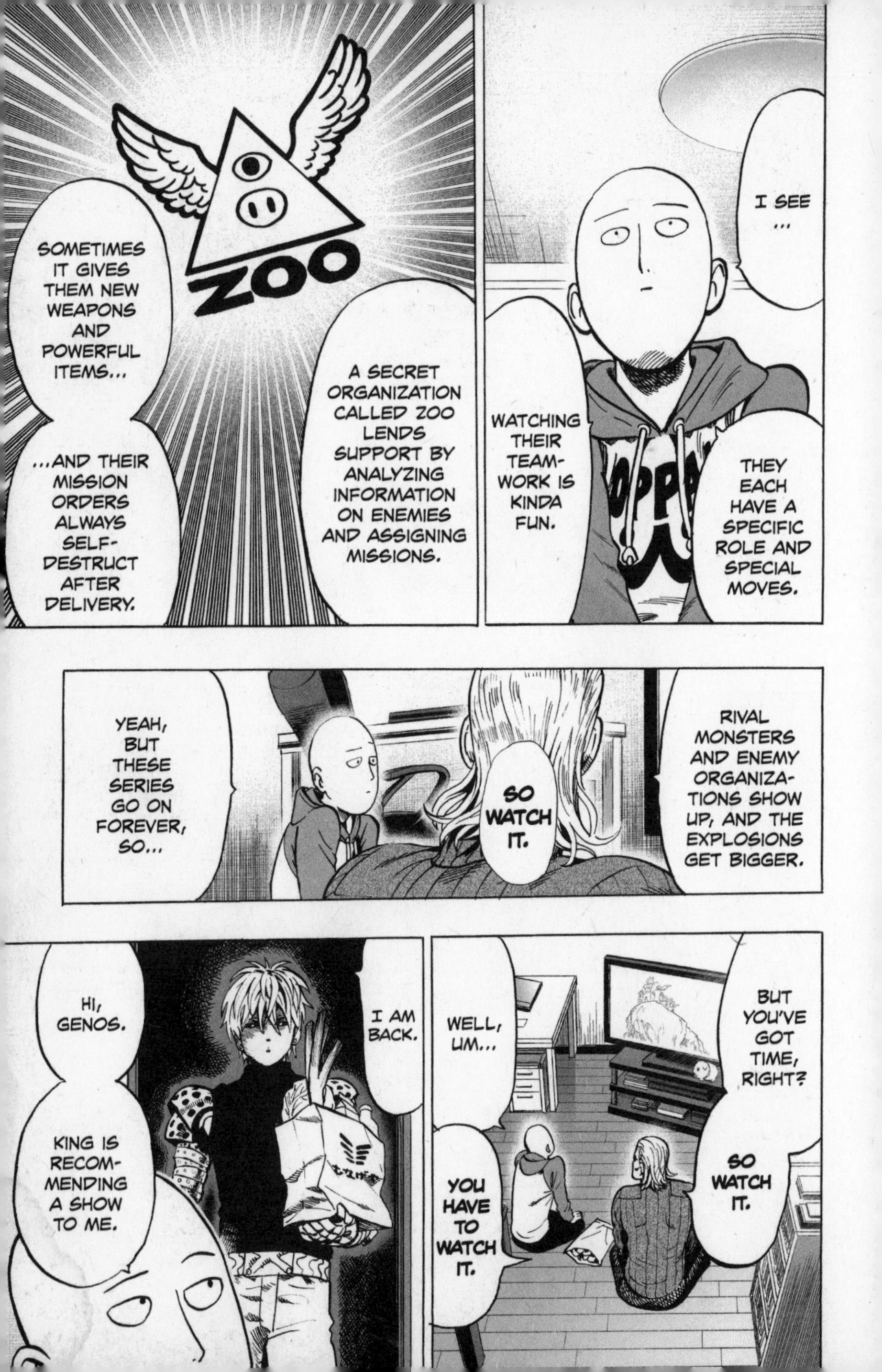
I SEE ...
THEY EACH HAVE A SPECIFIC ROLE AND SPECIAL MOVES.
WATCHING THEIR TEAM-WORK IS KINDA FUN.
A SECRET ORGANIZATION CALLED ZOO LENDS SUPPORT BY ANALYZING INFORMATION ON ENEMIES AND ASSIGNING MISSIONS.
ZOO
SOMETIMES IT GIVES THEM NEW WEAPONS AND POWERFUL ITEMS...
...AND THEIR MISSION ORDERS ALWAYS SELF-DESTRUCT AFTER DELIVERY.
RIVAL MONSTERS AND ENEMY ORGANIZA-TIONS SHOW UP, AND THE EXPLOSIONS GET BIGGER.
SO WATCH IT.
YEAH, BUT THESE SERIES GO ON FOREVER, SO...
BUT YOU'VE GOT TIME, RIGHT?
SO WATCH IT.
WELL, UM...
YOU HAVE TO WATCH IT.
I AM BACK.
HI, GENOS.
KING IS RECOM-MENDING A SHOW TO ME.

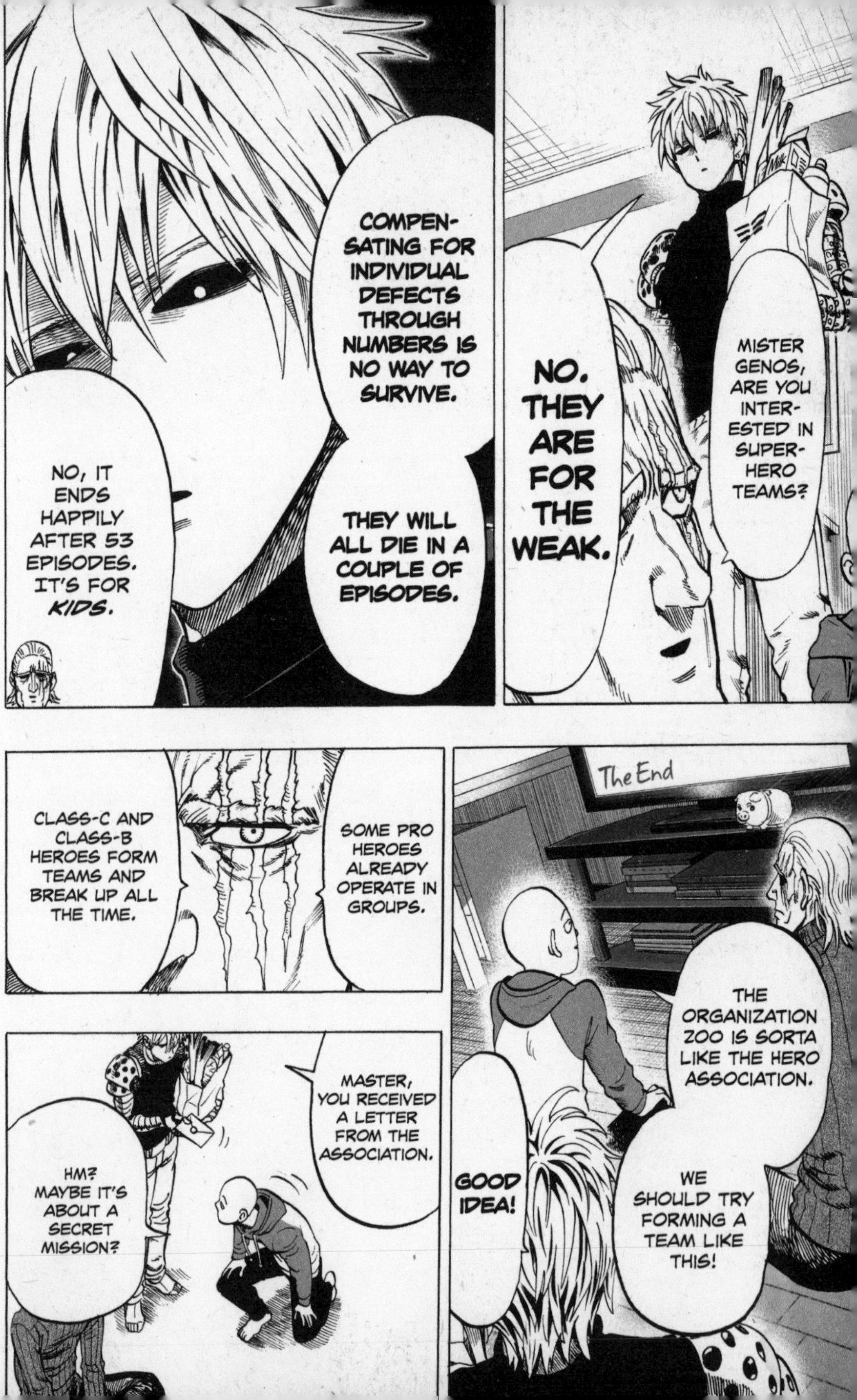
MISTER GENOS, ARE YOU INTER-ESTED IN SUPER-HERO TEAMS?
NO. THEY ARE FOR THE WEAK.
COMPEN-SATING FOR INDIVIDUAL DEFECTS THROUGH NUMBERS IS NO WAY TO SURVIVE.
THEY WILL ALL DIE IN A COUPLE OF EPISODES.
NO, IT ENDS HAPPILY AFTER 53 EPISODES. IT'S FOR *KIDS*.
The End
THE ORGANIZATION ZOO IS SORTA LIKE THE HERO ASSOCIATION.
WE SHOULD TRY FORMING A TEAM LIKE THIS!
GOOD IDEA!
SOME PRO HEROES ALREADY OPERATE IN GROUPS.
CLASS-C AND CLASS-B HEROES FORM TEAMS AND BREAK UP ALL THE TIME.
MASTER, YOU RECEIVED A LETTER FROM THE ASSOCIATION.
HM? MAYBE IT'S ABOUT A SECRET MISSION?

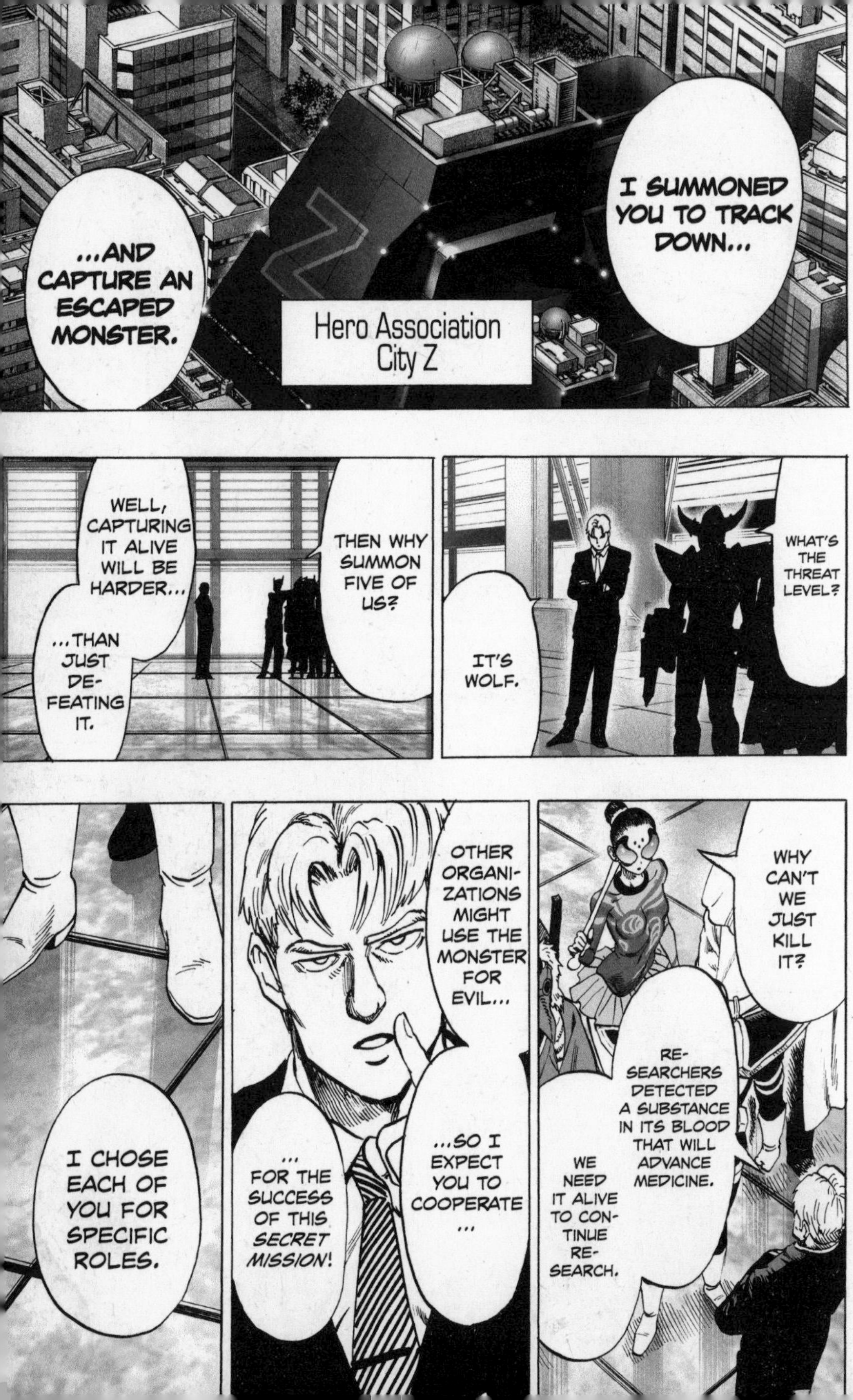
I SUMMONED YOU TO TRACK DOWN...
Hero Association City Z
...AND CAPTURE AN ESCAPED MONSTER.
WHAT'S THE THREAT LEVEL?
IT'S WOLF.
THEN WHY SUMMON FIVE OF US?
WELL, CAPTURING IT ALIVE WILL BE HARDER...
...THAN JUST DEFEATING IT.
WHY CAN'T WE JUST KILL IT?
RESEARCHERS DETECTED A SUBSTANCE IN ITS BLOOD THAT WILL ADVANCE MEDICINE.
WE NEED IT ALIVE TO CONTINUE RESEARCH.
OTHER ORGANIZATIONS MIGHT USE THE MONSTER FOR EVIL...
...SO I EXPECT YOU TO COOPERATE...
...FOR THE SUCCESS OF THIS *SECRET MISSION*!
I CHOSE EACH OF YOU FOR SPECIFIC ROLES.

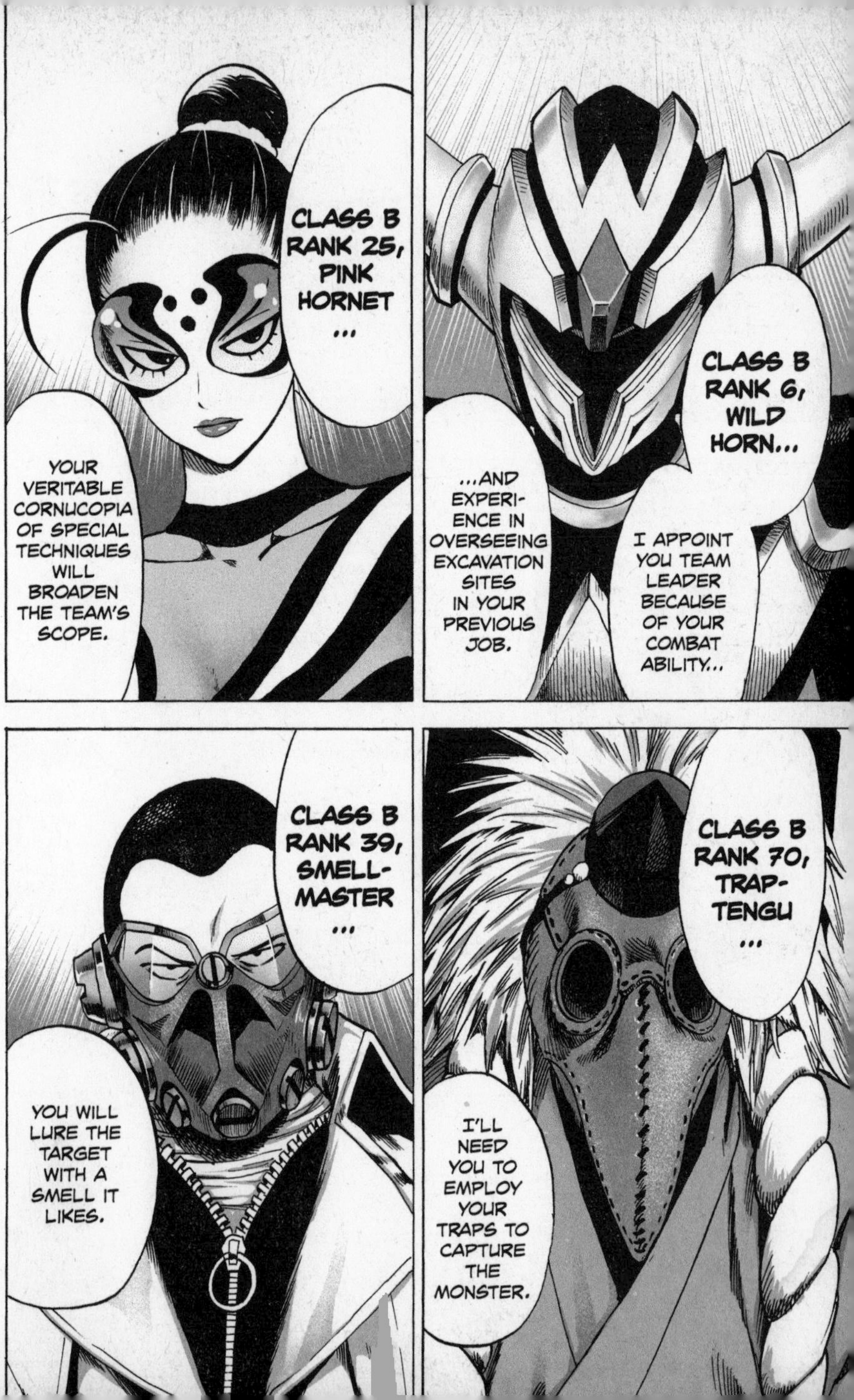
CLASS B RANK 6, WILD HORN...
I APPOINT YOU TEAM LEADER BECAUSE OF YOUR COMBAT ABILITY...
...AND EXPERIENCE IN OVERSEEING EXCAVATION SITES IN YOUR PREVIOUS JOB.
CLASS B RANK 25, PINK HORNET ...
YOUR VERITABLE CORNUCOPIA OF SPECIAL TECHNIQUES WILL BROADEN THE TEAM'S SCOPE.
CLASS B RANK 70, TRAP-TENGU ...
I'LL NEED YOU TO EMPLOY YOUR TRAPS TO CAPTURE THE MONSTER.
CLASS B RANK 39, SMELL-MASTER ...
YOU WILL LURE THE TARGET WITH A SMELL IT LIKES.

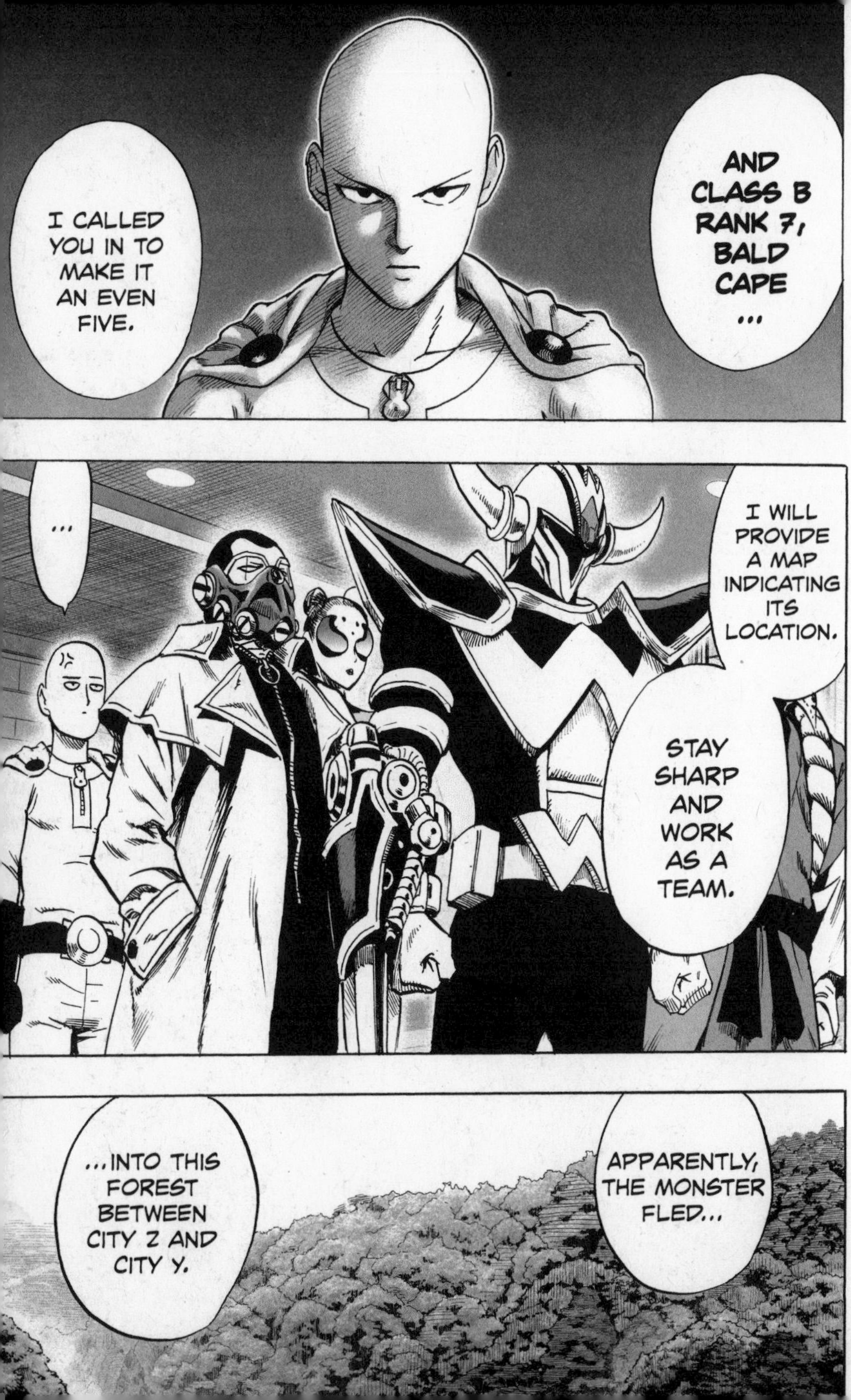
AND CLASS B RANK 7, BALD CAPE ...
I CALLED YOU IN TO MAKE IT AN EVEN FIVE.
I WILL PROVIDE A MAP INDICATING ITS LOCATION.
STAY SHARP AND WORK AS A TEAM.
...
APPARENTLY, THE MONSTER FLED...
...INTO THIS FOREST BETWEEN CITY Z AND CITY Y.

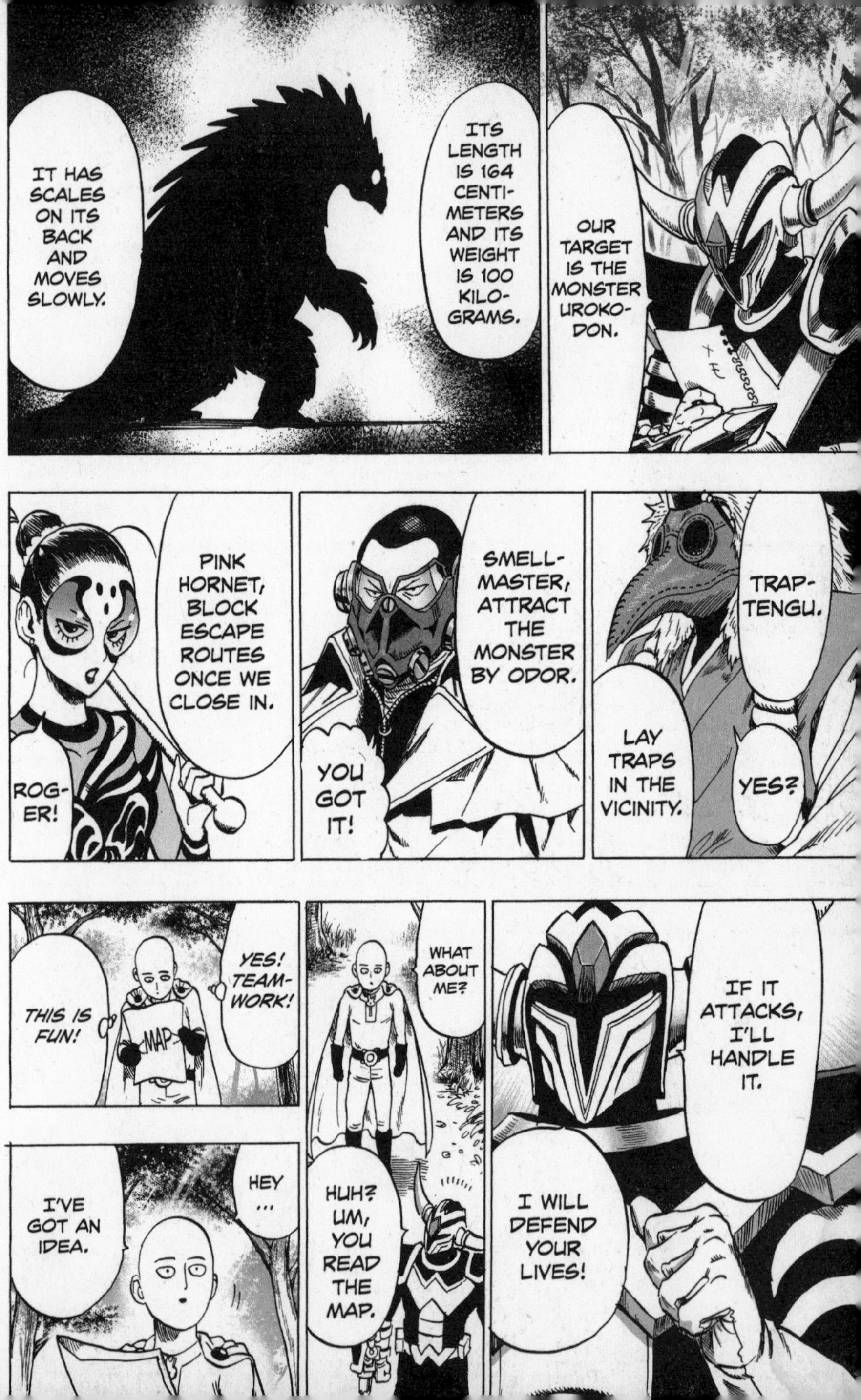
OUR TARGET IS THE MONSTER UROKODON.
ITS LENGTH IS 164 CENTIMETERS AND ITS WEIGHT IS 100 KILOGRAMS.
IT HAS SCALES ON ITS BACK AND MOVES SLOWLY.
TRAP-TENGU.
YES?
LAY TRAPS IN THE VICINITY.
SMELL-MASTER, ATTRACT THE MONSTER BY ODOR.
YOU GOT IT!
PINK HORNET, BLOCK ESCAPE ROUTES ONCE WE CLOSE IN.
ROG-ER!
IF IT ATTACKS, I'LL HANDLE IT.
I WILL DEFEND YOUR LIVES!
WHAT ABOUT ME?
HUH? UM, YOU READ THE MAP.
YES! TEAMWORK!
THIS IS FUN!
MAP
HEY...
I'VE GOT AN IDEA.

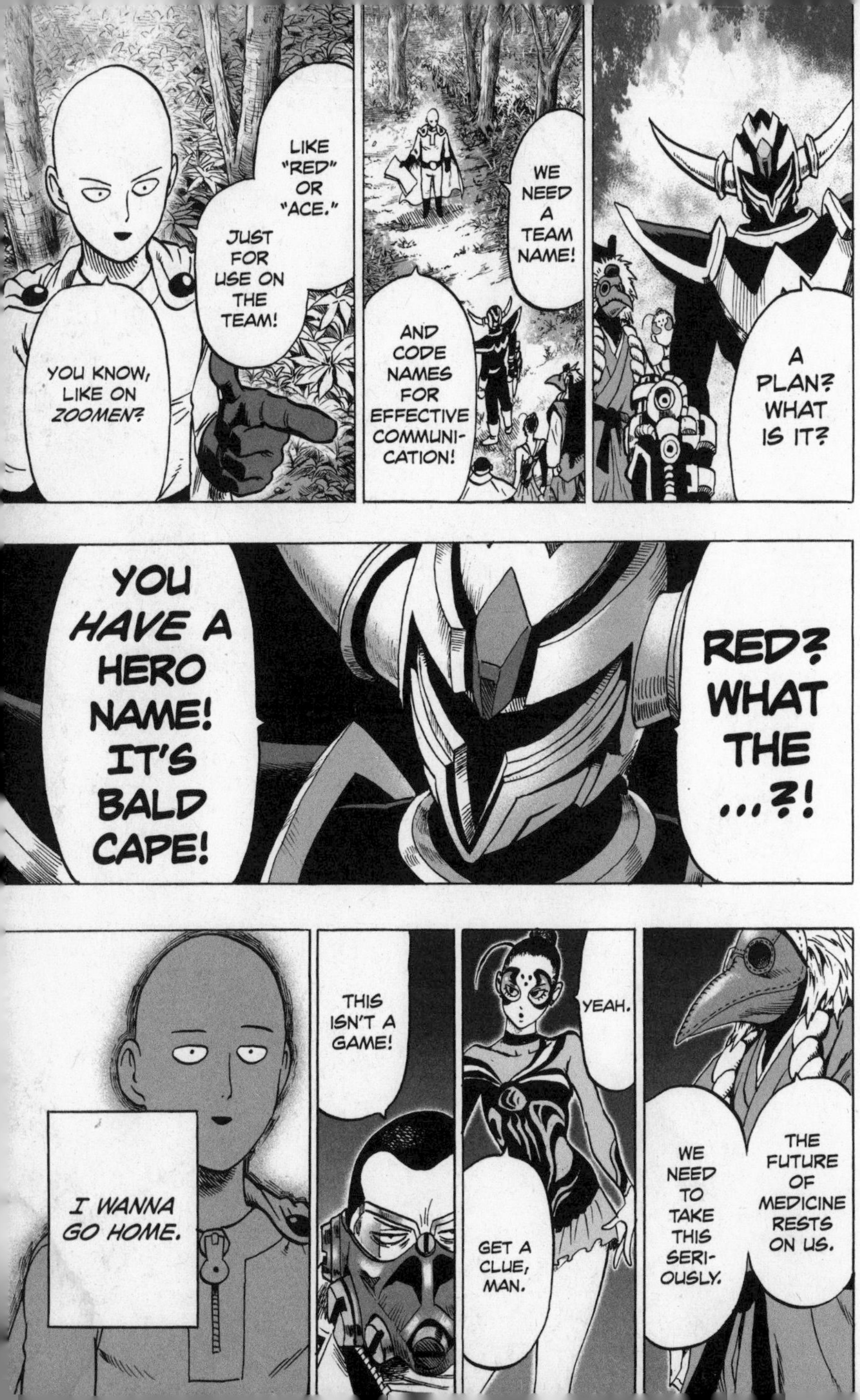
A PLAN? WHAT IS IT?
WE NEED A TEAM NAME!
AND CODE NAMES FOR EFFECTIVE COMMUNI-CATION!
LIKE "RED" OR "ACE."
JUST FOR USE ON THE TEAM!
YOU KNOW, LIKE ON *ZOOMEN*?
RED? WHAT THE ...?!
YOU *HAVE* A HERO NAME! IT'S BALD CAPE!
THE FUTURE OF MEDICINE RESTS ON US.
WE NEED TO TAKE THIS SERI-OUSLY.
YEAH.
GET A CLUE, MAN.
THIS ISN'T A GAME!
I WANNA GO HOME.

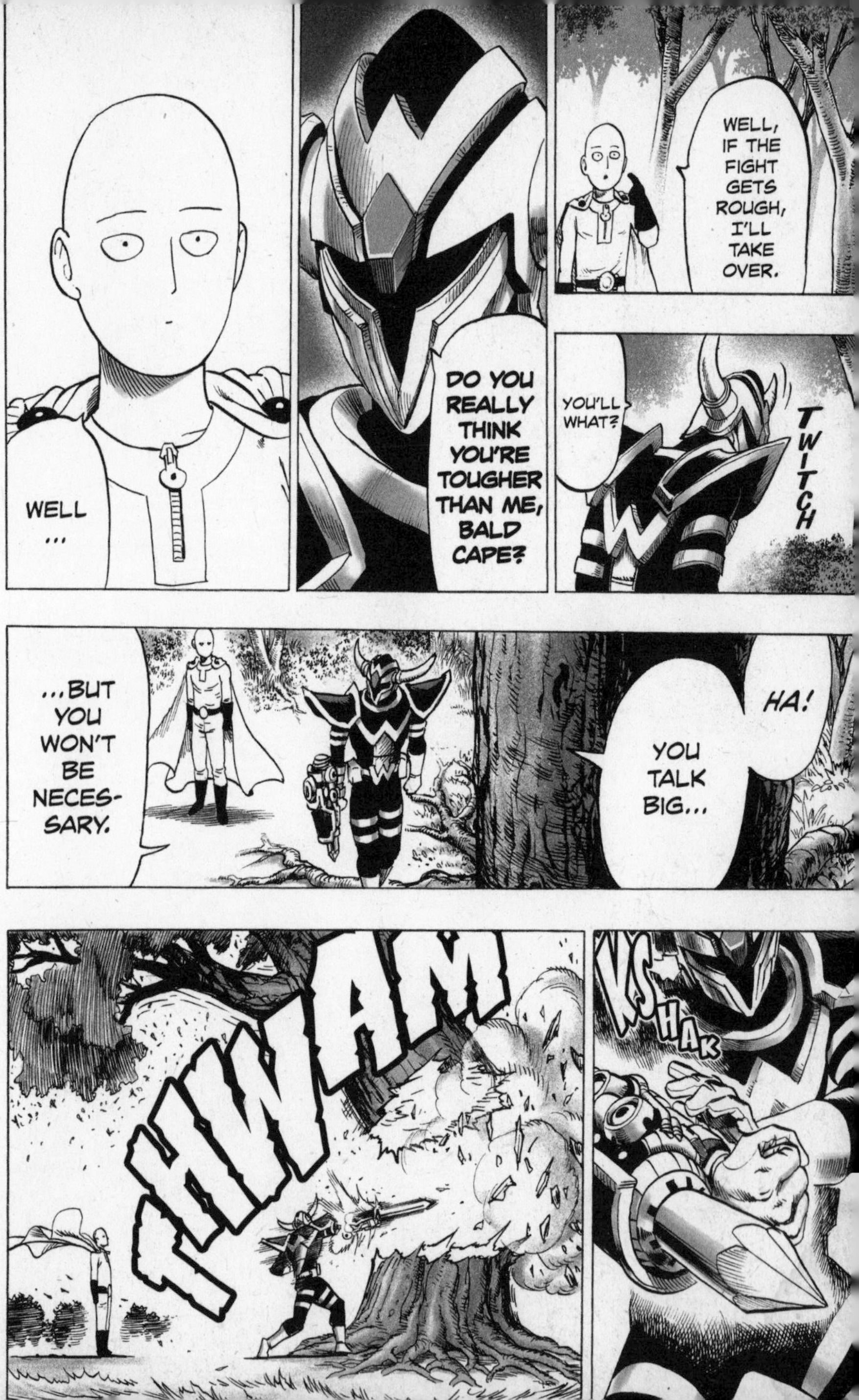
WELL, IF THE FIGHT GETS ROUGH, I'LL TAKE OVER.
YOU'LL WHAT?
TWITCH
DO YOU REALLY THINK YOU'RE TOUGHER THAN ME, BALD CAPE?
WELL ...
HA!
YOU TALK BIG...
...BUT YOU WON'T BE NECES-SARY.
KSHAK
THWAM

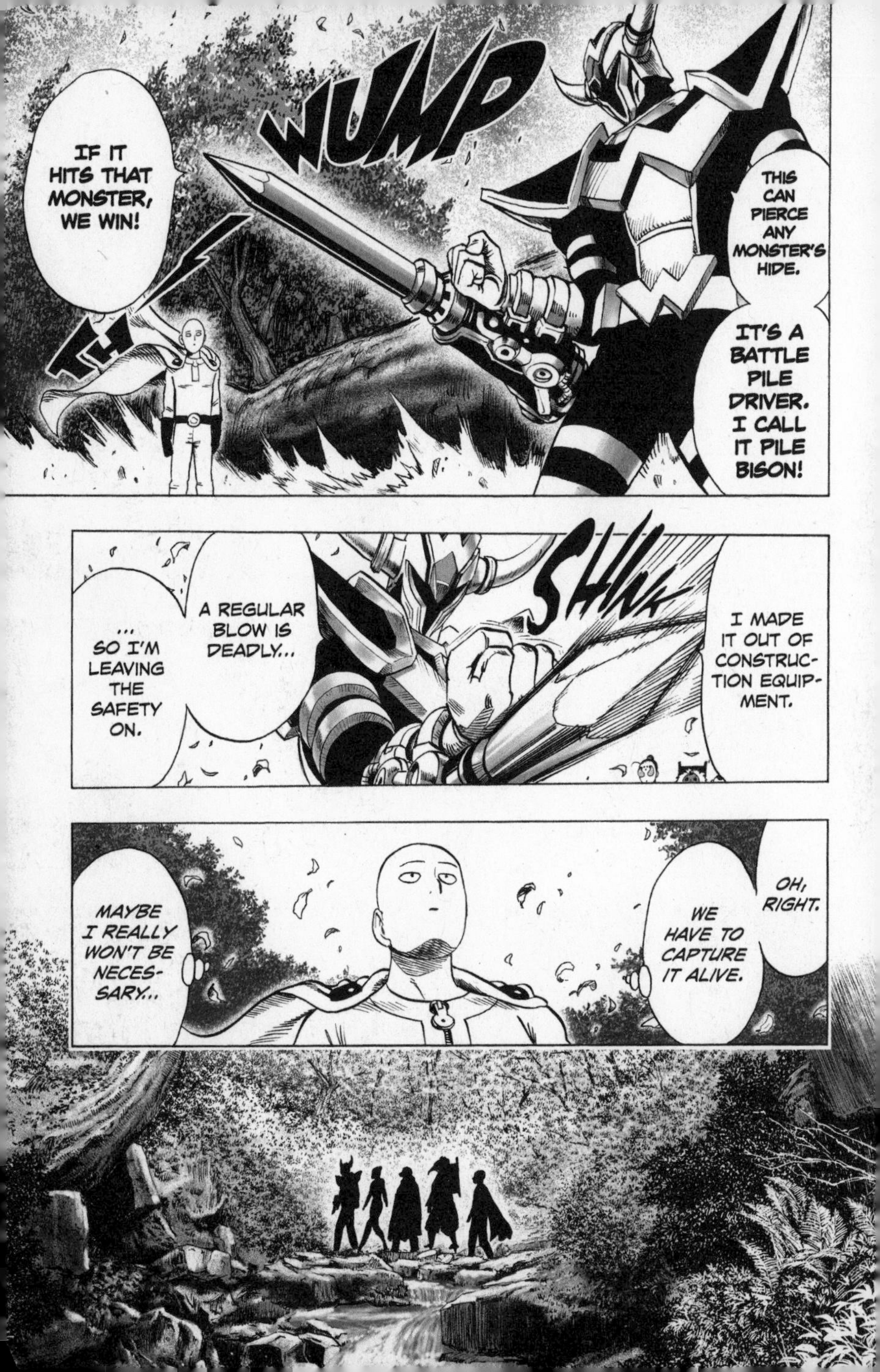
WUMP
THIS CAN PIERCE ANY MONSTER'S HIDE.
IT'S A BATTLE PILE DRIVER. I CALL IT PILE BISON!
IF IT HITS THAT MONSTER, WE WIN!
SHINK
I MADE IT OUT OF CONSTRUCTION EQUIPMENT.
A REGULAR BLOW IS DEADLY...
... SO I'M LEAVING THE SAFETY ON.
OH, RIGHT.
WE HAVE TO CAPTURE IT ALIVE.
MAYBE I REALLY WON'T BE NECESSARY...

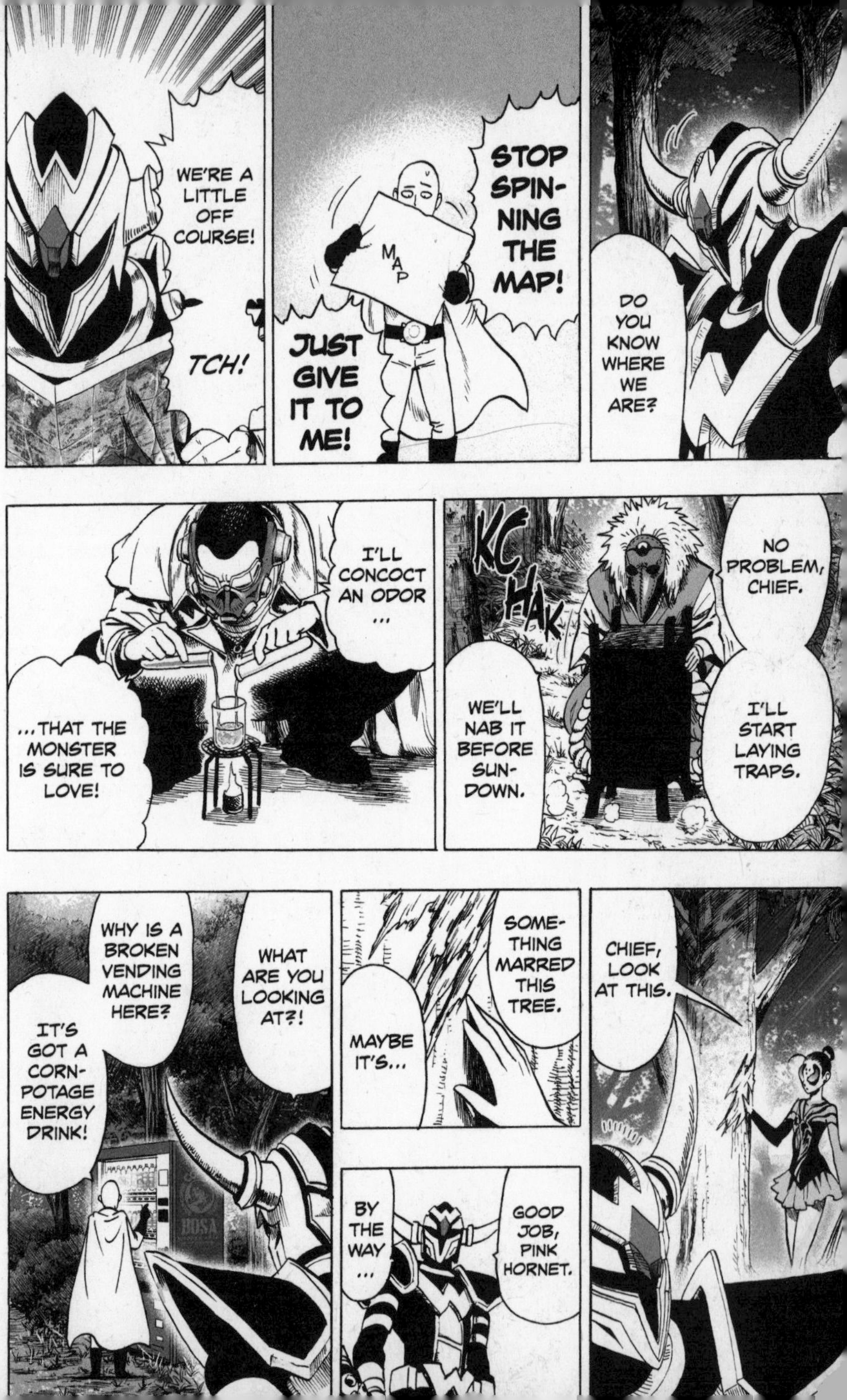
DO YOU KNOW WHERE WE ARE?
STOP SPIN-NING THE MAP!
MAP
JUST GIVE IT TO ME!
WE'RE A LITTLE OFF COURSE!
TCH!
NO PROBLEM, CHIEF.
I'LL START LAYING TRAPS.
KCHAK
WE'LL NAB IT BEFORE SUN-DOWN.
I'LL CONCOCT AN ODOR...
...THAT THE MONSTER IS SURE TO LOVE!
CHIEF, LOOK AT THIS.
SOME-THING MARRED THIS TREE.
MAYBE IT'S...
GOOD JOB, PINK HORNET.
BY THE WAY...
WHAT ARE YOU LOOKING AT?!
WHY IS A BROKEN VENDING MACHINE HERE?
IT'S GOT A CORN-POTAGE ENERGY DRINK!

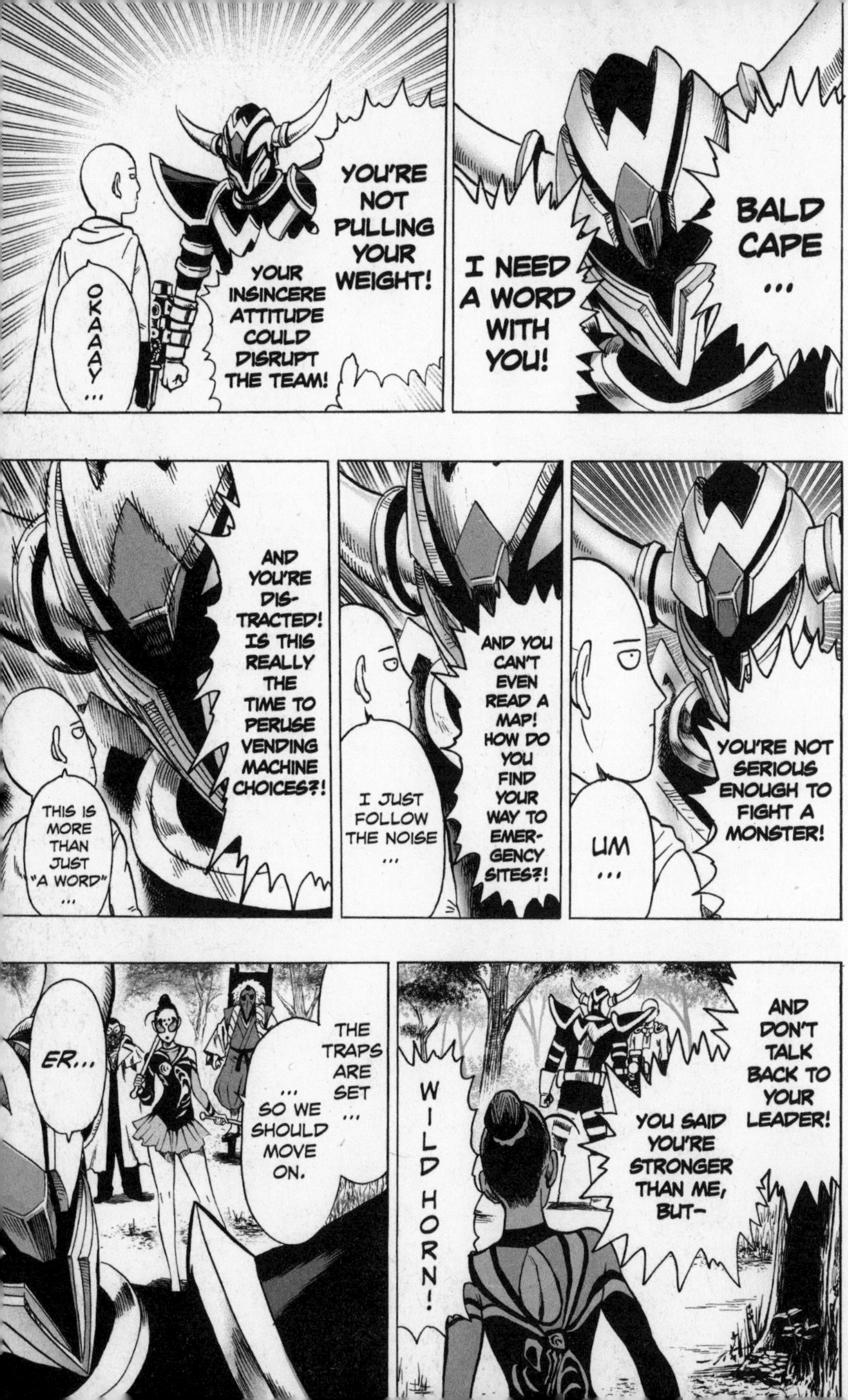
BALD CAPE ...
I NEED A WORD WITH YOU!
YOU'RE NOT PULLING YOUR WEIGHT!
YOUR INSINCERE ATTITUDE COULD DISRUPT THE TEAM!
OKAAAY ...
YOU'RE NOT SERIOUS ENOUGH TO FIGHT A MONSTER!
UM ...
AND YOU CAN'T EVEN READ A MAP! HOW DO YOU FIND YOUR WAY TO EMER-GENCY SITES?!
I JUST FOLLOW THE NOISE ...
AND YOU'RE DIS-TRACTED! IS THIS REALLY THE TIME TO PERUSE VENDING MACHINE CHOICES?!
THIS IS MORE THAN JUST "A WORD" ...
AND DON'T TALK BACK TO YOUR LEADER!
YOU SAID YOU'RE STRONGER THAN ME, BUT—
WILD HORN!
THE TRAPS ARE SET ...
... SO WE SHOULD MOVE ON.
ER...

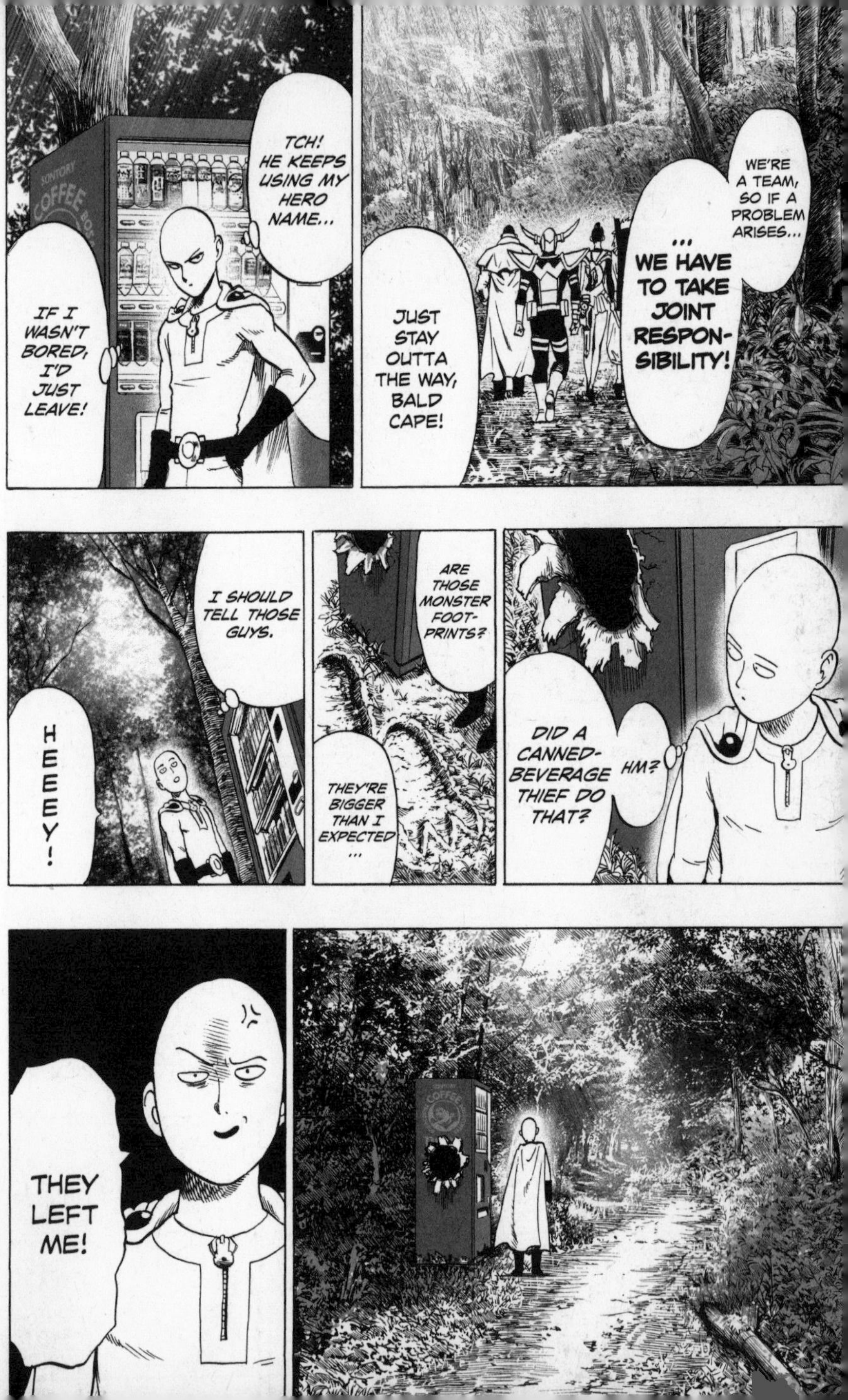
WE'RE A TEAM, SO IF A PROBLEM ARISES...
...WE HAVE TO TAKE JOINT RESPON-SIBILITY!
JUST STAY OUTTA THE WAY, BALD CAPE!
TCH! HE KEEPS USING MY HERO NAME...
IF I WASN'T BORED, I'D JUST LEAVE!
HM?
DID A CANNED-BEVERAGE THIEF DO THAT?
ARE THOSE MONSTER FOOT-PRINTS?
THEY'RE BIGGER THAN I EXPECTED...
I SHOULD TELL THOSE GUYS.
HEEEEY!
THEY LEFT ME!

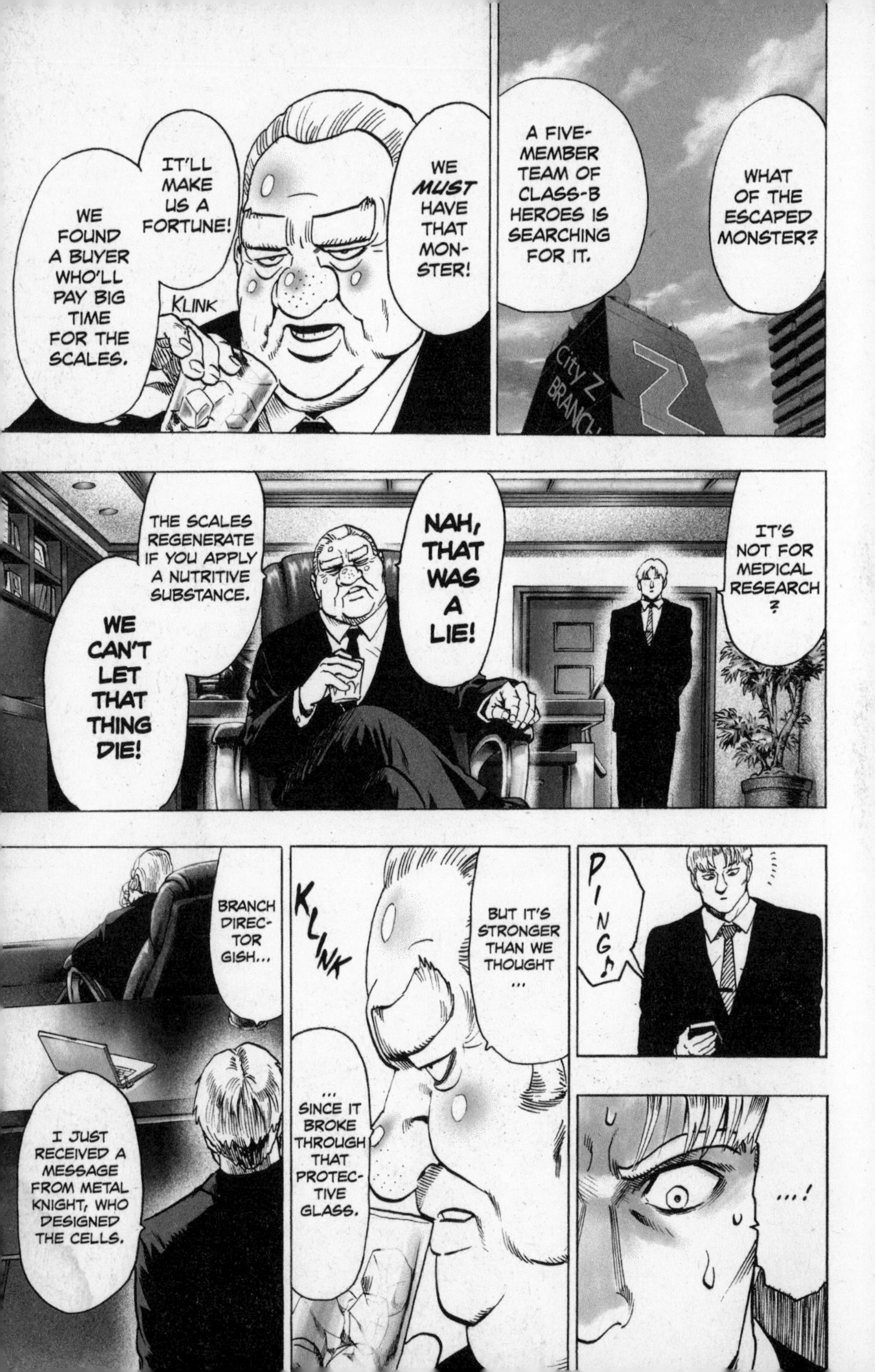
WHAT OF THE ESCAPED MONSTER?
A FIVE-MEMBER TEAM OF CLASS-B HEROES IS SEARCHING FOR IT.
City Z BRANCH
WE MUST HAVE THAT MONSTER!
IT'LL MAKE US A FORTUNE!
KLINK
WE FOUND A BUYER WHO'LL PAY BIG TIME FOR THE SCALES.
IT'S NOT FOR MEDICAL RESEARCH?
NAH, THAT WAS A LIE!
THE SCALES REGENERATE IF YOU APPLY A NUTRITIVE SUBSTANCE.
WE CAN'T LET THAT THING DIE!
PING♪
...
...!
BUT IT'S STRONGER THAN WE THOUGHT...
KLINK
...SINCE IT BROKE THROUGH THAT PROTECTIVE GLASS.
BRANCH DIRECTOR GISH...
I JUST RECEIVED A MESSAGE FROM METAL KNIGHT, WHO DESIGNED THE CELLS.

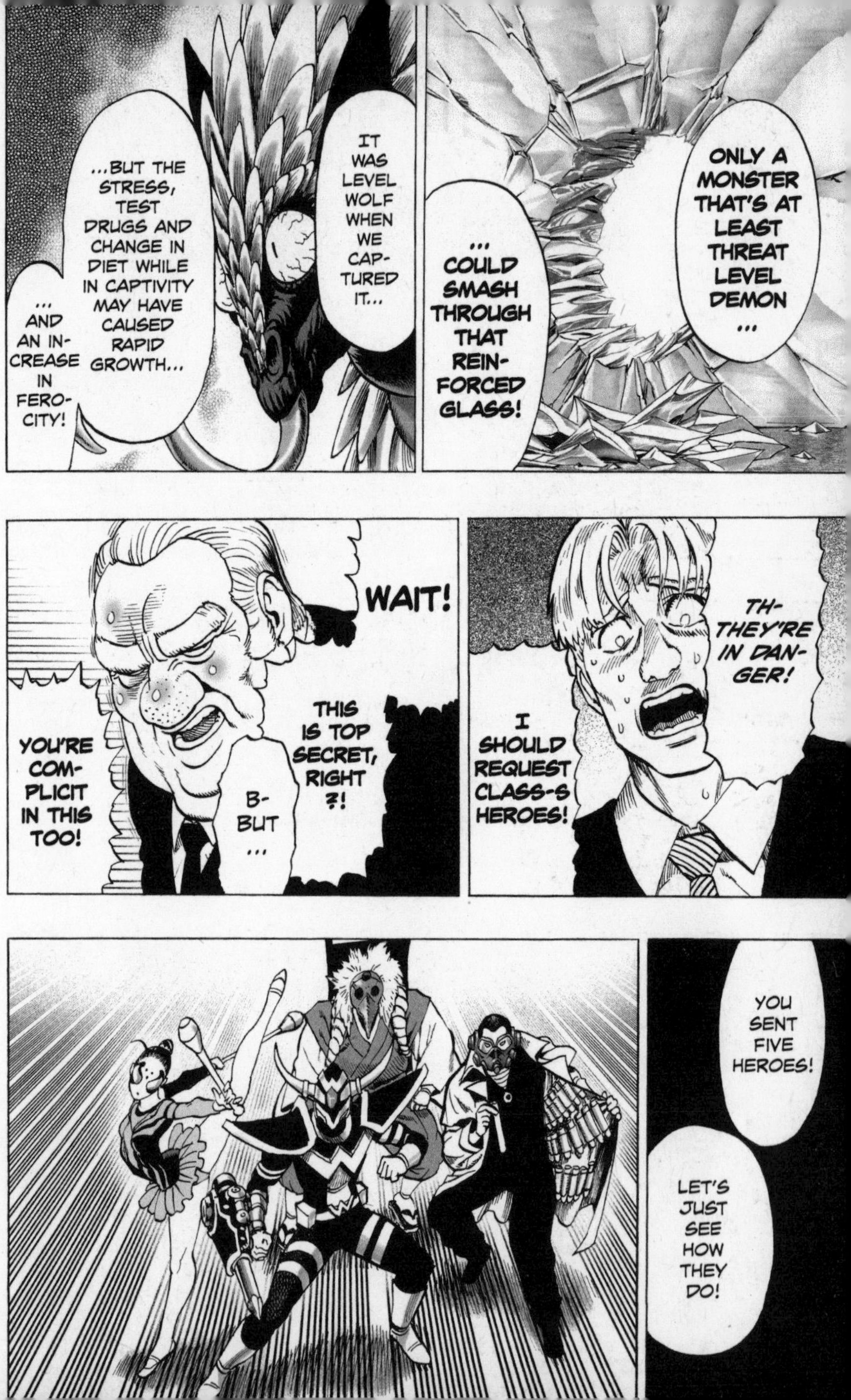
ONLY A MONSTER THAT'S AT LEAST THREAT LEVEL DEMON...
...COULD SMASH THROUGH THAT REINFORCED GLASS!
IT WAS LEVEL WOLF WHEN WE CAPTURED IT...
...BUT THE STRESS, TEST DRUGS AND CHANGE IN DIET WHILE IN CAPTIVITY MAY HAVE CAUSED RAPID GROWTH...
...AND AN INCREASE IN FEROCITY!
TH-THEY'RE IN DANGER!
I SHOULD REQUEST CLASS-S HEROES!
WAIT!
THIS IS TOP SECRET, RIGHT?!
B-BUT...
YOU'RE COMPLICIT IN THIS TOO!
YOU SENT FIVE HEROES!
LET'S JUST SEE HOW THEY DO!

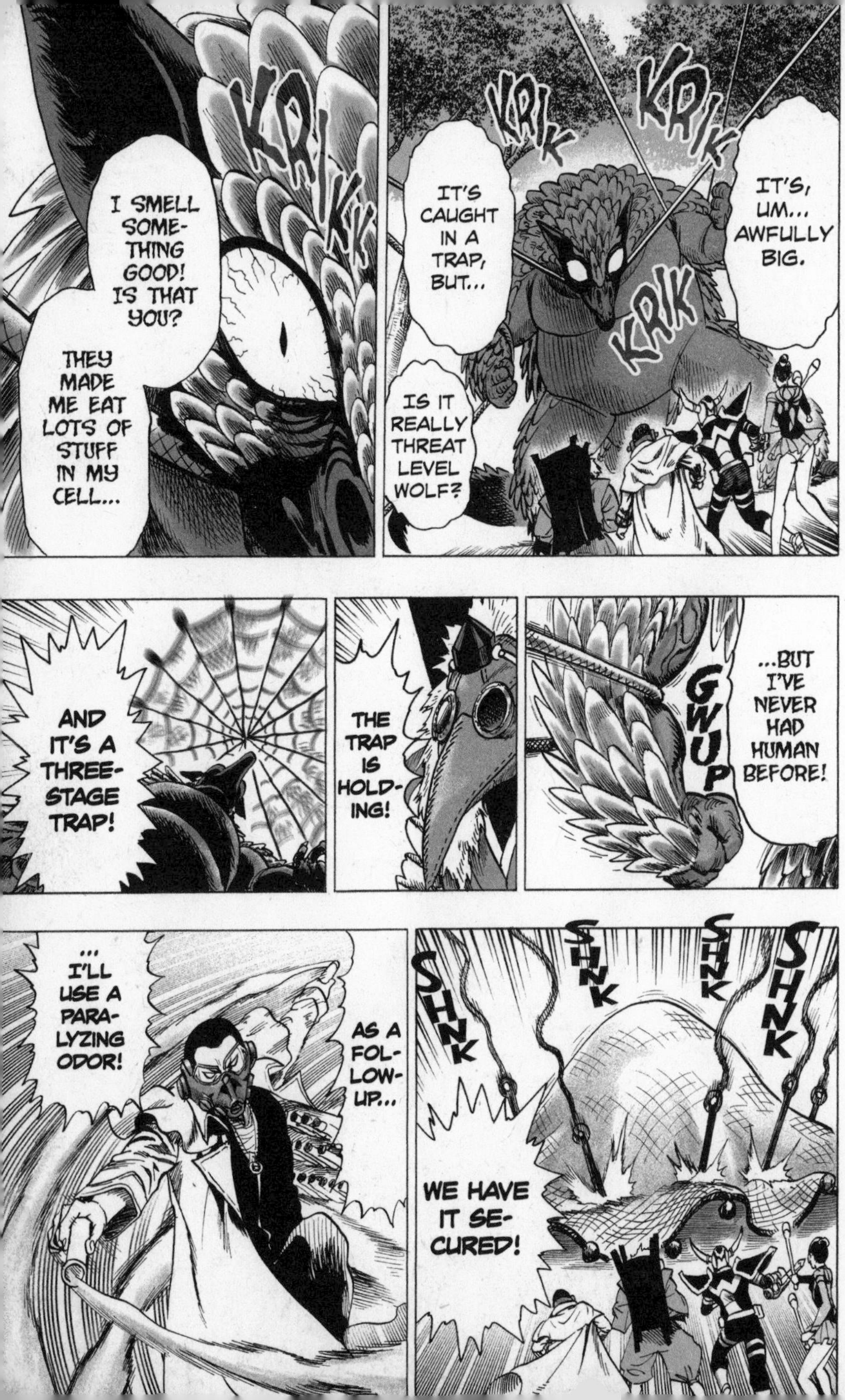
KRIK
KRIK
IT'S, UM... AWFULLY BIG.
IT'S CAUGHT IN A TRAP, BUT...
KRIK
IS IT REALLY THREAT LEVEL WOLF?
KRIKKK
I SMELL SOMETHING GOOD! IS THAT YOU?
THEY MADE ME EAT LOTS OF STUFF IN MY CELL...
...BUT I'VE NEVER HAD HUMAN BEFORE!
GWUP
THE TRAP IS HOLDING!
AND IT'S A THREE-STAGE TRAP!
SHNK
SHNK
SHNK
SHNK
WE HAVE IT SECURED!
AS A FOLLOW-UP...
...I'LL USE A PARALYZING ODOR!

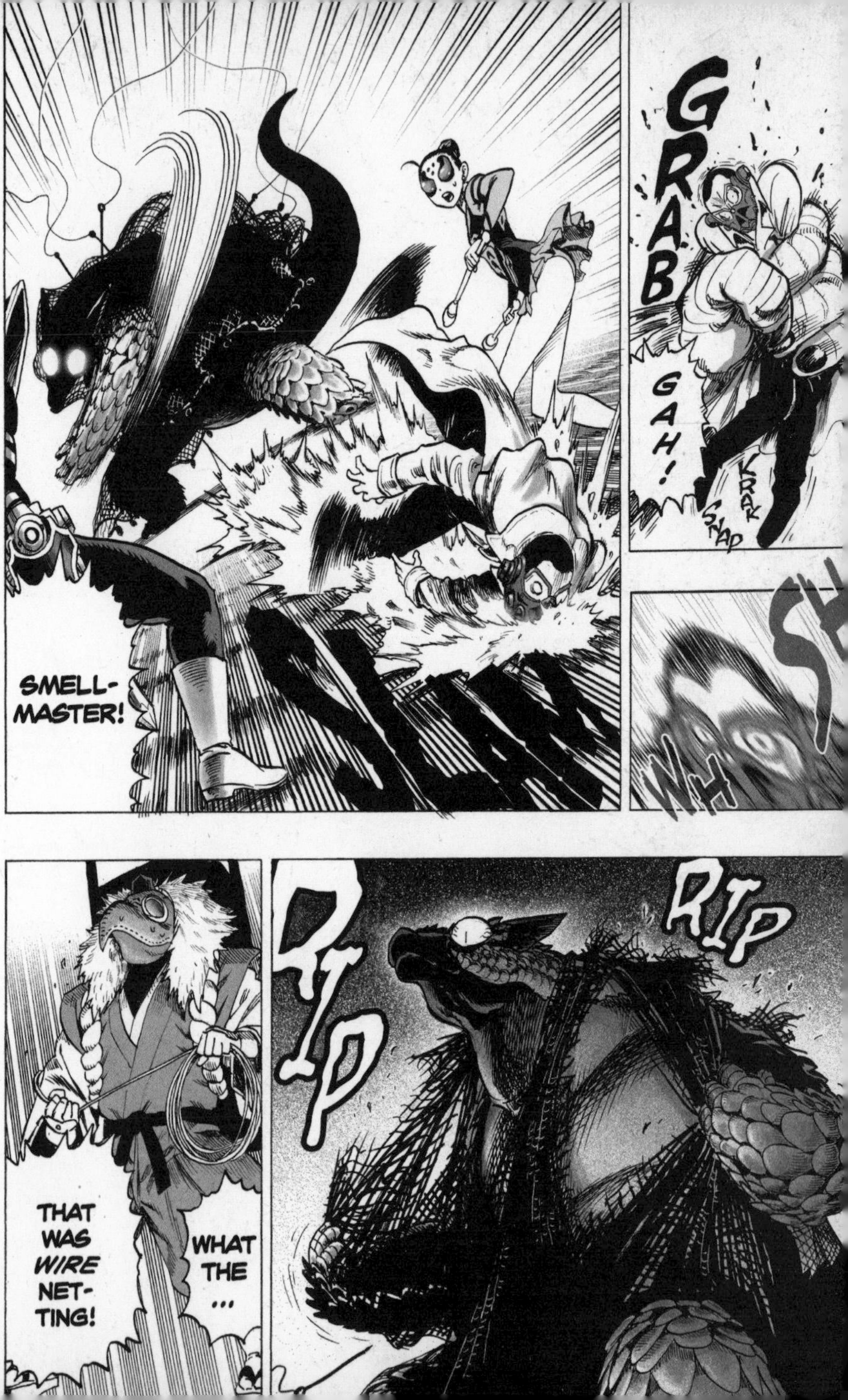
GRAB
GAH!
KRAK
SNAP
SMELL-MASTER!
DRIP
RIP
WHAT THE ...
THAT WAS *WIRE* NET-TING!

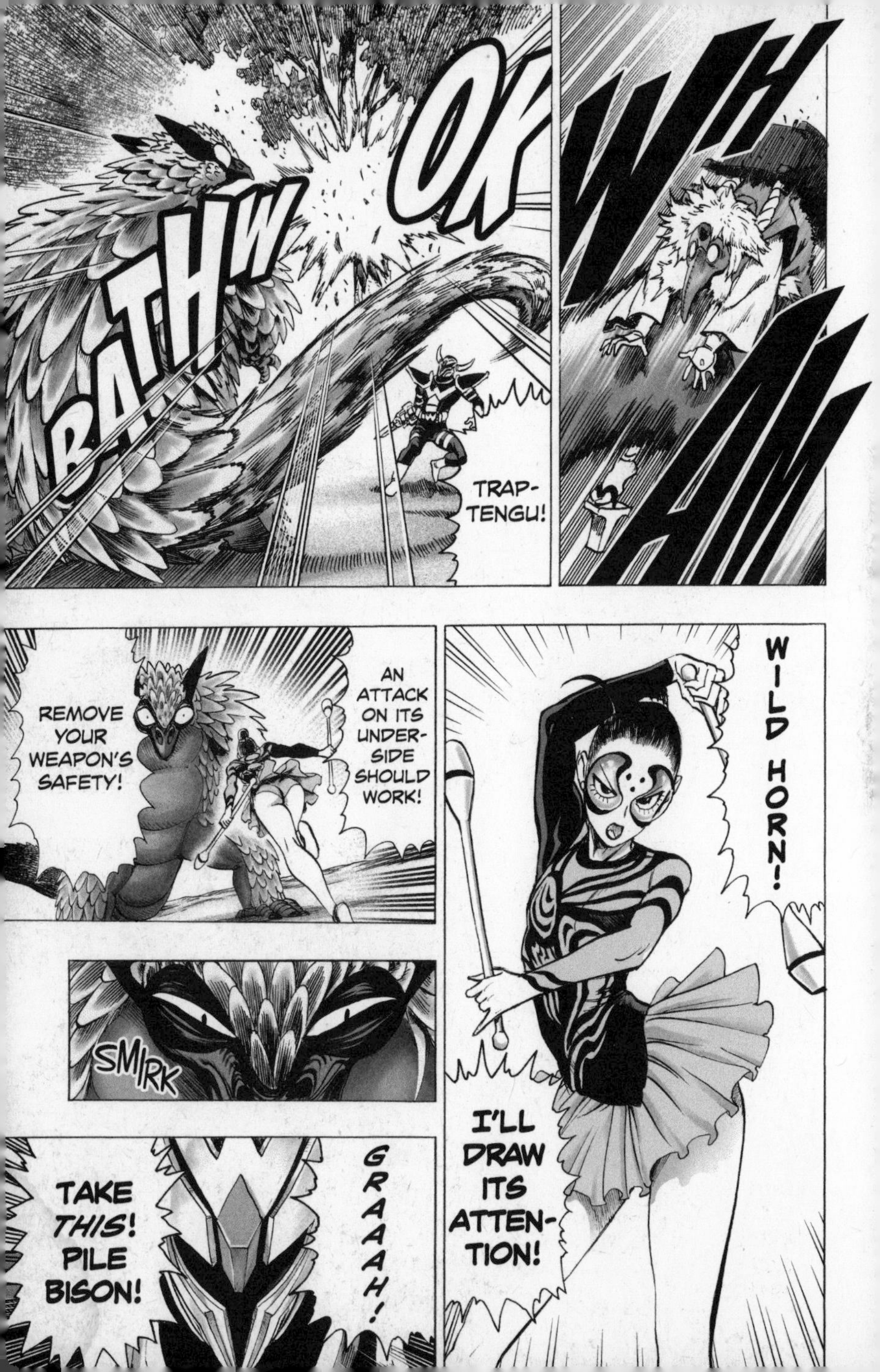
WHAM
BATHWOK
TRAP-TENGU!
WILD HORN!
I'LL DRAW ITS ATTENTION!
AN ATTACK ON ITS UNDERSIDE SHOULD WORK!
REMOVE YOUR WEAPON'S SAFETY!
SMIRK
GRAAAH!
TAKE *THIS*! PILE BISON!

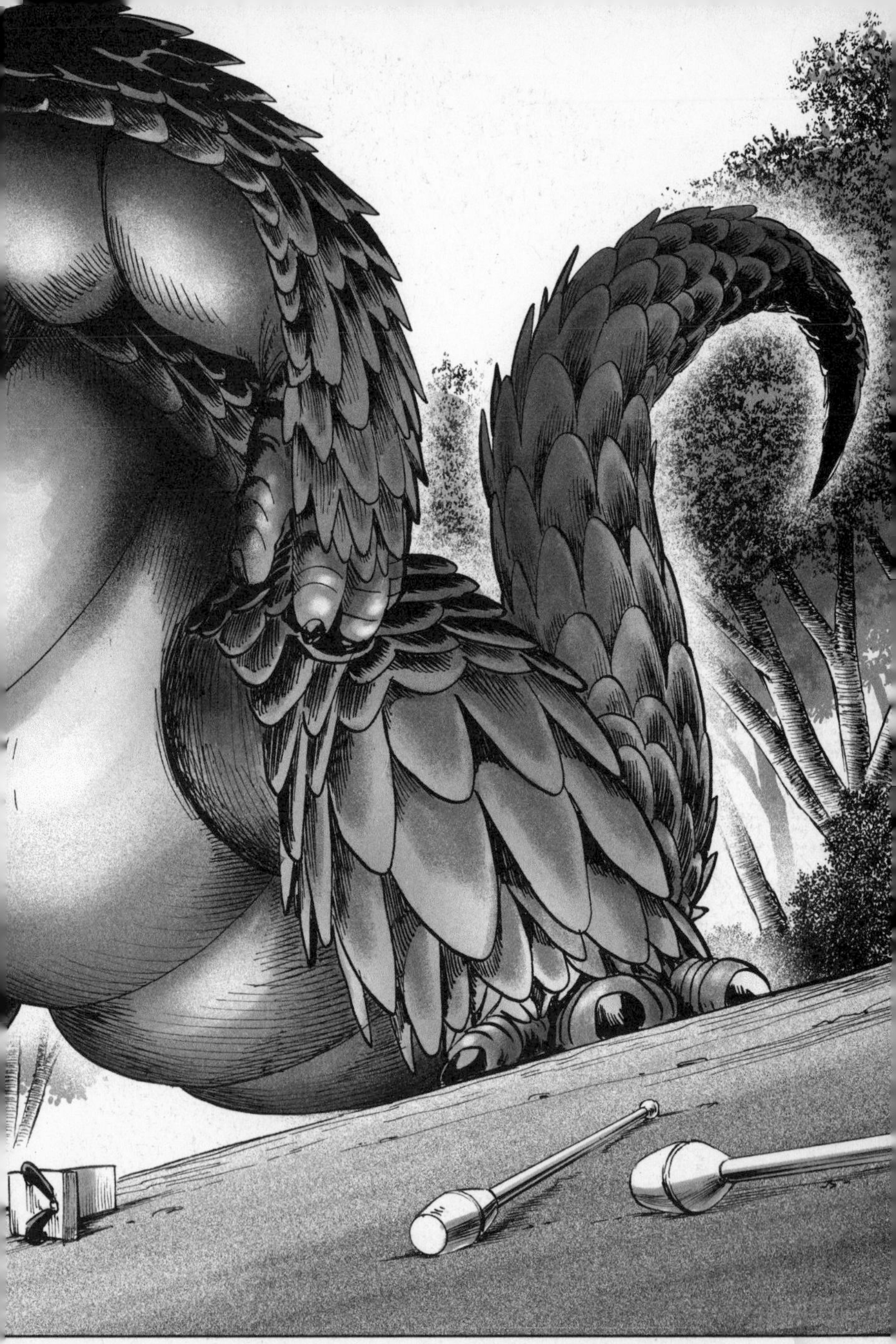

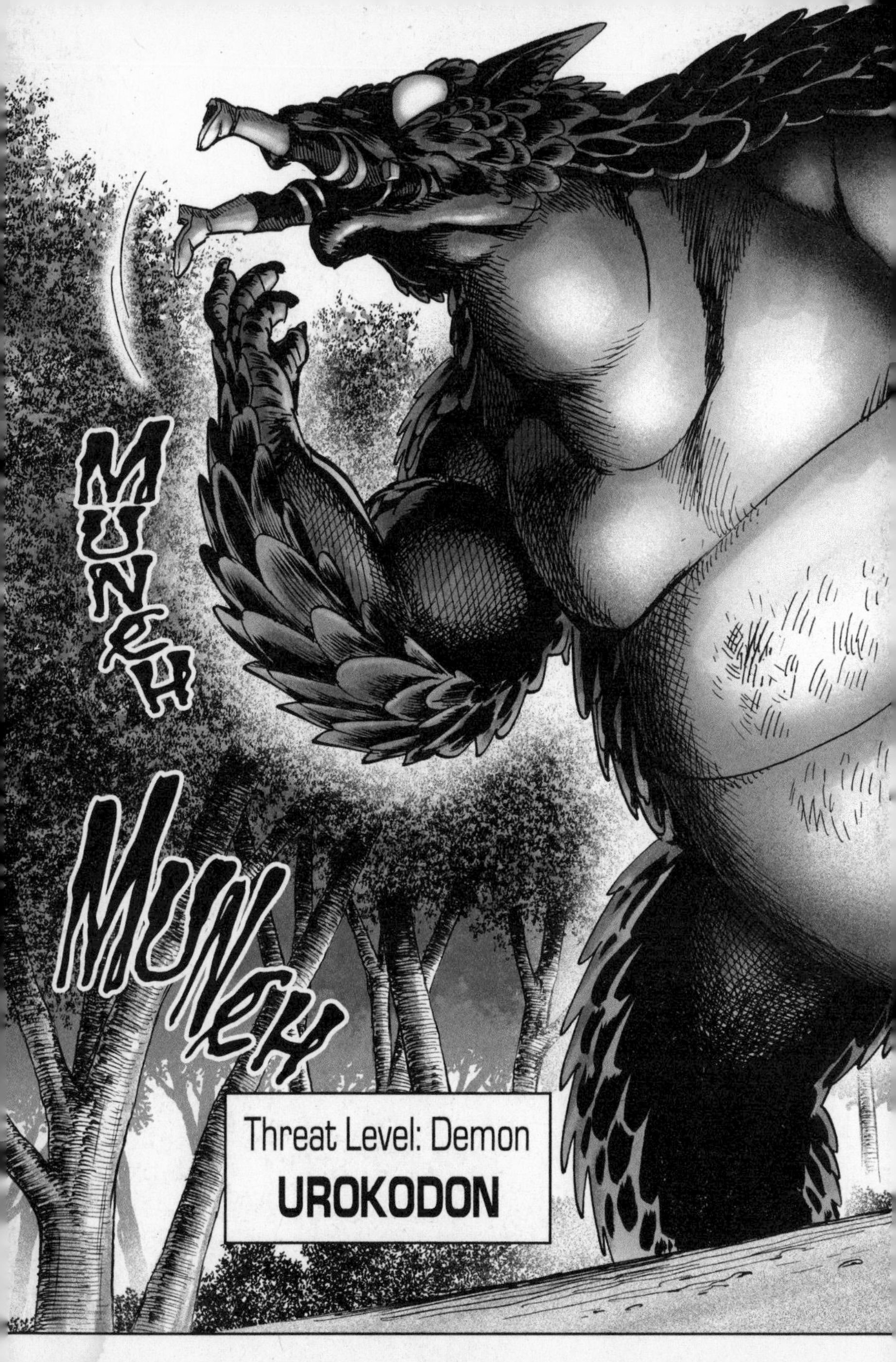
MUNCH
MUNCH
Threat Level: Demon
UROKODON

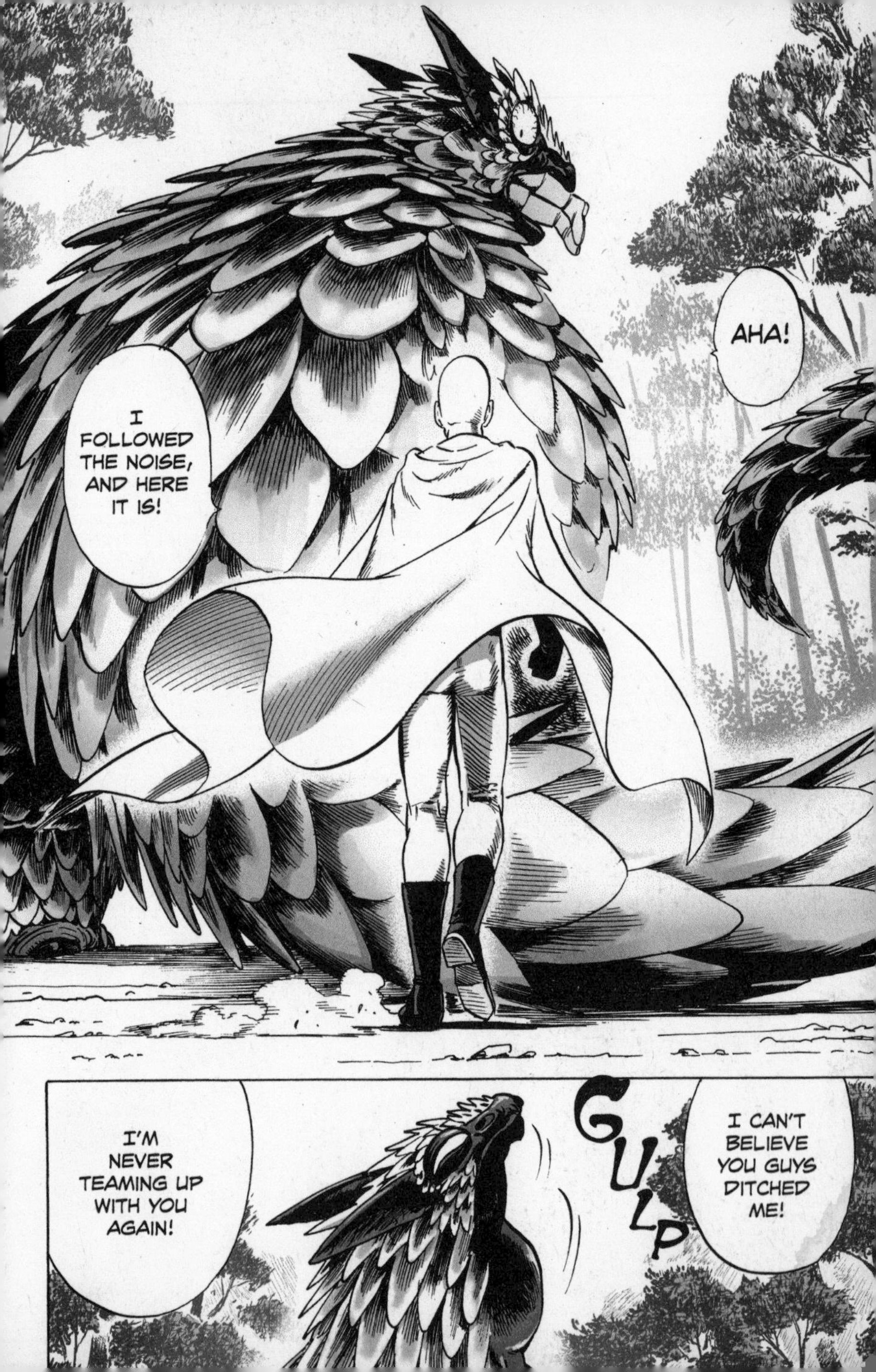
AHA!
I FOLLOWED THE NOISE, AND HERE IT IS!
I CAN'T BELIEVE YOU GUYS DITCHED ME!
GULP
I'M NEVER TEAMING UP WITH YOU AGAIN!

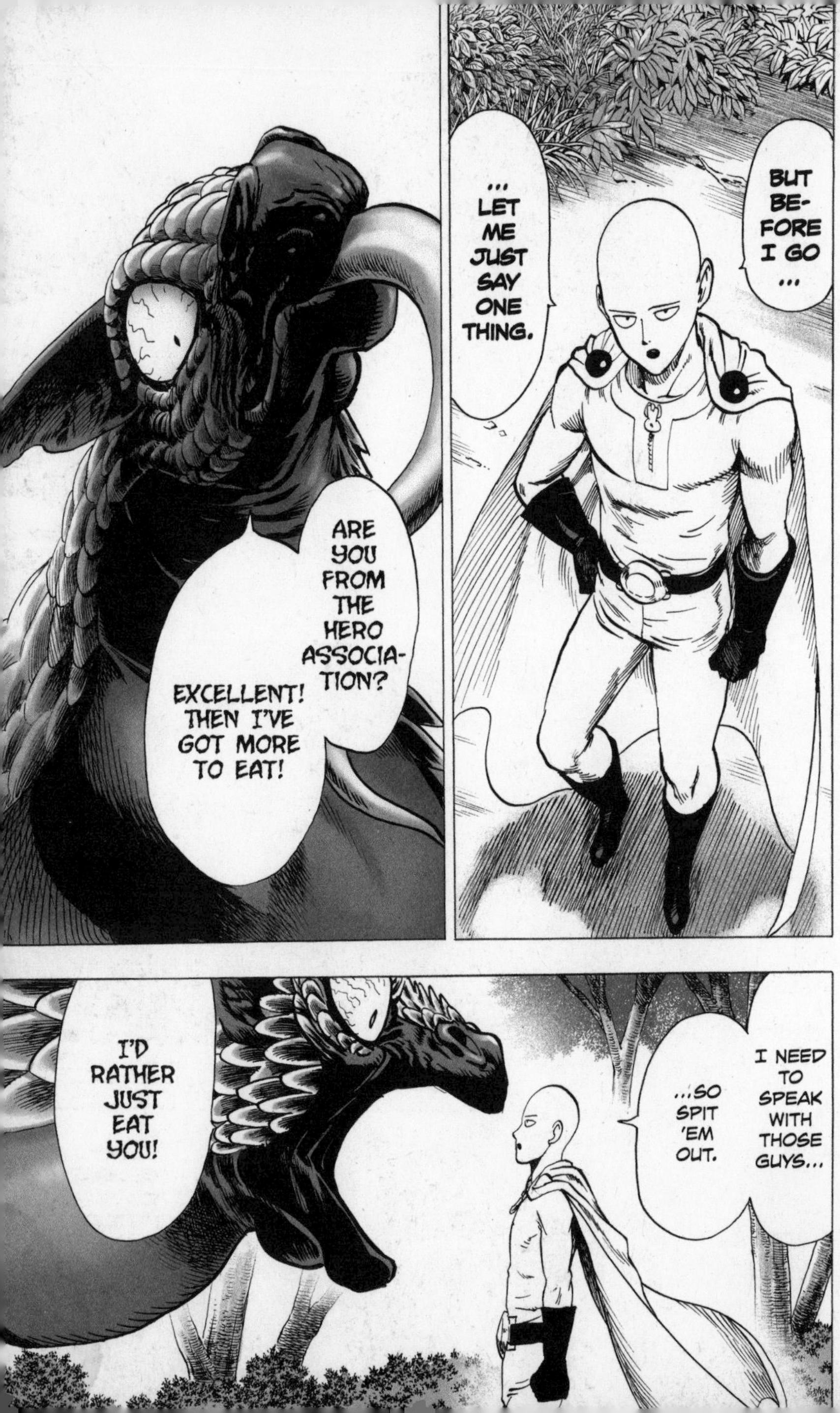
BUT BE-FORE I GO ...
... LET ME JUST SAY ONE THING.
ARE YOU FROM THE HERO ASSOCIA-TION?
EXCELLENT! THEN I'VE GOT MORE TO EAT!
I NEED TO SPEAK WITH THOSE GUYS...
...SO SPIT 'EM OUT.
I'D RATHER JUST EAT YOU!

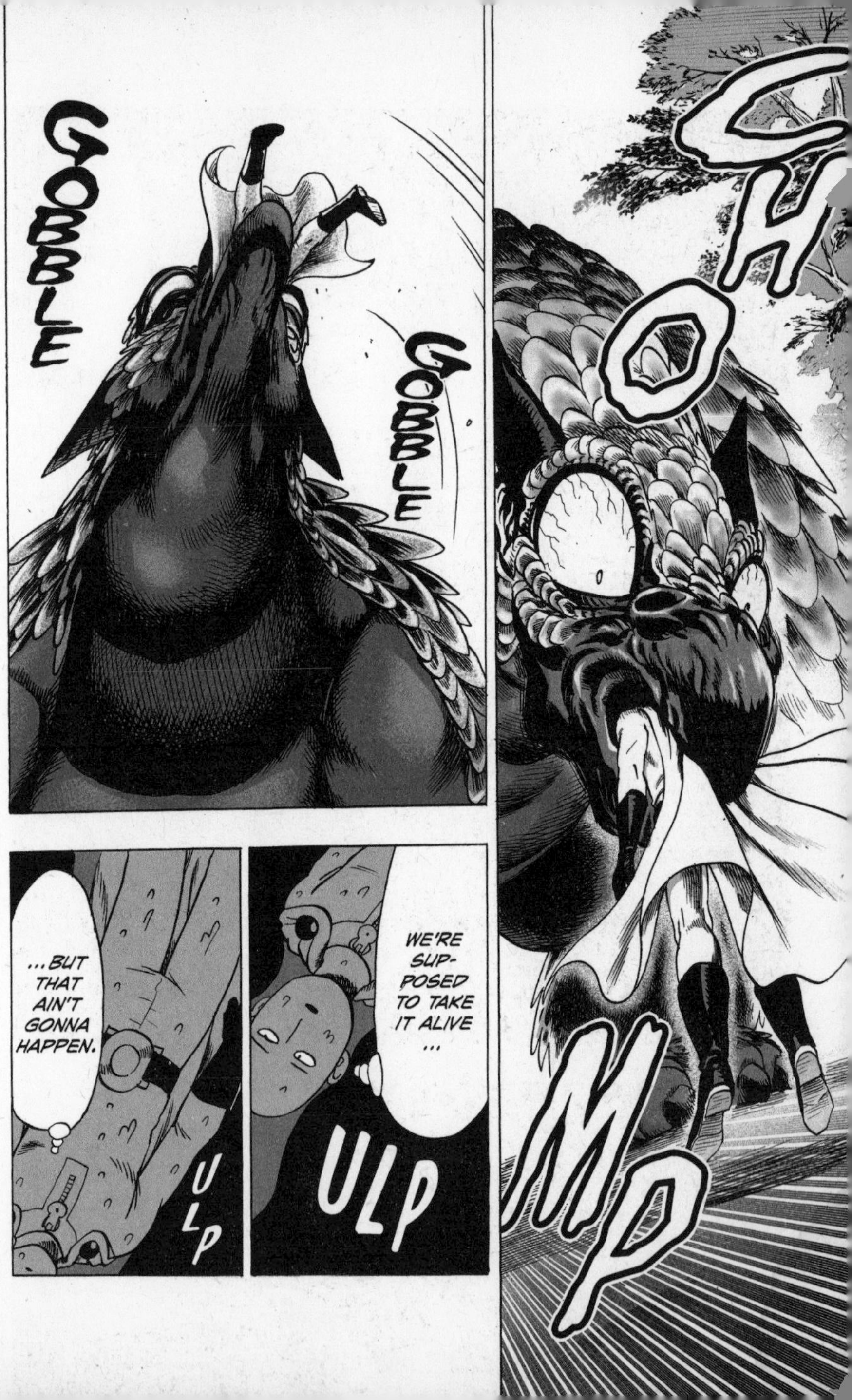
CHOMP
GOBBLE
GOBBLE
WE'RE SUP-POSED TO TAKE IT ALIVE ...
ULP
...BUT THAT AIN'T GONNA HAPPEN.
ULP

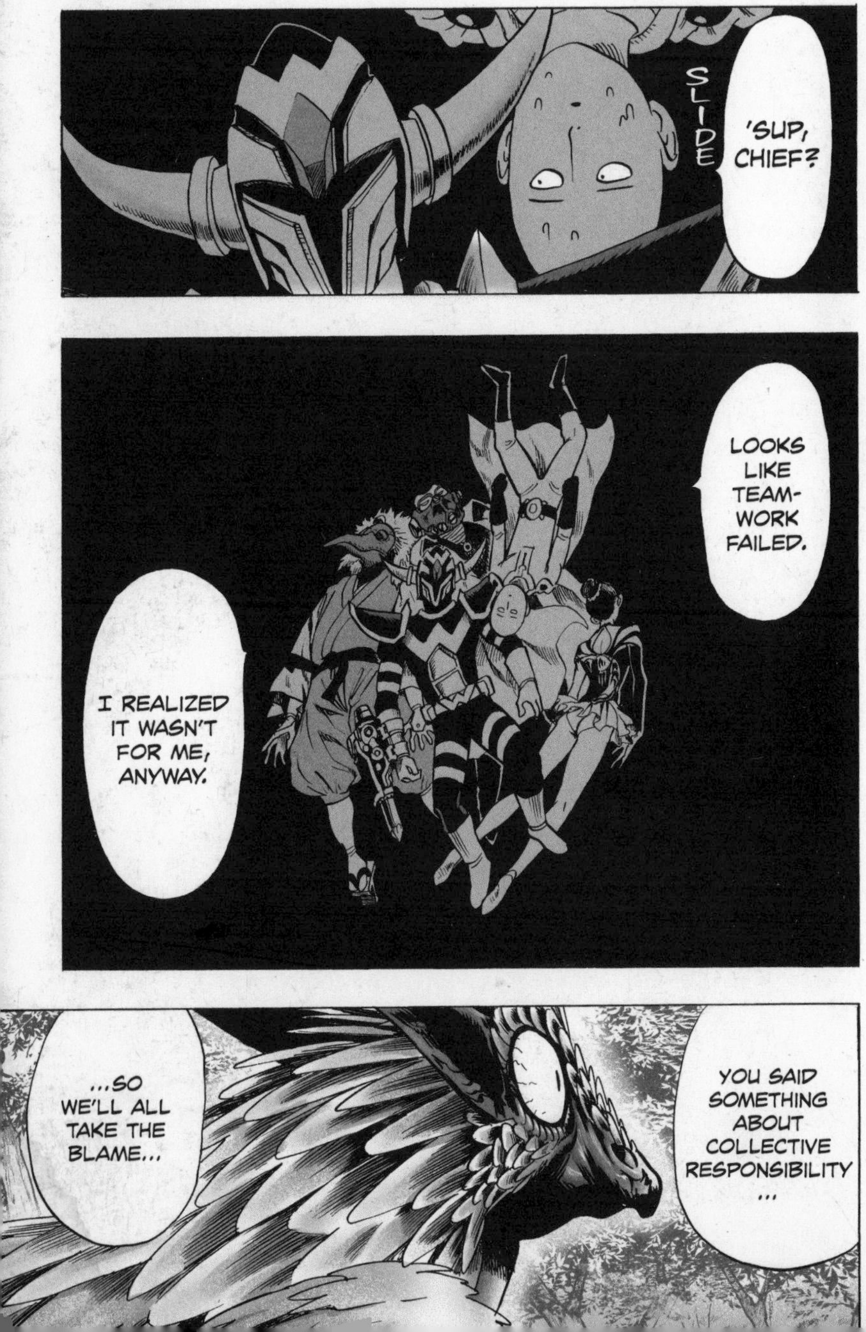
SLIDE
'SUP, CHIEF?
LOOKS LIKE TEAM-WORK FAILED.
I REALIZED IT WASN'T FOR ME, ANYWAY.
YOU SAID SOMETHING ABOUT COLLECTIVE RESPONSIBILITY ...
...SO WE'LL ALL TAKE THE BLAME...

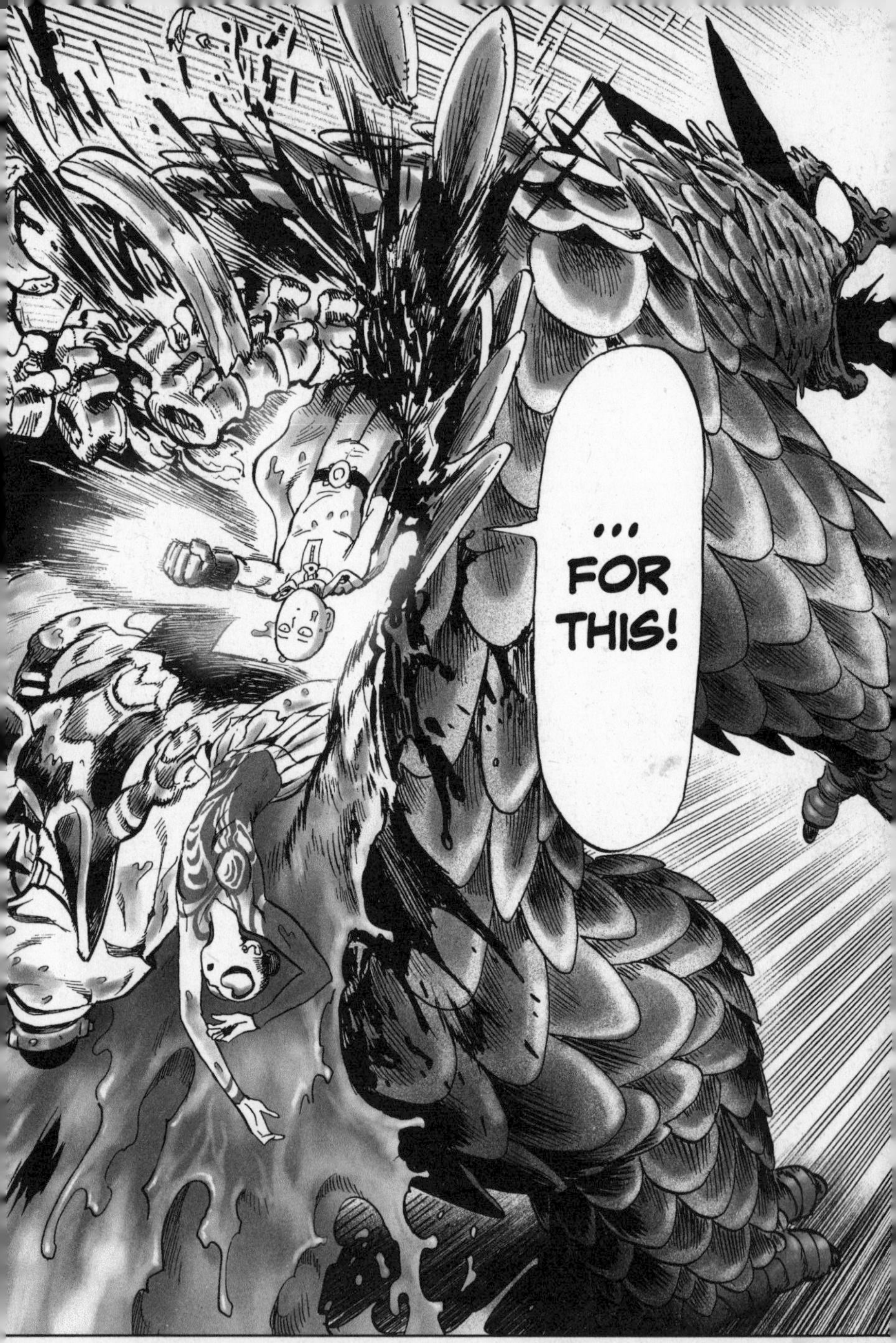
...FOR THIS!

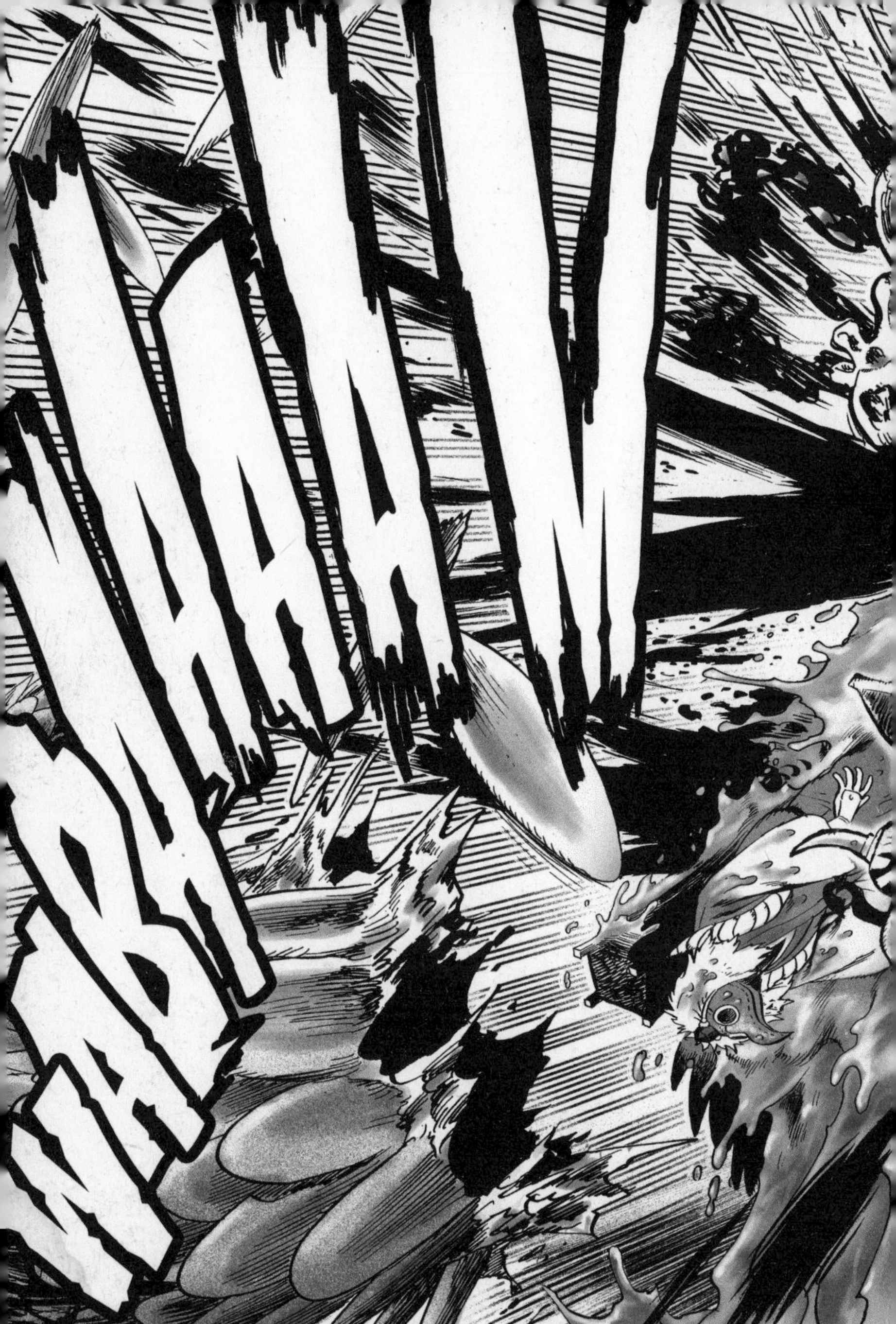

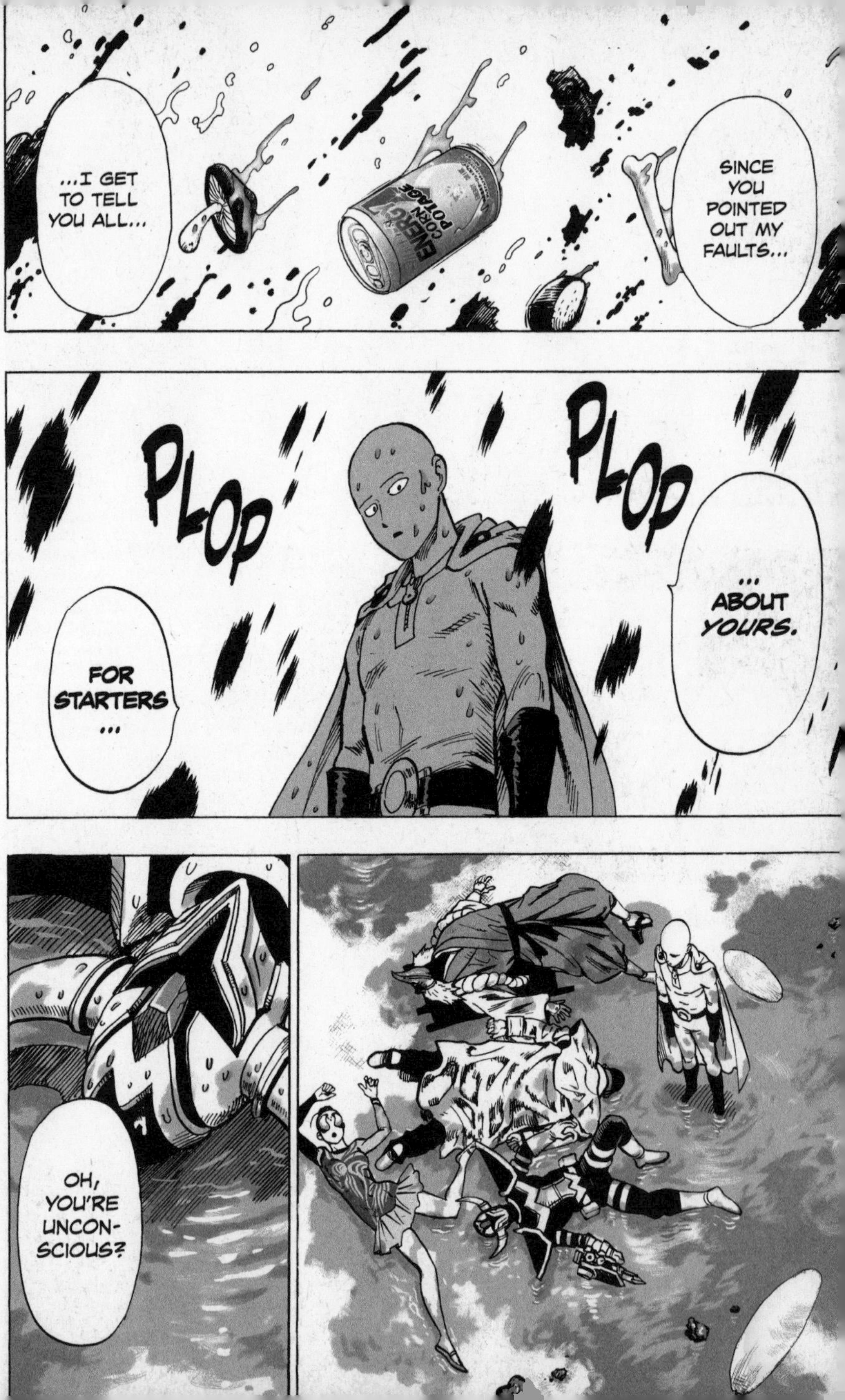
SINCE YOU POINTED OUT MY FAULTS...
...I GET TO TELL YOU ALL...
ENERGY CORN POTAGE
PLOP
...ABOUT YOURS.
PLOP
FOR STARTERS...
OH, YOU'RE UNCONSCIOUS?

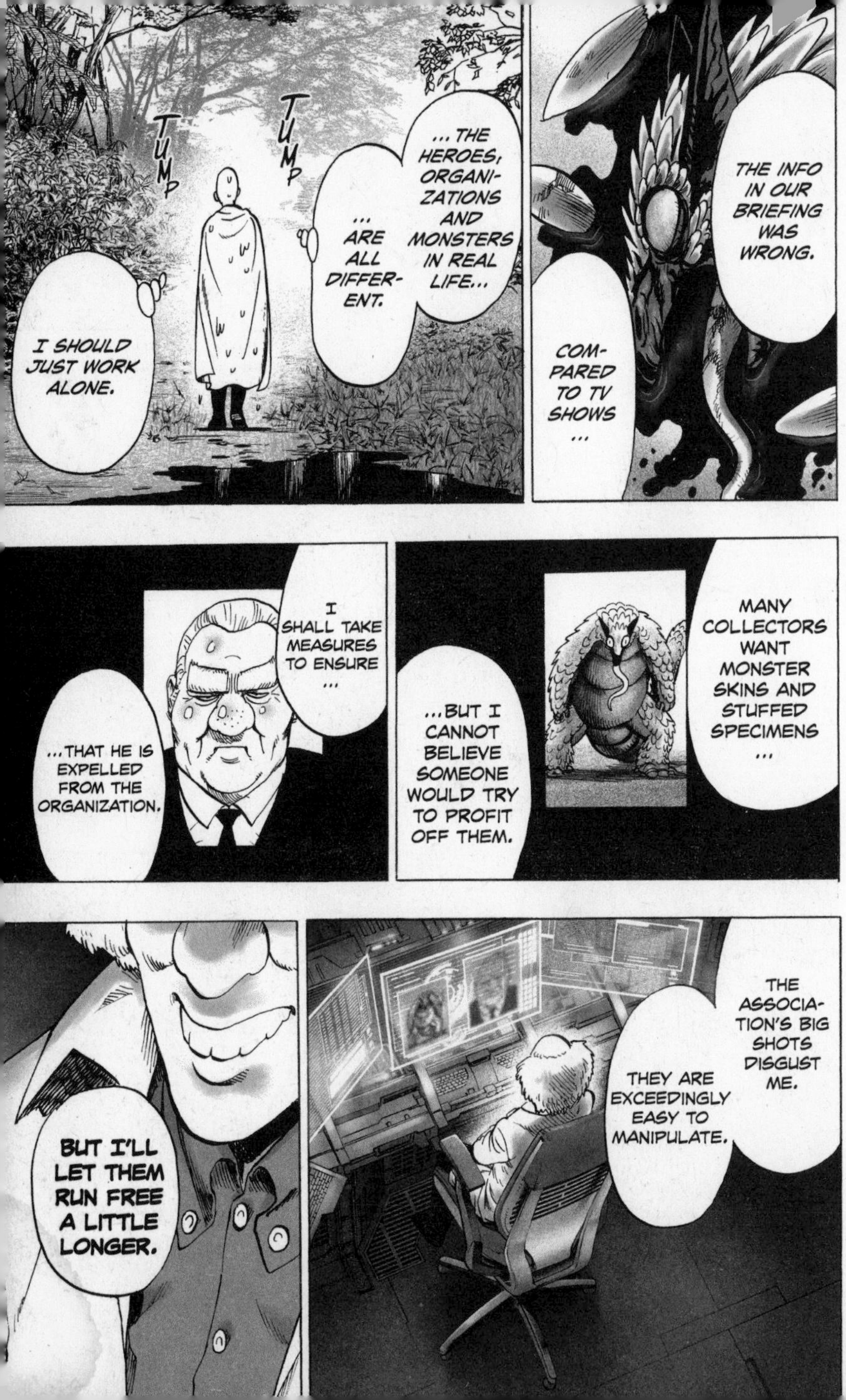
THE INFO IN OUR BRIEFING WAS WRONG.
COMPARED TO TV SHOWS...
TUMP
TUMP
...THE HEROES, ORGANIZATIONS AND MONSTERS IN REAL LIFE...
...ARE ALL DIFFERENT.
I SHOULD JUST WORK ALONE.
MANY COLLECTORS WANT MONSTER SKINS AND STUFFED SPECIMENS...
...BUT I CANNOT BELIEVE SOMEONE WOULD TRY TO PROFIT OFF THEM.
I SHALL TAKE MEASURES TO ENSURE...
...THAT HE IS EXPELLED FROM THE ORGANIZATION.
THE ASSOCIATION'S BIG SHOTS DISGUST ME.
THEY ARE EXCEEDINGLY EASY TO MANIPULATE.
BUT I'LL LET THEM RUN FREE A LITTLE LONGER.

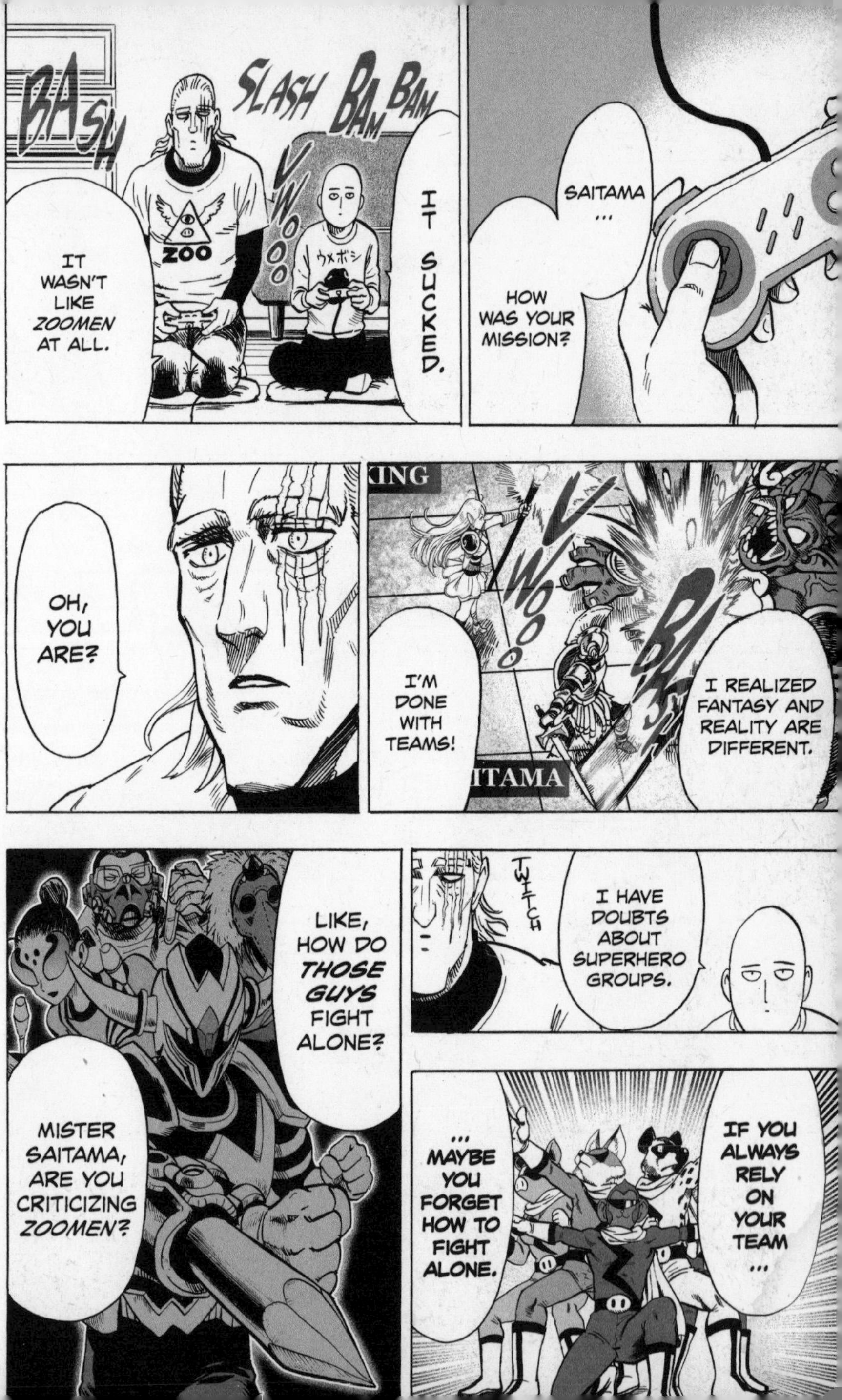
SAITAMA ...
HOW WAS YOUR MISSION?
IT SUCKED.
BASH
SLASH
BAM
BAM
VWOOO
ZOO
ウメボシ
IT WASN'T LIKE *ZOOMEN* AT ALL.
I REALIZED FANTASY AND REALITY ARE DIFFERENT.
KING
VWOOO
BASH
ITAMA
I'M DONE WITH TEAMS!
OH, YOU ARE?
I HAVE DOUBTS ABOUT SUPERHERO GROUPS.
TWITCH
IF YOU ALWAYS RELY ON YOUR TEAM ...
... MAYBE YOU FORGET HOW TO FIGHT ALONE.
LIKE, HOW DO *THOSE GUYS* FIGHT ALONE?
MISTER SAITAMA, ARE YOU CRITICIZING *ZOOMEN*?

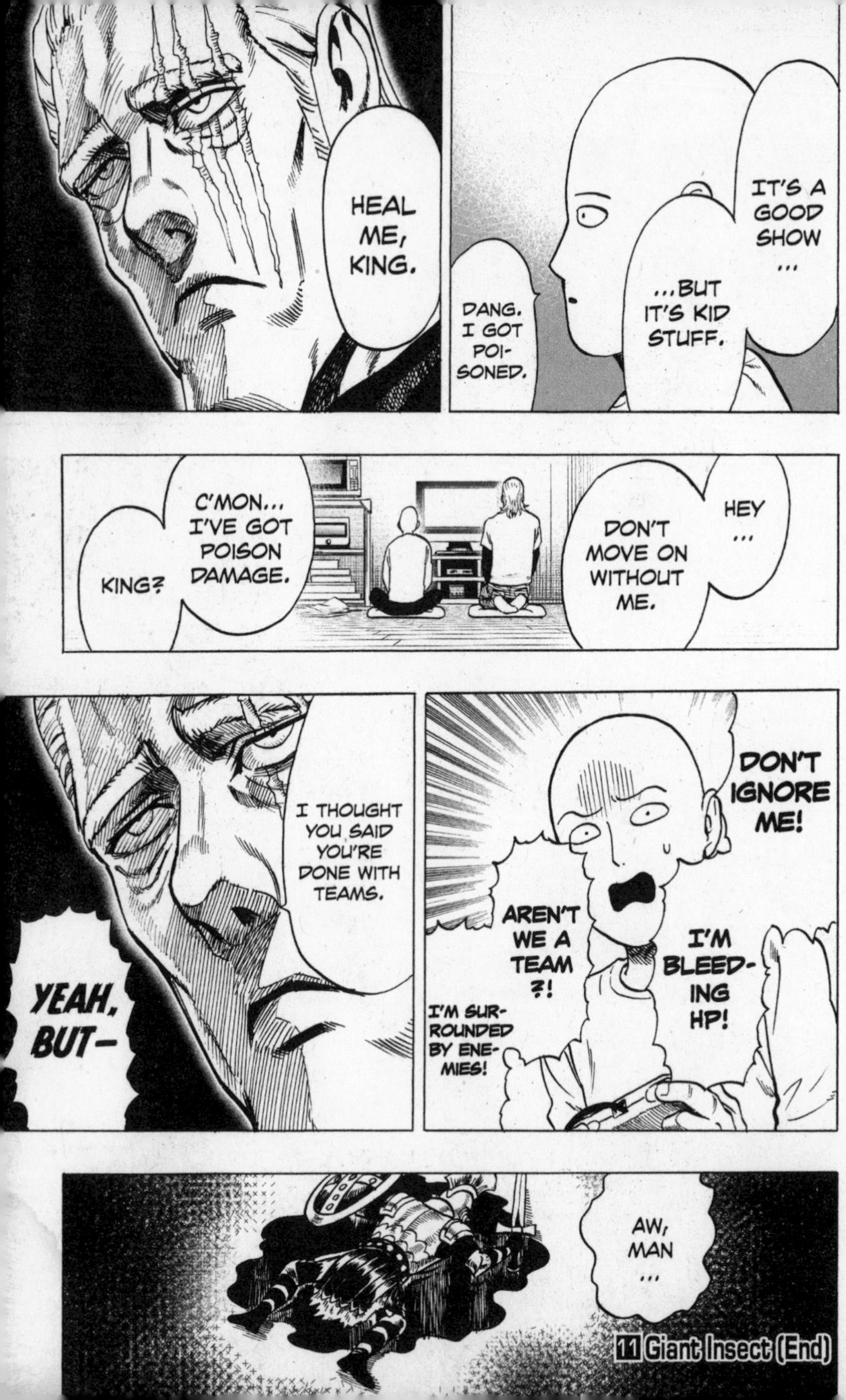
IT'S A GOOD SHOW...
...BUT IT'S KID STUFF.
DANG. I GOT POI-SONED.
HEAL ME, KING.
HEY...
DON'T MOVE ON WITHOUT ME.
C'MON... I'VE GOT POISON DAMAGE.
KING?
DON'T IGNORE ME!
I'M BLEED-ING HP!
AREN'T WE A TEAM?!
I'M SUR-ROUNDED BY ENE-MIES!
I THOUGHT YOU SAID YOU'RE DONE WITH TEAMS.
YEAH, BUT—
AW, MAN...
11 Giant Insect (End)

BONUS MANGA: WEAPON

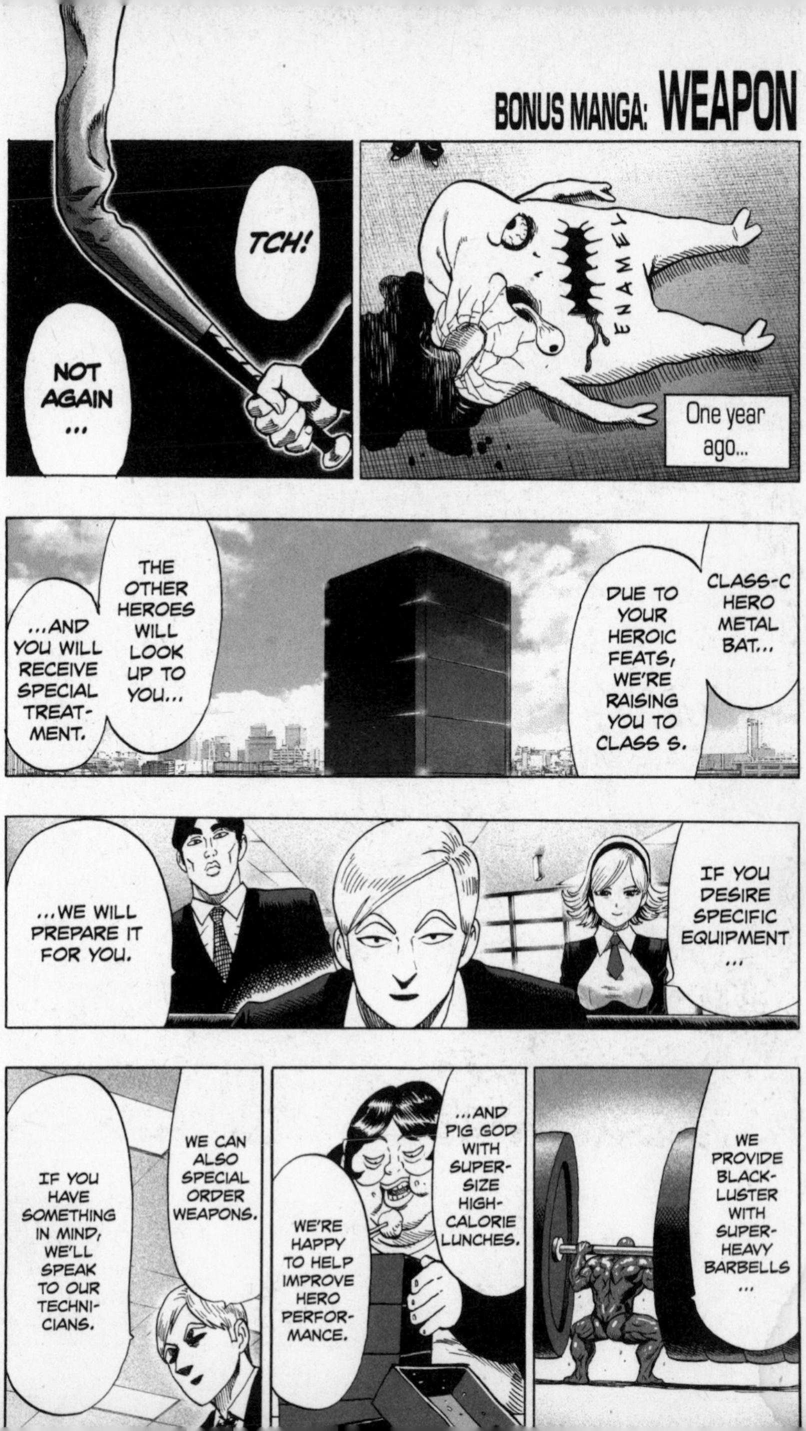
ENAMEL
One year ago...
TCH!
NOT AGAIN ...
CLASS-C HERO METAL BAT...
DUE TO YOUR HEROIC FEATS, WE'RE RAISING YOU TO CLASS S.
THE OTHER HEROES WILL LOOK UP TO YOU...
...AND YOU WILL RECEIVE SPECIAL TREAT-MENT.
IF YOU DESIRE SPECIFIC EQUIPMENT ...
...WE WILL PREPARE IT FOR YOU.
WE PROVIDE BLACK-LUSTER WITH SUPER-HEAVY BARBELLS ...
...AND PIG GOD WITH SUPER-SIZE HIGH-CALORIE LUNCHES.
WE'RE HAPPY TO HELP IMPROVE HERO PERFOR-MANCE.
WE CAN ALSO SPECIAL ORDER WEAPONS.
IF YOU HAVE SOMETHING IN MIND, WE'LL SPEAK TO OUR TECHNI-CIANS.

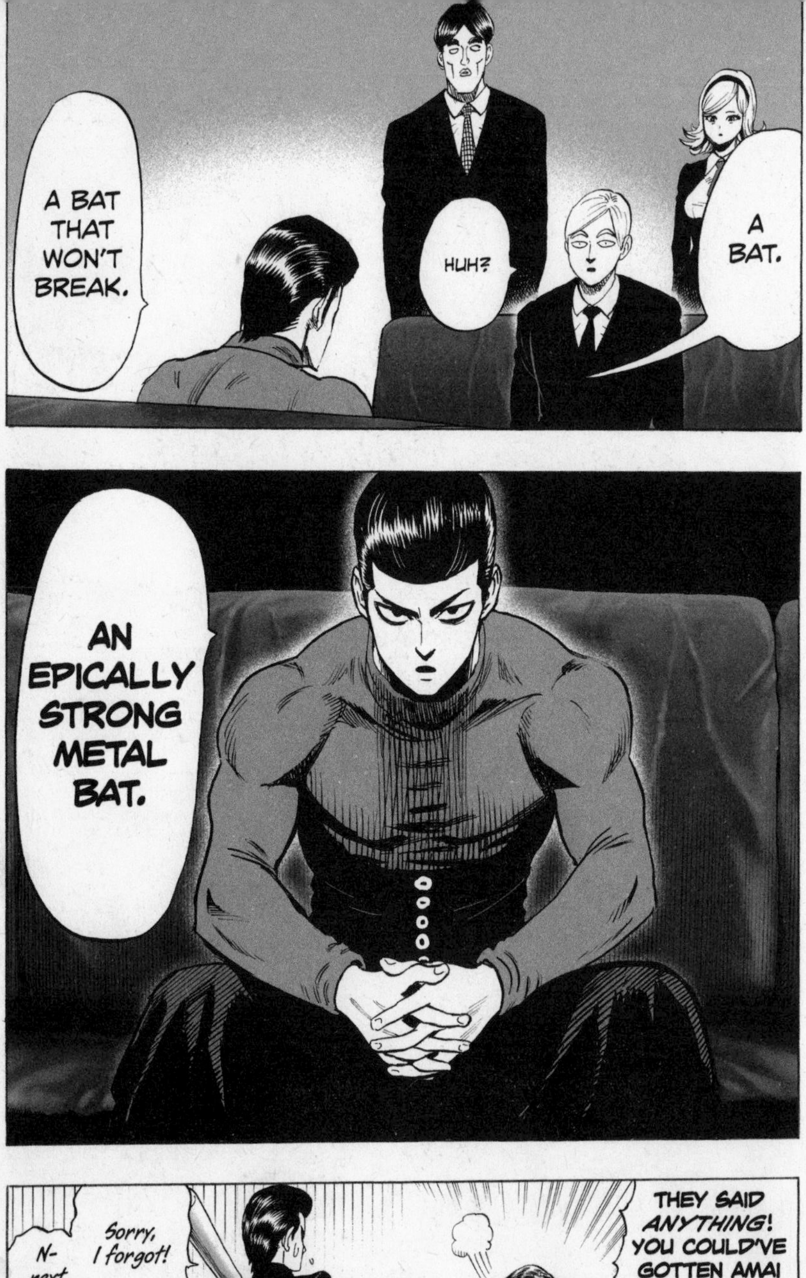
A BAT.
HUH?
A BAT THAT WON'T BREAK.
AN EPICALLY STRONG METAL BAT.
THEY SAID *ANYTHING*! YOU COULD'VE GOTTEN AMAI MASK'S SIGNATURE!
Sorry, I forgot!
N-next time, okay?

CONT'D FROM COVER

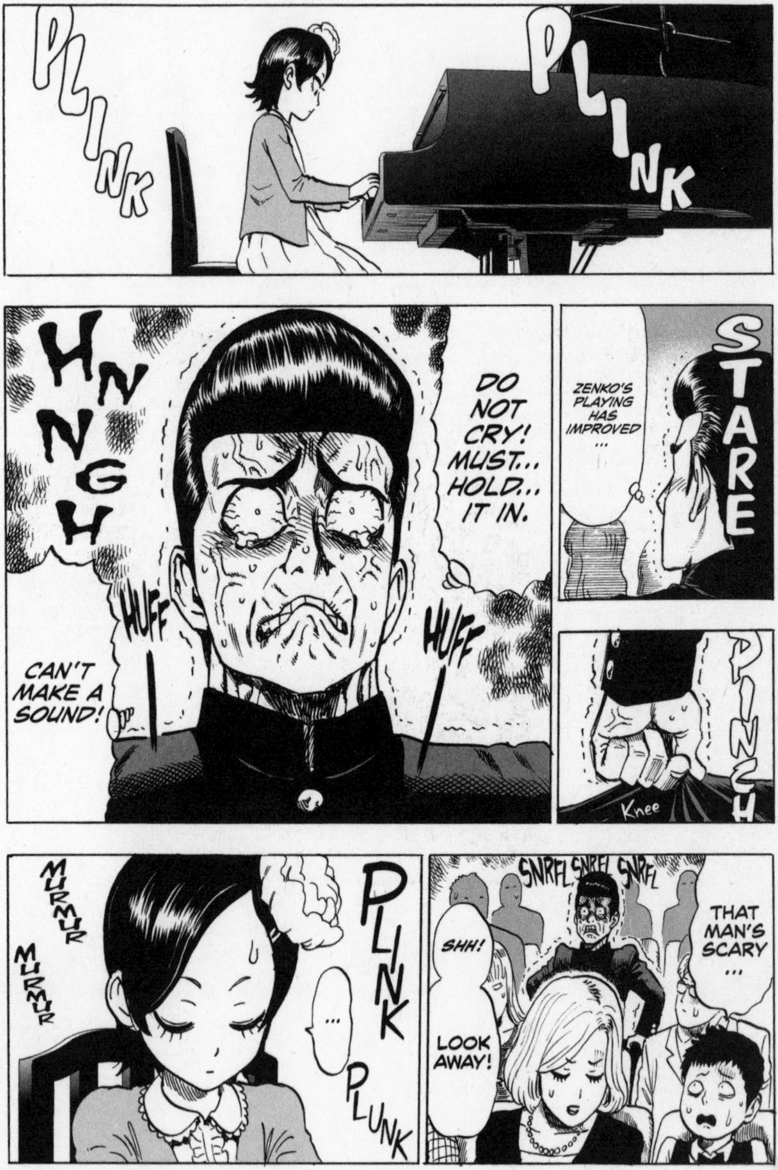
PLINK
PLINK
STARE
ZENKO'S PLAYING HAS IMPROVED ...
PINCH
Knee
DO NOT CRY! MUST... HOLD... IT IN.
HNNGH
HUFF
HUFF
CAN'T MAKE A SOUND!
SNRFL SNRFL SNRFL
THAT MAN'S SCARY ...
SHH!
LOOK AWAY!
PLINK
...
MURMUR
MURMUR
PLUNK

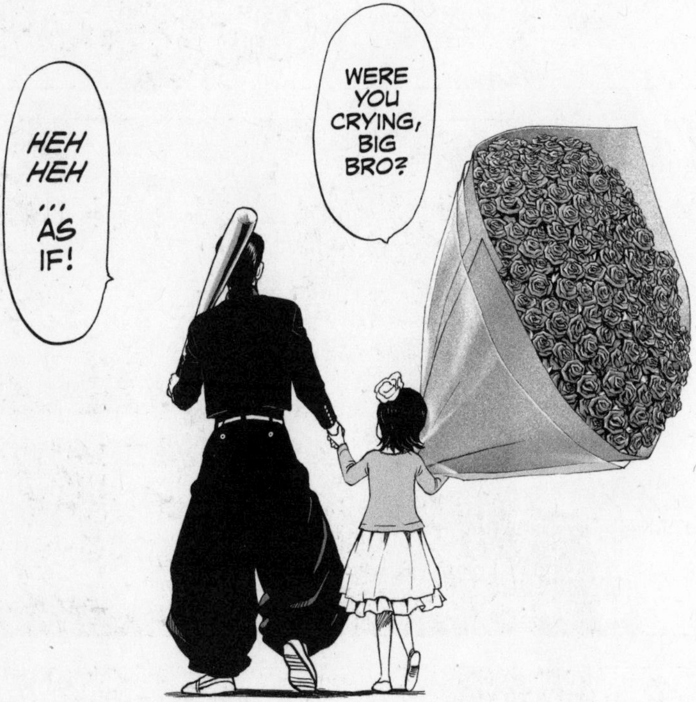
WERE YOU CRYING, BIG BRO?
HEH HEH ... AS IF!

END NOTES

PAGE 49, PANEL 1:
The kanji on his stomach is a pun. It can be read as "to break" or "to smash." and it is also a homonym for rhino in Japanese.

PAGE 145, PANEL 4:
His helmet says "do not light."

PAGE 174:
The BakuDonald's on the cup and bag is play on McDonald's. McDonald's is pronounced *Makudonarudo* in Japanese. *Baku* means "explosion."

PAGE 204, PANEL 2:
Saitama's shirt says "pickled plum."

ONE-PUNCH MAN
VOLUME 11
SHONEN JUMP MANGA EDITION

STORY BY | ONE
ART BY | YUSUKE MURATA

TRANSLATION | JOHN WERRY
TOUCH-UP ART AND LETTERING | JAMES GAUBATZ
DESIGN | SHAWN CARRICO
SHONEN JUMP SERIES EDITOR | JOHN BAE
GRAPHIC NOVEL EDITOR | JENNIFER LEBLANC

ONE-PUNCH MAN © 2012 by ONE, Yusuke Murata
All rights reserved.
First published in Japan in 2012 by SHUEISHA Inc., Tokyo.
English translation rights arranged by SHUEISHA Inc.

Printed in the U.S.A.

Published by VIZ Media, LLC
P.O. Box 77010
San Francisco, CA 94107

10 9 8 7 6 5 4 3 2 1
First printing, March 2017

www.viz.com

www.shonenjump.com

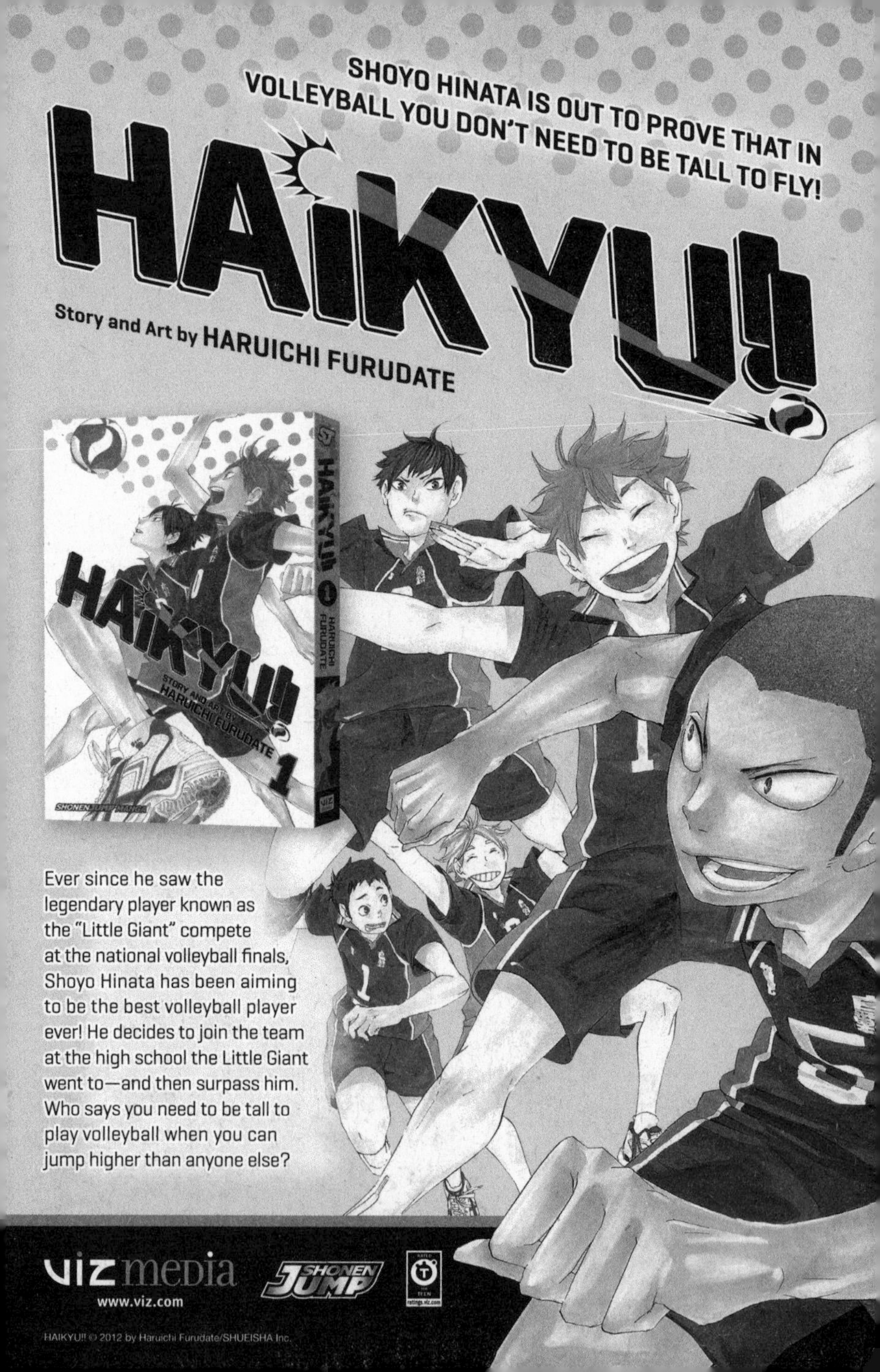
SHOYO HINATA IS OUT TO PROVE THAT IN VOLLEYBALL YOU DON'T NEED TO BE TALL TO FLY!
HAIKYU!!
Story and Art by HARUICHI FURUDATE
HAIKYU!! STORY AND ART BY HARUICHI FURUDATE 1
SHONEN JUMP MANGA
Ever since he saw the legendary player known as the "Little Giant" compete at the national volleyball finals, Shoyo Hinata has been aiming to be the best volleyball player ever! He decides to join the team at the high school the Little Giant went to—and then surpass him. Who says you need to be tall to play volleyball when you can jump higher than anyone else?
VIZ media
www.viz.com
SHONEN JUMP
ratings.viz.com
HAIKYU!! © 2012 by Haruichi Furudate/SHUEISHA Inc.

STOP!

YOU'RE READING THE WRONG WAY!

★ ONE-PUNCH MAN READS FROM RIGHT TO LEFT, STARTING IN THE UPPER-RIGHT CORNER. JAPANESE IS READ FROM RIGHT TO LEFT, MEANING THAT ACTION, SOUND EFFECTS, AND WORD-BALLOON ORDER ARE COMPLETELY REVERSED FROM ENGLISH ORDER.

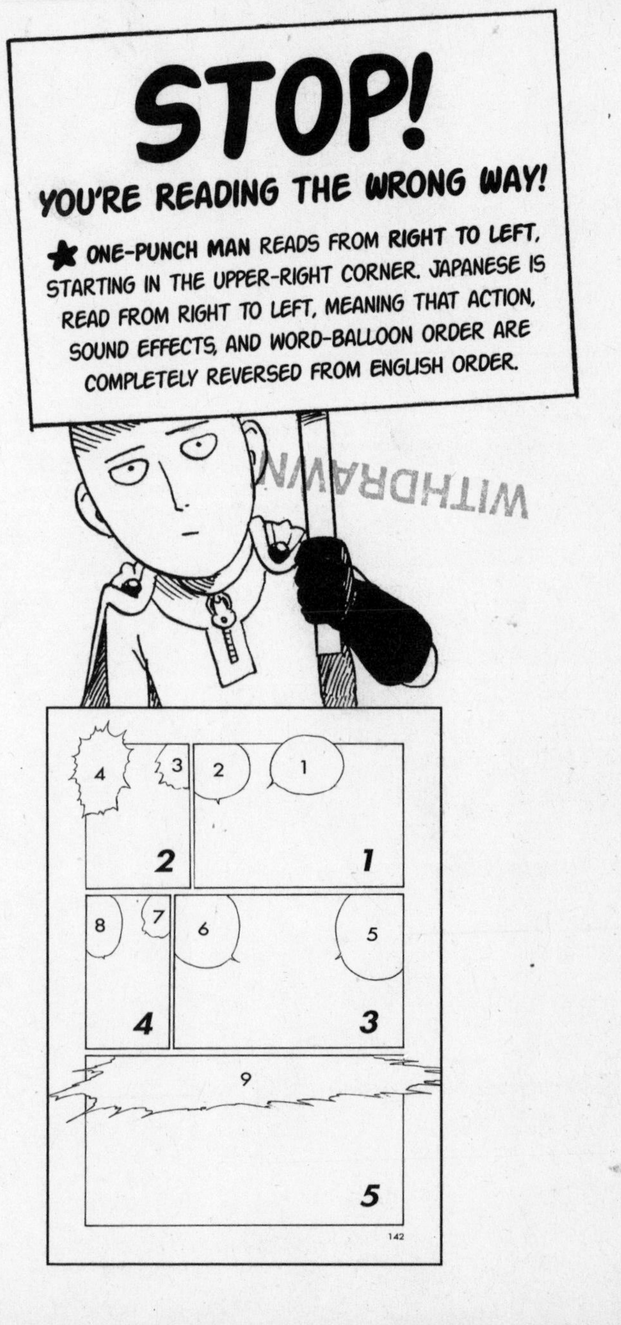